Popular Memories of the Mao Era

Popular Memories of the Mao Era

From Critical Debate to Reassessing History

Edited by Sebastian Veg

Hong Kong University Press
The University of Hong Kong
Pokfulam Road
Hong Kong
www.hkupress.hku.hk

© 2019 Hong Kong University Press

ISBN 978-988-8390-76-2 (*Hardback*)

All rights reserved. No portion of this publication may be reproduced or transmitted in any form or by any means, electronic or mechanical, including photocopying, recording, or any information storage or retrieval system, without prior permission in writing from the publisher.

British Library Cataloguing-in-Publication Data
A catalogue record for this book is available from the British Library.

10 9 8 7 6 5 4 3 2 1

Printed and bound by Paramount Printing Co. Ltd., Hong Kong, China

Contents

Acknowledgments — vii

1. Introduction: Trauma, Nostalgia, Public Debate — 1
   Sebastian Veg

Part I. Unofficial Memories in the Public Sphere: Journals, Internet, Museums

2. Writing about the Past, an Act of Resistance: An Overview of Independent Journals and Publications about the Mao Era — 21
   Jean-Philippe Béja

3. *Annals of the Yellow Emperor*: Reconstructing Public Memory of the Mao Era — 43
   Wu Si

4. Contested Past: Social Media and the Production of Historical Knowledge of the Mao Era — 61
   Jun Liu

5. Can Private Museums Offer Space for Alternative History? The Red Era Series at the Jianchuan Museum Cluster — 80
   Kirk A. Denton

Part II. Critical Memory and Cultural Practices: Reconfiguring Elite and Popular Discourse

6. Literary and Documentary Accounts of the Great Famine: Challenging the Political System and the Social Hierarchies of Memory — 115
   Sebastian Veg

7. Filmed Testimonies, Archives, and Memoirs of the Mao Era: Staging Unofficial History in Chinese Independent Documentaries — 137
   Judith Pernin

8. Visual Memory, Personal Experience, and Public History: The Rediscovery of Cultural Revolution Underground Art — 161
   Aihe Wang

Part III. Unofficial Sources and Popular Historiography: New Discourses of Knowledge on the Mao Era

9. The Second Society 183
    Frank Dikötter
10. Case Files as a Source of Alternative Memories from the Maoist Past 199
    Daniel Leese
11. Popular Memories and Popular History, Indispensable Tools for Understanding Contemporary Chinese History: The Case of the End of the Rustication Movement 220
    Michel Bonnin

List of Contributors 235

Index 238

Acknowledgments

The present book grew out of two conferences bringing together contributions on everyday history and unofficial memory of the Mao era: the first held in Paris in December 2014 at the Maison des sciences de l'homme and the Centre d'études et de recherches internationales and the second held in Hong Kong in November 2015 at the University of Hong Kong.

The two conferences, as well as the some of the original research published in the present volume, were funded by a research grant from the Research Grants Council (Hong Kong) and the Agence nationale de la recherche (France) under the France–Hong Kong collaborative scheme, within the project "New Approaches to the Mao Era: Everyday History and Unofficial Memory." The project's main aim, as reflected in this book, was to confront social science studies of popular memory of the Mao era in present-day China, with research carried out by historians on the everyday history of the Mao era. This path has been a sometimes challenging, but always fruitful, one, and it is to be hoped that other studies will pursue it as well.

The editor would like to thank all participants and discussants in the conferences for their contributions, as well as two anonymous external reviewers for the present volume.

1

Introduction

Trauma, Nostalgia, Public Debate

Sebastian Veg

On May 2, 2016, a few days before the fiftieth anniversary of the May 16 circular that signaled the launch of the Cultural Revolution in 1966, a lavish concert titled "In the Fields of Hope" (Zai xiwang de tianye shang 在希望的田野上) was organized in the Great Hall of the People in Beijing by a private promoter (Fifty-Six Flowers troupe); it was sponsored by several state- and party-affiliated units. Slogans like Mao's Korean War–era call "People of the world unite to defeat the American invaders and their lackeys" and Cultural Revolution songs like "Sailing the Seas Depends on the Helmsman" featured prominently.[1] However, news and photos of the concert, spreading through social media, provoked an unexpected outcry, and prominent members of the group of "red progeny" (*hong erdai* 紅二代) spoke out against the attempt—bolstered by the scale and venue of the event—to relegitimize the Cultural Revolution. In the absence of endorsement from higher up, the organizers scrambled to justify themselves, each attempting to shift the blame to others.[2] This incident, though anecdotal, points to the continued lack of consensus within Chinese society about how to remember the Mao era, the years from the foundation of the People's Republic of China (PRC) in 1949 to the Chairman's death in 1976.

Although the official narrative of this period has not undergone any significant shift since 1981, and despite ongoing restrictions in the official media and academia, new and diverse expressions of unofficial memories of the Mao era have appeared over approximately the last decade, in print and internet publications, on film, and among amateur historians. They include unofficial testimonies, oral histories, and investigative studies, often focused on the everyday lives of ordinary people, which had not been adequately documented, as well as attempts to question some of the

---

1. *Ming Pao* Reporter, "Hongge yanchanghui beizhi fubi Wenge" [Red Song Gala accused of rehabilitating Cultural Revolution], *Ming Pao*, May 5, 2016, http://news.mingpao.com/pns1605061462470682787.
2. Wang Xiangwei, "Political Winds Raise Red Flags over Cultural Revolution-Style Gala," *South China Morning Post*, May 8, 2016, http://www.scmp.com/news/china/policies-politics/article/1942545/political-winds-raise-red-flags-over-cultural. By contrast, May 16 went by almost without mention in the Chinese press, apart from a *People's Daily* article reaffirming the official verdict formulated in 1981.

larger narratives of the Mao era.³ The most well-known single publication is probably *Tombstone*, the study of the Great Famine of 1959–1961 by retired Xinhua journalist Yang Jisheng, published in 2008 in Hong Kong, but there are many other examples of reportage and autobiographical writing by first-hand witnesses about the Mao era. These accounts are often published as "self-printed books" (*ziyinshu* 自印書, a literal translation of *samizdat*) or simply posted to the internet. Informal memory groups began to appear in the 1990s, focused on specific historical episodes (in particular the Educated Youth movement during the Cultural Revolution, but also the Anti-Rightist Movement), as well as registered journals devoted to publishing testimony and recollections like *Annals of the Yellow Emperor* (Yanhuang chunqiu 炎黃春秋, Beijing, 1991–), *Old Photographs* (Lao Zhaopian 老照片, Jinan, 1996–), *Looking at History* (Kan Lishi 看歷史, Chengdu, 2010–2013).⁴ The last ten years have seen an outpour of unofficial, mainly unregistered, journals disseminated via the internet, like *Remembrance* (Jiyi 記憶, Beijing, 2008–), *Remembering Five Black Elements* (Hei Wu Lei Yijiu 黑五類憶舊, Beijing, 2010–2011), and *Yesterday* (Zuotian 昨天, Chongqing, 2012–).⁵ While there had been one or two isolated bottom-up (non-state-initiated) attempts to document the Mao era on film in the 1990s (in particular Wu Wenguang's seminal *1966, My Time in the Red Guards*, 1992), beginning roughly with Hu Jie's *Looking for Lin Zhao's Soul* in 2004, dozens of independent documentary films, made by ordinary individuals thanks to cheap equipment, began to document family histories and personal memories of the Mao era, from the Land Reform to the Cultural Revolution. Finally, in the field of historical inquiry, new archival documents and new studies by amateur historians—a term which can refer to journalists or other people without formal academic training in history or to historians whose field of study is not officially the Mao era—some of whom practice oral history (often among family or village members), have contributed to this new wave of memory. Most recently, over the last few years, a wave of spontaneous apologies by former Red Guards has sparked further debates.⁶

The question thus arises: how do these popular initiatives reconfigure our understanding of the Mao era? How do they differ from previous expressions? This

---

3. The first unofficial histories appeared as early as the late 1970s, but they were rare and their reliability varied widely. See Michael Schoenhals, "Unofficial and Official Histories of the Cultural Revolution: A Review Article," *Journal of Asian Studies* 48, no. 3 (Aug. 1989): 563–72.
4. This journal began in 2007 as *Guojia Lishi* [National history], became *Kan Lishi* in 2010; after its ban in 2013 it became an online publication under the title *Women de lishi* [Our history], however no issues seem to have been published after late 2014. See the journal website: http://ourhistory.blog.21ccom.net/.
5. Several of these (and some others) are archived on the PRC History Group website; see http://prchistory.org. The issues of *Heiwulei yijiu* (bimonthly, 1–17) are available on the website *China in Perspective*: http://www.chinainperspective.com/ArtShow.aspx?AID=13903. On *Jiyi*, see also Ian Johnson, "China's Brave Underground Journal II," *The New York Review of Books*, December 18, 2014, http://www.nybooks.com/articles/2014/12/18/chinas-brave-underground-journal-ii/.
6. The trend of apologies by former Red Guards began around 2008 in *Annals of the Yellow Emperor*; two important public apologies were the ones by Chen Xiaolu (Chen Yi's son) in August 2013 and Song Binbin in January 2014. See Zhao Jie, "Too Little? Too Late?" *News China*, November 2013, http://www.newschinamag.com/magazine/too-little-too-late.

volume will explore three main fields in which the new forms of memory have been expressed: journalism, including the print media and internet; cultural production, including literature, film, and visual art; and amateur history, including memoirs or autobiographical writings, archives, and oral history, and how they are used by historians to reassess the Mao era. These forms of memory can be characterized as both popular and critical. They are popular in the sense that they originate largely outside the scope of the state, in the realm of *minjian* 民間 ("unofficial" society or, more literally, "among the people"). They are also critical in that they question the accepted narrative of the Mao era in new ways. This in particular sets them aside from the popular memories of the 1990s, which were tinged with a strong feeling of nostalgia. It will be argued that popular memories of the Mao era have followed a classic three-tiered evolution: the first stage in the 1980s gave rise to the expression of mainly traumatic but closely controlled narratives, the second stage in the 1990s was dominated by nostalgia, while the third stage investigated below evinces a turn toward public debate and critical memory.

History and Memory

The distinction between history and memory is a classic one, and is often traced back to the work of Maurice Halbwachs and, more recently, Pierre Nora. Halbwachs defined collective memory as a social construction of the past according to the "beliefs and spiritual needs of the present" and carried by different groups.[7] Pierre Nora, working from the French case, noted that memory sacralizes the past, whereas history tends to rationalize it: for him, memory is encapsulated in state rituals that seek to unify the national community, while critical history as social science is a product of society. As modern societies replace organic communities, memory slowly fades in the face of critical history, but the "places of memory" remain as rituals in a society without rituals.[8] By contrast, in authoritarian and in particular socialist contexts, a distinction is often drawn between "official history" and "popular memory": since history is monopolized by the state, memory is construed as the "authentic" expression of civil society, the "unorthodox transmission of unapproved pasts."[9] It has thus been noted that the "underground memories" of the socialist era have often formed the basis for the new national narratives in post-socialist states.[10] It may therefore be useful to distinguish between the state's

---

7. Maurice Halbwachs, *The Collective Memory* (New York: Harper and Row, 1980), 7, 84–85.
8. Pierre Nora, "Entre mémoire et histoire, la problématique des lieux," in *Les lieux de mémoire, I. La République* ed. Pierre Nora (Paris: Gallimard, 1984); "Between Memory and History: Les Lieux de Mémoire," *Representations* 26 (Spring 1989): 7–24.
9. Rubie Watson, "Memory, History and Opposition under State Socialism," in *Memory, History and Opposition under State Socialism*, ed. Rubie Watson (Santa Fe: School of American Research Press, 1994), 8. See also Michael Schoenhals, "Unofficial and Official Histories of the Cultural Revolution: A Review Article," 564.
10. Rubie Watson, "Memory, History and Opposition," 4.

Table 1.1
Summary of types of relation to the past

Types of relation to past	Memory	History
State-led	State rituals	State historiography
Society-led	Popular commemorations Underground memories	Inquiry-based historiography

and society's uses of memory and history. This distinction can be summarized in the table above (Table 1.1). It should be noted that whereas, in democratic contexts, the opposition is often between state rituals and inquiry-based historiography (top left vs. bottom right), in authoritarian contexts, the main opposition seems to run between state historiography and popular commemoration (top right vs. bottom left). We may further note that, in recent years, the situation in China has become increasingly complex, with all four types of relation to the past appearing in the public sphere.

The 1980s saw a worldwide interest in the specific form of traumatic memory, which appeared in connection with the field of Holocaust Studies. In particular, the most "authentic" expression of "trauma" was now situated in the body, as the place of deeper memory, as opposed to its narrative rendering which already constitutes a rationalization.[11] Oral history, which allows for the reenactment of "mimetic trauma," became a new object of contention between those who believed that it encapsulated a deeper truth, and those who pointed to its factual errors and subjective biases.[12] More recently, studies of oral history have pointed to the fact that, while it cannot replace other methodologies, it plays an important role in establishing the multiplicity of viewpoints on any given historical event, and in highlighting that the narrator-historian cannot disappear behind an "objective" history that exists independently. Oral history therefore serves to qualify the position of the observing historian, who is always already part of the story.[13] In relation to the Holocaust, Saul Friedländer, himself both a historian and a survivor, has called to reconcile the deep memory of the survivor and the dispassionate discourse of the historian, underscoring that discounting the factual errors of the witness leads to ignoring the contingency of events.[14] Ultimately, as will be argued below, both history and memory rely to express themselves on a public sphere, in which society can contest state narratives, but also in which different social narratives can freely debate and contend among each other.[15]

---

11. Ana Douglass and Thomas Vogler, eds., *Witness and Memory: The Discourse of Trauma* (New York: Routledge, 2003), 5–14.
12. Raul Hilberg, *Sources of Holocaust Research: An Analysis* (Chicago: Ivan Dee, 2001), 48–49.
13. Alessandro Portelli, *The Death of Luigi Trastulli and Other Stories* (Albany: SUNY Press, 1991), 57.
14. Saül Friedländer, *Memory, History, and the Extermination of the Jews of Europe* (Bloomington: Indiana University Press, 1993); James Young, "Between History and Memory: The Voice of the Eyewitness," in *Witness and Memory*, ed. Ana Douglass and Thomas Vogler, 275–83.
15. Rubie Watson, "Memory, History and Opposition," 13.

The End of the Mao Era: Official History vs. Popular Memory

The expression of popular memory predated the official verdict on the Mao era, with the April 5 protest on Tiananmen Square in 1976 as well as the many spontaneous criticisms of the Cultural Revolution that appeared on the Democracy Wall in Xidan in 1978–1979. When coming to power in 1978, Deng Xiaoping originally encouraged the ongoing debates in Xidan to criticize Mao's rule. However, as part of his consolidation of power, and having been himself closely involved in episodes like the Anti-Rightist Movement, Deng prevented any further discussions through the "Resolution on certain questions in the history of our Party since the Foundation of the PRC," adopted at the 6th Plenum of the 11th Central Committee on June 27, 1981, and modeled on a similar text adopted in 1945.[16] Its goal was as much to mark a break with Mao's regime as it was to put a stop to political criticisms that touched on the nature of Party rule. It thus salvaged the first seven years of "basic completion of the socialist transformation" as "entirely correct" (§11), while the ten following years (1956–1966) suffered from "serious faults and errors" (§17), and the Cultural Revolution decade, "initiated and led by Comrade Mao Zedong," is described as "responsible for the most severe setback and the heaviest losses suffered by the Party, the state and the people since the founding of the People's Republic" (§19). It is attributed to an "entirely erroneous appraisal of the prevailing class relations and political situation in the Party and state" (§20), for which the chief responsibility lies with Mao. The resolution thus effectively closes off the "Mao era" by establishing a "new historical period" (§32). Nonetheless, despite Mao's "gross mistakes during the 'Cultural Revolution,'" the resolution maintains that "his contributions to the Chinese revolution far outweigh his mistakes" (§27).

The content of the resolution reflected a consensus between critical intellectuals and inner-Party reformers that held up throughout the 1980s, according to which the Cultural Revolution, designated as a "grave blunder" (§8), could be conveniently framed as "benighted" (*yumei* 愚昧) and "backward" (*luohou* 落後). Though carried out in the name of socialism, it was in fact the expression of peasant tradition and "feudalism" (*fengjian zhuyi* 封建主義) that gave rise to irrational economic policies, violent political persecutions, and a cult of Mao's personality. It could now be overcome by promoting "enlightenment," opening up to the world, and economic development, three tenets of Deng's new policy. This narrative also conveniently vilified popular democracy and people's political participation, which Deng wished to associate with the Cultural Revolution, an elitist discourse that found a sympathetic echo among intellectuals. On the other hand, while mistakes were recognized in persecuting intellectuals and other "black categories," Mao's contribution to improving

---

16. "Resolution on Certain Questions in the History of Our Party since the Founding of the People's Republic of China," http://www.marxists.org/subject/china/documents/cpc/history/01.htm. For the Chinese original, see "Guanyu jianguo yilai dang de ruogan lishi wenti de jueyi," http://news.xinhuanet.com/ziliao/2002-03/04/content_2543544.htm.

the life of "ordinary people" was largely upheld in Party discourse, and connected to Deng's "reform and opening up," which could thus be presented as the continuation of the same goal through different means. The resolution also reaffirmed the Party's monopoly on historiography, literary and artistic creation, and laid out the borders of acceptable critical discussion, which have remained broadly unchanged up to the present. In 1984, the authorities conducted a campaign to "thoroughly negate" the Cultural Revolution, aimed at "three types of people" (*san zhong ren* 三種人): followers of Lin Biao and the Gang of Four, factionalists, and "smashers and grabbers."[17] By focusing the discussion around the question of "negating" (*fouding* 否定) the Cultural Revolution, the authorities were able to successfully preclude a deeper discussion of the questions it raised about the regime itself and to maintain the monopoly over history that characterizes communist states.[18]

In this context, society was mainly limited to voicing "underground memories" to express a counter-hegemonic narrative of the Mao era.[19] While "silent disagreement" was common in a situation in which the public sphere belonged to the state, occasionally resistance would take the forms of commemoration, ritual mourning and other forms of performance (such as on April 5, 1976).[20] While the state tried to privatize such rituals, "evocative transcripts,"[21] in which calculated ambiguity allowed participants to bring private memories into the public domain controlled by the state, sometimes made it possible for participants to create "shared meaning." Literature and film were also a useful vector for such intricate allusions, which were by necessity quite elitist.[22] Much of the intellectual critique of the Mao era in the 1980s took place through scar literature (*shanghen wenxue* 傷痕文學) and later forms that derived from it, in which intellectuals were depicted as the main victims of the Red Years. Trauma and suffering were the main modalities of the first wave of writing. Many of the narrative or performative expressions of counter-hegemonic memory in the 1980s were therefore expressions of membership in a group of victims of a shared trauma. Halbwachs had underscored precisely this role of collective memory in defining a community.

However, not all forms of underground memory are neatly counter-hegemonic, and compliance is not always coerced from above. As Ann Anagnost has noted, scar literature was heavily indebted to the Party's own hegemonic discourse. The practice

---

17. Yang Guobin, "Days of Old Are Not Puffs of Smoke: Three Hypotheses on Collective Memories of the Cultural Revolution," *The China Review* 5, no. 2 (Fall 2003): 19.
18. Rubie Watson points out that the primary justification of communist rule is inevitability based on the Marxist claim to scientific knowledge of history. "Memory, History and Opposition," 1.
19. Rubie Watson, "Memory, History and Opposition," 4.
20. Rubie Watson discusses the significance of commemorative ceremonies for Zhou Enlai in 1976 and Hu Yaobang in 1989: "Making Secret Histories: Memory and Mourning in Post-Mao China," in *Memory, History and Opposition*, 65–85.
21. Caroline Humphrey gives this name to expressions that are ambiguous by design, by contrast with James Scott's "hidden transcripts," which are produced by enduring groups within their own space. "Remembering an 'Enemy': The Bogd Khaan in Twentieth-Century Mongolia," in *Memory, History and Opposition*, 21–44.
22. Jonathan Unger, "Introduction," in *Using the Past to Serve the Present: Historiography and Politics in Contemporary China* (Armonk, NY: M. E. Sharpe, 1993), 1–8.

of "narrating bitterness" (*suku* 訴苦), designed by the Party during the Civil War and the early years of the PRC, in which peasants were encouraged to phrase their grievances within the theoretical framework of Marxist history, "was not simply an imposition of a narrative structure on the speaking subject. It represented for the party the process of merging the consciousness of the party with that of 'the people,' which legitimated its claim to represent the voice of the masses."[23] Institutionalized and controlled critique of the past could take place under the premise of enthusiastic affirmation of the glorious present and future. However, as Anagnost further notes, "this use of the body did not end with the establishment of a new social order but was . . . again transcribed into literature in the literature of the wounded (*shanghen wenxue*) of the early post-Mao period, which displayed insults to the bodies of intellectuals, who then turned to writing as a means to redress the injuries of the past."[24] In this sense, scar literature in some ways replicated the Party's early exploitation of *suku*, in that it allowed the traumatic narrative of victimhood to be rephrased and rationalized within the hegemonic narrative of Marxist progress.

Nostalgic and Contentious Uses of Memory in the 1990s

The economic reforms of the 1990s coincided with an unexpected turn from a traumatic and repressed toward a nostalgic and contentious form of memory. In connection with Mao's centenary in 1993, Mao's persona underwent commodification and trivialization, partly engineered, but also partly as the object of an authentic popular cult "never entirely harnessed by Party propagandists, despite various efforts to 'channel' it in the Party's favor."[25] Expressed in talismans, objects, and "red" songs sung in karaoke bars, the cult was reminiscent of folk religion but was also marketed as part of a new consumer culture that the Party wished to encourage. Barmé views it as both an expression of nostalgia for a "beguiling era, appearing in retrospect as a time of greater simplicity, purity, and idealism" and no less an "ironic inversion" indicating "a further rejection or devaluing of ideology."[26] "Red culture" entered the mainstream of commercial entertainment, notably through remakes of "red classics," which became a useful tool for the propaganda authorities, though it is not always easy to handle to the satisfaction of all audiences.[27] This turn coincided with a more precise form of nostalgia among former "educated youth" (*zhiqing* 知

---

23. Ann Anagnost, "Making History Speak," in *National Past-Times: Narrative, Representation and Power in Modern China* (Durham, NC: Duke University Press, 1997), 32. Brian DeMare also points out how propaganda novels eulogizing the Land Reform reproduced the narrative of *suku*. See Brian DeMare, "The Romance and Tragedy of Rural Revolution: Narratives and Novels of Land Reform in Mao's China," *Clio* 43, no. 3 (2014): 341–65.
24. Ann Anagnost, "Making History Speak," 19.
25. Geremie Barmé, *Shades of Mao: The Posthumous Cult of the Great Leader* (Armonk, NY: M. E. Sharpe, 1996), 13.
26. Geremie Barmé, *Shades of Mao*, 52, 49.
27. See Rong Cai, "Restaging the Revolution in Contemporary China: Memory of Politics and Politics of Memory," *The China Quarterly* 215 (Sept. 2013): 663–81.

青), which Yang Guobin dates back to a 1990 exhibition on the Great Northern Wilderness (Beidahuang), held in Beijing. In contrast with previous elite-inflected narratives, it marked the rise of ordinary voices, expressing nostalgia for heroism and an ambivalent attitude toward modernity defined by economic development.[28] As former *zhiqing* fell victims to the layoffs of the 1990s, they expressed resistance to marketization and reforms, and nostalgia for a more "authentic" or "meaningful" form of life. Like in the Mao cult, it was particularly ironic, as Yang points out, that market-based culture (nostalgic restaurants, memorabilia, cultural events) was massively used to challenge the advent of the market.[29]

The popular memories that emerged in the wake of Mao fever and of popular discontent with the economic reforms of the 1990s, defined new political communities engaged in new forms of struggles.[30] As society diversified, different communities articulated different versions of popular memories that were distinct from the "official" narrative. These narratives had a cognitive, but also a political dimension: as previously noted by Tilly, collective memories are always appropriated and reinterpreted for present action, defining groups that rely on frames of shared memory to formulate their claims.[31] Many contentious worker movements of the 1990s successfully mobilized such memories of socialism, against the rise of state-led capitalism. In the context of marketization and factory closures, the mobilization of references to the Revolution in order to fight against layoffs further stimulated a poetics of socialist nostalgia in literature and film. With the rise of the New Left on the intellectual scene, in the late 1990s, popular voices appeared calling for a positive reassessment of the Mao era.[32]

Nonetheless, the popular memories of the Mao era that appeared in the 1990s were not more welcomed by the state than the previous ones, as they directly challenged the state's economic policy. Nor were they necessarily uncritical of the Mao era, since the nostalgia for lost ideals or a more meaningful life was also contrasted with the failure of Mao's state to live up to the ideals of socialism and the expectations of the masses.[33] However, the popular memory of workers, especially in large state-owned factories, remained deeply embedded in the language of state

---

28. Yang Guobin, "China's Zhiqing Generation: Nostalgia, Identity, and Cultural Resistance in the 1990s," *Modern China* 29, no. 3 (July 2003): 267–96.
29. Yang Guobin, "Days of Old Are Not Puffs of Smoke: Three Hypotheses on Collective Memories of the Cultural Revolution," *The China Review* 5, no. 2 (Fall 2003): 19.
30. Ching Kwan Lee and Guobin Yang, "Introduction: Memory, Power, Culture," in *Re-envisioning the Chinese Revolution: The Politics and Poetics of Collective Memory in Reform China*, ed. Ching Kwan Lee and Guobin Yang (Washington, DC: Woodrow Wilson Press, 2007), 7.
31. Charles Tilly, "Afterword: Political Memories in Space and Time," in *Remapping Memory: The Politics of TimeSpace*, ed. Jonathan Boyarim (Minneapolis: University of Minnesota Press, 1994), 249.
32. An early example is Cui Zhiyuan's article "Mao Zedong 'wen ge' lilun de deshi yu xiandaixing de chongjian" [An assessment of Mao Zedong's Theory of Cultural Revolution and the reconstruction of Chinese modernity], *Hong Kong Journal of Social Sciences* 7 (1996): 60–74.
33. Kimberly Ens Manning, "Communes, Canteens and Crèches: The Gendered Politics of Remembering the Great Leap Forward," and Jonathan Unger and Anita Chan, "Memories and the Political Economy of a State-Owned Enterprise," in *Re-envisioning the Chinese Revolution*, 93–118, 119–40.

socialism, which the state has for a long time successfully mobilized to articulate subaltern interests.[34] In many cases, subalterns already speak in the language of the state, especially when moving away from the personal, everyday experience toward larger historical narratives.[35] It is therefore unsurprising that even critical memory narratives still rely on the language of the state to criticize the state. Overall, the nostalgic and contentious popular memories of the 1990s formed a contested field within both rural and urban society, with little consensus on whether the Chinese revolution had ultimately empowered workers and peasants or simply provided now opportunities for oppression.[36]

From Contentious to Critical Memory

Over the last decade, contentious social movements have shifted in emphasis and more rarely mobilize popular representations of socialism or of the "revolution," but increasingly reference the language of "rights." The intellectual scene has become more complex and many of its members have called for a more differentiated approach to the Mao era, one that is neither reduced to the trauma discourse of the 1980s, nor to the nostalgic discourse of the 1990s.[37]

More detailed forms of critical memory have appeared that precisely document key episodes of the Mao era like the Great Famine of 1959–1961. At the same time, new public spheres have formed and accommodated these memories. While the qualified nostalgia of the 1990s can be seen as a form of backlash against the crony capitalism of the post-Tiananmen decade, the new phenomena reflect both growing dissatisfaction with the authoritarian control over history exercised by the Chinese state, and the rise of new spaces for counter-hegemonic narratives provided by social media and the growing private economy in the 2000s. Private companies took important stakes in the publishing, media, and especially the internet sector, and even some individual private museums appeared. Furthermore, books could be either self-printed or printed outside mainland China and brought back in, respectively like *samizdat* and *tamizdat* in Soviet times.[38] Alternative memories are increasingly discussed publicly in a critical, historiographical manner, raising the question of how popular memories can translate into a new understanding of history. The mass of unofficial material being generated and increasingly discussed

---

34. Ching Kwan Lee, "What Was Socialism to Chinese Workers?" in *Re-envisioning the Chinese Revolution*, 141–65.
35. Gail Hershatter, "The Subaltern Talks Back: Reflections on Subaltern Theory and Chinese History," *positions* 1, no. 1 (Spring 1993): 108.
36. Lee and Yang, "Introduction: Memory, Power, Culture," 10–11.
37. For example, Han Shaogong, in "Why Did the Cultural Revolution End?" (*boundary 2*, vol. 35.2 [2008]: 93–106) proposes to tease out the democratic or egalitarian legacies of the Cultural Revolution rather than "negating" it.
38. See Peter Steiner, "Samizdat, Tamizdat, Magnitizdat and Other Strange Words That Are Difficult to Pronounce," *Poetics Today*, special issue on *samizdat*, 29, no. 4 (2008): 613–28.

has begun to inflect the popular understanding of Mao-era politics towards a reconfiguration of the relation between elite and subaltern narratives.[39]

In this perspective, popular memory is not only an alternative to official history, or a tool for political mobilization, but also a mechanism for the social construction of knowledge. Memory encompasses a broad set of narratives dealing with the past, mainly produced by individuals, which overlap to constitute communities of shared memories that are often contentious rather than consensual. By contrast, history can be defined more narrowly as a body of socially and politically sanctioned knowledge about the past, underpinned by a measure of professional or social consensus. In examining the critical popular memories of the 2000s, the present collection therefore focuses more precisely on the processes of private production, public dissemination, and social sanctioning of narratives of the past, whereby memory is transformed into history. It is not sufficient to label a statement as "true" to make it into the accepted version of history. The social and institutional negotiations inherent in "sharing" private narratives in a tightly controlled but nonetheless expanding public sphere, the definition of criteria of (popular) "authenticity" and (elite) "scientificity" are at the heart of the mechanisms by which individual narratives come to enter the public sphere. Without denying the contentious nature of the competition between narratives, it is also important to understand how some of these come to be more widely "shared" than others. Three main aspects of popular memory will be successively examined.

Firstly, there has been a clear shift in the boundaries between private and public spheres: counter-hegemonic memories that used to be confined to hidden transcripts are increasingly becoming part of a growing public debate on history, fuelled by the technological advances of the internet and the sinophone publishing industry outside mainland China.[40] The most obvious example is the Great Famine of 1959–1961, not previously a suitable subject for academic or media inquiry, which has been publicly debated several times on the mainland in the last decade.[41] Unofficial journals, the internet, private museums are all venues in which the borders have

---

39. Felix Wemheuer contrasts the situation in China, where social groups like peasants and local cadres have "filled the gaps" in the official narrative with their own memories, with Ukraine, where the counter-hegemonic memory of the famine became the new national narrative after 1991. Felix Wemheuer, "Regime Changes of Memory: Creating the Official History of the Ukrainian and Chinese Famine under State Socialism and after the Cold War," *Kritika: Explorations in Russian and Eurasian History* 10, no. 1 (2009): 31–59. Contrary to Hershatter, he also finds that peasant memories are formulated in words not strongly influenced by Party discourse. Felix Wemheuer, "Dealing with Responsibility for the Great Leap Famine in the People's Republic of China," *The China Quarterly* 201 (2010): 176–95.
40. For an early discussion of the role of the public sphere, see Mary Mazur's description of a public debate on Cultural Revolution history in 1996, in connection with the journal *Annals of the Yellow Emperor*. Mary Mazur, "Public Space for Memory in Contemporary Civil Society: Freedom to Learn from the Mirror of the Past?" *The China Quarterly* 160 (Dec. 1999): 1019–35.
41. An obvious example of such social validation of non-mainstream narratives is the May 2012 issue of *Nanfang Renwu Zhoukan*, with the title "Da Jihuang" (the Great Famine) and a graph of production statistics for 1959–1961 on the cover, which evinces the influence of Yang Jisheng's book without quoting it. There are other examples, like interviews with former rightists or survivors of Jiabiangou Reeducation Through Labor Camp.

been expanded. This shift, though still often challenged by censorship or even state violence, qualifies the nature of the control that the socialist state can exercise over history.

The chapters in Part I, dedicated to the print media (Jean-Philippe Béja, Wu Si), the internet (Jun Liu), and museums (Kirk Denton) analyze the process of negotiation that take place between private production and public dissemination of alternative narratives. Jean-Philippe Béja studies three types of independent historical material—official journals, unofficial journals, and self-printed books (*ziyinshu*)—arguing that the acts of private citizens who make public their interpretations of the past attest the pluralization of society. Wu Si, the former editor of one of these journals, *Annals of the Yellow Emperor*, describes the journal as a kind of nexus between state and society, both privately supported and state-owned, which through careful negotiation with the authorities was for a time able to construct what he terms a "public memory" of the Mao era. Jun Liu explores the structural change brought about by social media in the formation of social memory. Because it enables the accumulation and wide dissemination of alternative historical material (often from private sources), it contains a mechanism for production of knowledge through crowdsourcing of historical materials, and favors the aggregation of individual testimony into counter-narratives. Private museums, discussed in a case study by Kirk Denton, yield ambiguous conclusions, as the absence of a master narrative allows relative interpretive freedom, but produces a polyphonic juxtaposition that can appear to be more oriented toward consumption than critical reflection. This is a typical dilemma of an embryonic public sphere, subject to the controls of both politics and the market.

Secondly, intellectual and cultural productions dealing with the Mao era suggest that the relationship between elite and popular memory has been reconfigured. While intellectuals have long been spokespersons and proxies for the state throughout traditional and revolutionary China, this close connection has been eroded in the decades since the repression of the Tiananmen democracy movement. The "scar literature" of the 1980s was to a large extent the product of intellectuals' internalized acceptance of the official narrative and was read through the lens of trauma suffered by loyal and innocent intellectuals, sometimes at the hands of violent and hostile peasants. By contrast, more recent textual and visual productions have challenged this disconnect between elite and popular memory, either by highlighting the guilt of intellectuals who were closely involved in carrying out revolutionary violence (for example in Yan Lianke's novel, *Four Books*) or by bringing subaltern discourse or memory into the public sphere. Previous critical narratives of the Mao era focused on elite suffering during the Cultural Revolution, while peasant suffering in the famine of the Great Leap Forward had long remained mute, a contrast that has been ascribed to a difference in social class.[42] Cultural texts of the 2000s, though still

---

42. Susanne Weigelin-Schwiedrzik, "Trauma and Memory: The Case of the Great Famine in the People's Republic of China (1959–1961)," *Historiography East and West* 1, no. 1 (2003): 52. Commenting on interviews

produced by an elite, now often focus on the famine and on the persecution of the peasants. The ostensible claim by some documentary filmmakers to "reestablish the truth" in fact often translates into subtle struggles to redraw social hierarchies and responsibility. For example, the films dedicated to the survivors of Jiabiangou labor camp focus on the price paid by ordinary people in remote areas with little connection to national politics.[43] The Folk Memory Project at Caochangdi Documentary Film Workstation, conceived and coordinated by Wu Wenguang since 2010, has given a group of young film directors the initiative to return to their villages and gather firsthand testimony about the Great Famine from ordinary villagers, as part of a series of projects addressing the rural-urban divide in today's China. Many of these testimonies were transcribed and made available on the Caochangdi website, while films and theatre productions are used to "perform" and disseminate the main insights of these investigations.

The chapters in Part II examine the reconfiguration of elite and popular memory in the social discourses encapsulated in literature (Sebastian Veg), documentary film (Judith Pernin), and visual art (Aihe Wang). Using the examples of Yang Xianhui, Yang Jisheng, and Yan Lianke, Sebastian Veg shows how writers in the last decade have broken with earlier writing about the Mao era by turning to the 1950s and critically confronting both the PRC state in its foundations and their own role in sustaining its legitimacy. Rather than a self-vindication in the form of a personal memoir of persecuted intellectuals, they construct self-reflexive discussions encompassing a plurality of viewpoints. Judith Pernin, analyzing several independent documentary films that grapple with memories of the Mao era, highlights the authenticating strategies used by directors to validate unofficial and counter-hegemonic narratives. Their rejection of mainstream documentary techniques that use archival footage and voice-over to construct master narratives compels them to find other techniques for authenticating subaltern discourses, in particular by resorting to objects or by establishing connections with a textual source. Aihe Wang, excavating and rereading visual art produced by ordinary workers—including herself—during the Cultural Revolution, shows how a form of painting, understood as purely private at the time, can now enter the public sphere as testimony of the everyday life of ordinary people erased by the pervasive narratives of elite politics. This ordinary experience, because it is private and apolitical, can be reread as a form of quotidian resistance in an era saturated with politics.

Thirdly, popular and elite memories have also interacted to produce new discourses of knowledge. While early historiography of the Mao era was pioneered by scholars based outside of China, the last decade has seen new research on the early

---

conducted in 2005 with former students of Agricultural University who had first-hand experience of the famine in the countryside, Felix Wemheuer notes that "intellectuals" like his interviewees tend to see the famine as a mistake rather than a crime and show little moral introspection. However, they do acknowledge political manipulation and coercion. See F. Wemheuer, "Der Weg in die Hungersnot," *Asien* 25 (2005): 25–41.

43. Following Wang Bing's two films (documentary *Fengming, a Chinese Woman* and feature film *The Ditch*), Ai Xiaoming dedicated a five-part documentary to the survivors, titled *Jiabiangou Elegy* in 2017.

years of the PRC from both abroad and within China, where a small group of historians have investigated everyday life far from the leadership struggles in Beijing.[44] Works of popular historiography and "unofficial sources" like legal proceedings or archival material obtained by independent investigators have contributed to changing popular perceptions of the history of the Mao era. Memoirs and other autobiographical documents have become increasingly available, bringing intimate experiences into the public realm.[45]

Chapters in Part III demonstrate how the historiography of the Mao era has been transformed as changes appeared in the memory culture. Personal memoirs can be used together with archival sources to document the existence of an underground network of social practices in the late stages of the Cultural Revolution. Frank Dikötter uses both literary/autobiographical sources and declassified investigation reports or other archives to document the duality of outward compliance and inner dissent during the late Cultural Revolution. Memoirs by both participants and former officials are also used by Michel Bonnin to question the government's motivation in bringing the Rustication (Educated Youth) movement to an end in 1980, while official sources still celebrated it as a great success. Unofficial material from petition files by Shanghai *zhiqing* who were stranded in Xinjiang can in this way become a socially sanctioned source of historical knowledge. Finally, historical archives themselves can be depositories that bear the mark of contested memories, when documents (fake or "black" materials used to frame certain individuals) have been removed or changed during the revision of "unjust, false and mistaken cases" that took place after the Cultural Revolution. The judicial records studied by Daniel Leese contain snippets of personal narrative statements—confessions, self-criticisms, self-explanations—that show how victims of persecution strategically reframed their discourse according to the political circumstances. Here too, the construction of historical knowledge relies on sifting through different layers of discourse (confessions extracted under duress, petitions requesting rehabilitation during the reassessment of verdicts) to understand the experience of victims of persecution. This part shows that alternative everyday history is not only preserved in oral memories but can also be reconstructed through documents. This process leads to the social validation by elite knowledge discourses of alternative narratives that originate from the popular realm.

All these memoirs, archival materials, citizen investigations, testimonies, literary, or filmic works made by ordinary citizens, and published or disseminated

---

44. See, for example, work by Dong Guoqiang, Feng Xiaocai, Jin Dalu, Yang Kuisong, and, in English, Zhou Xun's oral history investigations.
45. A similar tendency has been noted in the Soviet and post-Soviet context. See Benjamin Nathans, "Talking Fish: On Soviet Dissident Memoirs," *The Journal of Modern History* 87, no. 3, *Literary and Visual Arts in the European Public Sphere* (September 2015): 579–614; Jochen Hellbeck, "Working, Struggling, Becoming: Stalin-Era Autobiographical Texts," *The Russian Review* 60 (July 2001): 340–59. See also the discussion of a memoir by a "rural intellectual" who supported the CCP and felt betrayed in Paul Pickowicz, "Memories of Revolution and Collectivization in China: The Unauthorized Reminiscences of a Rural Intellectual," in *Memory, History, and Opposition*, 127–48.

through various channels including the internet, contribute to challenging the existing historiography of the first thirty years of the People's Republic, with deep-reaching consequences. Indeed, the challenge has not gone unnoticed by the regime. In the interval since most of the chapters in the present volume were originally written, a backlash has taken place explicitly targeting "historical nihilism." The alleged "Central document no. 9" leaked in early 2013 singles out Party history as one of the "unmentionable topics" in the mainland media.[46] It was followed by a series of concrete measures targeting historical narratives critical of the Party, culminating during the fiftieth anniversary of the Cultural Revolution in 2016, which saw the shutdown of the social media (Weibo and public Weixin) accounts of the Folk Memory Project in June 2016 (Caochangdi station B accounts were reopened in September), the state takeover of *Annals of the Yellow Emperor* in July,[47] the closure of the privately run Cultural Revolution Museum in Shantou,[48] and finally the shutdown of the influential website *Consensus* (Gongshiwang) in September after its associated journal *Leader* published a special commemorative issue on the Cultural Revolution in July.[49] Yang Jisheng's new book on the Cultural Revolution was published in Hong Kong in December 2016, but any reference was actively removed from the Chinese internet, and the author was reportedly under significant pressure to halt the publication.[50]

While unofficial memories call into question some of the basic tenets that justify the Party's claim to power since 1949, the CCP sticks to its narrative of "liberation" of the oppressed classes, such as workers and peasants, and of empowering subaltern groups in the new political order. Violence against "class enemies," while its degree may be retrospectively recognized as excessive, remains justified, in the Party's view, as a necessary means to the goal of advantaging the victims of previous political regimes. Unofficial memories however, give credence to a rival narrative, highlighting widespread violence, including against many poor members of the rural population, and the establishment of a new class hierarchy in post-1949 China, in which a small new elite was able to exercise power without restraints, and enjoyed unprecedented privilege.[51] As Qin Hui wrote in 2004: "Compared to the short-lived (though of course cruel) attacks endured by the 'faction in power,' the

---

46. See "Document no. 9: A Chinafile translation," November 8, 2013, http://www.chinafile.com/document-9-chinafile-translation.
47. See Sebastian Veg, "Debating the Memory of the Cultural Revolution in China Today," *Modern Chinese Literature and Culture*, August 8, 2016, http://u.osu.edu/mclc/online-series/veg2/.
48. Didi Kirsten Tatlow, "Fate Catches up to a Cultural Revolution Museum in China," *New York Times*, October 2, 2016, http://www.nytimes.com/2016/10/03/world/asia/china-cultural-revolution-shantou-museum.html.
49. Oiwan Lam, "Chinese Authorities Shutter 'Gongshi' Intellectual Website, Leading Netizens to Ask: Is This 'The End of Consensus'?," *Global Voices*, October 5, 2016, https://advox.globalvoices.org/2016/10/05/as-authorities-shutter-gongshi-intellectual-website-netizens-ask-has-china-reached-the-end-of-consensus/.
50. See Chris Buckley, "Historian's Latest Book on Mao Turns Acclaim in China to Censure," *New York Times*, January 21, 2017, https://www.nytimes.com/2017/01/21/world/asia/china-historian-yang-jisheng-book-mao.html.
51. For a characterization of the post-1949 regime as a new status system, see Jean-François Billeter, "The System of 'Class Status,'" in *The Scope of State Power in China*, ed. Stuart Schram (London: SOAS, 1985), 127–69.

suffering of those ten years [1966–1976] was mainly sustained by the lower rungs of society, in particular the outcasts [*jian min* 賤民] (five black elements, rightists) who had continually been persecuted before the Cultural Revolution."[52] Such a counter-narrative obviously challenges the very foundations of the CCP's historical legitimacy.

Bringing together material from a great variety of sources, this volume probes how new forms of popular memory are transforming our understanding of recent Chinese history. After a period of post-traumatic outpour, followed by commodified nostalgia, popular memory in recent years has shown signs of moving towards more critical discussions, which have begun, despite the recent backlash, to transform the mainstream narrative of the Mao era in China.

Bibliography

"Document no. 9: A Chinafile Translation." November 8, 2013. http://www.chinafile.com/document-9-chinafile-translation.

"Resolution on Certain Questions in the History of Our Party since the Founding of the People's Republic of China." http://www.marxists.org/subject/china/documents/cpc/history/01.htm. [Chinese original: "Guanyu jianguo yilai dang de ruogan lishi wenti de jueyi." http://news.xinhuanet.com/ziliao/2002-03/04/content_2543544.htm.]

Anagnost, Ann. "Making History Speak." In *National Past-Times: Narrative, Representation and Power in Modern China*, 17–44. Durham, NC: Duke University Press, 1997.

Barmé, Geremie. *Shades of Mao: The Posthumous Cult of the Great Leader*. Armonk, NY: M. E. Sharpe, 1996.

Billeter, Jean-François. "The System of 'Class Status.'" In *The Scope of State Power in China*, edited by Stuart Schram, 127–69. London: SOAS, 1985.

Buckley, Chris. "Historian's Latest Book on Mao Turns Acclaim in China to Censure." *New York Times*, January 21 2017. https://www.nytimes.com/2017/01/21/world/asia/china-historian-yang-jisheng-book-mao.html.

Cai, Rong. "Restaging the Revolution in Contemporary China: Memory of Politics and Politics of Memory." *The China Quarterly* 215 (Sept. 2013): 663–81.

Cui Zhiyuan. "Mao Zedong 'wen ge' lilun de deshi yu xiandaixing de chongjian" [An assessment of Mao Zedong's Theory of Cultural Revolution and the reconstruction of Chinese modernity]. *Hong Kong Journal of Social Sciences* 7 (1996): 60–74.

DeMare, Brian. "The Romance and Tragedy of Rural Revolution: Narratives and Novels of Land Reform in Mao's China." *Clio* 43, no. 3 (2014): 341–65.

Douglass, Ana, and Thomas Vogler, eds. *Witness and Memory: The Discourse of Trauma*. New York: Routledge, 2003.

Friedländer, Saül. *Memory, History, and the Extermination of the Jews of Europe*. Bloomington: Indiana University Press, 1993.

---

52. Qin Hui, "Women gai zenyang fansi wenge" [How we should reflect on the Cultural Revolution], *Wenti yu zhuyi: Qin Hui wenxuan* (Changchun: Changchun Press, 1999), 10–11. See also Yang Jisheng's description of how luxury villas were built for visiting leaders all around the country at the worst of the famine in *Tombstone*, 460.

Halbwachs, Maurice. *The Collective Memory*. New York: Harper and Row, 1980.
Han, Shaogong. "Why Did the Cultural Revolution End?" *boundary 2*, vol. 35.2 (2008): 93–106.
Hellbeck, Jochen. "Working, Struggling, Becoming: Stalin-Era Autobiographical Texts." *The Russian Review* 60 (July 2001): 340–59.
Hershatter, Gail. "The Subaltern Talks Back: Reflections on Subaltern Theory and Chinese History." *positions* 1, no. 1 (Spring 1993): 103–30.
Hilberg, Raul. *Sources of Holocaust Research: An Analysis*. Chicago: Ivan Dee, 2001.
Humphrey, Caroline. "Remembering an 'Enemy': The Bogd Khaan in Twentieth-Century Mongolia." In *Memory, History and Opposition under State Socialism*, edited by Rubie Watson, 21–44. Santa Fe: School of American Research Press, 1994.
Johnson, Ian. "China's Brave Underground Journal II." *The New York Review of Books*, December 18, 2014. http://www.nybooks.com/articles/2014/12/18/chinas-brave-underground-journal-ii/.
Lam, Oiwan. "Chinese Authorities Shutter 'Gongshi' Intellectual Website, Leading Netizens to Ask: Is This 'The End of Consensus'?" *Global Voices*, October 5, 2016. https://advox.globalvoices.org/2016/10/05/as-authorities-shutter-gongshi-intellectual-website-netizens-ask-has-china-reached-the-end-of-consensus/.
Lee, Ching Kwan. "What Was Socialism to Chinese Workers?" In *Re-envisioning the Chinese Revolution: The Politics and Poetics of Collective Memory in Reform China*, edited by Ching Kwan Lee and Guobin Yang, 141–65. Washington, DC: Woodrow Wilson Press, 2007.
Lee, Ching Kwan, and Guobin Yang, eds. *Re-envisioning the Chinese Revolution: The Politics and Poetics of Collective Memory in Reform China*. Washington, DC: Woodrow Wilson Press, 2007.
Manning, Kimberly Ens. "Communes, Canteens and Crèches: The Gendered Politics of Remembering the Great Leap Forward." In *Re-envisioning the Chinese Revolution: The Politics and Poetics of Collective Memory in Reform China*, edited by Ching Kwan Lee and Guobin Yang, 93–118. Washington, DC: Woodrow Wilson Press, 2007.
Mazur, Mary. "Public Space for Memory in Contemporary Civil Society: Freedom to Learn from the Mirror of the Past?" *China Quarterly* 160 (Dec. 1999): 1019–35.
Ming Pao Reporter. "Hongge yanchanghui beizhi fubi Wenge" [Red Song Gala accused of rehabilitating Cultural Revolution]. *Ming Pao*, May 5, 2016. http://news.mingpao.com/pns1605061462470682787.
Nathans, Benjamin. "Talking Fish: On Soviet Dissident Memoirs." *The Journal of Modern History* 87, no. 3, *Literary and Visual Arts in the European Public Sphere* (September 2015): 579–614.
Nora, Pierre. "Between Memory and History: Les Lieux de Mémoire." *Representations*, no. 26, *Special Issue: Memory and Counter-Memory* (Spring, 1989): 7–24. [French original: "Entre mémoire et histoire, la problématique des lieux." In *Les lieux de mémoire, I. La République*, edited by Pierre Nora, xvi–xlii. Paris: Gallimard, 1984.]
Pickowicz, Paul. "Memories of Revolution and Collectivization in China: The Unauthorized Reminiscences of a Rural Intellectual." In *Memory, History, and Opposition: Under State Socialism*, edited by Rubie Watson, 127–48. Santa Fe: School of American Research Press, 1994.

Portelli, Alessandro. *The Death of Luigi Trastulli and Other Stories*. Albany: SUNY Press, 1991.
Qin Hui. "Women gai zenyang fansi wenge" [How we should reflect on the Cultural Revolution]. *Wenti yu zhuyi: Qin Hui wenxuan*, 10–11. Changchun: Changchun Press, 1999.
Schoenhals, Michael. "Unofficial and Official Histories of the Cultural Revolution: A Review Article." *Journal of Asian Studies* 48, no. 3 (Aug. 1989): 563–72.
Steiner, Peter. "Samizdat, Tamizdat, Magnitizdat and Other Strange Words That Are Difficult to Pronounce." *Poetics Today*, special issue on *samizdat*, 29, no. 4 (2008): 613–28.
Tatlow, Didi Kirsten. "Fate Catches up to a Cultural Revolution Museum in China." *New York Times*, October 2, 2016. http://www.nytimes.com/2016/10/03/world/asia/china-cultural-revolution-shantou-museum.html.
Tilly, Charles. "Afterword: Political Memories in Space and Time." In *Remapping Memory: the Politics of TimeSpace*, edited by Jonathan Boyarim, 249. Minneapolis: University of Minnesota Press, 1994.
Unger, Jonathan. "Introduction." In *Using the Past to Serve the Present: Historiography and Politics in Contemporary China*, edited by Jonathan Unger, 1–8. Armonk, NY: M. E. Sharpe, 1993.
Unger, Jonathan, and Anita Chan. "Memories and the Political Economy of a State-Owned Enterprise." In *Re-envisioning the Chinese Revolution: The Politics and Poetics of Collective Memory in Reform China*, edited by Ching Kwan Lee and Guobin Yang, 119–40. Washington, DC: Woodrow Wilson Press, 2007.
Veg, Sebastian. "Debating the Memory of the Cultural Revolution in China Today." *Modern Chinese Literature and Culture*, August 8, 2016. http://u.osu.edu/mclc/online-series/veg2/.
Wang, Xiangwei. "Political Winds Raise Red Flags over Cultural Revolution-Style Gala." *South China Morning Post*. May 8, 2016. http://www.scmp.com/news/china/policies-politics/article/1942545/political-winds-raise-red-flags-over-cultural.
Watson, Rubie. "Making Secret Histories: Memory and Mourning in Post-Mao China." In *Memory, History and Opposition under State Socialism*, edited by Rubie Watson, 65–85. Santa Fe: School of American Research Press, 1994.
Watson, Rubie. "Memory, History and Opposition under State Socialism." In *Memory, History and Opposition under State Socialism*, edited by Rubie Watson, 1–20. Santa Fe: School of American Research Press, 1994.
Weigelin-Schwiedrzik, Susanne. "Trauma and Memory: The Case of the Great Famine in the People's Republic of China (1959–1961)." *Historiography East and West* 1, no. 1 (2003): 41–67.
Wemheuer, Felix. "Dealing with Responsibility for the Great Leap Famine in the People's Republic of China." *The China Quarterly* 201 (2010): 176–95.
Wemheuer, Felix. "Der Weg in die Hungersnot: Erinnerungen chinesischer Intellektueller an den ländlichen 'Großen Sprung nach vorne' (1958–1961)." *Asien* 25 (2005): 25–41.
Wemheuer, Felix. "Regime Changes of Memory: Creating the Official History of the Ukrainian and Chinese Famine under State Socialism and after the Cold War." *Kritika: Explorations in Russian and Eurasian History* 10, no. 1 (2009): 31–59.
Yang, Guobin. "China's Zhiqing Generation: Nostalgia, Identity, and Cultural Resistance in the 1990s." *Modern China* 29, no. 3 (July 2003): 267–96.

Yang, Guobin. "Days of Old Are Not Puffs of Smoke: Three Hypotheses on Collective Memories of the Cultural Revolution." *The China Review* 5, no. 2 (Fall 2003):13–41.

Young, James. "Between History and Memory: The Voice of the Eyewitness." In *Witness and Memory: The Discourse of Trauma*, edited by Ana Douglass and Thomas Vogler, 275–83. New York: Routledge, 2003.

Zhao Jie, "Too little? Too Late?" *News China*, November 2013. http://www.newschinamag.com/magazine/too-little-too-late.

Part I

Unofficial Memories in the Public Sphere

Journals, Internet, Museums

2
Writing about the Past, an Act of Resistance
An Overview of Independent Journals and Publications about the Mao Era

Jean-Philippe Béja

On February 26, 2014, the Standing committee of the NPC passed a bill to make December 13 the Nanjing Massacre Memorial Day.[1] Through this decision, the Chinese Communist Party (CCP) showed that it attached a great importance to history. This decision followed a long campaign during which Chinese leaders had denounced the Japanese government's militarism, and called on the heads of World War II Allied states to oppose Prime Minister Abe's historical revisionism. This attitude is not surprising as anti-Japanese resistance has been at the center of the CCP's propaganda for about thirty years: a quick look at Chinese television series shows communist heroes fighting the invaders and leading the people in their struggle for the liberation of the motherland. Documentaries on the Sino-Japanese war are innumerable, and the media often remind their audience of this episode of contemporary history.

However, when it comes to the history of the People's Republic, the Party does not display the same enthusiasm; whereas many TV series celebrate communist heroes' courage in their fight against the Kuomintang, mainstream media do not show series or films about the Land Reform, the cooperativization, the Great Leap Forward, or the Great Proletarian Cultural Revolution.[2] And in fact, apart from October 1, which marks the foundation of the People's Republic, not a single official holiday commemorates an event that took place after 1949. History books present only sketchy and simplistic versions of the history of the People's Republic, and the subject is confined to the political study courses that are compulsory in high school and university.

Party history remains the field of specialists, and the authorities strive to prevent open discussions on the subject. As a matter of fact, from the Party's point

---

1. "China ratifies national days on anti-Japanese war victory, Nanjing Massacre," *Xinhua*, February 27, 2014, http://news.xinhuanet.com/english/china/2014-02/27/c_133147713.htm.
2. An exception is Zhang Yimou's latest film, *Coming Home* (*Guilai*), which tells the story of a rightist who escapes reeducation in a labor camp to go back home during the Cultural Revolution, and is turned in by his own daughter, which causes a deep trauma to his wife. For once, an official film director tackles the question of memory of the Maoist period.

of view, any challenge to the official version of history amounts to a challenge to Party legitimacy: without any other means to assert its right to rule, the CCP regularly repeats that it was "chosen by the people" during the war of liberation. The people's support allowed the Party to defeat the Kuomintang, to reunify China, and to make what was then a weak "feudal" country subjected to foreign imperialism into a great power widely respected on the international scene.

The Interpretation of History: A Weapon in Intraparty Struggle

All political regimes ground their legitimacy in history: in France, General de Gaulle justified his right to rule by pointing to his role in the victorious struggle of the French people against German occupiers. Therefore, for many years, he denied the importance of collaboration. However, the legitimacy of a democratic government is periodically verified by an election, whereas the CCP regime can only rely on the Marxist-Leninist assumption that, as the vanguard of the proletariat, it represents history's march forward. Therefore, control of the interpretation of history is essential to legitimacy, and the Party cannot afford to let ordinary citizens and specialists freely question the official vision of the past. Under these circumstances, in totalitarian and post-totalitarian regimes, writing on contemporary history can become an act of resistance.[3] However, opportunities for debate can occur in specific circumstances: for example, when a change of leadership takes place, the emerging leaders often base their legitimacy on the previous dissenters' visions of history. Rehabilitation of purged cadres accompanied Khrushchev's as well as Gorbachev's rise to power. In the late 1980s, Mikhail Gorbachev allowed the publication of Roy Medvedev's historical research in order to delegitimize the Brezhnevian vision of history, and to legitimize his new political line. In 1987, he also allowed the creation of Memorial, an association devoted to the denunciation of Stalin's crimes, which collected personal accounts of the persecutions endured by ordinary citizens, painting a very gloomy picture of the "glorious revolutionary period."[4]

What was true for the USSR has also been true for China. Succession periods make it much less dangerous for dissenters to publish their visions of history, as most instances of the "struggle between two lines" centered on conflicts of interpretation of historical developments.[5]

This chapter will only succinctly present the conflict of interpretations that followed Mao's demise: after the coup that toppled the Gang of Four in October 1976, the new leadership needed to renew its legitimacy. As most of its members had been victims of the Cultural Revolution, they were more than willing to reevaluate this

---

3. See Claude Lefort, *Un homme en trop* (Paris: Belin, 2015).
4. Interview with Arseny Roginsky, founder and leader of Memorial, Paris, 2003.
5. For example, many decisions made by the Party during the last ten years of Mao Zedong's rule were criticized after his death. Similarly, during the Cultural Revolution, the first seventeen years of the People's Republic were denounced as "revisionist."

period. In 1978, Hu Yaobang, acting under Deng Xiaoping's leadership, encouraged critical reflection on the ideological developments that had made it possible for Lin Biao and the Gang of Four to launch all-around attacks on the so-called "revisionist cadres and capitalist roaders." Denunciation of class struggle, assertions according to which "practice [was] the only criterion for the truth," allowed cadres and intellectuals to question official ideology and the official interpretation of history.[6] After Hu Yaobang became secretary of the CCP organization department, he encouraged the victims of Mao's campaigns (*yundong* 運動) to fight for their rehabilitation.[7] In official journals and on the *dazibao*, which flourished on the walls of big cities, accounts of the repression of intellectuals, peasants, and workers, and denunciations of the Anti-Rightist Movement, the Cultural Revolution, and even of the Three- and Five-Anti Campaigns and Land Reform, brought to the public a completely new interpretation of contemporary history, which contradicted the previous orthodox narrative.[8]

This reflection was encouraged by the Party as it legitimized its new political line: emphasis on class struggle and on continued revolution was now regarded as an erroneous interpretation of Marxism-Leninism and of Mao Zedong thought. The "revisionist cadres," "rightist intellectuals," and "rightist opportunists" who had been jailed and ostracized because of their criticism of the Great Helmsman's policies were now regarded as exponents of the correct political line. This revision of history culminated in 1979 when Zhang Zhixin 張志新 (1930–1975)—a cadre who had dared criticize Jiang Qing, Lin Biao, and the Cultural Revolution in 1969, and had been executed for this crime—was presented as a national hero.

At the end of the 1970s, debate on the Maoist period was rife and was taking place in the official press. Ordinary citizens were also allowed to present their analyses of contemporary history on the *dazibao* and unofficial journals that appeared in 1978–1979.

However, there were limitations to the freedom of expression and questioning the Party's right to rule was out of the question. Writers were allowed (encouraged) to say that the leadership had erred, but were supposed to conclude that the Party, by showing its ability to correct its past mistakes, had demonstrated that it was the only organization that could lead the country on the road to socialism. These critical historical accounts helped reinforce Deng Xiaoping's position in the power struggle, but once the Maoists known as "whateverists" had been toppled, the new leader put an end to the free discussion of the recent past: the "Resolution on Certain Questions in the History of Our Party Since the Founding of the People's Republic of China," passed in 1981,[9] presented the official interpretation of Mao's

---

6. Cf. Ruan Ming, *L'empire de Deng Xiaoping: chronique d'un empire* (Arles: Picquier, 1992).
7. Dai Huang, *Hu Yaobang yu pingfan yuan jia cuo an* [Hu Yaobang and the rehabilitation of the unjust, fake, wrong cases] (Beijing: Sanlian chubanshe, 2013).
8. Victor Sidane, *Le printemps de Pékin* (Paris: Gallimard, Archives, 1980).
9. "Resolution on Certain Questions in the History of Our Party Since the Founding of the People's Republic of China," https://www.marxists.org/subject/china/documents/cpc/history/01.htm.

rule, which, from then on, was not to be challenged. A new orthodoxy emerged, and articles, books, and films criticizing the "errors" committed by the Party in the past were suppressed. As the novelist Yan Lianke writes, describing what he calls "state-sponsored amnesia": "Anything negative about the country or the regime will be rapidly erased from the collective memory. This memory deletion is being carried out by censoring newspapers, magazines, television news, the Internet and anything that preserves memories. . . . The best way to achieve this type of amnesia is to develop tactics utilizing state power to shackle people's minds and block all memory channels by altering historical records, manipulating textbook content and controlling literature, art and performances in all forms."[10]

Enforcing amnesia is essential in order to preserve the Party power in totalitarian regimes, and George Orwell encapsulated this necessity when he wrote: "He who controls the past controls the future. He who controls the present controls the past" (*1984*). But, as Claude Lefort has shown, even the worst totalitarian regime is unable to achieve full control over society,[11] and despite the massive effort to enforce amnesia, some citizens have found ways to fight it by publishing their visions of the past. During the 1980s, a few Chinese intellectuals, especially writers, published novels and short stories that depicted the sufferings of the ordinary people during the first decades of the regime. After June Fourth, many elderly Party members, intellectuals, and ordinary victims of Maoism wrote about the tragedies China went through during the Great Helmsman's rule. They were well aware that their endeavors represented a challenge to the Party's legitimacy but were convinced that only by informing the young generations about the movements that had shaken China during the first three decades of the PRC, would it be possible to avoid the repetition of these tragedies.

In their works, they have tried to understand the reasons for the upheavals that had upset their lives: rightists, rusticated youths, and Red Guards have established networks where free discussion about the campaigns is taking place. Most of them are convinced that the CCP's monopoly on the interpretation of history has reinforced one-party rule and that their initiatives can contribute to weakening it: for them, ignorance of history paves the way to the repetition of the disasters that have marked the first decades of the People's Republic. They are deeply worried by the Maoist revival that has been taking place among the youth in recent years, and they think it is all the more necessary to reveal what they deem to be the true nature of the Great Helmsman's project.[12] Furthermore, they often uphold pluralism and are strongly committed to political reform.

---

10. Yan Lianke, "On China's State-Sponsored Amnesia," *New York Times*, April 2, 2013, http://www.nytimes.com/2013/04/02/opinion/on-chinas-state-sponsored-amnesia.html?pagewanted=all&_r=0.
11. Claude Lefort, "Reculer les frontières du possible," in *L'invention démocratique* (Paris: Le livre de poche, 1981), 344.
12. Interviews with Tie Liu, January 2014; Tan Chanxue, June 2014.

It was not until 1998 that a number of witnesses of Mao's rule, feeling the weight of the years, tried by all means possible to make public their visions of the past. That year Zhu Rongji, a former rightist, became premier, and Bill Clinton made a visit to China—the first by an American president since the Tiananmen massacre. The political atmosphere became more relaxed. Perspicacious publishers thought it was time to publish works on the 1957 Anti-Rightist Movement and the movement against Hu Feng. These accounts by elderly intellectuals did not become best sellers, but they aroused some interest among young students.[13]

The Rise of Unofficial History

These endeavors are not without danger, and they have often been criticized by the authorities. I can't resist the temptation to quote at length the reaction of Mei Ninghua, then director of *Beijing Ribao*, who declared in 2010:

> Some people display pragmatism (*shiyong zhuyi* 實用主義), historical nihilism and other trends, which manifest themselves in the following ways:
> 1) They deny and distort the history of the Chinese Revolution
> 2) They painstakingly doctor and hypothesize history. In order to deny the successes of the Chinese Revolution, they invent and expand so-called "man-made calamities," they fabricate "the number of abnormal deaths,"[14] which, in fact is an example of painstakingly doctoring history. Some people preconize "the rewriting of history," the use of a "modern point of view" to replace "the revolutionary point of view," they oppose revolution and modernization, and through this "deconstruction of history," the reform and revolution which took place during modern history become negative forces which produced social unrest, sabotaged economic development, and prevented social progress. These subjective ideas betray history and reflect their rash attitude towards history.
> 3) Pretending to "restore the historical truth," they do all they can to extol the old forces which have been discarded by history
> 4) They "ironize" or "blacken" history
> 5) They pursue so-called "value neutrality," and "pure objectivity."[15]

Just establishing an exhaustive bibliography of the publications targeted by Mei Ninghua would be a very significant research result. This work has been started by some institutions such as Chinese University of Hong Kong's Universities Service Centre and the History Department of East China Normal University, which have

---

13. Niu Han and Deng Jiuping, eds., *Jiyizhong de fanyoupai yundong* [The Anti-Rightist Movement in memory], a trilogy: *Liu Yue xue* [Snow in June], *Jingji lu* [A road filled with thorns], *Yuanshang cao* [Grass on the plain] (Beijing: Jingji ribao chubanshe, 1998).
14. This is a reference to the works that have been published on the famine that followed the Great Leap Forward in 1960–1961.
15. Mei Ninghua, "Qizhi xianmingde fandui lishi xuwuzhuyi" [Overtly oppose historical nihilism], *Zhongguo Gongchandang Xinwen wang*, May 24, 2010, http://dangshi.people.com.cn/GB/138903/138911/11676447.html.

already collected a great number of such publications. In this chapter, I will only present the most significant ones.

The publications can be divided into three categories, and I will present one or two examples in each; some official journals have persistently endeavored to publish memoirs and articles on the recent past despite the restrictions imposed by the authorities.[16] I have chosen to present the most representative of these official publications, the one which has been in existence for the longest period, *Yanhuang chunqiu* 炎黃春秋 (Annals of the Yellow Emperor), as well as a journal which had a very large circulation albeit a very short life, *Kan Lishi* 看歷史 (National history), before migrating to the internet and becoming *Women de lishi* 我們的歷史 (Our history).

The second category comprises unofficial journals (*minban kanwu* 民辦刊物), often circulated online, some of which endeavor to reach a high academic standard, like *Jiyi* 記憶 (Remembrance), while some are more militant and struggle to obtain rehabilitation for the victims of Mao's campaigns[17] and punishment for those who have labeled them counterrevolutionaries, such as *Wangshi weihen* 往事微痕 (Tiny scars of the past).

Apart from the journals, many books present alternative visions of contemporary history; some are published in Hong Kong or overseas (what the Soviets used to call *tamizdat*),[18] while some are self-published as *samizdat* in the PRC. I will present two *samizdat*, one that exposes a very little known Maoist campaign (*yundong* 運動) that took place in 1958, and the second, which is the autobiography of a rightist who took part in the creation of an underground journal while serving a period of "reeducation through labor" (*laodong jiaoyang,* 勞動教養). The landscape of unofficial history is pluralistic, insofar as the nature of the publications and the objectives of their publishers are concerned.

An Official Publication That Dares Challenge Orthodoxy

Annals of the Yellow Emperor is an official journal, as it has a publishing license (*kan hao* 刊號, literally "publication number"). It was founded in 1992 by Du Daozheng

---

16. For example, *Bainian chao* 百年潮 used to publish daring articles in the late 1990s, but it was taken over by the society for the history of the Communist Party (*Zhonggong dangshi xuehui*), which is directly under the Central Committee research unit on Party History (*Zhonggong zhongyang dangshi yanjiushi*). Interview with Yang Dongxiao, journalist at *Kan Lishi,* June 2014.
17. Mao's campaigns, or Maoist movements are *yundong*, exemplified by the 1942 *zhengfeng* (rectification), the Hundred Flowers Movement, the Cultural Revolution. The process follows the same pattern: the Chairman calls on the masses to express their opinions and criticisms of the Party, they reluctantly (or not) do so, and the Chairman denounces the counterrevolutionaries who used this campaign to attack the regime. In the episode that follows, the masses dig out the culprits, and mass meetings are organized to denounce them. See Roderick MacFarquhar, *The Origins of the Cultural Revolution* (Oxford: Oxford University Press, 1974), and Wang Ruoshui, "Work-Style Rectification Overwhelms Enlightenment: The Collision between the May Fourth Spirit and 'Party Culture,'" in *Contemporary Chinese Thought*, special issue edited by J-P. Béja and J-P. Cabestan, "The Challenge Facing Chinese Intellectuals in the 21st Century," 34, no. 4 (Summer 2003): 27–56.
18. In Russian, *tam* means "there," while *sam* means "by oneself"; *izdat* means "to publish."

who had been forced to resign from his post as head of the Bureau of Press and Publication after June Fourth. Du founded the Chinese Yellow Emperor Cultural Research Society (Zhonghua yanhuang wenhua yanjiuhui 中華炎黃文化研究會) with General Xiao Ke 蕭克 and National People's Congress Vice-President Zhou Gucheng 周谷城. Despite the fact that they had been marginalized by the new Party leadership, these leading cadres had no difficulty in obtaining a publishing license; when the then-director of the Central Committee research team on Party history, Wen Jize 溫濟澤, had to end the publication of *Martyrs of China* (Zhonghua Yinglie 中華英烈), a biographical journal he edited, they asked him to transfer his license to their new publication. This is how the *Annals of the Yellow Emperor* was founded. At the time, the journal's objective was to rally overseas Chinese around the Party that had been isolated by the sanctions that Western countries had passed in the wake of the June Fourth Massacre. However, as they had supported Zhao Ziyang during the spring of 1989, the new leadership didn't trust them and therefore didn't support the new journal. Du had to use his own money and to borrow from friends to launch it. Taking advantage of the fact that many members of the research society—the responsible unit for the journal—were high-level cadres, Du Daozheng appointed the members of the editorial board without asking the authorization of the organization department. This gave the new journal the flavor of an unofficial publication. At the beginning, the editors had planned to write on Chinese culture in order to attract overseas Chinese readership, hence the title of *Annals of the Yellow Emperor*. But when they realized that the Party would not support their endeavor, they decided to turn to contemporary history; as elder Party members, they were in a good position to write on this subject. In 1995–1996, they became convinced that, in order to further develop the necessary debate on the future of China, it was indispensable to correct the wrong interpretations of history that were widespread in society. They therefore started to publish articles by historians who contested the official line, according to which Chen Duxiu[19] had been a "bad element," Qu Qiubai[20] had been a traitor, and the CCP had been the main force in the anti-Japanese struggle. Then, using their own experience as Party leaders, and relying on their large network of relationships among old cadres, they decided to narrate their experiences without taking into account the political necessities of the moment. A new light was cast on crucial episodes of the struggles within the Party, which differed from the official line: for example, Wen Jize wrote numerous articles across more than a decade to ask for the rehabilitation of Wang Shiwei (finally partially obtained in 1992), the writer who had been labeled a Trotskyite during the Yan'an Rectification movement, and executed in 1947. The journal was also instrumental in establishing the truth

---

19. Chen Duxiu (1879–1942) was a leader of the May Fourth Movement, and the first general secretary of the Communist Party (1921–1927). He was denounced as a Trotskyite.
20. Qu Qiubai (1899–1935) became a Party member in 1923, and led the organization from 1927 until 1928. He was executed by the Kuomintang, but his confession, *Duoyu de hua* (Superfluous words) was criticized and he was considered a "renegade."

about the Great Leap Forward and the Great Famine that it provoked. The fact that the author of *Tombstone*, Yang Jisheng,[21] was a member of the editorial board can partially explain this interest.

The journal published numerous accounts of the August 1959 Lushan Plenum where Peng Dehuai was purged. These articles have helped readers understand a crucial event of the history of the People's Republic.[22] Publishing unadulterated first-hand accounts of contemporary history made *Yanhuang chunqiu* quite successful and it was selling forty to fifty thousand copies by the end of the 1990s. Direct testimonies by the victims of the Anti-Rightist Movement, texts written by their offspring, articles by former cadres in the security or propaganda apparatus present a multifaceted image of the campaign. The journal published more than seven hundred articles referring to that historical episode. I asked Wu Si, then executive editor of the magazine why, as he published edited books composed of articles published in the journal, he didn't publish books on specific movements: "It is too sensitive and would not be possible. Besides, it would uselessly attract the attention of the concerned departments."[23] This does not mean that the magazine editors do not reflect on the meaning of these movements, and on the nature of the regime. Wu Si explains the situation as follows: "At the turn of the century, it became clear that to make an assessment of history meant to analyze the consequences of despotism, totalitarianism, and of one-party dictatorship (whether the Communist Party's or the Kuomintang's). The founders of the journal were convinced that a better system could have helped lower the cost of historical developments."[24] Therefore, the journal's objective became clear: to redress the erroneous visions of history, and to show the necessity of political reform. According to the same Wu Si: "In 2007, Xie Tao's article entitled 'Social-Democracy and China's Future'[25] was a watershed: from that date on, the editors decided that the journal should not only publish articles on history, but should propose a program for the future. Since then, all the members of the editorial board have agreed that *Yanhuang chunqiu*'s goal is to restore historical truth, make an assessment of political reform, and push a program of democratic constitutionalism."[26] And it seems that readers subscribed to this new orientation, as the journal was selling 190,000 copies at the end of 2013. Most of the readers were teachers, middle-aged Party cadres, government employees, or retired civil servants

---

21. Yang Jisheng, *Tombstone: The Great Chinese Famine (1959–1961)* (London: Allen Lane, 2012).
22. More than a dozen articles deal with this subject. See, for example, Wen Ji, "Zhang Wentian zai Lushan huiyishang de kangzheng" [Zhang Wentian's resistance at Lushan plenum], *Yanhuang Chunqiu*, no. 12 (2000), http://www.yhcqw.com/html/cqb/2008/327/08327103248JGK1F251EAD3ECC1HC79G0F.html; Yang Dipu, "Lushan huiyi Zhou Xiaodan jianchi bu pi Peng Dehuai" [Zhou Xiaodan persists in refusing to criticize Peng Dehuai at the Lushan Plenum], *Yanhuang Chunqiu*, no. 1 (2001), http://www.yhcqw.com/html/qsp/2008/327/08327113627781I277H5IH9JDHIED0GEF.html.
23. Interview with Wu Si, 2010.
24. Interview with Wu Si, 2013.
25. Xie Tao, "Minzhu shehuizhuyi moshi yu Zhongguo qiantu" [The social-democratic model and the future of China], *Yanhuang Chunqiu*, no. 2 (2007), http://www.yhcqw.com/html/yjy/2008/420/08420105457EJH1I1817I1G7K2KICIH6BBC.html.
26. Interview with Wu Si, 2013.

who believed that restoring historical truth was a prerequisite to the establishment of a democracy.

As Wu Si declared in an interview: "To express a dissenting voice on history is a way to promote democracy. This is the reason why we opposed the closure of the Maoist website *Utopia*. Although they often denounced us vehemently, we were very sad when we heard the news. The more different voices can be heard, the larger the space for free expression."[27] *Yanhuang Chunqiu* continued to publish testimonies by rightists, by victims of the Cultural Revolution, by former secretaries (*mishu*) of state and Party leaders. Debates on the meaning of the campaigns launched by Mao (such as the Anti-Rightist Movement, the One Strike Three Anti Campaign, etc.)[28] still took place in its columns. It ran articles on Party culture and discussions on constitutionalism. It also dared to publish articles that provided insights on the decision-making process at the highest level. And the editors did not hesitate to touch taboo subjects, such as the preparation of the 13th Congress when Zhao Ziyang proclaimed his intention to enforce the separation between the Party and the government.[29] It was a platform that conveyed unofficial versions of contemporary history and, at the same time, provided debate on the political system and its future. To conclude with Wen Jize's own words:

> Today, if we want to hide the reality to the people, similar historical tragedies can be repeated! We, the old guys, cannot do much anymore. The only thing we can do is just that: tell the things we have been through, and leave for history and for our grandchildren a few real things. It is our responsibility. It is our absolute duty.[30]

However, *Yanhuang chunqiu* was often the target of censorship: if the fact that it had been founded, and was still supervised, by former superior Party cadres protected its freedom of expression, its existence remained under threat. The present Party leadership has reinforced its control over the press and the internet, and the journal has not been able to escape this new trend. In September 2014, Du Daozheng was summoned by the Ministry of Culture, and by the State General Administration of Press, Publication, Radio, Film, and Television, and informed that the journal should switch its affiliation from the Yanhuang Chunqiu Research Society to the Chinese National Academy of Arts—a unit under the Ministry of Culture—before the end of the year. Du declared: "If we agree to be restructured, I am afraid that our magazine's inherent editorial independence will be ruined. And all our articles written by outspoken authors will be expunged under the current

---

27. Interview with Wu Si, 2013.
28. *Yida sanfan* (strike counter revolutionaries, oppose corruption, speculation, and waste) was a movement launched in January 1970 to eliminate the "leftist" supporters of Chen Boda. According to official figures, in eleven months it resulted in 840,000 investigations, 284,800 arrests, and 9,000 executions.
29. Cf. Wu Wei, "Zhonggong shisan da baogao qicao shushi" [The truth about the preparation of the report to the 13th Congress], *Yanhuang chunqiu*, no. 4 (2014): 47–56.
30. Xu Qingquan, "'Wenqing' Wen Jize" [The warm-hearted Wen Jize], *Yanhuang chunqiu*, no. 3 (2014): 42.

censorship system."[31] The *minjian* (unofficial) aspect of the journal, which Wu Si insists made it different from official publications, was threatened by the change of affiliation. Besides, only two members of the editorial board were able to keep their positions in the new setup, as most of them were over sixty and forced to retire.[32] The new affiliation would also deprive the journal of the protection of the elderly cadres that had allowed it to survive storms unscathed. Finally, after months of struggle, a compromise emerged. Wu Si resigned at the beginning of 2015 and was replaced by Yang Jisheng, who was assisted by the outspoken historian Ding Dong, the editor of the magazine *Lao zhaopian* (Old photographs). The journal did register under the Chinese National Academy of Arts, but Du Daozheng was confirmed as the publisher. In June, Yang Jisheng resigned because, as a retired journalist (he is retired from the Xinhua news agency) he was not allowed to continue as the executive editor of a journal. New editors were hired, and, despite its shaky situation, the journal continued to be published, and its viewpoint remained outspoken. However, finally, Du, too, had to leave his position. The entire editorial board was replaced, and, after August 2016 the journal's content completely changed.[33] It now only publishes articles that glorify the Party's official heroes and its role during its ninety years of existence.

This offensive against a journal that was published for twenty years by Party veterans shows that the new Communist Party leaders have decided to reinforce their control on the interpretation of history, as they emphasize their position as heirs to the Party's "excellent tradition."

A Cooperative Specialized in the Writing of History: *Women de lishi* (Our History)

Modeled on American journals, *National History* (Kan lishi 看歷史), which was published from 2010 to early 2013, was quite different from *Yanhuang chunqiu* as it was not as much concerned with "sensitive" episodes in the Party's history. The majority of its articles dealt with the Chinese Republican period (1911–1949) and were mostly written by journalists rather than witnesses. However, when the editors decided to publish an issue focused on Chiang Ching-kuo and Taiwan's democratization, the work unit that sponsored the journal decided to close it (under a financial pretext). The editor Tang Jianguang then went on to found the Our History Cooperative (*Women de lishi hezuoshe* 我們的歷史合作社) with the objective of encouraging the development of unofficial historical research, especially the history

---

31. Minnie Chan, "Order to 'Realign' Outspoken Liberal Magazine Will End Its Independence, Says Publisher," *South China Morning Post*, September 19, 2014, http://www.scmp.com/news/china/article/1595608/order-realign-outspoken-liberal-magazine-will-end-its-independence-says?comment-sort=.
32. Interview with a Beijing intellectual, September 14, 2014.
33. "Former Editors of Liberal Chinese Magazine Sue Government after Being Forced Out in Takeover," *South China Morning Post*, August 16, 2016, http://www.scmp.com/news/china/policies-politics/article/2005030/former-editors-liberal-chinese-magazine-sue-government.

of individuals. The cooperative also pursued a task that had been started by the journal: it gives grants and prizes to high school students who write family or village histories, through the method of oral history.[34] The project sponsors aimed at recording the experiences of ordinary people during the early years of the People's Republic, experiences that they regarded as indispensable sources in order to write reliable accounts of this period. Tens of thousands of students have taken part in these projects, whose goal was to produce an unofficial (*minjian*) history based on first-hand accounts. This is reminiscent of the experience of the former Soviet organization Memorial,[35] which created a prize for the most truthful and complete accounts of contemporary history written by high school students.

The Our History cooperative also planned to organize classes to teach volunteers how to record individual experiences in order to develop a vision of history from the bottom. It aimed at training cohorts of young people who will be able to go into villages and gather oral histories.

The high school prize had existed since 2010 and has mobilized tens of thousands of history teachers in China's high schools. Other projects (classes, etc.) have yet to be developed. As the Party has increased its control of the public sphere, Tang has been forced to reduce his ambitions. The school prize was ended in 2014, and the interviews currently published on the website are much less controversial than before; individual accounts of the participants and victims of the recurrent political movements that have shaken China under Mao's rule have almost disappeared. Tang Jianguang's hope that his cooperative would be acknowledged as a reliable source by historians, whether official or not,[36] looks more and more like a distant dream.

The Rise of Online Unofficial Journals

With the development of the internet, a gray area has appeared, and official journals are not the only ones that try to present alternative visions of the history of Maoism. Unofficial periodicals, whether electronic or on paper, have appeared in the course of the last ten years. I won't give an exhaustive list of these publications, but will only limit myself to presenting a couple of the most representative.

Wangshi weihen 往事微痕 (Tiny scars of the past)

The motto of this journal is "Refuse to forget, face history, uphold reform, promote democracy." It was founded in Beijing by Tie Liu, a former *Sichuan Ribao* journalist

---

34. *Kanlishi* zazhi bianzhe [Kanlishi editors], *Kebenshang bu shuo de lishi: Zhongxuesheng bixia de bainian jiaguo jiyi* [The history which is not told in history books: The memory of the homeland under the pen of high school students] (Beijing: Citic Press, 2012).
35. See its website at: http://www.memo.ru/eng/.
36. Interview with Tang Jianguang, 2014.

who was labeled a rightist in 1957, and was reinstated in his position as a journalist in the 1980s after his verdict was "corrected" (*gaizheng* 改正), and left the newspaper to become a businessman. As he had made money, he was able to start his own journal: the first issue was published on July 10, 2008, more or less one year after the fiftieth anniversary of the Anti-Rightist Campaign. It was privately funded, and was created by and circulated among a network of former rightists who write personal recollections of the past, publish discussions on the meaning of the Anti-Rightist Movement, and discuss the future of the regime. They also debate the importance of the emergence of unofficial memory in its columns.

In its first issue, the journal's goals were stated as follows:

> We, who have reached a ripe old age, have always wanted to write accounts of the small and great facts of our experience for everyone (including ourselves) in a spirit of frankness, realism, and objectivity in order to restore historical truth and to show the goodness and beauty of the human heart. With this, we want to encourage the living, and warn future generations.[37]

The journal contained a great number of testimonies by victims of Maoist movements. The bulk was composed of rightists' accounts that could not be published officially, but Tie Liu did not limit the scope of his periodical to the experiences of his companions of misfortune. The first issue also contained an article by Wan Runnan, the former chairman of the Federation for a Democratic China created overseas after 1989, an article on home searches during the early days of the Cultural Revolution, and testimonies by rightists, especially Tie Liu's own experience with literary journalists at the *Sichuan Ribao*. Besides the witness accounts, the journal also ran analytical articles by famous rightists. Xie Tao (1921–2010), a veteran Communist who led Renmin University's research team on Marxism Leninism after 1949, was labeled a Hu Feng supporter in 1955, and spent ten years in jail for that "crime," regularly wrote analytical articles in the journal. This scholar, who was a luminary of the Chinese Academy of Social Sciences in the 1980s and wrote a famous article advocating social democracy in 2007,[38] consistently denounced Mao Zedong, the man, his theories, and his leadership style in the columns of the journal. He also wrote the introductory text to the journal's first issue, under the title "Reading *Tiny Scars of the Past* is Rewarding."[39]

The accounts, either by survivors or by their companions, paint a bleak picture of the Maoist years, when any autonomous thinking led either to jail or to *laogai* (reform through labor camps). Marxist authors in the journal accused Mao of being a feudal lord and a Stalinist, and these accusations were supported by the narrations of the various movements launched by the Great Helmsman. The journal published

---

37. *Wangshi weihen*, no. 1, July 10, 2008.
38. Xie Tao, "Minzhu shehui zhuyi moshi yu Zhongguo qiantu," 1–8.
39. *Wangshi weihen*, no. 1, July 10, 2008.

special issues on certain events, such as the Anti-Rightist Movement in Peking University, and on famous rightists.

Following the path of Arseny Roginsky, the founder of the Soviet organization Memorial, whose association started by collecting the testimonies of the victims of Stalin's rule and continued by denouncing human rights violations in Russia, Tie Liu published articles on the 1989 Tiananmen massacre and on the repression of human rights defenders. In early 2012, he launched a campaign of denunciation of Mao Zedong, and asked for the dismantling of his mausoleum on Tiananmen Square. In August 2012, on the eve of the 18th Party Congress, which was to see a complete change of leadership, he launched a petition to reiterate his demand that Mao be judged for crimes against humanity.[40] Tie Liu hoped that the new generation of leaders would be more ready to listen to criticism of the Great Helmsman. Therefore, after the Congress, he openly supported Xi Jinping's declarations on the importance of enforcing the constitution. In December 2013, Tie Liu wrote a letter to Politburo Standing Committee Member Wang Qishan to express his support for the struggle against corruption. But the journal not only expressed its support for positive aspects of the new rulers' policy, it has also published many articles asking for the enforcement of constitutionalism, which it regards as the only way to avoid the repetition of the tragedies of the past.

To Tie Liu, by providing a platform where facts can be freely presented and discussed, the journal acted in favor of the pluralization of Chinese society, the democratization of the regime, and the emergence of an autonomous civil society. What impact can a pluralistic memory of the Maoist period have on the evolution of the regime? Is it possible to organize public discussions of the recent past of the People's Republic under the present political circumstances? By publishing accounts of the past that escape strict official censorship, *Tiny Scars of the Past* contributed to the pluralization of the sociopolitical sphere. Its denunciation of the Anti-Rightist Campaign led it to fight assiduously for political reform.

Until the end of 2010, Tie sent the journal by mail to subscribers. He then decided to modernize and cut costs, and the first electronic issue, no. 65, was sent on January 25, 2011. By mid-March 2014, *Wangshi weihen* had published 113 issues, a remarkable feat for an unofficial journal. However, it was not published regularly, and during its last two years the time lag between issues grew longer. The endeavor became increasingly dangerous and came to an end in September 2014, when eighty-two-year-old Tie Liu was detained for "stirring quarrels and creating trouble."[41] After he spent a month in detention, in October of that year, the original charge was discarded, and he was accused of "engaging in illegal economic activities"

---

40. Tie Liu, "Bixu chedi qingsuan 'wenge' yuanxiong Mao Zedong de taotian zuixing" [We must completely eradicate the horrendous crimes of Mao Zedong, the executioner of the "Cultural Revolution"], email, September 2, 2012.
41. "Writer Tie Liu Detained," *BBC News*, September 15, 2014, http://www.bbc.com/news/world-asia-china-29204874.

for publishing *Tiny Scars of the Past*, although it was sent to subscribers for free. He was transferred to Chengdu detention center on November 24, 2014, and had to write a self-criticism. He also had to pledge that he wouldn't write any more articles on politics and would not take part in "rightist" activities. On February 22, 2015, he was sentenced to thirty months of jail time with a four-year reprieve, and to a fine of 30,000 yuan for having published an illegal publication. He was thereafter released, but he can be rearrested at any time.[42] The harassment of such an old man shows that the Party is serious when it comes to reaffirming its monopoly on the interpretation of history.

Jiyi 記憶 (Remembrance)[43]

This journal was founded in 2008 by film historian Wu Di. Since the passing of the 1981 Resolution on Party History, publishing accounts of the Cultural Revolution has become increasingly difficult, almost a "prohibited zone." Not willing to have a direct conflict with the authorities, the editors of *Jiyi* have been careful not to make their journal public: although it exists in electronic form, it is not accessible on the internet, and is circulated through an email list. Subscribers have to send an email to a member of the editorial board with their names and addresses. Then, they receive *Jiyi* by email. The number of readers is about one thousand. At first, it was published monthly, but the number of articles received by the board was such that in April 2014, with issue no. 111, it became a bimonthly. The objective of the journal is to provide a platform for discussion and research on the Cultural Revolution. Authors belong to various social categories: teachers, scholars, and cadres. The most active are witnesses of the movement who want to transmit their experiences to the younger generations, and to discuss with their peers the meaning of an experience that has determined their futures. Accounts by former Red Guards and descriptions of life in the villages by former educated youth represent the bulk of the publication. *Jiyi* often publishes special issues, such as one on Red Guard journals,[44] or on the Cultural Revolution in a specific high school.[45] Although it is concerned essentially with this historical event, it publishes articles on other episodes of Mao's rule. For example, in 2012, it published articles on Land Reform and on the Anti-Rightist Movement.[46] Wu Di, the editor declares: "Of course, we are especially interested in the Cultural Revolution, as I went through it. However, the Cultural Revolution

---

42. "Tanfang chuyu de gan yan zuojia Tie Liu" [Interview with the recently freed courageous writer Tie Liu], *Yazhou zhoukan*, no. 11, March 22, 2015, http://www.yzzk.com/cfm/content_archive.cfm?id=1426130971406&docissue=2015-11.
43. See Michael Schoenhals, "*Jiyi* (Remembrance), Edited by Wu Di (Beijing) and He Shu (Chongqing)," *China Quarterly* 197 (March 2009): 204–6.
44. Cf. *Hongweibing baokan yanlu* [Quotations from Red Guards journals], *Jiyi*, no. 111, April 15, 2014.
45. *Nü fuzhong wenge zhuanji* [Special issue on the Cultural Revolution at the girls' high school], *Jiyi*, no. 112, April 30, 2014; *Beijing sizhong* [Beijing no. 4 High School], *Jiyi*, no. 11, June 30, 2010.
46. Cf. Ren Donglin, "Tudi gaige qianhou de Hunan nongcun" [Hunan villages before and after the Land Reform], *Jiyi*, no. 84, May 31, 2012.

didn't come from the sky. It is a natural development of the previous years' history. If one wants to understand it, one has to analyze the Anti-Rightist Movement, and even to go back to the 1942 Yan'an rectification movement. This is the reason why we are concerned with the whole period of Mao's rule."[47] But by contrast with the above-mentioned journals, *Jiyi* limits itself to reflections on history and to the publication of witness accounts. It also carries reviews of books concerning the history of the PRC, whether they were published in China or overseas.

However, it doesn't publish analyses of the present situation and doesn't advocate political reform. All in all, it is more academic than the other periodicals that have been presented above. Recently, an official website has decided to regularly republish articles that had appeared in the journal. This shows that its academic value is recognized, and represents a kind of protection that might guarantee its long-term existence.

Despite the fact that it is mostly academic, it also provides a platform for authors to meet as it organizes conferences and commemorations of various events related to the Cultural Revolution.

We have noted above that since he became Secretary General of the CCP, Xi Jinping has reinforced its grip on publishing and on public opinion. The importance that the new leadership attaches to its monopoly over history has led the authorities to crack down on the expression of alternative visions of history. With the approach of the fiftieth anniversary of the Cultural Revolution, the public security reinforced its surveillance of unofficial publications, especially those that, like *Jiyi*, are devoted to the history of that movement. Pressure increased on its publishers.[48] During 2016, *Jiyi* did not organize any conference. However, it did not interrupt its publication.

Zuotian 昨天 (Yesterday)

Another electronic journal, *Zuotian* 昨天 (Yesterday) shares the goals of *Jiyi*. Founded in 2012, it aims at "resurrecting the memory of the Cultural Revolution, at gathering its archives, exchanging and encouraging research on the Cultural Revolution. Like autumn leaves, those who witnessed these events disappear, and as long as archives are not all accessible, collecting memoirs and documents of the movement represents the basic work of scholars."[49] It is interesting to note that journals devoted to the Cultural Revolution have a more academic slant than the ones launched by the former "rightists." This might have to do with the experience of the Cultural Revolution: at the time, Red Guards denounced academic research as bourgeois, and refused to engage in it. When they came of age, they reflected on their experiences and often concluded that this contempt for academic research

---

47. Interview with Wu Di, June 23, 2014.
48. Interviews in Beijing, June 2015.
49. *Zuotian*, no. 1, January 31, 2012.

had been a factor that had contributed to the disaster. Therefore, when they publish journals on the period, they are very careful to respect basic academic criteria, to show clearly that they have broken with the past. Of course, presenting oneself as an academic journal is also safer in the eyes of the authorities.

Chinese *Samizdats*

Besides the periodicals that are devoted to unofficial (*minjian*) history, other initiatives taken by victims of the various Maoist movements have appeared. A great number of rightists have published their memoirs in Hong Kong, and in some Hong Kong journals: *Kaifang* 開放 has hosted many of these memoirs which provide a vivid, and often tragic account of the sufferings of Mao's victims. The 57 Xueshe 五七學社 (1957 study association), founded by former rightists from Peking University,[50] also helps rightists to publish accounts of their experiences. Once again, the role of Hong Kong is invaluable as a locus for independent publishing. Hong Kong academic institutions also play an important role in the writing of an alternative history, especially the Universities Service Centre, which, at the initiative of Xiong Jingming, has collected an impressive number of unofficial accounts in its library. Xiong has also launched a website, called *minjian lishi* (unofficial history) where bibliographies, documents and testimonies can be found.[51] As an increasing number of historians, scholars, and intellectuals from the mainland often go to Hong Kong; the influence of this initiative on the production of unofficial history in the People's Republic is far from trivial.

But other initiatives need to be mentioned: the considerable lowering of the costs of printing on the mainland has allowed some ordinary citizens to print accounts of their lives and give them away or sell them in private circles of friends. Of course the quality of these works varies greatly according to their authors' talents—some of them are embellished accounts of their lives, some do not rigorously respect historical truth—but as long as archives are not open to the public, they represent a valuable corpus for the historians who want to write a balanced account of Mao's rule. If most of these works don't meet the criteria of scientific history, there are exceptions either because of the extraordinary experiences of their authors, or because they present materials that were unknown until they were written. The number of these works is impressive and I have chosen to present two of these as they describe little-known events that took place in the 1950s and in the 1960s.

---

50. See the 1957 Society website: http://www.57hk.org/.
51. See the Minjian Lishi website: http://mjlsh.usc.cuhk.edu.hk/.

Resisting by disclosing forgotten movements: *The 1958 Disaster* (*Wuba jie* 五八劫) and the socialist education movement in Chengdu[52]

In 2008, I met victims of a very-little-known movement that rocked the high schools of Sichuan in the winter of 1958. Although this socialist education movement (*shehuizhuyi jiaoyu yundong* 社會主義教育運動) existed at the national level, it was strongest in that province. Modeled after the Hundred Flowers and the Anti-Rightist Movements that had just taken place, it aimed at persuading high school students to sincerely criticize the new government, promising that they wouldn't be punished. Chinese Youth League cadres were directed to take the initiative in exercising criticism.

However, after two weeks, a rectification movement was launched and the students were classified into four categories: the third and the fourth groups were considered "dubious" and their members were subjected to reeducation. Some of them couldn't graduate, some were sent to reeducation through labor, all were given jobs in backward regions unrelated to their qualifications, and none of them were allowed to take the university entrance exam (*gaokao* 高考) and pursue a tertiary education. As they had not been labeled rightists or bad elements, their situation did not change when the rightist verdicts were "corrected" in 1979–1980, and most were in no position to return to their place of origin.

This movement came to my attention thanks to an exceptional character, Wang Jianjun, who has launched a protracted struggle to make the government acknowledge the sufferings it caused the teenagers of that period. Since he retired, Wang has unceasingly looked for classmates who, like himself, were victims of the campaign. He collected more than one hundred testimonies that he published in a series of three books. Obviously, these books were printed unofficially, and he used his own money to publish them. He had to find a printer in the countryside near Chengdu, and went to collect the books with a friend at night, to avoid being noticed by the authorities.

But Wang was not satisfied with simply publishing these recollections. Acting as a real historian, he managed to locate and publish the official documents related to this campaign: the letters that the Communist Youth League leaders sent to the organization cadres, urging them to take the initiative in criticizing the authorities, are particularly interesting. No historian in Party schools or in universities helped Wang do the job, he worked totally on his own. Now, he is trying to convince his former classmates to write longer autobiographies so that future generations will be aware of the campaign that ruined the lives of thousands of teenagers. He has engaged in this huge work in order to warn the future generations of the dangers of one-party rule and of the absence of freedom of expression. Wang is a very good example of the victims who do not want their suffering to remain useless.

---

52. Wang Jianjun, ed., *Wuba jie, Wuba jie (Xubian), Wo yu Wuba jie* [The 1958 disaster, The 1958 disaster continued, The 58 disaster and myself]. The three books have been self-published.

Disclosing past episodes of resistance: Tan Chanxue, *Qiusu* (Searching)

A large number of people who have been through the agitated period of Maoism have written autobiographies. In this huge bibliography, Tan Chanxue's 譚蟬雪 story[53] stands out because her book is not only an account of the sufferings endured by students who were labeled rightists in 1957. She describes the struggle by a small group of rusticated rightists to denounce the consequences of the Great Leap Forward. Her book provides first-hand material on the history of the 1960s. Like *58 jie*, it is a *samizdat*: a fake Hong Kong company served to get an ISBN number, but the author used her own money to publish the book.[54]

In 1957, Tan Chanxue was a student at Lanzhou University, and like most of her classmates, she took part in the great debate (*daming dafang* 大鳴大放) organized by the Party. During one of these meetings, she mentioned a saying that circulated among the peasants of her native village: "the KMT was corrupt, the CCP exploits the labor of the people." She wanted to point out the consequences of some errors committed by Party cadres during the previous movements. After June 1957, this was considered rightist talk, and Tan was labeled a rightist: she had to do manual work for two years in the University without a salary, and was then sent to a village in Tianshui (Gansu) to be reeducated by the peasants. During her stay in the countryside, she met Zhang Chunyuan, another rightist from her university who had also been sent down, and took part in the adventure of *Xinghuo* 星火 (The spark) a mimeographed journal that he had started in order to discuss his experiences with other rightists. Only twenty copies of the "journal" were printed and circulated among friends. This was enough to have its editors sentenced to long prison terms.[55]

In her book, Tan publishes the contents of the only two issues that ever saw the light of day. This journal was made famous by Hu Jie's film on Peking University rightist Lin Zhao, who published a long prose poem (*Haiou* 海鷗, The seagull) in its first issue.[56] But most interesting are the analyses of the Great Leap Forward and the Great Famine that it conveyed. The foreword of the first issue of *Xinghuo* is a good indication of the contents of the journal.

> Why, after hardly ten years in power, has a once progressive party become so corrupt and reactionary, so that on the domestic scene there is anger, noise, confusion, and rebellions everywhere while on the world scene it is surrounded by enemies all over? This is because it has made everything that belongs to the whole people its private property; and because everything—down to the smallest matter—is decided by Party members. . . . If one wants to call this despotic rule socialism, then it must be a State socialism monopolized by political oligarchs, it

---

53. Tan Chanxue, *Qiusu* [Searching] (Hong Kong: Hong Kong Tianma Ltd., 2010), 263.
54. I am grateful to the documentary film maker Hu Jie who introduced me to Tan Chanxue whom he had interviewed in his film *Xinghuo* 星火 (The Spark).
55. Tan Chanxue was sentenced to fourteen years, while Zhang Chunyuan was sentenced to life imprisonment. His sentence was changed during the Cultural Revolution and he was executed in 1970.
56. Hu Jie has also made a documentary *Xinghuo* (Spark) which tells the story of the journal.

belongs to the same category as the Nazis' national-socialism, but has nothing in common with real socialism . . . Comrades who have already become aware, let us unite under the common goal of 'democratic socialism,' of 'scientific socialism,' and seize the opportunity to awaken the masses in order to fight for the complete destruction of this strong power's rule![57]

The articles published in the journal contain analyses of the way people's communes had deprived the peasants of all their rights and changed them into serfs who depend on the State for everything.[58] Most of the articles criticize the collectivization enforced after the Great Leap Forward and denounce the People's communes as a form of militarization of the countryside: "Because they have been deprived of everything (including their fundamental human rights) peasants have become a proletariat, this is utterly obvious."

The workers' situation is no better: with the exception of a few large factories, their working conditions are bad, their work quotas are very high, their salaries are low, and "discontent and resistance among the working class are also growing."[59] After having described the intellectuals' situation, the author concludes:

> The buds of a brand new bureaucratic stratum had already appeared before 1957, but it is only after that year that its characteristics have become clear and perfect. The ruling bureaucracy's features are the following: in the political, spiritual and economic fields, it enjoys privileges, and practices repression, pillage and enslavement.[60]

The journal also contains denunciations of the movement against rightist opportunism, and defends Peng Dehuai's position at the Lushan plenum.[61] Tan Chanxue's book shows that as early as 1960, some rightists had not only seen through the Great Leap Forward, but had also started to take action. They had also convinced some local cadres who decided to work with them in order to prevent the extension of the Great Famine that had started to affect their district. Wushan Party Vice-Secretary Du Yinghua was one of them: he used the rightists' insights and was influenced by their criticisms of the people's communes. In 1960, he was sentenced to three years in jail as a rightist opportunist.[62]

---

57. Introductory article to *Xinghuo*, "Give Up Your Illusions, Prepare for the Struggle," *Xinghuo*, no. 1, reprinted in Tan Chanxue, *Qiusu*, 28.
58. Zhang Chunyuan, "Nongmin, nongnu he nongli, dangqian nongcun peishi zhiyi" [Peasants, serfs and slaves, an analysis of the present countryside, part 1], *Xinghuo*, no. 1, in Tan Chunxue, *Qiusu*, 55.
59. Xiang Chengqian, "Muqian xingshi ji women renwu" [The present situation and our task], *Xinghuo*, no. 1, 33.
60. Xiang Chengqian, "Muqian xingshi ji women renwu," 34.
61. At the Lushan Plenum in 1959, Marshall Peng Dehuai, then minister of defense, wrote a letter to Mao Zedong to denounce the consequences of the Great Leap Forward. Mao circulated the letter among the members of the Central Committee and demoted Peng. He then launched the campaign against "rightist opportunists."
62. Tan Chanxue, *Qiusu*, 100–101. While in jail, Du, who was a "free employee" communicated with Zhang Chunyuan who was in the same jail, and was therefore sentenced to death and executed with Zhang. Wang Zhongyi, *Chi zi zhenqing* [The truth about the revolutionary words] (Longcheng: self-published, 2012).

Tan's book casts a light on resistance at the grassroots, a phenomenon that is little known by historians of the period. The author is convinced that *Xinghuo*'s experience can be useful at present: it shows that even under Mao's rule, when there was no autonomous public opinion, in the countryside, some citizens had been able to analyze the situation and to take steps to start resistance, despite the fact that they had been deprived of their basic freedoms.[63]

Writing history from a personal point of view, without respecting the official guidelines repeatedly published by the Party, is in itself an act of resistance, as it challenges the narrative on which the regime legitimacy is built. In this article, we have presented a selection of initiatives taken by private citizens to present their visions of contemporary history. Far from being exhaustive, this survey nevertheless shows the plurality of these initiatives. Most of them have something in common: their authors are convinced that, by making public their own interpretation of the past, they contribute to the pluralization of Chinese society, and that this pluralization itself is a defense against the possible repetition of the tragedies that ruined their lives.

One of the characteristics of these endeavors is that they are not the works of professional historians, but in the majority of cases, of citizens who went through the period, either as actors or as victims of the movements. They have launched these publications because they wanted to let future generations know what they have been through, and provide them with the knowledge that would help them avoid the repetition of the tragedies. These lessons vary according to the generations and according to personalities: whereas rightists and old Party members advocate a deep political reform and democratization, former Red Guards tend to avoid directly political discourse and emphasize the academic level of their endeavors. But whatever their avowed motivations, they all work to break the monopoly exercised by the Party on the writing and the interpretation of contemporary history. This, in itself, is an act of resistance. It contributes to the structuring of the pro-democracy movement, as the absence of memory of past struggles is one of its major weaknesses.

However, the regime is vigilant, and over the last year, many of the writers who published unofficial accounts of recent history have run into problems: as we have seen, *Yanhuang chunqiu*, one of the major official publications, has been suppressed, while Tie Liu, the initiator of *Tiny Scars of the Past*, has been detained. Writing about past resistance, or writing about past suffering, has remained an act of resistance. For, as Liu Xiaobo wrote:

> Man is a spiritual animal, memory is the foundation of spiritual life, an individual without memory is a vegetable, and for a nation, not having memory is a kind of spiritual suicide. If after every catastrophe, survivors are not able to reflect over the disaster, they are, at best, useless bodies. And even if they enjoy the

---

63. Interview with Tan Chanxue, Shanghai, May 2014.

happiness of relative prosperity, what they enjoy is only the happiness of the pigs in a pigsty.[64]

Bibliography

Chan, Minnie. "Order to 'Realign' Outspoken Liberal Magazine Will End Its Independence, Says Publisher." *South China Morning Post*, September 19, 2014. http://www.scmp.com/news/china/article/1595608/order-realign-outspoken-liberal-magazine-will-end-its-independence-says.

Dai Huang. *Hu Yaobang yu pingfan yuan jia cuo an* [Hu Yaobang and the rehabilitation of the unjust, fake, wrong cases]. Beijing: Sanlian chubanshe, 2013.

Kanlishi zazhi bianzhe [Kanlishi editors]. *Kebenshang bu shuo de lishi: Zhongxuesheng bixia de bainian jiaguo jiyi* [The history which is not told in history books: The memory of the homeland under the pen of high school students]. Beijing: Citic Press, 2012.

Lefort, Claude. "Reculer les frontières du possible." In *L'invention démocratique*. Paris: Le livre de poche, 1981.

Lefort, Claude. *Un homme en trop*. Paris: Belin, 2015.

Liu Xiaobo. "Meiyou jiyi, meiyou lishi, meiyou weilai—wei Beijing wenxue yu jiyi yantaohui er zuo" [Without memory, without history, there is no future—written for the Beijing Conference on Literature and Memory]. *Minzhu Zhongguo*, January 28, 2006. https://www.peacehall.com/news/gb/china/2006/01/200601281029.shtml

MacFarquhar, Roderick. *The Origins of the Cultural Revolution*. Oxford: Oxford University Press, 1974.

Mei Ninghua. "Qizhi xianmingde fandui lishi xuwuzhuyi" [Overtly oppose historical nihilism]. *Zhongguo Gongchandang Xinwen wang*, May 24, 2010. http://dangshi.people.com.cn/GB/138903/138911/11676447.html.

Niu Han, and Deng Jiuping, eds. *Jiyizhong de fanyoupai yundong* [The Anti-Rightist Movement in memory], a trilogy: *Liu Yue xue* [Snow in June], *Jingji lu* [A road filled with thorns], *Yuanshang cao* [Grass on the plain]. Beijing: Jingji ribao chubanshe, 1998.

Ren Donglin. "Tudi gaige qianhou de Hunan nongcun" [Hunan villages before and after the Land Reform], *Jiyi*, no. 84, May 31, 2012.

Ruan Ming. *L'empire de Deng Xiaoping: chronique d'un empire*. Arles: Picquier, 1992.

Schoenhals, Michael. "*Jiyi* (Remembrance), Edited by Wu Di (Beijing) and He Shu (Chongqing). Bi-weekly non-commercial electronic publication (distributed via the internet to Cultural Revolution historians worldwide). Twelve issues by mid-January 2009 (each issue approximately 64 pp.)." *China Quarterly* 197 (March 2009): 204–6.

Sidane, Victor. *Le printemps de Pékin*. Paris: Gallimard, Archives, 1980.

Tan Chanxue. *Qiusu* [Searching]. Hong Kong: Hong Kong Tianma Ltd., 2010.

Tie Liu. "Bixu chedi qingsuan 'wenge' yuanxiong Mao Zedong de taotian zuixing" [We must completely eradicate the horrendous crimes of Mao Zedong, the executioner of the "Cultural Revolution"], email, September 2, 2012.

---

64. Liu Xiaobo, "Meiyou jiyi, meiyou lishi, meiyou weilai—wei Beijing wenxue yu jiyi yantaohui er zuo" [Without memory, without history, there is no future—written for the Beijing Conference on Literature and Memory], *Minzhu Zhongguo*, January 28, 2006, https://www.peacehall.com/news/gb/china/2006/01/200601281029.shtml.

Wang Jianjun, ed. *Wuba jie, Wuba jie (Xubian), Wo yu Wuba jie* [The 1958 disaster, the 1958 disaster continued, the 58 disaster and myself]. No publisher, no date.

Wang Ruoshui. "Work-Style Rectification Overwhelms Enlightenment: The Collision Between the May Fourth Spirit and 'Party Culture.'" In *Contemporary Chinese Thought*, special issue edited by J-P. Béja and J-P. Cabestan, "The Challenge Facing Chinese Intellectuals in the 21st Century" 34, no. 4 (Summer 2003): 27–56.

Wang Zhongyi. *Chi zi zhenqing* [The truth about the revolutionary words]. Longcheng: self-published, 2012.

Wen Ji. "Zhang Wentian zai Lushan huiyishang de kangzheng" [Zhang Wentian's resistance at Lushan plenum]. *Yanhuang Chunqiu*, no. 12 (2000). http://www.yhcqw.com/html/cqb/2008/327/08327103248JGK1F251EAD3ECC1HC79G0F.html.

Wu Wei. "Zhonggong shisan da baogao qicao shushi" [The truth about the preparation of the report to the 13th Congress]. *Yanhuang chunqiu*, no. 4 (2014): 47–56.

Xie Tao. "Minzhu shehuizhuyi moshi yu Zhongguo qiantu" [The social-democratic model and the future of China]. *Yanhuang Chunqiu*, no. 2 (2007): 1–8. http://www.yhcqw.com/html/yjy/2008/420/08420105457EJH1I1817I1G7K2KICIH6BBC.html.

Xu Qingquan. "'Wenqing' Wen Jize" [The warm-hearted Wen Jize]. *Yanhuang chunaiu*, no. 3 (2014): 42.

Yang Dipu. "Lushan huiyi Zhou Xiaodan jianchi bu pi Peng Dehuai" [Zhou Xiaodan persists in refusing to criticize Peng Dehuai at the Lushan Plenum]. *Yanhuang Chunqiu*, no. 1 (2001). http://www.yhcqw.com/html/qsp/2008/327/083271136277811277H5IH9JDHIED0GEF.html.

Yang Jisheng. *Tombstone: The Great Chinese Famine (1959–1961)*. London: Allen Lane, 2012.

Yan Lianke. "On China's State-Sponsored Amnesia." *New York Times*, April 2, 2013. http://www.nytimes.com/2013/04/02/opinion/on-chinas-state-sponsored-amnesia.html?pagewanted=all&_r=0.

3
Annals of the Yellow Emperor
Reconstructing Public Memory of the Mao Era

Wu Si

From 2013 to 2014,[1] the journal *Yanhuang Chunqiu* (Annals of the Yellow Emperor) was involved in a dispute over the Great Famine. On one side was Jiangsu Normal University Professor Sun Jingxian, and on the other side were the journal's deputy editor, Yang Jisheng, and executive editor, Hong Zhenkuai.

Professor Sun published an article in *Chinese Social Sciences Today* (Zhongguo shehui kexue bao)[2] pointing out at least eight data errors in Yang Jisheng's *Tombstone*,[3] and on that basis he dismissed Yang's estimate of more than thirty million starvation deaths as mere rumor. Yang Jisheng responded with an article in the December 2013 issue of *Yanhuang Chunqiu* entitled "Rebutting the Claim that Thirty Million Starvation Deaths is Mere Rumor."[4] Sun Jingxian then further rebutted Yang Jisheng's arguments in conferences and on the internet, and Yang published another article in response: "Discussion on Population Loss during the Great Famine Years" (September 2014).[5] Hong Zhenkuai took Yang's side in the dispute with two articles in *Yanhuang Chunqiu*: "Great Famine Mortality Figures in Local Gazetteers" (May 2014)[6] and "New Fallacious Arguments Regarding the Great Famine: Viewing the Absurdity of 'Nutritional Mortality' of 2.5 Million People on the Basis of Sichuan's Official Figures" (November 2014).[7]

---

1. Translator's Note (TN): Wu Si resigned as chief editor of *Yanhuang Chunqiu* at the end of 2014.
2. TN: A publication of the Chinese Academy of Social Sciences.
3. TN: Yang Jisheng, *Mubei* (Hong Kong: Cosmos Books, 2008); English translation, *Tombstone: The Great Chinese Famine 1958–1962*, trans. Stacy Mosher and Guo Jian (New York: Farrar, Straus, and Giroux, 2012).
4. TN: Yang Jisheng, "Bo esi sanqianwan shi yaoyan" [Rebutting the claim that 30 million starvation deaths is mere rumor], 21ccom.net, December 14, 2013, accessed February 9, 2016, http://www.21ccom.net/articles/read/dushu/2013/1214/97011.html.
5. TN: Yang Jisheng, "Guanyu da jihuang niandai renkou sunshi de taolun" [Discussion on population loss during the Great Famine years], *Yanhuang Chunqiu* online, accessed February 9, 2016, http://www.yhcqw.com/html/zml/2014/99/1499152593JA8596114653IDEJEJH96AK.html.
6. TN: Hong Zhenkuai, "Difangzhi zhong de da jihuang siwang shuzi" [Great Famine mortality figures in local gazetteers], *Yanhuang Chunqiu* online, accessed February 9, 2016, http://www.yhcqw.com/html/wenzjc/2014/55/JI5D.html.
7. TN: Hong Zhenkuai, "Youguan da jihuang de xin miushuo: cong Sichuan guanfang shuju kan 'yingyangxing siwang' 250 wan ren de huangmiuxing" [New fallacious arguments regarding the Great Famine: Viewing the absurdity of "nutritional mortality" of 2.5 million people on the basis of Sichuan's official figures], *Yanhuang*

The dispute revived interest in the topic, resulting in a noticeable increase in articles about the Great Famine: nine in 2013, and eleven in 2014. These articles described the circumstances and details of the Great Famine from various angles, including cannibalism, referred to as "special cases."

Yanhuang Chunqiu enjoys disputes, and established a special column called "Record of Contention" (Zhengming lu). Controversial topics are good publicity. The number of clicks on *Yanhuang Chunqiu*'s Sina Weibo (microblog) for Hong Zhenkuai's "New Fallacious Arguments Regarding the Great Famine" reached 2.42 million within a month of its publication. On December 5 of that year, Sun Jingxian published another article in *Chinese Social Sciences Today*, "Refuting Hong Zhenkuai's 'New Fallacious Arguments Regarding the Great Famine.'"[8] It was presented on Sina News and reposted on the Sina Weibo *Headline News* (Toutiao xinwen), which has 36.96 million followers. Netizens suggested that the two men debate face-to-face, and on December 7, Hong Zhenkuai posted a Weibo challenge to Sun Jingxian. The link received 2.27 million hits within seven hours, but Sun did not respond to the challenge.

The story has continued to develop. In December 2015, the Chinese Academy of Social Sciences published an edited volume of almost three million characters, entitled *Selected Critiques of Historical Nihilism by the Chinese Academy of Social Sciences*,[9] which included Sun Jingxian's "The Origins and Development of the thirty Million Dead Story." The government imposes the label "historical nihilism" on any historical research that "smears the glorious history of the Chinese Communist Party and the accomplishments of socialism," claiming that it seriously threatens the ideological safety of the country.

In August 2016, the magazine *Qiushi*, published by Party Central, ran an article by Wang Junwei, director of the no. 2 research group of the CCP Central Document Research Office 中共中央文獻研究室第二編研部, under the title "The History of the Party's and the People's Struggles Forcefully Impels Us to Remember Our Original Aspirations and Continue Advancing."[10] The author begins by stating that deepening the struggle against historical nihilism is the best way to remain loyal while continuing to advance. The article argues that hostile forces within and without often use the history of the new China to create controversy, doing all they

---

Chunqiu online (in two parts), accessed February 9, 2016, http://www.yhcqw.com/html/csl/2014/1111/B59K.html, http://www.yhcqw.com/html/csl/2014/1111/6BIH.html.

8. TN: Sun Jingxian, "Bo Hong Zhenkuai 'youguan da jihuang de xin miushuo" [Rebutting Hong Zhenkuai's "New fallacious arguments regarding the Great Famine"], Chinese Social Sciences Net, accessed February 9, 2016, http://www.cssn.cn/index/index_focus/201412/t20141205_1430365.shtml.

9. TN: Chinese Academy of Social Sciences, ed., *Zhongguo shehuike xueyuan lishi xuwuzhuyi pipan wenxuan* [Selected critiques of historical nihilism by the Chinese Academy of Social Sciences] Beijing: Zhongguo shehui kexue chubanshe), December 1, 2015.

10. TN: Wang Junwei, "Dang he renmin fendou shi women buwang chuxin jixu qianjin de qiangda dongle" [The history of the party's and the people's struggles forcefully impels us to remember our original aspirations and continue advancing], *Qiushi*, August 2016, posted on QStheory.cn, August 15, 2016, accessed June 1, 2017, http://www.qstheory.cn/dukan/qs/2016-08/15/c_1119373309.htm.

can to attack, smear, and slander in the hope of overthrowing the leadership of the Communist Party and the socialist system. The author praises Sun Jingxian's research.

By contrast, *Yanhuang Chunqiu* has only come under increasing pressure. In July 2016, it was placed under direct management of the Chinese Academy of Arts under the Ministry of Culture, and the staff was entirely replaced. What can we conclude from this example? It allows us to make at least five observations.

First, the three-year Great Famine started out as a sensitive area, but thanks to *Yanhuang Chunqiu*'s incremental efforts, for a while it was no longer such a sensitive topic. More than ten years ago, I published an article in *Yanhuang Chunqiu* by Liao Gailong[11] that referred to more than thirty million starvation deaths during the Great Famine. As far as I know, this was the first time this figure was disclosed in a mainland publication. Although Liao Gailong enjoyed an elevated standing as deputy director of the CCP's Central Party History Research Office, I worried that this figure would bring trouble and didn't dare play it up. Flipping through past issues of *Yanhuang Chunqiu*, I see that we didn't publish a single article on the Great Famine in the year 2000, but in 2014 there was an article on that topic in nearly every issue. The accumulation of articles over the past decade or so has caused some topics to gradually become less sensitive. This was the daily work of *Yanhuang Chunqiu*.

Second, the government's original strategy in these sensitive areas was cover-up and amnesia—the "sensitive issues cannot be discussed" approach—and historical journals either rejected articles on these topics or watered them down. *Yanhuang Chunqiu*, however, did all it could to reveal the true picture. Later, the official strategy seemed to have been adjusted, evincing a willingness to provoke disputes. *Yanhuang Chunqiu*'s response has been to actively participate in these disputes and investigate the truth, and if the journal was proven wrong, it had the courage to acknowledge it.

Third, the space for dispute remains limited to only a handful of publications: on the one side *Yanhuang Chunqiu*, and on the other side *Chinese Social Sciences Today* and *Red Flag Manuscripts* (Hongqi wengao). These publications seem to have a "special zone" status. Ordinary magazines, newspapers, and books are unable or afraid to join the debate, and television likewise. Publications such as those in the Southern News Group that used to join in such debates experienced increasing editorial clampdowns after the 18th Congress. But the internet is enormous, and all kinds of entities have joined the debates, creating new space for influencing and reconstructing memory.

---

11. TN: Liao Gailong, "Mao Zedong haozhao 'jinjing gankao' huimou" [A backward glance at Mao Zedong's appeal for "proceeding to the capital to take the civil service exam"], *Yanhuang Chunqiu*, no. 3 (2000): 30, states, "According to statistics for this period [the three years of extraordinary hardship], unnatural deaths reached 40 million."

Fourth, there's been an awakening and reconstruction of memory. On the subject of the Great Famine, the official version is that China experienced three years of hardship due to three years of natural disaster and the Soviet Revisionists chasing China for repayment of its debts. There was originally no mention of a human factor, but eventually the government acknowledged the errors of the Great Leap Forward and the campaign against Right deviation. The government originally provided no mortality figures, but eventually the research sphere acknowledged a population loss of more than ten million. *Yanhuang Chunqiu*, for its part, stated in multiple articles that this was a man-made disaster, and provided various estimates of population loss in the area of thirty million.

The once popular formulation of "three years of natural disaster" seldom appears in the news media anymore. Many people who survived the Great Famine have disseminated their individual experiences nationwide, and there is a more profound understanding of its causes. Many young people's interest in history has been aroused by controversies, and those who are willing to search for the truth are able to find it on the internet. The existence of *Yanhuang Chunqiu* and its participation in this controversy has added new content to the depository of public memory, and has brought public memory closer to the truth, which the public is also finding easier to understand.

Extending this case to the overall situation, who is reconstructing the memory of the Mao era? The government usually describes it without much detail. In terms of unofficial participants, most articles in *Yanhuang Chunqiu* are submitted by two kinds of people. The first type consists of people who lived through this era, mainly veteran cadres and elderly intellectuals; victims of the Cultural Revolution and Anti-Rightist Movement have been particularly active. The second type is scholars or people who carry out research in their spare time, most having liberal tendencies. Very few people in society's lower strata have taken part, and only a dozen or so articles have been written by people belonging to the Five Black Categories[12] or by the offspring of landlords or rich peasants. Popular memory of this type has always existed, but without easy access to the public sphere. *Yanhuang Chunqiu*'s role has been to open the public sphere to the popular memory that the government has attempted to cover up, and to participate in the reconstruction of public memory by focusing attention on these memories and disseminating them to a wider audience.

Lastly, the reconstruction of memories that threaten the legitimacy of the rulers is viewed by officials as a political struggle. The Party's central ideology organs have eagerly participated in the debate, but given the poor quality and suboptimal results of their productions, they have resorted to political methods to eliminate the organizations rebuilding memory. The topic of the Great Famine has once again fallen into silence; it is no longer mentioned in the press, and the large-scale rebuilding of memory has come to a halt. Nonetheless, related articles continue to circulate in

---

12. TN: In the Mao era, the "five black categories" referred to people classified as landlords, rich peasants, counterrevolutionaries, bad elements, and rightists.

isolation on the internet or on WeChat. In the text that follows I will describe the general situation of *Yanhuang Chunqiu*, the realm of reconstructing memory, and conflicts in the reconstruction of memory.

The Basic Situation of *Yanhuang Chunqiu*

Founded in 1991, *Yanhuang Chunqiu* is an oddity within China's publication management system and is nearly impossible to categorize. The person who proposed establishing the magazine was the chairman of the Yanhuang [Yellow Emperor] Cultural Research Association and former vice-chairman of the Chinese People's Political Consultative Conference, Xiao Ke. Research associations are considered civil society organizations within China's system, and fall under the supervision of the Ministry of Culture. The actual founder of the journal was Du Daozheng, who was vice-chairman of the research association's standing committee, and who retired with honors as Director of the General Administration of Press and Publication (GAPP). If not for Du's status and background, it would have been virtually impossible to obtain a periodical registration number. A periodical registration number is equivalent to franchise rights. Due to this influential backing, the Ministry of Culture and GAPP gave the journal a green light and humored these elderly officials by renaming a defunct magazine *Yanhuang Chunqiu*. In this sense, *Yanhuang Chunqiu* can be categorized as the journal of a civil society organization.

Government franchise rights are a precious resource, monopolistic and granted only to state-owned enterprises, and in fact the magazine was registered as a state-owned entity.

At the time of the journal's founding, Du Daozheng said the state wasn't providing any support in terms of funding or editorial staff. He borrowed 300,000 *yuan* from the slush funds of the Xinhua News Agency's domestic news department, and turnover was enough for him to eventually repay the loan in full. The editors, most of them retired cadres drawing pensions, came and went, and as of autumn 2014 they made up nine of the magazine's sixteen staff. In terms of investment and personnel, therefore, *Yanhuang Chunqiu* can be classified as a privately run publication.

After it began publication, *Yanhuang Chunqiu* referred to itself as a "peer publication" (*tongren kanwu*); as with Chen Duxiu's *New Youth*,[13] all of the editors had an equal vote. Eventually this system developed and matured into a seven-person association committee in which every member has an equal vote. In terms of the editorial work, each editor also has an equal vote. But China's peer publications became extinct in 1957 because the government didn't recognize that kind of organizational system. In short, *Yanhuang Chunqiu* was both a publication of a state-owned unit and the journal of a private association; it was both a private publication and a

---

13. TN: Chen Duxiu, cofounder of the Chinese Communist Party, founded the magazine *New Youth* (*Xin Qingnian*) in 1915. The magazine launched the New Culture Movement and was an important vehicle for spreading the influence of the May Fourth Movement.

peer publication. This makes it unique and impossible to classify; in other words, it resembled neither a work unit nor a company, neither a state-run company nor a privately run company.

This system of "four non-resemblances" placed *Yanhuang Chunqiu* on the boundaries of official territory, making it difficult for officials to intervene in personnel or budget matters. A forceful intervention would challenge retired leaders of an older generation and higher rank. Officials below the ministerial level would not take the initiative to interfere with the journal, while those on a higher level had many controversies with *Yanhuang Chunqiu* but were not able to reach a consensus to restrict it. The journal thus continued to develop and strengthen within the cracks of the system.

Before 2005, the print run hovered around 40,000 or 50,000 copies, by the fall of 2014, the actual print run was 195,000 copies, with 138,000 subscriptions sent through the mail. If the average reading ratio is about three people per copy, the journal would have had around 600,000 readers. The journal's main readership consisted of people in their fifties or sixties or older, and most were old cadres or elderly intellectuals. After 2007, the readership gradually expanded to include middle-aged cadres and intellectuals.

In 2008, the magazine began operating a *Yanhuang Chunqiu* website, and hits on individual articles reached nearly ten million. *Yanhuang Chunqiu* attracted a total of 11,125,000 followers through Sina, Tencent, Netease, Sohu, People's Daily Online, and other platforms. The magazine cooperated with other websites to promote its online edition, and it reached a circulation of 3,315,000 through iPad, iPhone, and mobile phone editions. Furthermore, *Yanhuang Chunqiu* established reposting relationships with Phoenix, 21ccom.net, Netease, Sohu, Sina, Yahoo, Tencent, and other websites. Its online readers were probably somewhat younger than its print subscribers, but the magazine lacks statistical data on their demographics. The above summarizes *Yanhuang Chunqiu*'s history, fringe status, target audience, and scope of influence.

Between September 2014 and the beginning of 2017, a series of momentous events took place at *Yanhuang Chunqiu*. Firstly, in September 2014, the government forcibly changed the supervisory unit of the journal from the private Yellow Emperor Cultural Research Association to the Academy of Arts, directly subordinate to the Ministry of Culture. After three or four months of bargaining, the journal withdrew its legal complaint and signed an agreement with the Academy, marking its incorporation into the state.

Secondly, in the process of changing its supervisory unit, major differences of opinion appeared, entailing a split in how to handle decision-making and differing viewpoints within the journal. These differences resulted in about half of the editorial board resigning. I resigned my position of executive publisher and chief editor, and the legal representative of the journal was subsequently changed. In June 2015, Yang Jisheng, who had replaced me as chief editor, was also forced to resign under pressure from the authorities, and the publisher, Du Daozheng, became chief editor as well.

Thirdly, between January 2015 and May 2016, *Yanhuang Chunqiu* encountered frequent direct conflicts with several government departments regarding the publication of certain articles. The authorities repeatedly sent teams to the printer to prevent printing and arbitrarily rejected articles. Printed copies were scrapped. This had never happened before.

Fourthly, in July 2016, the Academy of Arts appointed two cadres as chief editor and publisher of the journal, ordered Du Daozheng to retire, and sent people to forcibly occupy the journal's editorial offices and place editorial and financial documents under seal. Existing staff resisted without effect, and their attempt to file a lawsuit was rejected by the court; finally, they refused to obey the orders of the new leaders. Subsequent issues of the journal had completely different content, which now sang the praises of the leadership and disseminated the Party's glorious and correct history. The journal became the creator of historical memory authorized by the state, and a guardian of the ideological front.

Finally, after word spread of the state takeover, many old cadres cancelled their subscriptions. The authorities sent people around the country to distribute the journal, so that at the end of the year the print-run had not dropped. However, mail subscriptions had plummeted, reportedly falling by 30 percent. The content published after reorganization was seen as too "red" by even some officials, who suggested adjusting and softening it.

The Realm of Reconstructing Memory

From its founding in 1991 until 2014, *Yanhuang Chunqiu* published 273 issues totaling more than 5,000 articles, which can be divided into three types: the first type narrates historical facts, the second introduces and discusses major theoretical viewpoints, and the third takes stands on various political, economic, and social issues. Reconstructing public memory of the Mao era mainly relied on articles of the first type regarding the true situation at that time. However, the theoretical viewpoints and stands expressed in the other two types also played a part in reconstructing memory because they made people observe, unearth, and interpret new historical facts from a new perspective. Likewise, new historical facts also supported new viewpoints and standpoints. I will now briefly describe *Yanhuang Chunqiu*'s participation in reconstructing public memory of the Mao era.

The Mao era before the CCP took power

A large portion of articles in *Yanhuang Chunqiu* touch on sensitive topics in the history of the Chinese Communist Party (CCP): for example, the USSR's role in founding the CCP, the campaign against the AB League,[14] Land Reform and expansion of the Red Army in the Chinese soviet areas, the West Route Army, confidential cables during the Long March, the campaign to eliminate Trotskyites, the Yan'an Rectification Movement and "emergency rescue" campaign, the actual role of the Yan'an Forum on Art and Literature, trade in "special products" (i.e., opium) in Yan'an, the CCP's role in the War of Resistance against Japan and the Kuomintang's frontline battles, rectification of deviations in Land Reform, the role of the underground Party, and so on.

The CCP's calls for democracy and constitutional government before it took power, and its experience in building democracy and safeguarding human rights in the base areas, are expressions of a weak vein in CCP tradition. *Yanhuang Chunqiu* published multiple articles exploring and discussing these issues in depth, and proceeded from there to the particular experience of "truth at both ends."[15]

The Mao era after the CCP took power

There were constant political campaigns after the People's Republic of China was founded in 1949. Articles published in *Yanhuang Chunqiu* covered nearly all of these major historical incidents, especially through narratives by those who experienced them: Land Reform, the Korean War, the campaign to Suppress Counterrevolutionaries, the campaign to Eliminate Counterrevolutionaries, the Three-Antis and Five-Antis campaigns,[16] the campaign against the Hu Feng Clique,[17] the campaign against the Gao-Rao Anti-Party Clique,[18] collectivization of agriculture, joint state-private ownership, the Anti-Rightist Movement, the Great Leap Forward, the campaign against Right-deviation, the Great Famine, the 7,000 Cadre Conference, the Four Cleanups campaign,[19] various stages of the Cultural Revolution, and so on.

---

14. TN: The Anti-Bolshevik (AB) League, an intelligence agency of the Nationalist government, was largely defunct by the time Mao led a campaign against it in the Chinese soviet areas in 1930 and 1931.
15. TN: Yang Jisheng proposed the concept of "truth at both ends" in a January 2001 article entitled "Lun ziyouzhuyi yu Xinzuopai—Zhongguo de yichang kua shiji zhenglun" [On liberalism and the New Left: A century-spanning controversy in China]. In that article, Yang wrote of people who pursued truth in their youth and old age while being sidetracked by their blind faith in Maoism in their middle years. See Chen Ziming, "Suowei 'liangtou zhen': minzhu–zhuanzheng–minzhu" [So-called "truth at both ends": Democracy–dictatorship–democracy], 21ccom.net, June 30, 2013, accessed February 9, 2016, http://www.21ccom.net/articles/rwcq/article_2013063086608.html.
16. TN: A campaign against corruption, waste, and bureaucracy in 1951, and a campaign targeting the capitalist class, specifically bribery, theft of state property, tax evasion, shortchanging government contracts, and stealing state economic information, in 1952.
17. TN: The campaign against the writer and literary theorist Hu Feng in 1955 eventually resulted in investigations against more than 2,100 intellectuals labeled members of his "counterrevolutionary clique."
18. TN: Senior cadres Rao Shushi and Gao Gang were targeted in 1954 for alleged "splittist" activities.
19. TN: The Four Clean-Ups Campaign, also called the Socialist Education Movement, targeted "unclean" manifestations of capitalism in the cities and countryside from 1962 to 1966.

Articles on the Cultural Revolution constituted a major topic. The government limits publication of such articles, which are seldom seen in mainland Chinese periodicals. Comparatively speaking, *Yanhuang Chunqiu* covered this topic extensively and in-depth: the historical play *Hai Rui Dismissed from Office*, the Three Family Village,[20] the Red Guard Movement, Red August,[21] mass killings in various localities, power seizures in various localities and work units, armed battles, May 16th,[22] the Inner Mongolian People's Revolutionary Party,[23] the Cleansing of the Class Ranks, the Ninth National Party Congress,[24] the Lin Biao incident,[25] the campaign to criticize Lin Biao and Confucius, the incident in Shadian, Yunnan Province,[26] the April Fifth Movement,[27] the unseating of Deng Xiaoping, the campaigns to learn from Dazhai and Daqing,[28] and the smashing of the Gang of Four. Little has been missed, and most of the material came from first-person accounts.

Reviewing and appraising the Mao era

On the question of how to assess Mao Zedong since the reform and opening-up policy was adopted, the government's approach, coupled with reflections by private individuals, has strongly influenced the reconstruction of memory of the Mao era.

---

20. TN: "Notes from a Three Family Village" was the name of a column in the journal *Frontline* that published essays by leading Beijing officials Deng Tuo, Wu Han, and Liao Mosha in the early 1960s. Wu, a historian, was author of the historical play *Hai Rui Dismissed from Office*. After that play was targeted as an attempt to "use the past to criticize the present" in 1965, the writers of the Three Family Village column also came under attack. The controversy became the "blasting fuse" for the Cultural Revolution.
21. TN: An outbreak of violence by Red Guards in August 1966 resulting in numerous fatalities.
22. TN: The May 16 Circular, issued by the Politburo on that day in 1966, summarized Mao's ideological justification for the Cultural Revolution. A small group of Beijing college students who formed an organization named for the circular in 1967 was suppressed by the central leadership when it was deemed too "radical," setting off a nationwide, multiyear witch hunt that incriminated more than a million alleged members of the defunct group.
23. TN: From the latter half of 1967 until May 1969, a purge of counterrevolutionaries was carried out in the Inner Mongolian Autonomous Region, and interrogation under torture was used to classify hundreds of thousands of people as members of the Inner Mongolian People's Revolutionary Party.
24. TN: The congress was held in April 1969 at the height of the Cultural Revolution, at a time when most members of the Eighth Central Committee were under investigation or in prison and could not attend. Lin Biao represented the Central Committee in presenting a political report centered on the theory of "continuous revolution under the dictatorship of the proletariat," and which criticized the "bourgeois headquarters" headed by Liu Shaoqi.
25. TN: Lin Biao, Mao's "closest comrade-in-arms and successor," was killed along with his family in a plane crash in Mongolia while fleeing China on September 13, 1971.
26. TN: Shadian, populated by members of the Muslim Hui minority, mounted a resistance when the People's Liberation Army closed down its mosques and burned religious books in 1974. The PLA attacked the town in July 1975, resulting in the deaths of more than 1,000 of the town's 7,200 residents and the destruction of 4,400 homes.
27. TN: Crowds gathered at Tiananmen Square on the day of the Qingming Festival, April 5, 1976, to mourn the passing of Premier Zhou Enlai in January that year. Leaders of the Cultural Revolution ordered a military crackdown, and Deng Xiaoping, an ally of Zhou Enlai, was placed under house arrest. Deng was not rehabilitated until after the death of Mao and the fall of the Gang of Four in October 1976.
28. TN: Mao called for all of China to learn from the accomplishments of Dazhai, Shanxi Province, in agriculture and Daqing, Heilongjiang, in industry.

Yanhuang Chunqiu published many articles on this topic as well: For example, the large number of articles discussing "practice as the test of truth," as well as articles on redressing unjust cases and the persecution of Rightists, on the adjustment of rural policies, on internal discussions of resolutions on the Party's historical problems, on adjustments to Mao's diplomatic line, and so on.

Reconfiguring memory of the Mao era, forming new historical viewpoints and world views

The most influential article published by *Yanhuang Chunqiu* was "The Democratic Socialist Model and China's Future" (February 2007),[29] written by the former vice-president of People's University, Xie Tao. This article outlined a view of world history in which democratic socialism is the genuine Marxism, and in which liberalism constitutes the mainstream of modern civilization, while the Leninist-Stalinist-Maoist road falls under Left-deviating revisionism that diverged from Marxist orthodoxy and ultimately resulted in failure. According to this worldview, the CCP's reform and opening-up policy constitutes China's reversion to democratic socialist orthodoxy from Left-deviating revisionism and has merged it into the mainstream of world civilization.

This viewpoint gave a meaningful context of world history to the life experience of those who had failed in practicing their ideals. It held that the core values and concept system of these failed idealists could with slight adjustment be merged into the mainstream of world culture, allowing the people of those generations to locate their position in history. This historical position was not on the right course, but their motivations weren't evil or trivial and were consistent with their self-realization. Starting off from this position allowed them to revert to the right course at little cost and with dignity, and to advance toward the future. This historical interpretation was enthusiastically received by middle-aged Chinese and reconfigured the worldview of that generation. The enormous influence of this article has made it a symbol of the emergence of democratic socialism in China.

This article even triggered a great debate over "what flag to raise and which road to take" that generated articles totaling nearly 300,000 words in mainland periodicals. Maoists convened twelve meetings all over the country to denounce the article. The CCP's top officials and Central Committee publications joined in the debate to varying degrees. The official policy was to not repost the article, to criticize it minimally and obliquely, and to mainly take the approach of positive guidance. *Yanhuang Chunqiu* published more than a dozen articles during this discussion, and, apart from one supporting the Maoists, all of them supported the democratic socialist viewpoint. This led to the magazine being seen as representing

---

29. TN: Xie Tao died on August 25, 2010 at the age of 89. His article (Minzhu shehuizhuyi moshi yu Zhongguo qiantu) is not posted on the *Yanhuang Chunqiu* website and does not seem to be available online at this time.

a democratic socialist faction within the Party, and it constructed the subjectivity of *Yanhuang Chunqiu* in this period.

Another effort *Yanhuang Chunqiu* made toward constructing a historical view and worldview was through a new interpretation of the theory of New Democracy. This group of theorists holds that Mao's advocacy of New Democracy was correct, and that New Democracy came from Lenin's New Economic Policy.[30] Stalin and Mao later diverged from Lenin's correct road and embarked on socialism too early, and the reform and opening policy was a reversion to New Democracy. The theory of the first stage of socialism is the modern version of the theory of New Democracy. Modern China is a society under New Democracy. Du Runsheng's articles, such as "Modern China and the Structure of New Democracy,"[31] express this viewpoint. This standpoint triggered a response among a group of people inside the Party, and prior to the 18th Party Congress it gave rise to a fairly substantial political discussion that drew the participation of many media organs and the attention of senior government officials.

After 2012, *Yanhuang Chunqiu*'s efforts to construct a worldview were directed toward democracy, rule of law, and civil rights, including universal values. Throughout 2013, apart from a suspension of the journal at the government's insistence in November, every issue included articles discussing implementation of the 1983 revision of the Chinese Constitution. The political background to this discussion was an internal government document proposing "seven topics that cannot be discussed," which imposed increasingly severe restrictions on discussing constitutional government.

Encouraging repentance

Starting in 2006, *Yanhuang Chunqiu* took note of essays expressing repentance, especially by participants of the Cultural Revolution. The journal launched a special column that published more than twenty of these confessions from 2008 onward, as well as advertisements by people expressing their regrets. These advertisements triggered a series of confessions and apologies throughout China that became a focus of extensive media reporting. This kind of moral force stimulated greater public participation and supported the reconstruction of public memory.

---

30. TN: Lenin devised his New Economic Policy in 1921 in order to provide the state with an influx of capital until the economy was strong enough to achieve socialism.
31. TN: Du Runsheng, "Minzhu shehuizhuyi moshi yu Zhongguo qiantu" [Modern China and the structure of New Democracy], *Yanhuang Chunqiu*, no. 2 (2008), Yanhuang Chunqiu online, accessed February 10, 2016, http://www.yhcqw.com/html/yjy/2008/422/08422151332D26A020628B1148JCFBE5K8J.html.

Conflicts in Reconstructing Memory: Boundaries and Self-Discipline

In the periodical and publication sphere, the government uses a system of sponsoring and management units to establish access barriers in news and publishing. It then relies on the system of sponsoring and management units to carry out internal management of the personnel, finances, and content of media within the system. These measures more or less ensure that periodicals and publishing houses carry out the government's intentions in shaping public memory.

As described earlier, *Yanhuang Chunqiu* occupied a fringe position and didn't fit into any standard classification. As it was relatively impervious to control of its personnel and finances, the main control measure was content management. This consisted of two aspects: the first was a system for recording the intention to publish material on important topics (*zhongda xuanti bei'an zhidu* 重大選題備案制度), and the second was content review and informal notice (*da zhaohu* 打招呼).

On the aspect of recording the intention to publish material on important topics, there are three departmental regulations for classification purposes, which can be found in *Anthology of Laws and Regulations for Periodical Publishing*, published by the Encyclopedia of China Publishing House. The "important topic" domain directly related to *Yanhuang Chunqiu* includes:

1. The writings, lives, and work of current and former Party and state leaders; 2. China's defense build-up and key people and campaigns, battles, operations, and living conditions at various stages in the history of the Chinese military; 3. the Cultural Revolution; 4. major historical events and key historical personages in the history of the Chinese Communist Party; 5. leaders of the Kuomintang and other high-ranking targets of the united front; 6. major events and key leaders of the former Soviet Union, Eastern Europe, and other fraternal parties and nations.

According to the above stipulations, nearly all of the articles published in *Yanhuang Chunqiu* required registration of intention to publish, and these articles could not be published without obtaining a positive response from the authorities. The system of recording intention to publish actually turned into a system of examination and approval.

China's periodicals management system is rather complex and requires some explanation.

Article 35 of the Constitution of the People's Republic of China stipulates that the citizens of the PRC enjoy freedom of the press, and the Chinese government denies the existence of a news censorship system. On paper, this is factual. One step below the Constitution are laws, but up to now the Chinese government has been unwilling to formulate a Press Law; the main consideration is that it is unable to deprive citizens of freedom of the press without violating the Constitution. The highest level law or regulation in China's news and publishing sphere is the State Council's "Regulations on Publication Administration," which fall under the category of administrative regulations and do not require ratification by the National

People's Congress. These regulations stipulate that the GAPP will only accept applications for permission to publish periodicals that are submitted through a sponsoring unit, which must be a government organ at a particular level. This method deprives privately published periodicals of the right to apply, and publication becomes an impossibility. The regulations also stipulate that content touching on important topics must be reported in advance to news and publication management organs. In departmental regulations that are classified a level lower than the "Regulations on Publication Administration," such as "Measures for Reporting Intention to Publish on Important Topics," the GAPP requires that articles subject to such reporting may not be published before a response is received. By establishing the condition of "response," the system for reporting intention to publish effectively becomes a system of examination and approval, i.e., censorship. Thus, in terms of content and subject, citizens are tacitly stripped of their freedom of the press.

After intention to publish is reported, the government's standard for examining the content of articles is mainly the "Resolution Regarding Certain Historical Problems since the Founding of the Country," passed by the CCP Central Committee in June 1981. The Resolution holds that accomplishments make up the chief part of the Mao era, and that the achievements of socialist transformation were glorious. Following that logic, it would be sufficient to revert to the seventeen years prior to the Cultural Revolution, and the reform and opening policy would be unnecessary. The vigorous development of the market economy under the push of Reform and Opening and Deng Xiaoping's Southern Tour in 1992 has made wholesale application of this standard unfeasible, and grey areas exist in the criteria for official censorship.

There is no norm for implementing the system for reporting intention to publish. According to written regulations, a reply must be given within thirty days of a report of intent to publish, but it took an average of three months to receive replies on fourteen articles that *Yanhuang Chunqiu* reported in 2013. Furthermore, not a single one of the fourteen articles was granted approval for publication.

If a periodical does not abide by the reporting system for important topics, it will have difficulty passing its annual inspection. That was usually the case for *Yanhuang Chunqiu* from 2004 onward. If a magazine strictly adheres to the regulations, it cannot survive, but if it doesn't adhere to the regulations, it won't pass the inspection. *Yanhuang Chunqiu* therefore resorted to following the regulations, but not to the letter, while the government likewise took the approach of executing the regulations, but not to the letter.

How could the boundary be determined? The magazine dealt with the situation by shrinking the ambiguous scope of the sensitive zone to eight "untouchables": June Fourth, problems relating to current and immediately former Party and state leaders and their families; the multi-party system; nationalization of the military;[32]

---

32. TN: That is, shifting the allegiance of the military from the party to the state, effectively placing the military under the control of the state.

separation of powers; independence for Tibet, Xinjiang, or Taiwan; Falun Gong; and Charter 08 and Liu Xiaobo. On these topics that the government is most concerned about, the magazine stated directly and explicitly that it would not cross the boundaries and asked the authorities to put their minds at rest. The magazine determined over the course of long-term and repeated "chess moves" that these were the government's core interests. Clarifying these core interests brought a sense of freedom in other areas; both sides were relatively at ease, and excessive vigilance was reduced.

Between the eight untouchables and the system for reporting intention to publish there existed a gray expanse where the specific boundaries are far from clear. Both sides advanced and retreated in this area, as manifested in content review and informal notification, the writing of examination and correction reports, the submission of a minimal number of reports of intent to publish, and failure to pass the initial annual inspection but ultimately not being closed down. This is a very long story.

Within the Central Propaganda Department and the GAPP (now reorganized as the State Administration of Press, Publication, Radio, Film and Television, SAPPRFT), there are specific reviewing teams. The *Nanfang Group* publications and *Yanhuang Chunqiu* are both important publications with dedicated staff. The reviewers (*yuepingyuan* 閲評員) prepare a reading report for every issue, pointing out any problems, and submit it to the supervisory unit. According to the severity of the identified problems, the leaders of the supervisory unit will inform the person responsible for the publication. For example, when the supervisory unit of *Yanhuang Chunqiu* was the Yellow Emperor Cultural Research Association, the vice-chairman of the association would get in touch with me as chief editor and ask me to take note of certain problems. We would further discuss our assessment of how severe the problem was, and prepare a reply proposing adjustments.

At the beginning of each year, when all Beijing publications must pass an annual inspection with the municipal Bureau of Press and Publications, all the problems would be compiled on a yearly list, determining whether we could pass the inspection. Each year, *Yanhuang Chunqiu* was criticized for not respecting the system for reporting intention to publish on important topics, and was told it could not pass the inspection. After submitting a rectification and improvement report through its supervisory unit to the SAPPRFT, *Yanhuang Chunqiu* would generally be allowed to pass the inspection before the date at which it would automatically become an illegal publication. In this manner, the authorities were able to maintain maximum pressure without completely killing off the journal. In this process, *Yanhuang Chunqiu* usually engaged in one or two rounds of negotiations with the highest officials of SAPPRFT, which had a strong flavor of bargaining, for example about how many articles had to be submitted in advance, which type had to be submitted and which type could be dealt with internally, how much time was needed to receive a reply, etc. Sometimes the Beijing municipal bureau and the supervisory unit also took part in such talks as related parties.

In terms of the larger trend in my more than a decade of publishing this magazine, I sensed that the sensitive territory gradually shrank and the boundaries of freedom gradually expanded, and that public memory was gradually being reconstructed. However, following the 18th Congress in 2012, the government took the posture of tightening the boundaries and displayed more aggressiveness.

This aggressiveness was manifested first of all in the general realm of ideology, as symbolized by the publication of the rules on "seven unmentionables," which included a critique of historical nihilism. The government thus made a point of attacking writers or periodicals that focused more extensively on flaws and errors in Party or national history, and denounced them for "historical nihilism," which was established as a crime in central government documents. *Yanhuang Chunqiu* fought back by publishing a series of articles describing the origins and evolution of historical nihilism, and investigating exactly who has been engaging in historical nihilism on a massive scale. These articles attracted a critical essay in *Red Flag Manuscripts* by the chairman of the Association of Chinese Historians, who called for legal measures to be taken against *Yanhuang Chunqiu*.

Consequently, the frequency of informal notifications increased noticeably from 2012 onward. They generally came through the leaders of the supervisory unit, but sometimes officials from the SAPPRFT also made direct contact. These new developments may have been the result of *Yanhuang Chunqiu* testing new boundaries, but also of the government's enhanced management and tightening of these boundaries. Or perhaps both sides had entered a new realm where new boundaries needed to be established, such as for example the difference between constitutional government (*xianzheng* 憲政) and constitutional rule (*xianzhi* 憲治). Finally, the authorities began to employ political and organizational methods to take over *Yanhuang Chunqiu*. In short, the system and atmosphere within which *Yanhuang Chunqiu* functioned deteriorated all around, and in a comprehensive manner.

Conclusion

Taking advantage of its systemic marginality, and drawing support from the special status and political influence of former senior officials within the system, *Yanhuang Chunqiu* played a significant part in reconstructing modern China's public memory, and even led this effort to a very great extent. This reconstruction of memory has also reconstructed the public image of the Communist Party and the public image of China to a certain degree. It has provided new answers to questions of identity such as who we are, who the CCP is, and who China is, and has even reconstructed our worldview. In this sense, *Yanhuang Chunqiu* has had a hand in reconstructing the subject and the self.

In this process, *Yanhuang Chunqiu* also played a role in constructing and expanding the power of democracy and rule of law, and at the same time constructed itself as a reformist faction within the system, a reformist faction in political reform, and a promoter of democratic constitutional government. But *Yanhuang Chunqiu*'s reconstruction efforts were strictly limited to the realm of concepts and memory, and it firmly refused to engage in any organized activity. For example, the magazine had no contact with, nor did it encourage, participate in, or follow the activities of *Yanhuang Chunqiu* reading groups. Organizing and liaising is an extremely sensitive area. At the same time, *Yanhuang Chunqiu* took the initiative to propose eight "untouchable" topics, promising to engage in self-discipline so the authorities could relax.

On the political level, as power concentrated at the highest level, it became easier to reach a negative consensus on the case of *Yanhuang Chunqiu*, which had long proved elusive, and the influence of some very senior old cadres declined. In this situation, *Yanhuang Chunqiu* refused to make any large-scale concessions. For example, on the issue of constitutionalism, the journal did not obey the "seven unmentionables," and even chose the "implementation of the 1982 constitution" as its annual topic. This type of steadfastness changed the nature of the journal in the eyes of the authorities, and its liberal flavor, as well as its non-party and non-system flavor and its oppositional nature became more pronounced.

In addition, between 2014 and 2017, an investigative article that appeared in *Yanhuang Chunqiu* on the "Five Heroes of Langya Mountain" triggered a libel lawsuit that attracted the attention of the highest level of leadership. The leadership viewed this case as a battle to protect Party and Army heroes. The state absolutely refused to allow the subversion of this area of memory, and for this reason added paragraph 185 in the new Civil Code promulgated in 2017, which states: "Sullying the name, image, reputation, or honor of heroes and martyrs harms the common interest of society, and the authors of such acts must bear civil liability for them." By publishing an article that touched on the historical image of a strongly conservative institution such as the military, compounded by the editor taking the initiative to sue for libel after suffering personal attacks, *Yanhuang Chunqiu* triggered a forcible response, since not only the system's interests, but also the personal interests of the victims' families had been harmed.

At that point, a journal that had played a leading role in reconstructing the public's historical memories for twenty years was sacrificed to political pressure. At the same time, *Yanhuang Chunqiu* itself became part of the political memories associated with the Chinese Communist Party.

Revised on May 4, 2017.
(Translated by Stacy Mosher and Sebastian Veg)

Bibliography

Chen Ziming. "Suowei 'liangtou zhen': minzhu–zhuanzheng–minzhu" [So-called "truth at both ends": Democracy–dictatorship–democracy], 21ccom.net, June 30, 2013. Accessed February 9, 2016. http://www.21ccom.net/articles/rwcq/article_2013063086608.html.

Chinese Academy of Social Sciences, ed. *Zhongguo shehuike xueyuan lishi xuwuzhuyi pipan wenxuan* [Selected critiques of historical nihilism by the Chinese Academy of Social Sciences]. Beijing: Zhongguo shehui kexue chubanshe, 2015.

Du Runsheng. "Minzhu shehuizhuyi moshi yu Zhongguo qiantu" [Modern China and the structure of New Democracy]. *Yanhuang Chunqiu*, no. 2 (2008). Accessed February 10, 2016. http://www.yhcqw.com/html/yjy/2008/422/08422151332D26A020628B1148JCFBE5K8J.html.

Hong Zhenkuai. "Difangzhi zhong de da jihuang siwang shuzi" [Great Famine mortality figures in local gazetteers]. *Yanhuang Chunqiu*, no. 5 (2014). Accessed February 9, 2016. http://www.yhcqw.com/html/wenzjc/2014/55/JI5D.html.

Hong Zhenkuai. "Youguan da jihuang de xin miushuo: cong Sichuan guanfang shuju kan 'yingyangxing siwang' 250 wan ren de huangmiuxing" [New fallacious arguments regarding the Great Famine: Viewing the absurdity of "nutritional mortality" of 2.5 million people on the basis of Sichuan's official figures]. *Yanhuang Chunqiu*, no. 11 (2014) (in two parts). Accessed February 9, 2016. http://www.yhcqw.com/html/csl/2014/1111/B59K.html, http://www.yhcqw.com/html/csl/2014/1111/6BIH.html.

Liao Gailong. "Mao Zedong haozhao 'jinjing gankao' huimou" [A backward glance at Mao Zedong's appeal for "proceeding to the capital to take the civil service exam"]. *Yanhuang Chunqiu*, no. 3 (2000).

Sun Jingxian. "Bo Hong Zhenkuai 'youguan da jihuang de xin miushuo" [Rebutting Hong Zhenkuai's "New fallacious arguments regarding the Great Famine"]. *Chinese Social Sciences Net*. December 5, 2014. Accessed February 9, 2016).http://www.cssn.cn/index/index_focus/201412/t20141205_1430365.shtml.

Wang Junwei. "Dang he renmin fendou shi women buwang chuxin jixu qianjin de qiangda dongle" [The history of the party's and the people's struggles forcefully impels us to remember our original aspirations and continue advancing]. *Qiushi*, August 2016, posted on QStheory.cn, August 15, 2016. Accessed June 1, 2017. http://www.qstheory.cn/dukan/qs/2016-08/15/c_1119373309.htm.

Xie Tao. "Minzhu shehuizhuyi moshi yu Zhongguo qiantu" [The social-democratic model and the future of China]. *Yanhuang Chunqiu*, no. 2 (2007): 1–8.

Yang Jisheng. "Bo esi sanqianwan shi yaoyan" [Rebutting the claim that 30 million starvation deaths is mere rumor]. 21ccom.net, December 14, 2013. Accessed February 9, 2016. http://www.21ccom.net/articles/read/dushu/2013/1214/97011.html.

Yang Jisheng. "Guanyu da jihuang niandai renkou sunshi de taolun" [Discussion on population loss during the Great Famine years]. *Yanhuang Chunqiu*, no. 9 (2014). Accessed February 9, 2016. http://www.yhcqw.com/html/zml/2014/99/1499152593JA8596114653IDEJEJH96AK.html.

Yang Jisheng. "Lun ziyouzhuyi yu Xinzuopai—Zhongguo de yichang kua shiji zhenglun" [On liberalism and the New Left: A century-spanning controversy in China]. January 6, 2001 (see, for example, reprint on *Duli Pinglun*). Accessed July 31, 2017. http://www.duping.net/XHC/show.php?bbs=11&post=471270.

Yang Jisheng. *Mubei*. Hong Kong: Cosmos Books, 2008.
Yang Jisheng. *Tombstone: The Great Chinese Famine 1958–1962*. Translated by Stacy Mosher and Guo Jian. New York: Farrar, Straus, and Giroux, 2012.

4
Contested Past
Social Media and the Production of Historical Knowledge of the Mao Era*

Jun Liu

> Since memory is actually a very important factor in struggle . . . if one controls people's memory, one controls their dynamism.[1]

Introduction

In the summer of 2015, Chinese authorities launched a full-scale national propaganda campaign to "rectify the names of the heroes."[2] Key official news organizations, including Xinhua News Agency, China National Radio, *People's Daily* (Renmin ribao 人民日報), *Guangming Daily* (Guangming ribao 光明日報), *China Daily*, and *Global Times*, are all engaging in the campaign with a cascade of reports responding to widespread skepticism about the stories of the heroes and growing cynicism towards these stories on Weibo, the Chinese social media platform.[3] These events exemplify a relevant, but less investigated topic about the political influence of social media in contemporary China: in addition to facilitating protests in contemporary contentious events,[4] social media aids the emergence, dissemination, and dissension of contested historical information. These emergent narratives may

---

* This chapter is a revision of the paper "Who Speaks for the Past? Social Media, Social Memory, and the Production of Historical Knowledge in Contemporary China," *The International Journal of Communication* 12 (2018): 1675–95.
1. Michel Foucault, "Film and Popular Memory," *Edinburgh Magazine* 2 (1977): 22.
2. Guanghui Ni, "We and the Heroes Are Together," *People's Daily*, July 27, 2015, 6.
3. For instance, "Xinhuashe Tuichu 'Wei Yingxiong Zhengming' Xilie Baodao Yinfa Qianglie Fanxiang" 新華社推出《為英雄正名》系列報道引發強烈反響 ["The series of reports on 'rectification of heroes' by Xinhua News Agency evoke a strong response,"], *Xinhua*, July 7, 2015, last modified May 20, 2017, http://news.xinhuanet.com/politics/2015-06/23/c_1115700082.htm. "War heroes under fire," *Global Times*, May 13, 2015, last modified May 22, 2017, http://www.globaltimes.cn/content/921505.shtml. "Making Fun of War Martyr Online Lands Internet User in Court," *China Daily*, July 9, 2015, last modified May 22, 2017, http://europe.chinadaily.com.cn/2015-07/09/content_21238079.htm.
4. For instance, Ronggui Huang and Xiaoyi Sun, "Weibo Network, Information Diffusion and Implications for Collective Action in China," *Information, Communication & Society* 17 (2014): 86–104. Jingrong Tong and Landong Zuo, "Weibo Communication and Government Legitimacy in China," *Information, Communication & Society* 17 (2014): 66–85.

challenge the authorized knowledge of the past in society and force the authorities to respond to this information.

To fill this gap, this chapter investigates the influence of social media—Weibo 微博 in this case—on the social memory and the production of historical knowledge of the Mao era in contemporary China. More specifically, it looks at how people use Weibo to interrogate the official knowledge of the past, articulate their individual memories, and reconstruct social memory, all of which shape the production of historical knowledge of the Mao era in a society. I first introduce a theoretical framework of social media, social memory, and the production of historical knowledge. Second, I briefly elaborate our methodological issues, and follow this with an overview of selected cases on Weibo—several contested debates over an historical event (i.e., the Great Famine)[5] and historical figures in the Mao era, such as Lei Feng 雷鋒, Huang Jiguang 黃繼光, and Qiu Shaoyun 邱少雲, once national role models but now controversial figures on Weibo. Third, I dissect how people use Weibo both to question and satirize the official discourse and knowledge of this event and figures, and to articulate and disseminate alternative historical stories and counter-narratives of the past that the public had previously never been able to know about. I conclude with thoughts on the political influence and implications of Weibo on the (re)construction of social memory and the mechanism of production of historical knowledge in contemporary China.

Social Memory in Social Media: A Research Agenda

Halbwachs in his work *On Collective Memory*[6] establishes a foundational framework for the study of societal remembrance. Collective memory represents a society's understanding of its past, defines the relationship between the individual and society, and enables a community to preserve its self-image and to transfer it through time. However, as Halbwachs explicates, "collective memory must be *distinguished from* history."[7] Instead, it is "essentially a *reconstruction* of the past in the light of the present."[8] In this process, for individuals, memories are *de facto* a manipulated construction of those who maintain power and status and who supervise the images of the past. More specifically, Halbwachs underlines the key role of the "social frameworks for memory,"[9] within which individuals localize, organize, understand, and remember commemorative events in mnemonic landscapes. As Halbwachs argues, "it is to the degree that our individual thought places itself in

---

5. For more information, see Jisheng Yang, *Tombstone: The Great Chinese Famine, 1958–1962*, trans. Stacy Mosher and Jian Guo (New York: Macmillan, 2012).
6. Maurice Halbwachs, *On Collective Memory*, trans. Lewis A. Coser (Chicago: University of Chicago Press, 1992).
7. Halbwachs, *On Collective Memory*, 222, emphasis added.
8. Lewis A. Coser, "*Introduction: Maurice Halbwachs 1877–1945*," in *On Collective Memory*, ed. Maurice Halbwachs (Chicago: University of Chicago Press, 1992), 34, emphasis added.
9. Halbwachs, *On Collective Memory*, Chapter 1.

these frameworks and participates in this memory that is it capable of the act of recollection."[10]

In the following decades, scholars advanced Halbwachs's work in various ways, in particular, elucidating the relation between power and the (re)construction of memory. In their seminal review on social memory studies, Olick and Robbins observe the politics of memory contestation and stress that "explicitly past-oriented meaning frameworks are prominent modes of legitimation and explanation."[11] In this sense, the memorial presence of the past becomes both a tool and an object of power that is subject to contestation, appropriation, and transformation at different points in time.

Although the dominant may exert considerable influences on the framing of the memory, as Steiner and Zelizer[12] point out, collective memory is a *process* that is constantly unfolding, changing, and transforming.[13] In practice, the process of (re-)shaping collective memory is thereby "dynamic and unexpected."[14] One particularly vibrant area of discussions concerning this kind of memory negotiation and contestation emerges from Foucault's notion of "counter-memory," which refers to memories that runs different from, and often counter to, the official (frameworks of) history.[15] In particular, counter-memory involves the memorialization—the politics of mnemonic practices—of *forgotten, suppressed,* or *excluded* histories as a crucial way of resisting oppression and dominant ideologies.[16] Memory contestation thus epitomizes the struggle between the dominant and the subordinate in a society and influences the production of historical knowledge.

Among many factors, Information and Communication Technologies (ICTs) play an emerging role in the process of formatting, constructing, and mediating memory and commemorative practices.[17] Given its technological assets, such as openness, accessibility, availability, and interactivity, social media not only enables

---

10. Halbwachs, *On Collective Memory*, 38.
11. Jeffrey K. Olick and Joyce Robbins, "Social Memory Studies: From 'Collective Memory' to the Historical Sociology of Mnemonic Practices," *Annual Review of Sociology* 24 (1998): 108.
12. Linda Steiner and Barbie Zelizer, "Competing Memories," *Critical Studies in Mass Communication* 12 (1995): 218–19.
13. Also see Iwona Irwin Zarecka, *Frames of Remembrance: The Dynamics of Collective Memory* (New York: Transaction Publishers, 1994).
14. Steiner and Zelizer, "Competing Memories," 221.
15. Michel Foucault, *Language, Counter-Memory, Practice: Selected Essays and Interviews* (Ithaca, NY: Cornell University Press, 1980).
16. For instance, see Daphne Berdahl, "'(N)Ostalgie' for the Present: Memory, Longing, and East German Things," *Ethnos* 64 (1999): 192–211. Jens Brockmeier, "Remembering and Forgetting: Narrative as Cultural Memory," *Culture & Psychology* 8 (2002): 15–43. Anthony L. Brown, "Counter-Memory and Race: An Examination of African American Scholars' Challenges to Early Twentieth Century K-12 Historical Discourses," *The Journal of Negro Education* 79 (2010): 54–65. Richard S. Esbenshade, "Remembering to Forget: Memory, History, National Identity in Postwar East-Central Europe," *Representations* 49 (1995): 72–96.
17. For instance, see Ekaterina Haskins, "Between Archive and Participation: Public Memory in a Digital Age," *Rhetoric Society Quarterly* 37 (2007): 401–22. Aaron Hess, "In Digital Remembrance: Vernacular Memory and the Rhetorical Construction of Web Memorials," *Media, Culture & Society* 29 (2007): 812–30. Mordechai Neiger, Oren Meyers, and Eyal Zandberg, *On Media Memory* (New York: Palgrave Macmillan, 2011). José van Dijck, *Mediated Memories in the Digital Age* (Stanford: Stanford University Press, 2007).

but also encourages alternative and counter-historical narratives to emerge and proliferate, giving rise to unofficial versions of history.[18] In the case of China, few studies note that digital media, including virtual museums and Bulletin Board Systems (BBS), allow ordinary people to engage in the narrative of localized histories and personal stories about, for instance, memories of the Cultural Revolution (CR).[19] As Yang observes, the memory boom facilitated by digital media—in particular, counter-narratives about the CR—leads to "the opening of China's political spaces."[20]

Existing studies, however, keep their focus on weblogs, giving less attention to the emerging role of Weibo in constructing the memorial presence of the past. To fill this gap, this study explores the role of Weibo in (re)shaping social memory in contemporary China. It dissects what kinds of narratives of the past have been articulated and circulated on Weibo. Who has been circulating these narratives? How are these narratives on Weibo different from the official narrative, or the dominant social framework for memory? And how and to what extent do the narratives of the past on Weibo challenge or change the social memory and further affect the production of historical knowledge in the long run in China?

Methods

This study employs a multiple-case study design[21] to look into the acts of memorialization on Weibo; in particular, how Weibo articulates (the query about) the narrative of the past and the ways in which it shapes social memory through these acts. Sampled cases were drawn from contestations of historical events and figures in the Mao era, including debates over the Great Famine[22] and over historical figures such as Lei Feng, Dong Cunrui 董存瑞, Huang Jiguang, and Qiu Shaoyun, who were once national role models or national martyrs but are now controversial figures on Weibo.[23]

---

18. For instance, see Michelle A. Amazeen, "The Politics of Memory: Contesting the 'Convention Night' Version of This Historic Day," *Media, Culture & Society* 36 (2014): 679–90. Christian Pentzold and Vivien Sommer, "Digital Networked Media and Social Memory," *Aurora. Revista de Arte, Mídia e Política* 10 (2011): 72–85. Anna Reading, "Digital Interactivity in Public Memory Institutions," *Media, Culture & Society* 25 (2003): 67–85.
19. Guobin Yang, "A Portrait of Martyr Jiang Qing: The Chinese Cultural Revolution on the Internet," in *Re-envisioning the Chinese Revolution: The Politics and Poetics of Collective Memories in Reform China*, ed. Ching-Kwan Lee and Guobin Yang (Stanford: Stanford University Press, 2007), 287–316. Lan Yang, "Memory and Revisionism: The Cultural Revolution on the Internet," in *Memories of 1968: International Perspectives*, ed. Ingo Cornils and Sarah Waters (Oxford: Peter Lang, 2010), 249–79. Junhua Zhang, "China's Social Memory in a Digitalized World-Assessing the Country's Narratives in Blogs," *Journal of Historical Sociology* 25 (2012): 275–97.
20. Guobin Yang, "Days of Old Are Not Puffs of Smoke: Three Hypotheses on Collective Memories of the Cultural Revolution," *China Review* 5 (2005): 33.
21. Robert K. Yin, *Case Study Research: Design and Methods* (London: Sage, 2009).
22. Hui Zhao and Jun Liu, "Social Media and Collective Remembrance: The Debate Over China's Great Famine on Weibo," *China Perspectives* 1 (2015): 41–48.
23. For instance, see Siqi Cao, "Mainstream Media Hit Back at Defamation of War Heroes," *Global Times*, April

I present data collected through participant observation and immersion[24] in the cases on Sina Weibo, the most popular social media platform in China with more than five hundred million users, or over one-third of the Chinese population. This methodology can be described as ethnography in virtual worlds. I also gathered the tweets and postings by doing keyword searches (including Zhibo Lin 林治波, "Da Jihuang" 大饑荒 [great famine], "Sannian Ziran Zaihai" 三年自然災害 [three years of natural disasters], and "Sannian Jingji Kunnan" 三年經濟困難 [three years of economic difficulty] in the case of the Great Famine and the names of the figures in the remaining cases) on Sina Weibo. The tweet corpus included 354 tweets after the cleanup (e.g., removing spam tweets such as advertisements and other unrelated tweets) from a total of 428 tweets. I also collected information from publications and media reports about the debates on the cases as objects of analysis.[25]

I then conducted an analysis of data from Weibo and traditional media. Two native Chinese speakers read the tweets, looked for core themes, categorized them, and highlighted key phrases and statements to identify explanations that would respond to the research questions and that helped us develop new insights. We did not develop a systematic representation of the codes and calculate their frequency. While there was not an explicit test of intercoder reliability for assuring consistency of content interpretation[26] and the frequency of the thematic elements given the inductive nature of this study, there was broad agreement with regard to the discussions that were found. I also integrated our field notes into the analysis.

After data collection, an explanation-building approach and a cross-case synthesis[27] were employed to dissect various mnemonic practices on Weibo through which people engaged with narratives of the past. The cases highlight issues of special relevance for an understanding of the long-term influence of Weibo on social memory, beyond a simple realization of sporadic contentious possibility.

22, 2015, accessed May 22, 2017, http://www.globaltimes.cn/content/918056.shtml. Daguang Li, "War Heroes Should Never Be Insulted," *China Daily*, April 28, 2015, accessed May 22, 2017, http://www.chinadaily.com.cn/opinion/2015-04/28/content_20565221.htm. "State Media Play Good Cop/Bad Cop to Wrest PLA Reform Narrative," *Want China Times*, April 30, 2015, last modified May 22, 2017, http://www.wantchinatimes.com/news-subclass-cnt.aspx?id=20150430000135&cid=1101 (no longer accessible).

24. Tom Boellstorff et al., *Ethnography and Virtual Worlds: A Handbook of Method* (Princeton: Princeton University Press, 2012), Chapter Five.

25. For instance, Cao, "Defamation of War Heroes," *China Daily*, "Doubts over Heroes' Authenticity Grow with Widening Internet Access," *China Daily*, July 9, 2015, accessed May 20, 2017, http://m.chinadaily.com.cn/en/2015-07/09/content_21229059.htm. Li, "War Heroes Should Never Be Insulted," Meng Liu, "Iconoclasm Controversy Leads Some to Realize Their Spirit is Still Needed," *Global Times*, February 23, 2015, accessed May 22, 2017, http://www.globaltimes.cn/content/697129.shtml. Liu, "War Heroes under Fire," Ni, "We and the Heroes Are Together."

26. Matthew Lombard, Jennifer Snyder-Duch, and Cheryl Campanella Bracken, "Content Analysis in Mass Communication: Assessment and Reporting of Intercoder Reliability," *Human Communication Research* 28 (2002): 587–604.

27. Yin, *Case Study Research*.

Debating Historical Events and Figures in Mao Era on Weibo: The Cases

The cases include the debates covering two types of historical narratives, memories, and descriptions of the past: one focuses on a historical topic such as the Great Famine.[28] The other discusses historical figures. In general, the debate demonstrates a distinct disjunction and disarticulation between individual narratives and memories and the authorized narratives and frameworks of the past.

The debate over the Great Famine

The debate over the Great Famine on Weibo was triggered by Lin Zhibo, the head of the Gansu Province branch of the *People's Daily*, the mouthpiece newspaper of the Chinese Communist Party (CCP). Using his verified account stating his affiliation and with over 230,000 Weibo followers, on April 29, 2012, Lin questioned reports that the Great Famine death toll, between 1960 and 1962, reached into the multimillions. He asserted that this number was a conspiracy "to defile Chairman Mao by utilizing the exaggerated slander of millions of people dying of starvation."[29]

Lin's tweet quickly ignited outrage among Weibo users, with strong criticism directed towards his denial of the starvation and deaths of millions in the early 1960s. The tweet was retweeted over 7,000 times within the four hours after it was first published, with the original tweet receiving more than 5,000 comments, most of which were scorching critiques. Weibo users also started to explore and distribute various kinds of historical materials that demonstrated conclusively that millions of deaths occurred in the early 1960s due to the famine, which has long been a politically taboo topic in China.[30] These materials included, among others, previously hard-to-access CCP archives and documents, rarely seen government statistics, banned or censored academic works, documentary films, and long-forgotten personal memoirs, stories, and shared memories about that period.[31] The various mnemonic activities related to the exploration of the Great Famine on Weibo articulated a contrapuntal memory of the period against the official one that never admitted that the famine actually happened, which fundamentally contributed to the process of recognition and reconstruction of the social memory of the famine.

---

28. Zhao and Liu, "Social Media and Collective Remembrance," 43–44.
29. Lin's tweet read: "Some people, to defile Chairman Mao, use the exaggerated slander of tens of millions of people dying of starvation between 1960 and 1962. And thus someone visited many of the villages in Henan and Anhui that were hardest-hit by the famine in those years, and the situation was nothing like what people slander it as. The locals had only heard of people dying of starvation, but had not personally witnessed any such deaths, and very few people can be directly confirmed to have starved to death" [14:17, April 29, 2012]; see also, "Numbers and the Great Famine," last modified August 20, 2014, http://www.thechinastory.org/archive/china-time/.
30. Tania Branigan, "China's Great Famine: The True Story," *The Guardian*, January 1, 2013, accessed May 22, 2017, https://www.theguardian.com/world/2013/jan/01/china-great-famine-book-tombstone.
31. For instance, "Denial from People's Daily Branch Head Ignited Fury and Discussions," last modified May 20, 2017, http://offbeatchina.com/denial-from-peoples-daily-branch-head-ignited-furious-discussion-of-the-great-famine.

For instance, an online survey after the debate, with over 12,000 Weibo users participating, showed that seven out of ten participants believed the conclusion that thirty million people—or even more—starved to death over the three-year period of 1959 through 1962, which is quite a bit more than the official narrative, which reported that about ten million died.[32] In this process, the term the "Great Famine," which calls for reflection upon the famine as a political calamity that was "born [out] of the system of totalitarianism,"[33] is gradually taking the place of the ones favored by the authorities that attribute millions of deaths by starvation to either natural disasters or the Soviet Union's treachery.[34]

The debates over historical figures on Weibo

The debates over historical figures on Weibo include doubts over their actual existence or details of their biographies, accusations that these heroes were actually corrupt and profligate, and cynicism toward the official narratives of their heroism. The debate over Lei Feng—an iconic Mao-era soldier who exemplified unswerving devotion to communist ideology and fanatic loyalty to the leader of the CCP[35]—fermented on Weibo at the beginning of March 2012, around the time that the government commemorated Lei Feng with the annual "Learn From Lei Feng Day," on March 5, a holiday initiated by Mao Zedong in 1962.[36] The government's effort to exalt and resuscitate the unconditional self-sacrifice and obedient patriotism of Lei Feng, however, evoked unprecedented controversy, criticism, incredulity, and cynicism toward the authenticity of the historical story of Lei Feng on Weibo.[37] More specifically, some expressed their skepticism about the authenticity of his diaries that contain unsupported details about how he helped people and expressed his great spirit. For instance, many questioned how it was possible that Lei Feng, who was "nearly illiterate," could have composed voluminous diaries with literary flourish and flawless language.[38] Others doubted the authenticity of pictures shot by professional photographers of Lei Feng in the act of doing good deeds, even though he was at the time still an obscure soldier.[39]

32. Zhao and Liu, "Social Media and Collective Remembrance," 48.
33. Jonathan Mirsky, "Unnatural Disaster," *New York Times*, December 11, 2012, BR22.
34. Renmin Jiaoyu Chubanshe Lishishi 人民教育出版社歷史室 [The History Section of People's Education Press], *Zhongguo Jinxiandaishi (Xiace)* 中國近代現代史（下冊）[A modern and contemporary history of China (volume II) (Beijing: Renmin Jiaoyu Chubanshe, 2003), 109–10.
35. *China Daily*, "Lei Feng: Changing Role Models In China," *China Daily*, March 10, 2011, accessed May 20, 2017, http://www.chinadaily.com.cn/china/2011-03/10/content_12150057.htm.
36. For instance, see the propaganda campaign on Sina's Lei Feng special section, last modified May 20, 2017, http://news.sina.com.cn/z/leifeng35/.
37. For the official reports covering this issue, see Liu, "Iconoclasm Controversy."
38. For instance, see the tweet by He Weifang 賀衛方, a law professor with over 1.7 million Weibo followers, "Lei Feng Diary," 2 March 2012, http://www.weibo.com/1216766752/y80ZEoBSs?mod=weibotime&type=comment#_rnd1448010608477.
39. For instance, the tweet by Pu Zhiqiang 浦志強, a well-known human rights lawyer, underlined that "one of the biggest lies of the last 60 years is Lei Feng. He hoodwinked me for two decades, actively pandering to

Among others, Ren Zhiqiang 任志強, a property developer and a Weibo celebrity[40] with over 35 million Weibo followers, argued that

> as a tamed tool for class struggle, the image of Lei Feng has been established to meet the needs of the Cultural Revolution. After turning all citizens into screws that can be willfully placed anywhere,[41] there is no need for democracy, human rights, or freedom [in China]. [March 12, 2012][42]

Ren's tweet was forwarded over 27,000 times within 24 hours, with over 10,000 comments, most of which echoed his argument and backed it up with Weibo users' own reflections upon "the ridiculous brainwashing stories" from "the wretched propaganda campaigns" in their memories, such as the one about Lei Feng.[43]

Meanwhile, public cynicism proliferated towards the authorities' effort to "authenticate" Lei Feng and his life's tales.[44] For instance, after Zhang Jun 張峻, a retired military photographer who produced over two hundred images of Lei Feng, died of a heart attack while speaking out against suspicions about the authenticity of Lei Feng's stories and photos—"I will die on the spot if I have had half-a-word lie!"—Weibo users noted satirically that "Zhang finally paid the price after he was a liar his whole life (about Lei Feng's story)."[45] Although the authorities launched a national campaign to combat the widespread controversy and cynicism regarding Lei Feng's story, the debate continues on Weibo as an increasing number of suspicions of the official narrative spring up. Along with the debate, more and more Weibo users are refusing to regard Lei Feng as an unquestionable role model as in the official narrative of commemoration.

Similar to the incredulity over the authenticity of Lei Feng's stories, skepticism has raged on Weibo about the truth of the tales of several historical figures, such as Huang Jihuang, who hurled himself against an enemy machine gun to block its fire, Qiu Shaoyun, who chose to burn to death to protect his unit's location, and Dong

---

his promoters, his diaries a collective creation. A monthly allowance of seven or eight yuan and he's making 100-yuan donations—either that's fiction or there's corruption involved. Back then 30 million died from starvation, people my age might have taken a single photograph, and yet when he's up late at night studying Mao with a flashlight, there are people taking pictures! He left thousands of photos behind! Beijing police, if you want to arrest hidden forces, go arrest the hidden forces behind Lei Feng" [12:03:17, June 8, 2013].

40. Weibo users with millions of followers on Weibo.
41. Lei Feng wrote in his dairy: "I will be a screw that never rusts. Wherever the Party chooses to place me, I will shine."
42. The original tweet by Ren has been censored later, one of the retweeted post (October 10, 2014) can be seen here: http://www.weibo.com/1975447693/Bss4lEzio?type=comment#_rnd1448011800859.
43. For instance, Qin Zhihui 秦志晖, a Weibo celebrity with the nickname Qin Huohuo 秦火火, deemed Lei Feng to be corrupt and profligate, as he "spent 90 yuan on his clothes while his soldiers' salary was only 6 yuan." Qin was arrested later by the police for "making rumors slanderous to the image of Lei Feng." See Neil Thomas, "China's two Greatest Internet Rumor Mongers and 'Black PR' Philanderers Arrested," last modified May 22, 2017, http://www.danwei.com/chinas-two-greatest-internet-rumor-mongers-and-black-pr-philanderers-arrested/.
44. For instance, Ying Xie, "Man or Myth?" *News China*, May 2012, accessed May 22, 2017, http://old.newschinamag.com/magazine/man-or-myth.
45. See, for instance, tweet by Shiguang Huangfeishi 時光荒廢師 [Time waster], May 27, 2015, http://www.weibo.com/1928820545/CjHey4wMr?type=comment#_rnd1447532222577.

Cunrui, who sacrificed his life with his left hand lifting a package of explosives under an enemy's bunker until it detonated.[46] Some challenged the idea that Qiu's ability to remain silent while burning to death defies their understanding of human physiology. Others argued that Huang's story was fabricated because it was impossible to block bullets fired by a strafing machine gun using one's body. For Dong Cunrui, Weibo users believed the improbable heroic deed was pure imagination because nobody saw it. This doubt and questioning of historical heroes' authenticity snowballed on Weibo, despite the government's effort to "authenticate the historical stories of these heroes" by large-scale propaganda campaigns.

Findings and Discussions

In the debates over this particular historical event and these public figures, Weibo provides a platform for individuals to participate in narrating the past in different ways. Abundant historical materials that were previously either unavailable to the public or banned from publication due to the censorship—in particular, individual memories and experiences that have been unknown to people up to now—finally came to light as the debate evolved. As counter- and alternative frameworks for social memories, the articulation, dissemination, and aggregation of these materials emerge, develop, and proliferate on Weibo very quickly, with enormous influence on society. These frameworks argue against, query, or satirize the official, orthodox frameworks for historical narratives, further generating and superimposing new historical knowledge. The archiving and storage of these materials on Weibo also allows them to be easily retrieved and reactivated. In this way, Weibo cultivates the dynamics of social remembering as a crowdsourcing, continuous, accumulating, and latent process, which shapes the commemoration of historical issues in Chinese society in the long run.

The engagement of individuals into the practice of narrating the past

With the development of digital technologies, the emergence of weblogs allows witnesses of historical events to share their memories without depending on mass communication.[47] Different from digital media such as weblogs or BBS, social media further open up opportunities for individuals to engage in narrating the past via various mnemonic practices.[48]

In China, sites dedicated to the maintenance and (re)production of the historical past, such as educational institutions, museums, and mass media, were once monopolized by the party-state. This allowed the authorities to claim to speak

---

46. For instance, *China Daily*, "Doubts over Heroes' Authenticity," Yao and Yang, " Internet User in Court."
47. In the case of China, see Yang, "Memory and Revisionism," Zhang, "China's Social Memory."
48. Emily Keightley and Philip Schlesinger, "Digital Media—Social Memory: Remembering in Digitally Networked Times," *Media, Culture & Society* 36 (2014): 745–47.

about the past in the voice of the nation, while leaving the ordinary person almost no space to speak up without accepting and following the official frameworks for memory. In the cases we have presented here, however, a large number of individuals have involved themselves in various mnemonic practices of the historical issues on Weibo. More specifically, the participants in the debates include not only those who previously monopolized or had access to the narrative of the past, such as the government and its controlled mass media (via their verified Weibo accounts), but also people from all walks of life, whether they experienced these historical events or not. For instance, in the case of the Great Famine, both Weibo celebrities[49] and ordinary users joined the debate by articulating, commenting, and distributing narratives, stories, memoirs, and numbers over the historical period to a wider scope.

Most importantly, this process characterizes the emergence and recognition of the *individual* narrative, memoir, and memory of the past, be it from a Weibo celebrity or from an ordinary person. For instance,

> @Kai-fu Lee 李開復: In 1960, my grandma died of hunger. Both my uncle and his two kids passed away in those years. [Although I am] not sure if the reason was starvation, but their deaths definitely had something to do with the environment of that time. [17:53, April 29, 2012]
>
> @Z Chunlei @Z 春雷 [Weibo nickname]: I was born in the 1980s, so I did not have any experience with the famine. However, my mother who was born in the 1950s often told me stories of starvation during that period [from 1959 to 1961] . . . The most impressive one is that a beggar begged my grandma for something to eat, which my grandma refused. The beggar kept on walking for less than 500 meters and then died at the entrance of the village.
>
> @Bei Dafei @被打飛 [Weibo nickname]: My parents' hometown is located in the northern part of Suzhou city. I called them and asked whether there were people who died of hunger during the Great Famine. My father said that one hungry cousin came to visit his neighbor for something to eat. However, the neighbor did not have extra food to give him. After a few days, the cousin died of hunger. My mother said that quite a few children ate too much potherb and were poisoned to death, including the little daughter of her high school headmaster.[50]

The tweets embody the point that Weibo users—no matter if they are a celebrity or an ordinary person—and their family members, including those that experienced the Great Famine period but had *never* shared their experiences, stories, and memories with others as they did not have Weibo accounts or due to the lack of internet access, joined the debate, directly or indirectly, as individuals by speaking out about their personal memories. These individual historical narratives introduce

---

49. Such as Yu Jianrong 于建嶸, a professor from Chinese Academy of Social Sciences with 1.8 million Weibo followers, and Kai-Fu Lee, a Taiwanese IT entrepreneur with over 51 million Weibo followers.
50. For more tweets and discussions, see Manzi Xue 薛蠻子, "Wangji Lishi Dengyu Beipan" "忘記歷史等於背叛" [Forgetting history is a betrayal!], May 1, 2012, http://blog.sina.com.cn/s/blog_78ebb6ad01015p9j.html (no longer available).

concrete human beings and their experiences of suffering into the commemoration of the past, a perspective that has been largely missing from existing narratives and memories of the past.[51]

Similar incidents have occurred in the debates over historical figures, during which Weibo has offered unprecedented opportunities for individuals to question, criticize, or satirize the official historical narratives. This process consequently breaks the regime's monopoly on the access to narratives of the past by acknowledging and integrating individuals' remembrances and mnemonic practices into the recollection of the past, and by introducing and accumulating alternative and counter-frameworks of memory against the official one.

The establishment of counter- and alternative frameworks for memories

The debates on Weibo engender the articulation, accumulation, and proliferation of alternative and counter-historical narratives about the historical period and figures through crowdsourcing, with Weibo users voluntarily involving themselves in different kinds of mnemonic practices through various media texts.

More specifically, Weibo allows its users to post and distribute information in various modes, such as text, photos, music, short videos, or a combination of multimodal contents. It is also possible to embed long-form content and links from other websites into the tweet. Tweets on Weibo, therefore, become content-rich, descriptive, and vivid. Many of the historical archives and documentaries that were previously unavailable to the public have now been presented on Weibo and exposed to the public for the first time.

For instance, in the case of the Great Famine, historical materials, including the CCP's documents and archives,[52] books that had been censored by the government,[53] and overseas documentaries that people rarely encountered before, have recently been tweeted and diffused to a wide audience to testify to the existence of the famine.

Among them, one of the most prominent materials includes stories from *Tombstone: An Account of Chinese Famine in the 1960s* (Mubei: Zhongguo liushi niandai dajihuang jishi 墓碑——中國六十年代大饑荒紀實), hereafter *Tombstone*.[54] Uncovering a series of colossal tragedies, including instances of cannibalism, and the continued systematic efforts of the CCP to cover up the history of the Great Famine, *Tombstone* has been banned in the Chinese mainland. Nevertheless, its

---

51. Zhao and Liu, "Social Media and Collective Remembrance," 44.
52. For instance, the copy of "the special report" by the central patrol group reporting that over 1,700 people died of starvation in Zhao Temple group in Anhui Province from the winter of 1959 to the summer of 1960, see the tweet by Feng Yan 嚴鋒, April 29, 2012, http://www.weibo.com/1687198333/ygSubmNrk#_rnd1408465965414.
53. For instance, see Frank Dikötter, *Mao's Great Famine: The History of China's Most Devastating Catastrophe, 1958–1962* (New York: Walker & Co., 2010). Jisheng Yang, *Mubei* (Hong Kong: Cosmos, 2008).
54. Yang, *Mubei*. Yang, *Tombstone*.

influence has snowballed in debates over the Great Famine on Weibo, after people quoted it or referred to the stories in it. For instance,

> @Huoshan Baiyang @火山白楊 [Weibo nickname, verified as a journalist from Xinhua News Agency]: I was born in the mid-1970s . . . so I did not have any experience with the famine deaths in the 1960s. But my elders told me quite a few stories, and I also read Yang Jisheng's *Tombstone*. I believed in what they said. [4:52, April 30, 2012]

Similarly, in the debates over historical figures, Weibo users dug up and further tweeted lesser-known texts, a majority of which had never appeared or been circulated in the media before. For instance, the image of Lei Feng on a motorcycle in front of Tiananmen Square immediately attracted extraordinary attention and distribution on Weibo, as the official narrative never associates Lei Feng with the concept of "luxury"—having a motorcycle in 1960s.

Most importantly, the accumulation of these historical materials entails a fundamentally different narrative of the historical period and figures from this time than those provided by the dominating official discourse as the prescribed, authorized social framework of memory. Criticism and cynicism towards the official, orthodox—and previously hegemonic—framework accordingly emerged, and were widely diffused.

For instance, the historical materials and archives crowdsourced by Weibo users about the Great Famine not only highlight the enormous number of thirty million as the population that suffered from starvation during the period of 1959 to 1962, but also excoriate both the CCP's mistaken policy and the practice of holding back the truth about these mistakes made by the authorities. These narratives are significantly different from the official discourse and the dominant memorial framework of the period, which, according to either the official chronicle of the CCP[55] or historical textbooks,[56] never used the term "The Great Famine." Instead, in describing this period as the "Three Years of Economic Difficulty" or the "Three Years of Natural Disasters," the official narrative of the historical period between 1959 and 1961 attributes the fact that around ten million population were wiped out by starvation to a series of unavoidable natural disasters and the Soviet Union's "perfidious" withdrawal of experts and technicians from China and its request for payment for its industrial hardware, which exacerbated an already difficult situation and sped up the loss of population.[57]

---

55. Zhonggong Zhongyang Dangshi Yanjiushi 中共中央黨史研究室 [The Central Party History Research Office], *Zhongguo Gongchangdang Lishi (Di'erjuan)* 中國共産黨歷史（第二卷） [History of the Chinese Communist Party (volume II, 1949–1978)] (Beijing: Zhonggong dangshi chubanshe), 2011.
56. Renmin Jiaoyu Chubanshe Lishishi 人民教育出版社歷史室 [The History Section of People's Education Press], *Zhongguo Jinxiandaishi (Xiace)* 中國近代現代史（下冊） [A modern and contemporary history of China (volume II)], 109.
57. Renmin Jiaoyu Chubanshe Lishishi 人民教育出版社歷史室 [The History Section of People's Education Press], *Zhongguo Jinxiandaishi (Xiace)* 中國近代現代史（下冊） [A modern and contemporary history of China (volume II)], 109–10.

However, a totally different narrative of the period has been established on Weibo, with its users speaking up and accumulating counter- and alternative narratives of the period against the official framework. For one thing, people aggregated alternative stories, memoirs, and memories either from their own experiences or from their family to testify to the actual existence of the famine, which had been denied by the authorities and questioned by Lin's tweet. These stories and memories, previously largely unknown to the public, had thereby been a relevant part of the proof of the famine and became known to more people. For instance,

> @Lu Gongmin @盧公民 [Weibo nickname]: Between 1958 and 1960, my great-grandmother, seven people in my grandparents' generation, my aunt and my uncle, a total of ten people, starved to death, one by one, in Tongwei County, Gansu Province. [10:09, May 1, 2012]

> @Coding worker Zhao Ye @碼農趙野 [Weibo nickname, verified as a journalist]: Just ended a call with my father, who mentioned that during the Great Famine period in 1960s . . . there were over one hundred people who died in our village . . . in Caohu Village, Anhui Province . . . @Lin Zhibo If Director Lin is interested, I can bring you to my hometown and carry out some interviews. People there aged sixty or older all have similar memories [of the Great Famine] during that period. [23:23, May 1, 2012]

Alternative historical narratives also came from memoirs of Party cadres. For instance, @Qinglou Zhishang @青樓直上 (Weibo nickname) quoted the memoir by a veteran cadre Li Lei, the then-secretary of the party committee in Linxia state, Gansu Province, in which Li revealed that "588 people ate 337 human bodies in ten communes in Linxia city" during the Great Famine.[58]

Moreover, Weibo users collected different materials to argue against the death toll in the dominant framework of memory, which only admitted that around ten million of the population starved to death.[59] For instance, with over two million Weibo followers, economist Mao Yushi 茅于軾 proposed his way of accounting for the death toll and estimated that the number would be thirty-six million [19:56, April 30, 2012]. Historical scholar Lei Yi 雷頤, who has over 270,000 followers, introduced two published works—demographer Cao Shuji's article and Dutch historian Frank Dikötter's book—which estimated that the death toll was either 32.5 million (Cao) or 45 million (Dikötter) [9:19, May 1, 2012]. Ordinary Weibo users also offered statistics they read from academic and historical documents and demonstrated their opinions about the death toll. Xiyue Jianglang 西嶽江郎 (Weibo nickname), for instance, presented the numbers raised by American Sinologist Basil Ashton and Ansley J. Coale, former chair of the Population Association of America.

---

58. See more discussions, for instance, the tweet by Xinjing Ziranhao 昕靜自然好 [Silence is gold], May 1, 2012, http://www.weibo.com/1782415244/yhbGrztXs#_rnd1408436255362.
59. Zhonggong Zhongyang Dangshi Yanjiushi 中共中央黨史研究室 [The Central Party History Research Office], *Zhongguo Gongchangdang Lishi (Di'erjuan)* 中國共產黨歷史（第二卷） [History of the Chinese Communist Party (volume II, 1949–1978)], 368–69.

According to his tweet, Ashton estimated that there were around "thirty million excess deaths and about thirty-three million lost or postponed births," while Coale believed the death toll to be closer to twenty-seven million. As more and more Weibo users participated in searching, posting, and forwarding various historical materials, they further aggregate into alternative and counter-frameworks. Such frameworks not only greatly challenge the authorities' framework for memory by shaping the online debate, but also establish the concept of the Great Famine, which gradually replaced the "Three Years of Economic Difficulty" and the "Three Years of Natural Disasters" terms in later online surveys.

Apart from the emergence of alternative and counter-frameworks, doubt and cynicism over the established historical narrative also force authorities to revise official narratives of the figures or to admit to shallow propaganda efforts in those years. In the case of Lei Feng, authorities modified their narrative, albeit not fundamentally, of Lei as a god-like ideal after the photo of him riding on a motorcycle in front of Tian'anmen went viral and drew criticism on Weibo.[60] Instead, they acknowledged that Lei Feng was also a fashionable young man, and accordingly he "did almost all the fashionable things of his day," such as "wearing a fashionable leather jacket" and "riding on a borrowed motorcycle" to take a photo—all of which would have been considered to be luxury items at the time. In the face of doubts over the authenticity of Lei Feng's impossibly squeaky-clean photos, the authorities admitted for the first time that some of these photos had been posed shots (*bupai* 補拍), instead of candid photos as they had previously asserted.[61] In short, the authorities' framework of historical narratives underwent gradual transformation in the face of alternative and counter-narratives and historical materials on Weibo. In this sense, Weibo entails a long-term influence on social remembrance and the framework for memory by facilitating the integration of newly emerging, crowdsourced information from diversified subjects into the production of historical knowledge.

The changing mechanism of the production of historical knowledge

The debate over the narrative of the past on Weibo, including the involvement of individuals that speak up about their memories, experiences, doubts, criticisms, and sense of cynicism toward the official historical narrative and the emergence of counter- and alternative frameworks against the once-monopolized official framework for memory, crystallizes a crucial influence of social media on society and politics in contemporary China. While social media such as Weibo empowers people to organize contentious activities in contemporary contested events, it also allows

---

60. China Daily, "Doubts over Heroes' Authenticity."
61. Jiang Wang, "Lishishang de Leifeng: Bupai yu Baipai Beihou de Zhenshi" 歷史上的雷鋒：補拍與擺拍背後的真實 ["Lei Feng in history: The truth behind posed shots afterward and make-up shots," March 5, 2014, http://image.fengniao.com/437/4376199.html?from=bdshare#0-tsina-1-52604-397232819ff9a47a7b7e80a40 613cfe1.

them to engage in various mnemonic practices, through which people (re)construct social memory and further shape the production of historical knowledge in the society. More specifically, social media entails the transformation of the mechanism of the production of historical knowledge from the following three perspectives.

First, social media invites individuals into the production of the knowledge of the past by expanding opportunities for them to join in various kinds of mnemonic practices. With social media, individuals, with or without alternative memories that differ from the official story, are able to act as active subjects of history and memory in commemorative activities—in our study, they speak up about previously unknown or lesser known memories and experiences, share alternative and counter-narratives, or question and challenge the authenticity of official stories. New knowledge of the past emerges and is disseminated in this process, which consequently challenges, if not ends, the monopoly of the memory production mechanism held by the authorities.

Second, social media offer a platform to aggregate individual mnemonic narratives and practices into alternative and counter-frameworks of the past. These frameworks not only challenge the hegemonic, official framework, but also encourage further participation of ordinary people in the process of social remembering. Alternative and counter-memories of the past serve as a political means—and, in some case, facilitate political challenges—against the dominant power and its ideologically constructed history. In practice, as more and more social media users join the process of crowdsourcing and distribution, the accumulation of these memories and frameworks aggregate previously isolated, fragmented, or unorganized individual stories and experiences against the official framework, making participants recognize that they are not a minority with (officially) unrecognized memories in a society. This accordingly encourages more people to stand up and speak up about their alternative memories and experiences. Moreover, as soon as these alternative and counter-memories, discourses, and frameworks are diffused on social media, to ban or delete them completely becomes impossible, which allows more people to read different voices from the official one and further join the discussion and participate in these mnemonic practices.

Third, by storing and archiving historical materials, including the debate, in a digitally networked sphere, social media make them easily retrievable with the potential to be reactivated. More specifically, people can easily search, retrieve, revisit, and reflect upon the material. In addition, the easy retrievability embeds the possibility to reactivate the process of narrating the past any time by reengaging people into the production of historical narratives.[62] In this way, the commemoration of the past is being continually produced, accessed, and updated. To summarize,

---

62. For instance, the debate over the Great Famine has been raised again in 2014, after Lanzhou University in northwest China appointed Lin Zhibo as the dean of its journalism school. Weibo users immediately recalled the debate and voiced strong criticism towards Lin, centering on his denial of the existence of the Great Famine and the deaths in that part of Chinese history.

Weibo cultivates the dynamics of social remembering as a crowdsourcing, continuous, accumulating, and latent process, which shapes the commemoration of historical issues in Chinese society in the long run.

Conclusion

The growing ubiquity of digital media has facilitated changes in political culture and power structure around the world. This chapter looks at the use of social media in the production of (alternative) historical knowledge and the (re)formation of social memory in contemporary China. It takes several contested debates over historical events and figures in the Mao era on Weibo as cases to understand how social media enable individuals to articulate and accumulate their experiences and memories, question and interrogate the established framework for memory, and shape social memory in contemporary China. This study shows that social media embrace wide and diversified subjects to engage in the production of historical knowledge and facilitate the dissemination of alternative frameworks of memory as counter-hegemonic discourse. The integration of fragmented, individual experiences and memories into the general historical knowledge and the facilitation of diversified mnemonic practices accordingly constructs the social memory of the society and facilitates *long-term* social and cultural changes in contemporary China.

Acknowledgments

The author deeply appreciates Hui Zhao's help in data collection and thanks Sebastian Veg and the two anonymous reviewers for their comments which helped to improve the manuscript.

Funding

This work was supported by Dr.phil. Ragna Rask-Nielsen Grundforskningsfond and S. C. Van Fonden [reference numbers 1267, 1503].

Bibliography

Alia. "Denial from People's Daily Branch Head Ignited Fury and Discussions." Offbeat China, 3 May 2012. http://offbeatchina.com/denial-from-peoples-daily-branch-head-ignited-furious-discussion-of-the-great-famine. No longer accessible.

Amazeen, Michelle A. "The Politics of Memory: Contesting the 'Convention Night' Version of This Historic Day." *Media, Culture & Society* 36 (2014): 679–90.

Berdahl, Daphne. "'(N)Ostalgie' for the Present: Memory, Longing, and East German Things." *Ethnos* 64 (1999): 192–211.

Bodnar, John E. *Remaking America: Public Memory, Commemoration, and Patriotism in the Twentieth Century*. Princeton: Princeton University Press, 1994.

Boellstorff, Tom, Bonnie Nardi, Celia Pearce, and T. L. Taylor. *Ethnography and Virtual Worlds: A Handbook of Method*. Princeton: Princeton University Press, 2012.

Bond, George C., and Angela Gilliam. *Social Construction of the Past: Representation as Power*. London: Psychology Press, 1994.

Branigan, Tania. "China's Great Famine: The True Story." *The Guardian*. January 1, 2013. Accessed May 22, 2017. https://www.theguardian.com/world/2013/jan/01/china-great-famine-book-tombstone.

Brockmeier, Jens. "Remembering and Forgetting: Narrative as Cultural Memory." *Culture & Psychology* 8 (2002): 15–43.

Brown, Anthony L. "Counter-Memory and Race: An Examination of African American Scholars' Challenges to Early Twentieth Century K-12 Historical Discourses." *The Journal of Negro Education* 79 (2010): 54–65.

Cao, Siqi. "Mainstream Media Hit Back at Defamation of War Heroes." *Global Times*, April 22, 2015. Accessed May 22, 2017. http://www.globaltimes.cn/content/918056.shtml.

Chen Xi, and Jian Tan. "Xinhuashe Tuichu 'Wei Yingxiong Zhengming' Xilie Baodao Yinfa Qianglie Fanxiang" 新華社推出《為英雄正名》系列報道引發強烈反響 [The series of reports on "rectification of heroes" by Xinhua News Agency evoke a strong response], *Xinhua*, June 23, 205. Accessed May 20, 2017. http://news.xinhuanet.com/politics/2015-06/23/c_1115700082.htm.

China Daily. "Doubts over Heroes' Authenticity Grow with Widening Internet Access." July 9, 2015. Accessed May 20, 2017. http://m.chinadaily.com.cn/en/2015-07/09/content_21229059.htm.

China Daily. "Lei Feng: Changing Role Models in China." March 10, 2011. Accessed May 20, 2017. http://www.chinadaily.com.cn/china/2011-03/10/content_12150057.htm.

Coser, Lewis A. *Introduction: Maurice Halbwachs 1877–1945*. In M. Halbwachs, *On Collective Memory*, 1–34. Chicago: University of Chicago Press, 1992.

Dikötter, Frank. *Mao's Great Famine: The History of China's Most Devastating Catastrophe, 1958–1962*. New York: Walker & Co., 2010.

Esbenshade, Richard S. "Remembering to Forget: Memory, History, National Identity in Postwar East-Central Europe." *Representations* 49 (1995): 72–96.

Foucault, Michel. "Film and Popular Memory." *Edinburgh Magazine* 2 (1977): 22.

Foucault, Michel. *Language, Counter-Memory, Practice: Selected Essays and Interviews*. Ithaca, NY: Cornell University Press, 1980.

Halbwachs, Maurice. *On Collective Memory*. Translated by L. A. Coser. Chicago: University of Chicago Press, 1992.

Haskins, Ekaterina. "Between Archive and Participation: Public Memory in a Digital Age." *Rhetoric Society Quarterly* 37 (2007): 401–22.

Hess, Aaron. "In Digital Remembrance: Vernacular Memory and the Rhetorical Construction of Web Memorials." *Media, Culture & Society* 29 (2007): 812–30.

Huang, Ronggui, and Xiaoyi Sun. "Weibo Network, Information Diffusion and Implications for Collective Action in China." *Information, Communication & Society* 17 (2014): 86–104.

Keightley, Emily, and Philip Schlesinger. "Digital Media—Social Memory: Remembering in Digitally Networked Times." *Media, Culture & Society* 36 (2014): 745–47.

Li Daguang. "War Heroes Should Never Be Insulted." *China Daily*, April 28, 2015. Accessed May 22, 2017. http://www.chinadaily.com.cn/opinion/2015-04/28/content_20565221.htm.

Liu, Meng. "Iconoclasm Controversy Leads Some to Realize Their Spirit Is Still Needed." *Global Times*, February 23, 2012. Accessed May 22, 2017. http://www.globaltimes.cn/content/697129.shtml.

Liu, Xin. "War Heroes under Fire." *Global Times*, May 13, 2015. Accessed May 22, 2017. http://www.globaltimes.cn/content/921505.shtml.

Lombard, Matthew, Jennifer Snyder-Duch, and Cheryl Campanella Bracken. "Content Analysis in Mass Communication: Assessment and Reporting of Intercoder Reliability." *Human Communication Research* 28 (2002): 587–604.

Mirsky, Jonathan. "Unnatural Disaster." *New York Times*. December 11, 2012. https://cn.nytimes.com/china/20121211/c11mirsky/en-us/.

Neiger, Mordechai, Oren Meyers, and Eyal Zandberg. *On Media Memory*. New York: Palgrave Macmillan, 2011.

Ni, Guanghui. "We and the Heroes Are Together." *People's Daily*. July 27, 2015, 6.

Olick, Jeffrey K., and Joyce Robbins. "Social Memory Studies: From 'Collective Memory' to the Historical Sociology of Mnemonic Practices." *Annual Review of Sociology* 24 (1998): 105–40.

Pentzold, Christian, and Vivien Sommer. "Digital Networked Media and Social Memory." *Aurora. Revista de Arte, Mídia e Política* 10 (2011): 72–85.

Reading, Anna. "Digital Interactivity in Public Memory Institutions." *Media, Culture & Society* 25 (2003): 67–85.

Renmin Jiaoyu Chubanshe Lishishi 人民教育出版社歷史室 [The History Section of People's Education Press]. *Zhongguo Jinxiandaishi (Xiace)* 中國近代現代史（下冊） [A modern and contemporary history of China (volume II)]. Beijing: Renmin jiaoyu chubanshe, 2003.

Staff Reporter. "State Media Play Good Cop/Bad Cop to Wrest PLA Reform Narrative." *Want China Times*, April 30, 2015. Accessed May 22, 2017. http://www.wantchinatimes.com/news-subclass-cnt.aspx?id=20150430000135&cid=1101. No longer accessible.

Steiner, Linda, and Barbie Zelizer. "Competing Memories." *Critical Studies in Mass Communication* 12 (1995): 213–39.

Thomas, Neil. "China's Two Greatest Internet Rumor Mongers and 'Black PR' Philanderers Arrested." *Danwei*, August 24, 2013. Accessed May 22, 2017. http://www.danwei.com/chinas-two-greatest-internet-rumor-mongers-and-black-pr-philanderers-arrested/.

Tong, Jingrong, and Landong Zuo. "Weibo Communication and Government Legitimacy in China." *Information, Communication & Society* 17 (2014): 66–85.

Van Dijck, José. *Mediated Memories in the Digital Age*. Stanford: Stanford University Press, 2007.

Wang Jiang. "Lishishang de Lei Feng: Bupai yu Baipai Beihou de Zhenshi" 歷史上的雷鋒：補拍與擺拍背後的真實 ["Lei Feng in history: The truth behind posed shots afterward and make-up shots." March 5, 2014. Accessed May 22, 2017. http://image.fengniao.com/437/4376199.html?from=bdshare#0-tsina-1-52604-397232819ff9a47a7b7e80a40613cfe1.

Xie, Ying. "Man or Myth?" *News China*. May 2012. Accessed May 22, 2017. http://old.newschinamag.com/magazine/man-or-myth.

Xue Manzi 薛蠻子. "Wangji Lishi Dengyu Beipan" 忘記歷史等於背叛 [Forgetting history is a betrayal!], May 1, 2012. Accessed May 22, 2017. http://blog.sina.com.cn/s/blog_78ebb6ad01015p9j.html.

Yang, Guobin. "A Portrait of Martyr Jiang Qing: The Chinese Cultural Revolution on the Internet." In *Re-envisioning the Chinese Revolution: The Politics and Poetics of Collective Memories in Reform China*, edited by C. K. Lee and G. Yang, 287–316. Stanford: Stanford University Press, 2007.

Yang, Jisheng. *Mubei*. Hong Kong: Cosmos, 2008.

Yang, Jisheng. *Tombstone: The Great Chinese Famine, 1958–1962*. Translated by S. Mosher and J. Guo. New York: Macmillan, 2012.

Yang, Lan. "Memory and Revisionism: The Cultural Revolution on the Internet." In *Memories of 1968: International Perspectives*, edited by I. Cornils and S. Waters, 249–79. Oxford: Peter Lang, 2010.

Yao, Yao, and Jie Yang. 2015. "Making Fun of War Martyr Online Lands Internet User in Court." *China Daily*. July 9, 2015. Accessed May 22, 2017. http://europe.chinadaily.com.cn/2015-07/09/content_21238079.htm.

Yin, Robert K. *Case Study Research: Design and Methods*. London: Sage, 2009.

Zarecka, Iwona Irwin. *Frames of Remembrance: The Dynamics of Collective Memory*. New York: Transaction Publishers, 1994.

Zerubavel, Eviatar. *Time Maps: Collective Memory and The Social Shape of the Past*. Chicago: University of Chicago Press, 2012.

Zhang, Junhua. "China's Social Memory in a Digitalized World-Assessing the Country's Narratives in Blogs." *Journal of Historical Sociology* 25 (2012): 275–97.

Zhao, Hui, and Jun Liu. "Social Media and Collective Remembrance: The Debate over China's Great Famine on Weibo." *China Perspectives* 1 (2015):41–48.

Zhonggong Zhongyang Dangshi Yanjiushi 中共中央黨史研究室 [The Central Party History Research Office]. *Zhongguo Gongchangdang Lishi (Di'erjuan)* 中國共產黨歷史（第二卷）[History of the Chinese Communist Party (volume II, 1949–1978)]. Beijing: Zhonggong dangshi chubanshe, 2011.

5
Can Private Museums Offer Space for Alternative History?
The Red Era Series at the Jianchuan Museum Cluster

Kirk A. Denton

Until recently, all museums in the People's Republic of China (PRC) were subsidized, supported, and monitored by the state. Only since the early 1990s have we seen the emergence of private museums. As of 2006, there were some 200 private museums in the PRC, a number that grew to 1,100 by 2015.[1] The majority of these new museums are fine arts museums dedicated to the display of paintings, porcelain, calligraphy, or avant-garde art, though private natural science museums or specialty museums are also common. The state seems to encourage these forms of private museums because they contribute to the cultural economy of cities and to a softening of the image of state power and authority, even as some of the art housed in these museums can be at odds, explicitly or implicitly, with the political interests of the state.

Given its long historiographic tradition and heightened consciousness of the political uses of history, history museums in China are subject to greater political scrutiny. In this essay, I examine whether a private history museum can assert memories that are normally proscribed in the highly controlled context of the single-party state in China. The museum in question is the Jianchuan Museum Cluster 建川博物館聚落, a private museum established by the real estate entrepreneur Fan Jianchuan 樊建川 in Anren 安仁, Sichuan, in 2005; it has developed enormously over the ensuing years and continues to grow as I write. Although the museum is not exclusively devoted to the Cultural Revolution, I focus on its representation of that period of Chinese history because of its political sensitivity, which makes for an excellent test case in gauging the latitude private museums do or do not have in expressing alternative historical views.

Scholars seem to disagree on the political meaning of this museum. Although he was conjecturing about its future, Michael Dutton sees postsocialist

---

1. See Song Xiangguang, "Sili bowuguan fazhan xuyao shehui zhichi" [The development of private museums requires social support], *Zhongguo wenwu bao* (Sept. 15, 2006): 6; and *Zhongguo siren bowuguan hangye fazhan baipishu, 2016 nian* [White paper on the development of the private museum industry in China, 2016] (Beijing: Zhongguo siren bowugan lianhe pingtai, 2016), 7.

Kirk A. Denton

commodification and nostalgia at play, not historical memories of an alternative nature.[2] Denise Ho and Jie Li, by contrast, suggest that the museum's exhibits "challenge and disrupt Mao-era history." But as Ho and Li also write, Fan Jianchuan had "originally intended to call his museum complex a 'museum supermarket,'" so they too acknowledge the commercial motivations behind the museum.[3] Zhang Ming 張鳴, a political scientist at Renmin University, recognizes the importance of the museum as a counter to the forgetting that takes place in "official history museums" in China. At the same time, he realizes the "limits" faced by private curators like Fan and recognizes that his museum "has still watered down the tragedy, helplessness, and loss of human life" of the Cultural Revolution.[4]

Although they do not rely on the state for subsidies, private museums like the Jianchuan Museum are still subject to state/party oversight, not to mention the demands of the market.[5] Private history museum developers must negotiate among their own desire to be true to the past, the limits the Chinese Communist Party (CCP) places on historical memory, and the need to develop a commercially viable enterprise. But what is the product of this negotiation? What happens to the trauma of the Cultural Revolution when it gets displayed in a space that is at once "private" and subject to public forces, both political and commercial? Do these forces contain and thus whitewash the trauma? And what happens to the very sensitive issue of personal responsibility—who is to blame for the Cultural Revolution—that is one of the key reasons the post-Mao state has been so reluctant to fully unleash memories of this and other sensitive facets of the Maoist past. Is the museum a cultural form that inherently reifies the past in such a way that trauma can never be presented in any tangible way? Would relegating memory of the Cultural Revolution to a narrative that is a product of present-day politics and neoliberal ideology merely serve to whitewash the past of its complexity, heterogeneity, and power to speak to the present? What kind of museum exhibit, if any, can do justice to this kind of past?

Ba Jin, the Museum of the Cultural Revolution, and Sites for Remembering the Cultural Revolution

As is well known, in 1986 the writer Ba Jin 巴金 proposed the establishment of an official, state-sponsored museum dedicated to the Cultural Revolution. He did this partly out of his own sense of guilt in contributing to the denunciation of other

---

2. Michael Dutton, "From Culture Industry to Mao Industry: A Greek Tragedy," *boundary 2* 32, no. 2 (2005): 165–66.
3. Denise Y. Ho and Jie Li, "From Landlord Manor to Red Memorabilia: Reincarnations of a Chinese Museum Town," *Modern China* 42, no. 1 (2016): 3.
4. See Joshua Frank, 2014, *Collecting Insanity*, Documentary film (9:34 min.). Chinafile.com (2014): min. 7:14. http://www.chinafile.com/multimedia/video/collecting-insanity.
5. One must apply through the local Bureau of Cultural Relics (文物局) to open a private museum, a process that includes submitting a list of artifacts to be displayed and an outline of the display organization. Museums are also subject to inspections by state officials.

intellectuals both before and during the Cultural Revolution, but his principal concern was the need for a nation to confront its past so as to not repeat it:

> So that everyone sees clearly and remembers clearly, it is necessary to build a museum of the Cultural Revolution, exhibiting concrete and real objects and reconstructing striking scenes which will testify to what took place on this Chinese soil twenty years ago! Everyone will recall the march of events there, and each will recall his or her behavior during that decade. Masks will fall, each will search his or her conscience, the true face of each one will be revealed, large and small debts from the past will be paid. If we free ourselves from our selfishness, we will no longer fear deception. Let us dare to proclaim the truth, and we will not so easily swallow such lies any longer. It is only by engraving in our memory the events of the Cultural Revolution that we will prevent history from repeating itself, that we will prevent another Cultural Revolution from occurring. The construction of this Cultural Revolution museum is absolutely necessary, because only those who do not forget the past will be masters of the future.[6]

To this day, that museum has not been realized and official memory of the Cultural Revolution continues to be a highly sensitive topic in China.[7] Indeed, in official exhibitionary spaces where one might expect at least some attention to the Cultural Revolution—for example, the Museum of Modern Chinese Literature in Beijing—there is a glaring blank. In the early 2000s, as the new National Museum of China was taking shape and curators were charged with revamping its exhibits for a renovated museum, I was told in interviews with curators that the Cultural Revolution would be treated seriously and forthrightly. But when the museum opened in the fall of 2011, the Cultural Revolution occupied but a single placard. In this official context, as I have argued elsewhere, the Maoist past is whitewashed of its trauma and turmoil, and "Mao is refashioned from a radical leftist into a modernizer whose policies in the 1950s laid the foundation for the explosive development of the Deng era."[8]

The absence of an official commemorative space does not, of course, mean that the Cultural Revolution is not remembered in China. There are numerous physical and virtual spaces where such remembering occurs: digital media, film and literature, avant-garde art, personal memoirs, private memorial spaces, etc. These remembrances take a variety of forms. There are those in the nostalgic mode, such as the "red classics" restaurants, which are decorated with Cultural Revolution memorabilia and often feature performances of revolutionary songs. Others, like

---

6. Ba Jin, "A Museum of the 'Cultural Revolution,'" trans. Geremie Barmé. CND.org, http://www.cnd.org/cr/english/articles/bajin.htm. Originally published as "Wenge bowuguan" [Cultural Revolution museum], in Ba Jin, *Suixiang lu* [Random thoughts], http://www.readers365.com/bajin/suixianglu/index.htm.
7. The Chinese Academy of Museums actually drew up plans for the museum, but the plans stalled because of bureaucratic inertia and fear. For an overview of these failed efforts, see Ye Yonglie, "'Wenge bowuguan' zhi meng" [The dream of a Cultural Revolution Museum], *Zhengming* no. 217 (Nov. 1995): 79–84.
8. Kirk A. Denton, "China Dreams and the Road to Revival," *Origins: Current Events in Historical Perspective* 8, no. 3, http://origins.osu.edu/article/china-dreams-and-road-revival.

the online journal *Remembrance* (記憶), discussed in Jean-Philippe Béja's chapter, are more academic in orientation, seeking to unearth the officially repressed truth of the Cultural Revolution. Reflective modes of remembrance make one ponder the continuity of the Maoist past into the present. The artist Yue Minjun's 嶽敏君 *Brain Sea* (腦海), for example, explicitly depicts the continuing place of Mao in the memories of the Chinese people, an image that is expressly at odds with, or a response to, state-enforced amnesia toward the Maoist past (Figure 5.1). The Cultural Revolution has in recent years returned as a subject to the screen, less as a direct depiction than as a haunting in the present. Zhang Yimou's 張藝謀 *Coming Home* (歸來), for example, tells the story of a woman who develops amnesia and fails to recognize her husband when he returns home after being rehabilitated following the end of the Cultural Revolution. Neo-leftists, such as those affiliated with the Wengewang.org site, reappropriate the Maoist past as a form of political critique of the neoliberal present.[9] Finally, a few former red guards, most notably Chen Xiaolu 陳小魯 and Song Binbin 宋彬彬, have made public apologies for their actions during the early years of the Cultural Revolution.[10]

Take, for instance, the Red Guard cemetery in Shapingba Park 沙坪壩公園, Chongqing. The cemetery was "saved" from destruction in 1985 by then Chongqing party secretary Liao Bokang 廖伯康, who was struck by the incongruous use of the word "martyr" on the sign to the entrance to the cemetery: "What kind of martyrs

Figure 5.1
Yue Minjun, "Brain Sea". Source: http://www.artnet.com/artists/yue-minjun/sea-of-the-brain-XZC2jr4n3bHRrv4z-t99zoA2.

---

9. The Wengewang website is based in the US and was established in 2005. It presents historical materials on the Cultural Revolution and is a platform for neo-leftists to meet virtually and share their views.
10. Anthony Kuhn, "Chinese Red Guards Apologize, Reopening a Dark Chapter," National Public Radio (Feb. 2, 2014), http://www.npr.org/sections/parallels/2014/01/23/265228870/chinese-red-guards-apologize-reopening-a-dark-chapter.

were they? A martyr is someone who sacrifices his life for the nation. To die in a mistaken political movement, to die by the guns of your own brothers, you can't use the word 'martyr' for that."[11] The cemetery is a site, if a rather physically marginal one, for memorializing the Cultural Revolution. Tian Taiquan 田太權 has used the site as a setting for his provocative photographs, which cause one to reflect on the relationship between the present and this violent past (Figure 5.2).

Some have argued that despite the state-imposed amnesia, the Cultural Revolution—and the Maoist past more generally—can be felt everywhere in China today. Perry Link, for example, sees the origins of the post-Mao reform movement not in policy prescriptions from above, but in the "widespread popular revulsion against the disastrous conditions that the Great Leap and the Cultural Revolution had left behind."[12] Tao Zhu sees the tendency to "build big" in China today—the "megaprojects" that can be found around the country—as a legacy of Maoist monumentalization, such as the construction of the "ten great buildings" during the Great Leap Forward era.[13] Other scholars have argued that the political activism that led to the 1989 movement can be traced back to the Red Guard/*zhiqing* experience during the Cultural Revolution.[14] In short, in the urban landscape, in modernization, and

Figure 5.2
Tian Taiquan photograph, with the Shapingba Red Guard Cemetery as backdrop. Source: http://www.mandarinfineart.com/photographers/tian-taiquan.

---

11. See Philip P. Pan, *Out of Mao's Shadow: The Struggle for the Soul of a New China* (New York: Simon and Shuster, 2008), 109. See also Jie Li, "Memorials and Museums of the Maoist Era: A Survey and Notes for Future Curators," in *Red Legacies in China: Cultural Afterlives of the Communist Revolution*, ed. Jie Li and Enhua Zhang (Cambridge, MA: Harvard University Asia Center, 2016), 319–54.
12. See "Fifty Years Later, How Is the Cultural Revolution Still Present in China," *China File* (April 19, 2016), http://www.chinafile.com/conversation/fifty-years-later-how-cultural-revolution-still-present-life-china.
13. Tao Zhu, "Building Big, with No Regret: From Beijing's 'Ten Great Buildings' in the 1950s to China's Megaprojects Today," in *Red Legacies in China: Cultural Afterlives of the Communist Revolution*, ed. Jie Li and Enhua Zhang (Cambridge, MA: Harvard University Asia Center, 2016), 56–84.
14. Guobin Yang, *The Red Guard Generation and Political Activism in China* (New York: Columbia University Press, 2017).

in youthful democratic aspirations, the Cultural Revolution has left its indelible mark. But this legacy is, of course, not explicitly or publicly recognized in China, resulting in a strange incongruence between the Cultural Revolution's omnipresence as a historical force and its haunting invisibility.

Although no official state Cultural Revolution museum exists in China, "semi-official" museums do. These museums tend to be far removed from the political center. One such site, reported on extensively in the foreign press,[15] is the Museum of the Cultural Revolution outside of Shantou, Guangdong (Figure 5.3). The museum was established by Peng Qi'an 彭啟安, a local official who suffered during the Cultural Revolution but rose in the post-Mao era to become deputy mayor of Shantou. The museum is lacking as a memorial site in several respects: its setting is remote, about an hour outside of Shantou, and visitors are few; it is swallowed up in the larger scenic and tourist destination of which it is a part; and its main exhibition hall contains few actual artifacts.[16] Still, the site manages, or at least it did until it was closed down in 2016,[17] in its dispersed style to draw attention to some of the

Figure 5.3
The building housing the main exhibits at the Shantou Cultural Revolution Museum. Photograph by Kirk A. Denton.

---

15. See Mark Mackinnon, "China's Cultural Revolution Museum: A Well-Kept Secret," *Toronto Globe and Mail* July 22, 2010, http://www.theglobeandmail.com/news/world/chinas-cultural-revolution-museum-a-well-kept-secret/article1389357/; Didi Kirsten Tatlow, "Talking 'bout a Revolution," *South China Morning Post*, June 19, 2005, http://www.scmp.com/article/505060/talking-bout-revolution; and "Cultural Revolution Museum Seeks 600,000 yuan for Extension," *South China Morning Post*, May 17, 2006, http://www.scmp.com/article/549184/cultural-revolution-museum-seeks-600000-yuan-extension.
16. The displays consist mostly of metal plates on which have been etched photographs taken from a book published in Hong Kong entitled *Cultural Revolution Museum*. See Yang Kelin, ed., *Wenhua dageming bowuguan* [Cultural Revolution museum] (Hong Kong: Dongfang, 1995).
17. Didi Kirsten Tatlow, "Fate Catches Up to a Cultural Revolution Museum in China," *New York Times*, October 2, 2016, https://www.nytimes.com/2016/10/03/world/asia/china-cultural-revolution-shantou-museum.html.

horrors of the period: it includes, for instance, a stone façade on which are etched the "100 tortures of the Cultural Revolution." There are at least three other museums around China—one each in Shanghai, Kunming, and Heihe—devoted to the fate of the youth that Mao "sent down" to rural areas during the Cultural Revolution.[18] In terms of scope and quality of artifacts, however, the Shantou Cultural Revolution Museum and these other sites pale in comparison to the Jianchuan Museum Cluster.

Fan Jianchuan and Connoisseurship

Fan Jianchuan (1957–), the founder of the Jianchuan Museum, made his fortune as a real estate developer in Chengdu, at one point rising to as high as number 406 on the Hurun list of China's wealthiest people.[19] Fan tells us in his autobiography that his "collecting consciousness" (收藏意識) arose during the Cultural Revolution, when he began amassing Mao badges and political flyers as a way of understanding the criticism against his father, who was a target of political persecution.[20] Fan's predilection for collecting thus predates by several decades his accumulation of wealth as a real estate developer. Still, Fan represents a new breed of entrepreneurs who have made enormous fortunes in the market economy and can afford to pursue more leisurely interests. He now spends all of his time engaged with the museum.[21] He has invested more than US$200 million in the project over the years, and says, with evident pride, that over 95 percent of the museums' more than eight million artifacts were purchased.[22]

As an entrepreneur-turned-collector, Fan is repeating an age-old pattern for Chinese merchants going back at least to the Ming.[23] Collecting and connoisseurship are forms of self-identity for the nouveau riche in the market economy, symbolic capital for entrepreneurs who may not have more established and institutional credentials, a public way to position themselves not just as cultured but as people of financial means.[24] Like some of his Ming predecessors, Fan is not just a dilettante; he

---

18. Magnus Fiskejö, "Review Essay: The Museum Boom in China and the State Efforts to Control History," *Museum Anthropology Review* 9, no. 2 (Fall 2015), https://scholarworks.iu.edu/journals/index.php/mar/article/view/19150/29099.
19. Fan's company is called the Jianchuan Enterprise Group (建川事業集團有限公司). Projects have included high-rise office buildings and apartment complexes in Chengdu and luxury housing and villas in Dujiangyan. See the Baidu baike entry for Fan Jianchuan: http://baike.baidu.com/view/639676.htm.
20. Fan Jianchuan, *Daguan nu: Fan Jianchuan de jiyi yu mengxiang* [Slave of big museums: Fan Jianchuan's memories and dreams] (Beijing: Sanlian, 2013), 108.
21. This, according to Fan's general manager, who now has taken charge of the company. Fan has sold his interests in the company and now devotes himself entirely to the museum.
22. See Fan, *Daguan nu*, 126. In a 2016 interview, Fan responds to the claim that, with 8 million, his museum has eight times as many artifacts as the National Museum of China. See Sun Hongyan, "Fan Jianchuan zhuanfang" (interview with Fan Jianchuan), *Kangri zhanzheng jinianwang*, November 18, 2016, http://www.krzzjn.com/html/40958.html.
23. Craig Clunas, *Superfluous Things: Material Culture and Social Status in Early Modern China* (Honolulu: University of Hawai'i Press, 2004).
24. Fan is at pains to draw attention to his financial straits and to stress that his museum project was an obsession, not a good business strategy. He quotes a friend as saying: "For a person to be done for, take drugs; for an

is a real expert who has published one book on Cultural Revolution porcelain and two on the War of Resistance.²⁵

Although not a native of Anren,²⁶ Fan must be considered its most prominent citizen; everyone knows him, and his presence and the presence of his museum are everywhere felt in the town. Indeed, he has even been made honorary mayor by town officials.²⁷ Town streets are emblazoned with banners advertising the museum complex. Following the establishment of the Jianchuan Museum, the town of Anren rebranded itself as "China's museum village,"²⁸ a term that refers both to Fan's museum complex and to Anren as a "living museum." Since 2009, with the financial backing of the Chengdu government,²⁹ the village has undergone a large-scale restoration, during which many of the town's old residences were converted to inns, art galleries, cafes, bars, and museums.³⁰ To celebrate the completion of the renovation, in April 2011, Anren put on what was billed as a "nostalgic light and scenery performance," which included performers dressed up in period costumes, horse-drawn carts, rickshaws, newspaper boys, and even a restored streetcar. The town particularly plays on this Republican-era past and the subtle, though faded, grandeur of its old residences. In this sense, the restoration of Anren can be seen as part of a larger nostalgia for the Republican era in contemporary China that is, of course, rooted in the market economy. Anren is, moreover, in the process of developing an official town museum that will further consolidate its brand as "China's museum village."³¹ Fan's connection to the town goes back to 2003: when looking for a site for the museum, he came to Anren and fell in love with it; the town government, for its part, embraced Fan's idea for the museum complex and happily sold him the land on which to build it.

Anren is, of course, most famous in China not as a well-preserved "museum village" or even as the location of the Jianchuan Museum, but as the home of Liu Wencai 劉文彩, a notorious evil landlord in Mao-era propaganda. Liu's mansion was turned into a museum in 1958, and, later, part of it was dedicated to displaying the Rent Collection Courtyard series of sculptures that depicted the evils of

---

entrepreneur to be done for, build museums." See Fan, *Daguan nu*, 176.
25. See Fan Jianchuan, *Wenge ciqi tujian* [Illustrated handbook of Cultural Revolution porcelain] (Beijing: Wenwu, 2002); *Yige ren de kangzhan* [One person's war of resistance] (Beijing: Zhongguo duiwai fanyi, 2000); and *Kangfu: Zhongguo kangri zhanfu xiezhen* [Resistance prisoners: The true story of prisoners during the War of Resistance] (Beijing: Zhongguo duiwai fanyi, 2006).
26. Although his father's ancestral home is in Shanxi, Fan was born and grew up in Yibin, Sichuan. He was for a while deputy mayor of Yibin.
27. Mou Naihong, "Fan Jianchuan he tade Jianchuan bowuguan" [Fan Jianchuan and his Jianchuan Museum], *Dang jian* (June 1, 2014): 57.
28. The marketing campaign was launched in 2011. See Cui Ran, "Anren Zhongguo bowuguan xiaozhen yiqi qihang" [The China Museum village at Anren phase one sets sail], Chengdu Quansousuo, April 28, 2011, http://news.chengdu.cn/content/2011-04/28/content_702542.htm.
29. According to one report, the Chengdu government invested 5 billion yuan in the project. See Cui Ran, "Anren Zhongguo bowuguan."
30. For information on Anren as a tourist destination, see its official website: http://www.anrentown.com/.
31. The Barcelona based architectural firm TCHV has a design plan for the museum on its website. See http://www.tchv.es/anren.html.

landlord oppression of the peasant class (Figure 5.4). The mansion is still a tourist site in Anren, but people now seem to visit it less to learn the lessons of class oppression than to revel in the opulence of Liu Wencai's home, perhaps fueling their own real estate dreams, dreams that Fan Jianchuan's company might just be able to fulfill. Fan was drawn to Anren partly because of its place in Cultural Revolution history, and that history needs to be considered in any analysis of the Jianchuan Museum.

One cannot help but ponder the irony of Fan Jianchuan, a landlord wealthier than anything Liu Wencai could have imagined, now the object of praise by the local government as a patriotic entrepreneur with an abiding passion for preserving China's past.[32] Fan's positive reputation in Anren parallels a radically revisionist view of Liu Wencai himself that the infamous landlord's grandson has been campaigning for on his long-dead grandfather's behalf.[33] The irony is not, it seems, lost on local residents. Denise Ho and Jie Li mention an encounter they had with a local pedicab driver in Anren who praised Fan as the "new landlord in town," as good as Liu Wencai because both created jobs and built public facilities.[34] This postsocialist

Figure 5.4
Part of the Rent Collection Courtyard sculptural display. Photograph by Kirk A. Denton.

---

32. Articles in local and provincial papers frequently cover and praise Fan's activities.
33. On Liu Xiaofei's 劉小飛 campaign, see Guo Wu, "The Social Construction and Deconstruction of Evil Landlords in Contemporary Chinese Fiction, Art, and Collective Memory," *Modern Chinese Literature and Culture* 25, no. 1 (Spring 2013): 131–64. The revisionist historian Xiao Shu has also sought to de-demonize Liu Wencai. See Xiao Shu, *Liu Wencai zhenxiang* [The true face of Liu Wencai] (Xi'an: Shaanxi shifan daxue, 1999) and *Xin shixue: da dizhu Liu Wencai* [New historiography: Big landlord Liu Wencai] (Guangzhou: Guangdong renmin, 2011).
34. Denise Y. Ho and Jie Li, "From Landlord Manor to Red Memorabilia," 28.

representation of the landlord class is starkly at odds with the demonization that was the norm in the Mao era.

In an interview, Fan praises the advent of private property in China as a stabilizing force that can prevent political upheaval and social chaos, like that of the Cultural Revolution, from occurring:

> When a person has property, they have roots, when they have roots, then they have a harvest. Then they don't want society to have revolutions, or become chaotic or have riots, or to fluctuate too much. These people say, I have property, are you going to destroy my 10,000 *kuai*, are you going to rob me? They want society to succeed. The greatest kind of stability is to have some people with property, and their numbers must be ever increasing.[35]

Here Fan is essentially supporting the market-oriented, neoliberal policies of the present regime. Seen in this light, his museum cluster and its attention to the Cultural Revolution is clearly not some subversive attempt to undermine the Party and its political legitimacy by drawing attention to the horrors committed in its name. For Fan, remembering the chaos of the past is a social mechanism for reinforcing a stable social and political system in the present, a system that has allowed him to become rich and will lead to an ever-larger middle class. For Fan, remembering the Cultural Revolution is, it goes without saying, also not about resurrecting a lost radicalism that can be turned against the injustices of the neoliberal economy. Nor is it about confronting a traumatic period of history in order to understand the political causes of that trauma. Rather, remembering the past is a means of maintaining social order and stability in the present and is thus not inconsistent with official state policy on the Cultural Revolution. This attitude may explain, at least partly, why the Jianchuan Museum can exist and the nature of what gets remembered in its exhibits.

The Cluster Concept

Jianchuan Museum Cluster is the umbrella term for what is a complex of many individual museums. As of 2017, the eighty-acre site consisted of twenty-eight museums, divided into four "series"—the War of Resistance series, the Red Era series, the Earthquake series (which focuses on the Wenchuan earthquake of 2008), and the Folk series—as well as several open-air memorial squares. It also boasts a reception center, a "red-era theme" hotel, a teahouse, and a cafeteria in the style of a People's Commune dining hall. The Jianchuan Museum Cluster is the largest private museum in China, and must be one of the largest in the world.[36]

---

35. See "The Legacy of Property provides Stability," Asia Society "China Boom project," http://chinaboom.asiasociety.org/period/emancipation/0/110. Full interview conducted on June 3, 2008 is available here: https://rucore.libraries.rutgers.edu/rutgers-lib/38534/.

36. This assertion is often made about the museum. Fan himself describes it as the largest completely self-funded museum in the world. See He Yue, "Fan Jianchuan: Yige juluo, yi zuo chengchi" [Fan Jianchuan: A cluster, a

Although he had earlier exhibited some of his collected artifacts in the Sichuan Provincial Museum in April and May 2001, and later in Beijing and Hong Kong, Fan opened the first five of his museums at the Anren site in 2005 on the sixtieth anniversary of the end of the War of Resistance. According to Fan, in the early development, there were financing issues, but since then he has added museums and artifacts at a furious pace.[37] Fan hired big-name architects—both domestic and foreign (e.g., Isozaki Arata 磯崎新, Xing Tonghe 刑同和, Liu Jiakun 劉家琨, and Zhang Yonghe 張永和)—to design the various buildings that make up the site. Modest in scale and designed sustainably to keep heating and cooling costs down, the museum buildings are not uniform in style, giving the compound an eclectic and heterogeneous look that is consistent with Fan's motivations behind the "cluster" concept.[38] Fan hired Zhang Yonghe and Liu Jiakun as his general planners, and then worked closely with the various architects to create buildings that were appropriate in style to the theme of the particular museum.[39] For example, the Prisoners of War museum, designed by Cheng Taining 程泰寧, is meant to look and feel prison-like (Figure 5.5).

The concept behind "cluster" (聚落)—a term that is conventionally used to describe a group of homes forming a village—suggests both that the compound is like a village and that in order to get at the truth of a historical period, one must approach it from a variety of perspectives and angles. In a conceptual volume published before the museum began to take physical shape, Fan describes "cluster" as a "sharp conceptual innovation [銳利的觀念創新]" centered on three main concepts. The first is described in the following way: "Twenty-five museums, scattered like stars in the firmament or like pieces on a chessboard [星羅棋布], mutually supporting each other, the beginning resonating with the end. They are chanting the same song, but it's not a solo, it's a chorus; not a concerto, but a symphony, full and of many colors."[40] In presenting an array of museums on a variety of historical periods and topics, the museum's approach is different from the distinctly narrative style of state history museums, where linear storylines shaped by politically driven, monolithic notions of truth dominate exhibitionary practice.

---

walled city], *Xin jin shang* (Sept. 5, 2014): 42–47.

37. Fan attributes these financial issues to the fact that because official approval had not been granted when the museum first opened, the media were not allowed to cover it, which led to a dearth of visitors. But the inauspicious opening forced Fan to understand the absolute importance of marketing work to the survival of the museum. See Fan, *Daguan nu*, 177. Fan has become over the years a master at exploiting the media to promote the museum: he has granted dozens, if not hundreds, of interviews; the museum has been the focus of numerous documentaries; he gets the media to cover visits to the museum by well-known politicians, cultural figures, and celebrities; and he has given a TED talk in Chengdu; see http://m.youku.com/video/id_XMTg4NTY2MjIzNg==.html.
38. Fan, *Da guan nu*, 146.
39. Liu and Fan were already close friends, probably connected through Fan's real estate business, and the former introduced the latter to Zhang Yonghe.
40. See Fan Jianchuan, *Jianchuan bowuguan juluo* [Jianchuan Museum Cluster] (Anren: Jianchuan bowuguan, n.d.), 12.

Figure 5.5
The Unyielding Prisoners Hall at the Jianchuan Museum. Photograph by Kirk A. Denton.

The second concept asserts, in language only a real estate marketer could compose, that the museum cluster would be "harmoniously unified with commerce, offices, and residences . . . History's diversity and today's happy life." It seems from a schematic I have found online that early designs for the museum complex even called for an integration of museums with residential and office spaces, creating a compound that would resemble a village. At the very least, the museum complex was intended to be a "continuation of the pattern of the old town of Anren."[41] As for the third concept, Fan writes: "to taste history and chew life, like the perfect unity . . . spirit and flesh, material products and noble spiritual consumption. . . . We are heading toward a well-off society, we will encounter prosperity, we will have leisure, we will experience things, we will have warmth, and we will know newness. In the end, we will be happy."[42] Here Fan forefronts the commercial dimensions of his concept, and the real estate developer comes to overshadow the historian. As mentioned earlier, Fan had originally intended to conceptualize the complex as a "museum supermarket" (博物館超市), but his idea was eventually rejected because "everyone opposed me"; despite the resistance, however, Fan continued to believe in the supermarket concept, which served his purpose of descralizing the museum as an elite cultural institution and making it speak to the average person.[43] His ideal museum as a polyphonic symphony of perspectives cannot be disconnected from the commercial economy's notions of leisure time and happiness through consumption; the multiplicity of historical perspectives is intertwined with a market economy that offers consumers an array of goods and services—history is a department store from which to consume memories. Fan says that he intentionally sought to keep the individual museums small so that the visitor would spend no more than forty-five minutes in each and thus not lose a sense of "freshness."[44]

To reduce Fan's cluster concept to nothing but a museum supermarket, however, would do it a disservice. In some regards, the museum offers a refreshing alternative

---

41. Liu Jiakun, "Anren Jianchuan bowuguan juluo sheji" [Design of the Jianchuan Museum Cluster in Anren], *Shidai jianzhu* 1 (2006): 37.
42. Fan, *Jianchuan bowuguan juluo*, 13.
43. Fan, *Daguan nu*, 137–38.
44. Fan, *Daguan nu*, 137.

to state museums. For instance, the Jianchuan complex has the only museums in China dedicated to the contributions of the Nationalist (KMT) army during the War of Resistance and to Chinese prisoners of war. It has a museum dedicated to the US military in the War of Resistance: the Flying Tigers Hall 飛虎奇兵館. Elements of all these things can be found in such state museums as the War of Resistance Memorial Hall outside Beijing, but to have dedicated museums to these topics gives them a significance and a prominence they do not have when embedded in larger exhibitions. Since the 1980s, as part of a softening of relations with Taiwan and an effort to prevent it from turning politically "green" (i.e., Democratic Progressive Party), state memorial sites have emphasized the Nationalist role in the war effort. To do so is to forge a shared history between the mainland and Taiwan and to counter the "desinicization" tendency among Taiwan nationalists. Fan has himself traveled to Taiwan several times and met with KMT officials, including Lien Chan 連戰, to talk about his museum project and solicit donations. Indeed, Lien Chan, former premier of the ROC and once head of the KMT, wrote the calligraphy of the characters that were to form the sign for the KMT war efforts hall.[45]

Cultural Revolutionary Memory in the Jianchuan Museum

What is most remarkable about Fan's museum cluster in terms of "alternative" historical memories is, however, his Red Era series devoted to the Cultural Revolution. It is this series that has garnered most of the media (at least in the West) and scholarly attention.

What stands out in the Red Era series museums is their relative lack of narrative line. State museums generally construct clear narratives according to a strong "guiding [political] principle" (綱領), structured into chapters (章) and units (單元) punctuated with placards that set the larger context and propel the narrative. Whereas "official" museums start with a "complete framework" (整體框架) and display artifacts to "prove" a point, Fan uses what one critic calls a "thematic exhibitionary style" (主題陳列式) that is intentionally fragmented and disparate.[46]

The absence of narrative lines is true both within individual museums (more about this below) and within the museum cluster as a whole. The museum buildings are not arranged in any way that might suggest a chronology or a coherent narrative of the history of modern China from the War of Resistance to the Mao era to the present. The complex is not divided into sections based on the four series; rather, museums from different series are interspersed with each other, giving the complex an almost random structure. Although the architectural advisors recommended to

---

45. Fan changed the name of the museum, so in the end the sign could not be used, but it is prominently displayed inside the museum.
46. On Fan's "thematic exhibitionary style," see Huang Zhanjin, "Lishi de lingyizhong jilu fangshi" [An alternative method of recording history], *Fenghuang zhoukan* 227 (Aug. 2006): 20–23.

Fan placing the series museums together, Fan stuck to his guns, saying "it must be mixed, not concentrated" (一定要混搭，不要集中).[47]

Interspersing the Red Era series museums, of which there are seven, with museums in the other series is part of Fan's strategy to make memory of the Cultural Revolution politically palatable. The cluster concept serves both to present multiple sides of history, as mentioned above, and to camouflage a sensitive period of Maoist history with other subjects that conform more closely to official discourse. The hall devoted to the CCP war efforts is at the "epicenter" of the compound: it is the first museum one arrives at after walking down the main entranceway, the first in the museum's official guidebook, and the place where tourists most often take photographs.[48] As such, this museum, which is called the Bulwark Hall (中流砥柱館), takes on a significance that other museums in the complex do not have and lends the entire complex an air of official legitimacy. "Bulwark" is Maoist discourse for the role of the CCP in saving and liberating the Chinese people from the Japanese army.[49]

This heroic patriotic mode is also conveyed in the huge "China Heroes Statues Square" (中國壯士群雕廣場) on which are placed more than two hundred slightly-larger-than-life-size steel statues of heroes who fought in the War of Resistance (Figure 5.6).[50] The figures are laid out in the shape of a map of China; figures are placed in locations with which they are historically associated. The square presents China in miniature, dotted with the heroes who fought and sometimes died to save the nation from external threat.

Juxtaposing the Red Era museums with those of the war, the earthquake, and folk culture allows Fan to couch the Cultural Revolution in a general atmosphere of patriotism, service to the nation, and love of one's local culture. Although the cluster structure may mitigate against the idea of the Cultural Revolution as a distinct historical period characterized by particular political issues, it lends a semblance of patriotism and party loyalty to Fan's revisionist museology.[51] Furthermore, one of the museums in the Red Era series is a memorial hall devoted to Deng Xiaoping,

---

47. Fan, *Daguan nu*, 145.
48. For the museum guidebook, see Fan Jianchuan, *Jianchuan bowuguan jiangjieci* [Text for guides at the Jianchuan Museum] (Anren: Jianchuan bowuguan, 2007).
49. The phrase has a classical provenance—the *Yanzi chunqiu* (晏子春秋). In pre-Mao usages, it can refer to a specific rock at Sanmen Gorge (三門峽) along the Yellow River or, metaphorically, to a sturdy presence that can withstand the currents running against it. It appears near the end of Mao's "On Coalition Government" (論聯合政府, 1945).
50. It should be pointed out that the square is also revisionist in including Nationalists and "local militia" (地方軍) alongside famous Communist martyrs.
51. The "patriotizing" process is enhanced in a 2010 CCTV News documentary "Memories of a Museum" (崢嶸歲月). The documentary was originally produced by Phoenix TV in Hong Kong and then rebroadcast in altered form on CCTV. In the prefatory section of the film, we see a throng of PLA soldiers standing before the Heroes Square. One soldier is holding a PRC flag, while triumphant music plays. Parts 8, 9, and 10 of the original documentary covered the Red Era series museums, but these segments were cut by CCTV. See Fan, *Daguan nu*, 196. The original ten-part version is no longer available on the Phoenix website. For the CCTV version, in five parts, see http://english.cntv.cn/program/storyboard/special/jianchuan_museum/.

Figure 5.6
China Heroes Statute Square. Photograph by Kirk A. Denton.

who was himself purged twice during the Cultural Revolution. His presence here sanctions the Red Era series' remembering of the Cultural Revolution as a healthy expression of what it means to be a modern and stable nation.

When a survey asked which of the museum series in the complex most attracted them, 48 percent of respondents cited the War of Resistance series, while 21 percent named the Red Era series, 15 percent named the Earthquake series, and 12 percent named the Folk series.[52] One can surmise that this preference for the war series museums reflects an obsessive attention to the war period in party discourse, as well as in TV serials and "main melody" commercial-propaganda films. The history of the war, as a time that China was both victimized and resisted heroically, sits more easily in the minds of Chinese today than does the Cultural Revolution, with its moral ambiguity and lack of clearly defined enemy.

At the same time, reading against the grain, we might say that putting a museum that treats the heroic resistance of the CCP against the Japanese next to a museum exhibiting Cultural Revolution artifacts or near one about the Wenchuan Earthquake might suggest to some viewers the discrepancy between the heroism of the past and the failures of the Party to live up to those ideals in more recent times. Tucked in a wooded area of the compound is a one-room museum devoted to a single victim of the Wenchuan Earthquake—one Hu Huishan 胡慧珊, a sixteen-year-old girl who died in Dujiangyan (Figure 5.7). The memorial hall is made up of

---

52. Zhai Qiying, "Jianchuan bowuguan juluo guanzhong yanjiu" [A spectator study of the Jianchuan Museum Cluster] (MA thesis, Zhongyang meishu xueyuan, Beijing, 2014), 31.

Figure 5.7
Hu Huishan Memorial Hall. Source: Arch Daily, http://www.archdaily.com/363718/hu-huishan-memorial-jiakun-architects.

a single pink room displaying some of Hu's personal possessions. It's a subtle and understated memorial that has no underlying political motivation in the way Ai Weiwei's 艾未未 monumental list of names of earthquake victims has.[53] But set in the larger context of the other museums in the Jianchuan complex and the many state museums around China that glorify communist heroes and martyrs, the very ordinariness of the life of this girl—a "common life" as a placard puts it—takes on an implicit political dimension; Hu Huishan becomes a martyr to the failures of the state to protect its innocent children.

Another juxtaposition we find in the complex as a whole is that between the "hard" remembering of the War of Resistance and the revisionism of the KMT and Flying Tigers exhibits, which focus more on conventional historical artifacts, photographs, and texts, with the more nostalgic remembrance of the Cultural Revolution in the Red Era series and its focus on daily life and its aestheticization of Maoist artifacts. One might go so far as to argue that the cluster concept hinges on the ironic juxtaposition of official and non-official discourses in the same exhibitionary space, though I'm not prepared to argue that this is how actual visitors interpret the museums in the cluster.[54]

The original concept for the museum, as outlined in an undated catalogue, was to have a total of twenty-five museums organized around three themes—the War of Resistance, the Cultural Revolution, and Folk Traditions.[55] In the beginning, Fan

---

53. Ai's *Names of the Student Earthquake Victims Found by Citizen's Investigation* has been displayed in museums around the world.
54. The two main earthquake museums are, in a sense, opposite: one gives the "rescue" story, a heroic narrative that is consistent with state discourse, and the other is more oriented toward personal stories, like that of Hu Huishan, and emphasizes the tragedies.
55. See Fan, *Jianchuan bowuguan juluo*.

used the term "Cultural Revolution," but government censors at the CCP Central Propaganda Department apparently objected to singling this period out.[56] Fan was forced to change the name of the porcelain hall, which was the first Cultural Revolution–related museum to open at the complex, to the "New China Porcelain Hall" (新中國瓷器館); he then had to dig out of his collection pieces of porcelain from the 1950s and early 1960s to add in some token content from the period before the Cultural Revolution. Later, again in response to demands from above, Fan changed the name of the whole series from the "Cultural Revolution" series (文革系列) to the "Red Era" series (紅色年代系列). The term "red era" generalizes the Maoist past and effaces the historical specificity and political resonances of period terms such as "Anti-Rightist Campaign," "Great Leap Forward," or "Cultural Revolution"; it also gives that past a more nostalgic aura and ties it into the post-socialist consumption of "red culture" and "red tourism" (紅色旅遊), a state sponsored effort initiated in 2004 to stimulate travel to sites of historical significance to the Communist revolution.[57]

The individual museums in the Red Era series have relatively little text and generally do not set the objects, as suggested earlier, in any kind of manifest narrative; they emphasize the artifacts themselves. Indeed, one of the aesthetic features of the exhibits is to impress the visitor with an abundance of artifacts. The porcelain hall, for example, presents shelf after shelf of teapots, mugs, and vases, as well as statues of Mao, of socialist heroes, and of characters from the model theater (Figure 5.8). With the exception of brief introductory and concluding remarks, there is almost no text. As Denise Ho and Jie Li mention in passing, one might look at these sorts of displays as forms of "mass ornament."[58] The concept of "mass ornament" comes from Siegfried Kracauer, who first applied it to capitalist modes of production and then linked it to a similar tendency in German fascism. Developing Ho and Li's remarks we can say that the quantity and uniformity of the objects, as well as the ways they are shaped into patterns and designs, suggest not just the Maoist totalitarian past, but also the commodity culture of the present.[59]

Presenting the artifacts in this way aestheticizes and dehistoricizes them, divorcing them from the violence and chaos of the history of the Cultural Revolution. In this sense, they become cultural commodities satisfying a consumerist pleasure

---

56. According to one anonymous source, Fan circumvented the provincial government and sought approval for the museum directly from the central government. Local governments, Fan's thinking might have been, would perhaps be warier of approving such a controversial museum. Fan also sought support for the project from various members of the so-called "red second generation," sons and daughters of high-ranking officials from the founding fathers' generation, many of whom may have been "sent-down youths" like Fan himself.
57. One study explicitly conceives of the museum complex in terms of "red tourism" and red tourism commodities. See Wang Bing, "Hongse lüyou shangpin de geming: yi Dayi xiang Anren zhen Jianchuan bowuguan qun lüyou jinianpin wei li" [The revolution in red tourism goods: The example of souvenirs at the Jianchuan Museum in Anren, Dayi County], *Lüyou zonglan* (Aug. 2014): 208–9.
58. Denise Y. Ho and Jie Li, "From Landlord Manor to Red Memorabilia," 30. Ho and Li do not mention that the source of this term is Siegfried Kracauer, *The Mass Ornament: The Weimar Essays* (Cambridge, MA: Harvard University Press, 1995).
59. Fan has some 50,000 pieces of porcelain in his collection; 7,000 are on display.

Figure 5.8
Display in the Red Era Porcelain Hall. Photograph by Kirk A. Denton.

or *objets d'art* stimulating aesthetic appreciation; as such, they may fail to provoke historical reflection in the visitor. At the same time, not couching the artifacts in a narrative frame offers freedom to the museumgoer to interpret the objects as s/he sees fit. As Jie Li argues, the museum "opens up a space for public remembrance and plural interpretations. Visitors might find endearing artifacts of their childhood or reminisce about 'the drab spiritual life in the ultra-leftist years.'"[60] One might add to these possible interpretations a revisionist desire to turn the Maoist past against the neoliberal present. Fan himself insists that the artifacts should speak for themselves. A museum sign warns the visitor, "We do not speak; let history speak."[61] The Red Era museums seem to recognize that different visitors will have different interpretations of the Cultural Revolution. The epilogue to the porcelain museum, for instance, couches the displays in rather vague, almost poetic, language: "those days that were both simple and complex, stable and yet frenzied, passionate yet disheartening, colorful yet monotonous, full of expectation yet hopeless, devoted yet mistrustful . . . Porcelain is breakable, yet history is permanent."

Despite this general tendency to let the artifacts speak for themselves, the Red Era series finds subtle ways of giving them significance as more than aesthetic objects or mass ornaments. Architectural design is one such way. Although it was in the end not used, the original design of the porcelain museum building, by Zhang Lei 張雷, had several long and deep cracks through the façade, an architectural

---
60. Jie Li, "Memorials and Museums of the Maoist Era," 331.
61. The sign can be seen in a shot in Frank, *Collecting Insanity*, min. 244.

detail that pointed to the cracks that inevitably come to mark porcelain, but that perhaps was also meant to capture the rupture of the Cultural Revolution.[62] In the end, Fan went with a more conservative design, in the style of the local Sichuan vernacular.[63] Consistent with the architectural style of the building, Fan made the main entrance out of a small old-style wooden door to create the sense that the spectator is entering someone's home—indeed, the first room one enters looks like a family's living room. But straight ahead sits a large statue of a waving Chairman Mao, positioned at a slight angle, which Fan says points the spectator into the main exhibit space.[64] The subtle positioning of the statue might also hint at the sense of *wai* 歪, meaning "askew," the opposite of *zheng* 正, correct or proper, a term that has clear moral and political implications in the Chinese cultural context. This use of the domestic space as a vestibule before entering the main exhibition space points to the breakdown of divisions between private and public space during the highly politicized atmosphere of the Cultural Revolution.

Individual displays also draw attention to how the Cultural Revolution is remembered today. For instance, the porcelain museum displays a white vase inscribed with short quotations. Fan invited a group of famous writers who had lived through the Cultural Revolution to comment on a famous "big-character poster vase": the vase, which is also included in the exhibit, visually depicts the story of a group of children who learn that a privately-raised duck has been secretly eating public grains; the duck is then hung on a tree along with a big character poster declaring that the person who raised the duck should be criticized. Fan had the writers' comments printed on a white porcelain vase. Liu Shahe 流沙河 wrote: "It's really hard to be a man," to which Shao Yanxiang 邵燕祥 humorously replied: "And not easy to be a duck, either." Zhang Xianliang 張賢亮 comment is "laughing out tears," to which Feng Jicai 馮驥才 replied: "Don't laugh, this is the reality of our generation."[65] The comments reflect on the absurd and tragicomic nature of the Cultural Revolution.

In the Badges section of the Badges, Clocks, and Seals Hall (章鐘印陳列館), there are thousands of Mao badges arrayed as mass ornaments, but in one display the curators have ingeniously arranged badges into huge black bas reliefs of Mao's head and used them to define the contours of his face, thus suggesting both the proliferation of Maoist imagery and the relation of iconography to political power (Figure 5.9). In other displays, Mao badges are placed on top of archival photographs of people during the Cultural Revolution. In this way, the exhibit reinserts the badges back into history and stresses that they are more than mere collectors'

---

62. Zhang Lei's design was never built, but one can find a schematic in Fan, *Jianchuan bowuguan juluo*, 84–85. Another design, perhaps Zhang's final one, can be found on Zhang's architectural firm's website: http://www.azlarchitects.com/en/project.aspx?SortID=36&ID=840. It remains to be seen why Zhang's design was not used.
63. The final building was designed by the Xu Shangzhi, an elder statesman in the world of Chinese architecture.
64. Fan, *Daguan nu*, 241.
65. For more on this, see Fan, *Daguan nu*, 242.

Figure 5.9
Display of Mao badges in the Badges, Clocks, and Seals Hall. Courtesy of Mark Bender.

items; they were part of the vibrant fabric of Cultural Revolution social and political life.

The Mirror Museum is particularly ingenious in its use of exhibitionary techniques to provoke thoughtful reflection on the Cultural Revolution. The museum features thousands of mirrors, many of which are imprinted with political slogans (Figure 5.10). As Julie Makinen describes it, it is a "disorienting maze reminiscent of a boardwalk-style Hall of Mirrors."[66] Taking Makinen's observation a step further, the display not only creates a sense of the chaos and disorientation of the Cultural Revolution, it inserts the visitor into that history by having their images reflected in the artifacts themselves, literally surrounded by the political discourse (and ideology) that often decorates these mirrors. As such, it asks of the spectator to contemplate the relationship between the past and the present, issues of personal responsibility, and the like. In one display, the spectator enters a maze-like space lined with mirrors. As Fan says of this exhibit: "It's more of an abstract, conceptual exhibit. Most people don't get it. Many people get lost in there and can't find their way out. They go in circles, calling 'Save us! We can't get out!' We have to go in there and rescue them."[67]

---

66. Julie Makinen, "Chinese Museum Builder Lets History Speak," *Los Angeles Times*, November 7, 2012, http://articles.latimes.com/2012/nov/07/world/la-fg-china-museums-20121108.
67. See Frank, *Collecting Insanity*, min. 5:13. This disorientation effect was intentional. Fan and the architect Li Xinggang (李兴钢) had wanted to take it a step further—including, for instance, a revolving door with mirrors instead of glass—but they were worried about older patrons falling down and hurting themselves. See Fan, *Daguan nu*, 156.

Figure 5.10
Display in the Mirrors Hall.
Courtesy of Mark Bender.

The Educated Youth Hall is more conventional than the other museums in the Red Era series in terms of depicting a chronological history. It traces the history of the *zhiqing* movement, displaying conventional artifacts such as diaries and photographs accompanied by textual explanations on placards. The exhibits are divided into four sections that cover the history of and the struggles encountered by *zhiqing*. One section is devoted to commemorating individual *zhiqing*, both the well-known and the obscure. As a whole the Educated Youth museum, with its green color scheme meant to represent youth, takes a nostalgic approach to its subject.

But this nostalgic tenor is countered by displays that express a strong sense of loss and waste. The entrance courtyard, for example, displays steles dedicated to ten female *zhiqing* who died in a fire in their dormitory in Yunnan, where they had been sent from Chengdu. This is the first display the spectator sees after entering the museum. Once inside the exhibition space, the spectator encounters a reproduction of He Duoling's 何多苓 famous oil painting *Youth* (青春; 1984). The painting, in muted colors, shows a *zhiqing* seated on a rock in a barren landscape, a hawk about to land on the dry and lifeless ground behind her. Her face shows a touch of melancholy, and she is staring directly at the spectator. The painting is usually seen as part of the "scar" cultural movement that expressed the confusion and sorrow of a generation of Cultural Revolution youth from a post-Mao political perspective. The painting and stele set a tone of loss—perhaps even of martyrdom—for the exhibits that follow.

In the museum's most provocative display, the ground of an open-air courtyard is strewn with broken and rusted pieces of farm tools and equipment interspersed among which are shattered pieces of mirrors covered with Mao images and Maoist slogans. A small grove of lush bamboo in the background provides a contrast to the "dead" artifacts in the foreground. Above the bamboo is the number "17,760,000," the number of youths sent to the countryside during the 1960s and 1970s. The display is meant to suggest, I think, the intrusion of politics into the normal agricultural life of the peasants. But it also speaks of wasted youth. Fan says that the display was deeply personal to him because he himself had been a *zhiqing* and that it can be interpreted from a variety of perspectives:

> As for the broken shards of Cultural Revolution-era mirrors, one can understand them as representing a lack of wholeness [不能重圓], mirror images of history, looking face to face with us, a reflection on history, all are possible . . . When you see this work, you feel a sense of suffocation, a stifling quality, ugliness, coarseness, a sense of loss, oppressiveness, disorder, crudeness, and a lack of culture . . . This work expresses my passionate feelings, my essential understanding of educated youths, my brothers and sisters.[68]

The detritus in the courtyard exhibit is consistent with the museum's opening displays and their depiction of loss. The exhibit ends with a blown-up quote, signed by Fan Jianchuan, that nicely captures the museum's duality—at once nostalgic for and regretful toward the *zhiqing* experience—and avoids taking a stand on its ultimate meaning: "Whether we have no regrets about it or see it as wasted time, it was our youth" (無論是無悔，還是蹉跎，總歸是我們的青春).

When this hall opened in 2011, the museum held a ceremony with some 500 *zhiqing* from various parts of the country in attendance. Hou Jun 侯雋, who had been a "model sent-down youth," gave the invocation in the entranceway courtyard, next to the stele commemorating the ten dead *zhiqing*. Fan Jianchuan presided over the ceremony. Clearly Fan sees this museum—and this applies to all the museums in the complex—not just as a building in which to house artifacts, but also as a site for active historical remembrance and commemoration among the living.[69]

The Daily Life Hall is also in a generally nostalgic mode, a mode that is embodied in its principal exhibitionary form: the diorama. Although the entranceway to the exhibits—a bright red tunnel with a ten-year timeline marked out on the floor (from 1966 to 1976) and a video monitor at the end broadcasting Cultural Revolution–era archival clips of Mao receiving throngs of Red Guards at Tiananmen—is somewhat ominous, the exhibits proper are centered on ordinary, daily life (Figure 5.11). As the visitor walks past the tunnel and up a set of stairs toward the exhibits, the bright red turns paler pink, hinting that one is about to enter a less politically charged space. The contrast between the bright red entranceway and the exhibits proper may be Fan's way of stressing that the Cultural Revolution was much more than rabid Red Guards exulting in a distant sight of Chairman Mao on Tiananmen, for example. Even as China was embroiled in a political maelstrom, people had to go on with the daily struggles of eating and working and continued to enjoy life's little

---

68. Fan, *Daguan nu*, 283.
69. See Long Min, "Yi hongse niandai: Dayi Jianchuan bowuguan Zhiqing shenghuoguan jinri longzhong kaiguan" [Remembering the red years: The Educated Youth daily life hall of the Jianchuan Museum, Dayi, has its grand opening today], Dayi Toufangwang, October 16, 2011, http://www.dytfw.com/a/201110/59734249858.html.

Figure 5.11
Entrance to the exhibits in the Daily Life Hall.
Source: http://www.yododo.com/area/guide/01407584DDD61F14402881D340757B3B.

pleasures. As a whole, this museum resonates with other museums in China, such as the Shanghai Municipal History Museum, that eschew grand narratives of war and revolution in favor of a sympathetic and nostalgic representations of daily life.[70] One exhibit, for example, shows a row of dioramas depicting typical homes of a worker, a peasant, a soldier, and a cadre.

Echoes of History (歷史回聲) is a visually powerful exhibit at the very end of the Badges, Clocks, and Seals Hall (章鐘印陳列館) (Figure 5.12). The room is in the form of a rotunda, with a large hole in the ceiling opening the space to the sky. The red brick wall is lined with numerous photographs of the Cultural Revolution running at face level around the circular room. The photographs show, among other things, officials being criticized and humiliated by predatory crowds. They are prefaced by a placard, one of the few such placards in the Red Era series museums, that presents in very "official" looking calligraphic script the 1981 Central Committee verdict on the Cultural Revolution.[71] On the floor are embedded hundreds of large bronze replicas of the round official seals used by Cultural Revolution revolutionary committees and rebel groups to assert their power and authority, and the rotunda itself, which imitates the shape of the official seals on the floor, is like a giant official seal. As the *Echoes of History* sign at the entrance way suggests, the room is also something of an echo chamber, a space in which official versions of the truth are repeated endlessly and unquestioningly. Perhaps this is Fan's way of representing the blind worship of political authority during the Cultural Revolution. But the echoes of history are meant to be "heard" by present-day spectators, who can add, quite

---

70. See Kirk A. Denton, *Exhibiting the Past: Historical Memory and the Politics of Museums in Postsocialist China* (Honolulu: University of Hawai'i Press, 2014), 88–92.
71. The text of the official CCP verdict on the Cultural Revolution is "Zhongguo gongchang dang zhongyang weiyuanhui guanyu jianguo yilai dang de ruogan lishi wenti jueyi" 中國共產黨中央委員會關於建國以來的若干歷史問題決議 [CCP Central Committee resolution on certain party historical problems since the founding of the nation], http://cpc.people.com.cn/BIG5/64162/71380/71387/71588/4854598.html. A partial English translation is found in *China's Cultural Revolution, 1966–1969: Not a Dinner Party*, ed. Michael Schoenhals (Armonk, NY: M. E. Sharpe, 1996), 296–303, and online: https://www.marxists.org/subject/china/documents/cpc/history/01.htm.

Figure 5.12
The rotunda in the Badges, Clocks, and Seals Hall. Courtesy of Mark Bender.

literally, their own voices into the mix. As has been emphasized in other exhibits, here Fan draws the contemporary spectator's attention to his/her relationship to the past.

In its minimalist aesthetic—in stark contrast to the "mass ornaments" on display in the other Red Era series museums—the exhibit serves as a completive space for the spectator to reflect on the Cultural Revolution, the state's official discourse on it, the national scope of the Cultural Revolution, and the nature of political power and authority and its abuse. Outside the rotunda, a winding hallway exhibits a "catacomb" of hundreds of clocks placed in niches, like small statuary in a Buddhist shrine (Figure 5.13).[72] The clocks, and the mesmerizing sound of their ticking, are, as the official guidebook informs us, "time-keeping devices, but they are also alarm clocks for the world. They reflect a unique moment in history, in politics. They are a warning to future generations."[73] The clock catacomb and the rotunda it leads to ask the visitor to reflect on the passing of time, the movement of history, and the relationship between the past and the present.

Another such contemplative space is the Newspaper Center, connected physically to the Badge, Clocks, and Seals Museum building but not thematically part of it. One can purchase copies of old issues of *People's Daily* from a large kiosk. Next to the reading room is the People's Commune Dining Hall, a striking space that resembles the nave of a church more than the utilitarian room one would associate with a

---

72. Fan makes this Buddhist connect explicit, calling the design the "thousand Buddha cliff." In the Phoenix TV documentary, these niches are referred as "shrines for ancestral tablets." See Fan, *Daguan nu*, 150.
73. Fan, *Jianchuan bowuguan jiangjieci*, 119.

Figure 5.13
Clock display in the Badges, Clocks, and Seals Hall. Courtesy of Mark Bender.

communal dining hall (Figure 5.14). In the altar-like space at the end of the hall is a large bust of Chairman Mao illuminated with natural light from a skylight above. The room conveys a strong sense of the religious deification of Mao during the Cultural Revolution. Combined with the Newspaper Center, the two spaces suggest the role of propaganda (i.e., the *People's Daily* and the propaganda posters that line the walls of the reading room) in fomenting that deification of political authority.

Another technique Fan uses to insert alternative memories into the museums is what Denise Ho and Jie Li call "guerilla exhibits," which treat "sensitive, unapproved materials and take semi-permanent and impermanent forms."[74] An example of the former is an alcove in the Red Era Daily Life museum that is devoted to the film actor Feng Zhe 馮喆, who either committed suicide or was beaten to death in Anren during the Cultural Revolution. As part of his original conception for the complex, Fan had intended to create a dedicated Feng Zhe Memorial Hall, to be included in the Folk Customs series.[75] Having a dedicated hall to this victim of the Cultural Revolution was perhaps too much for Fan's overseers, and the memorial was eventually scrapped and moved into a small room in the Daily Necessities Hall.[76] The exhibit displays photos and documents from Feng's family in a shrine-like space;

---

74. Denise Ho and Jie Li, "From Landlord Manor to Red Memorabilia," 29.
75. Fan, *Jianchuan bowuguan juluo*, 168–71.
76. In his discussion of this memorial space, Fan offers no explanation for this change. See Fan, *Daguan nu*, 238–40. On Feng Zhe's death, see Bu Ronghua, "Dianying Nanzheng beizhan yanyuanzhe Feng Zhe wenge hanyuan zisha zhi mi" [The mystery of the unjust suicide of Feng Zhe, the actor who played Battalion Commander Gao in *From Victory to Victory*]. Blog post (Jan. 31, 2016): http://blog.wenxuecity.com/myblog/70413/201601/542852.html.

Figure 5.14
The People's Commune Dining Hall. Photograph by Kirk A. Denton.

though the term is not used for obvious reasons, Feng Zhe is positioned as a "martyr" of the Cultural Revolution, and the exhibit serves as an emotional hook for the visitor to reflect on the injustices of the Cultural Revolution and to contrast Feng's martyrdom with the myriad CCP martyrs who are worshipped in official memorial sites around the country.[77] The Feng Zhe exhibit is now a permanent part of the Daily Necessities Hall, and in that sense can no longer be said to constitute a "guerilla exhibit." A better example of Fan Jianchuan's "guerilla exhibits" would be a temporary exhibit of photographs and posters from the Great Leap Forward held next to, perhaps ironically, given the horrendous famine it caused, the People's Commune Dining Hall.

Conclusion

In the present political climate in China, Fan cannot create the kind of museum that Ba Jin envisioned, one that would not only display the broad history of this traumatic period of China's past, but that would directly and explicitly address issues of moral responsibility. One of the unapproved museums that Fan plans to build is a comprehensive history of the Cultural Revolution. Indeed, the building for that museum, nicknamed the Anren Bridge Museum because the structure crosses over a stream, was completed in 2012 (Figure 5.15).[78] If approved, this museum might set

---
77. See Denton, *Exhibiting the Past*, 95–115.
78. Designed by Yung Ho Chang (Zhang Yonghe) of the Feichang Atelier, the building draws from multiple

Figure 5.15
The Anren Bridge Museum. Source: Arch Daily, http://www.archdaily.com/274329/1966-1976-museum-in-anren-atelier-feichang-jianzhuhui.

the other museums, which as I have shown are dominated by aesthetic, conceptual, and nostalgic modes of exhibition, in a larger historical narrative that includes artifacts pertaining to issues of injustice, persecution, and even mass killings. Indeed, Fan has collected innumerable diaries, letters, suicide notes, and official judgments that remain stored in his warehouse awaiting the day they can be displayed. These text-based artifacts concern real people and historical incidents in ways that porcelain, mirrors, clocks, and badges do not. They are also less easy to aestheticize and dehistoricize than the artifacts that presently fill his Red Era series museums. Fan understands the difference clearly. In an interview in a documentary film about his museum complex, he says: "It's not that the government won't let us open a new museum [a comprehensive history of the Cultural Revolution]. It's that we don't think it's the right time [不方便] to expand. For example, a museum about the violence during the Cultural Revolution. The reason we can't build one is simple: The perpetrators of the violence are still around, and there are a lot of them. You don't want to get their children tangled up in the issue. Society doesn't need that."[79]

---

architectural inspirations. For accounts of this structure, see Qiu Zheng, "Wei zhi jinianbei: Anren qiao guan" [As yet unknown monuments: The Anren Bridge Museum], *Yishu jie* 2 (2013): 42–45; and Javier Gaete, "1966–1976 Museum in Anren / Atelier FCJZ," *Arch Daily* (Sept. 25, 2012), http://www.archdaily.com/274329/1966-1976-museum-in-anren-atelier-feichang-jianzhu. The museum, to be formerly called the Ten Years Chronology Museum (十年大事記), does not appear anywhere on the official site of the Jianchuan Museum. One news item, dated July 13, 2010, on the site mentions Yung Ho Chang's visit to the museum complex to decide on a design and construction plan for the hall. The item also mentions that this building would house a "propaganda poster museum" in the form of a "chronological overview of the history of China during the ten years from 1966 to 1976." See http://www.jc-museum.cn/cn/info_100.html.

79. See Frank, *Collecting Insanity*, min. 8.

Although limited in what it can depict, one might argue that Fan Jianchuan's open-ended, if commercialized and aesthetic, exhibition of the Cultural Revolution is a better alternative to, say, a state-sponsored museum like the one Ba Jin envisioned, because it offers the visitor interpretive freedom. In displaying so many wonderful artifacts, Fan's Red Era series brings the Cultural Revolution to life, making it far more than just a narrative of political persecution and victimization, which is what it might have become in a state sponsored museum. It seems consistent with the view presented in some of the recent revisionist scholarship[80] on the Cultural Revolution as a period that "offered a diversity of cultural experience and an obscure sense of freedom," as Laikwan Pang puts it.[81] This is its strength as a memorial space. But is this freedom to interpret history that Fan offers his visitors merely an illusion propagated by the commercial ideology of a neoliberal economy? The opened-ended view of this private museum seems to posit a spectator who already knows about the Cultural Revolution or has personal experience of that past and can make an informed choice about how to view it and remember it. As is often reported, the state has done a fine job of erasing knowledge of the Cultural Revolution among young people in China. But how might young people with little knowledge of the Cultural Revolution look at these artifacts? A young visitor might well be wowed by the spectacle of all the artifacts, with their sheer abundance and colorful appearance, but emerge from the viewing experience with little appreciation for their importance or meaning as testimonies to a violent and traumatic past. The empty Anren Bridge Museum is thus a perfectly ironic monument to the Cultural Revolution itself, suggesting at once state-imposed amnesia and the possibility of becoming a storehouse of multiple memories.

Bibliography

Ba Jin 巴金. n.d. "A Museum of the 'Cultural Revolution.'" Translated by Geremie Barmé. CND.org. http://www.cnd.org/cr/english/articles/bajin.htm. Originally published as "Wenge bowuguan" 文革博物館 [Cultural Revolution museum]. In Ba Jin, *Suixiang lu* 隨想錄 [Random thoughts]. http://www.readers365.com/bajin/suixianglu/index.htm.

Bu Ronghua 蔔榮華. "Dianying Nanzheng beizhan yanyuanzhe Feng Zhe wenge hanyuan zisha zhi mi" 電影南徵北戰演員著馮喆文革含冤自殺之謎 [The mystery of the unjust suicide of Feng Zhe, the actor who played Battalion Commander Gao in From Victory to Victory]. Blog post (Jan. 31, 2016): http://blog.wenxuecity.com/myblog/70413/201601/542852.html.

Cui Ran 崔然. "Anren Zhongguo bowuguan xiaozhen yiqi qihang" 安仁中國博物館小鎮一期起航　夢回20世紀迷人風情 [The China Museum town at Anren phase one sets

---

[80]. An example of this scholarship is Barbara Mittler, *A Continuous Revolution: Making Sense of Cultural Revolution Culture* (Cambridge, MA: Harvard University Press, 2013).

[81]. Laikwan Pang, *The Art of Cloning: Creative Production during China's Cultural Revolution* (London: Verso, 2017), 1.

sail], Chengdu quansousuo, April 28, 2011. http://news.chengdu.cn/content/2011-04/28/content_702542.htm

Clunas, Craig. *Superfluous Things: Material Culture and Social Status in Early Modern China*. Honolulu: University of Hawai'i Press, 2004.

Denton, Kirk A. "China Dreams and the Road to Revival." *Origins: Current Events in Historical Perspective* 8, no. 3 (2014). Accessed July 24, 2015. http://origins.osu.edu/article/china-dreams-and-road-revival.

Denton, Kirk A. *Exhibiting the Past: Historical Memory and the Politics of Museums in Postsocialist China*. Honolulu: University of Hawai'i Press, 2014.

Dutton, Michael. "From Culture Industry to Mao Industry: A Greek Tragedy." *boundary 2* 32, no. 2 (2005): 151–67.

Fan Jianchuan 樊建川. *Daguan nu: Fan Jianchuan de jiyi yu mengxiang* 大館奴：樊建川的記憶與夢想 [Slave of big museums: Fan Jianchuan's memories and dreams]. Beijing: Sanlian, 2013.

Fan Jianchuan 樊建川. *Jianchuan bowuguan jiangjieci* 建川博物館講解詞 [Text for guides at the Jianchuan Museum]. Anren: Jianchuan bowuguan, 2007.

Fan Jianchuan 樊建川. *Jianchuan bowuguan juluo* 建川博物館聚落 [Jianchuan Museum Cluster]. Anren: Jianchuan bowuguan, nd.

Fan Jianchuan 樊建川, ed. *Kangfu: Zhongguo kangri zhanfu xiezhen* 抗俘：中國抗日戰俘寫真 [Resistance prisoners: The true story of prisoners during the War of Resistance]. Beijing: Zhongguo duiwai fanyi, 2006.

Fan Jianchuan 樊建川. *Wenge ciqi tujian* 文革瓷器圖鑒 [Illustrated handbook of Cultural Revolution porcelain]. Beijing: Wenwu, 2002.

Fan Jianchuan 樊建川. *Yige ren de kangzhan* 一個人的抗戰 [One person's war of resistance]. Beijing: Zhongguo duiwai fanyi, 2000.

Fiskejö, Magnus. "Review Essay: The Museum Boom in China and the State Efforts to Control History." *Museum Anthropology Review* 9, no. 2 (Fall 2015). https://scholarworks.iu.edu/journals/index.php/mar/article/view/19150/29099.

Frank, Joshua. *Collecting Insanity*. Documentary film (9:34 min.). Chinafile.com, 2014. http://www.chinafile.com/multimedia/video/collecting-insanity.

Gaete, Javier. "1966–1976 Museum in Anren / Atelier FCJZ." Arch Daily (Sept. 25, 2012). http://www.archdaily.com/274329/1966-1976-museum-in-anren-atelier-feichang-jianzhu.

Gao Yun 高雲. "Jianchuan bowugan juluo: zai yu siwang saipao de lushang jian bowuguan" 建川博物館聚落：在與死亡賽跑的路上建博物館 [The Jianchuan Museum Cluster: Racing against death by building museums]. *Mingri fengshang* (May 15, 2013): 54–67.

Hao Shuang 郝爽. "Siren bowuguan, nimen hai hao ma?" 私人博物館，你們還好嗎？ [Private museums, are you doing well?]. *Yishu shichang* (Jan. 25, 2013): 12–21.

He Yue 何悅. "Fan Jianchuan: Yige julu, yi zuo chengchi" 樊建川：一個聚落，一座城池 [Fan Jianchuan: A cluster, a walled city]. *Xin jin shang* (Sept. 5, 2014): 42–47.

Ho, Denise Y. *Curating the Revolution: Politics on Display in Mao's China*. Cambridge: Cambridge University Press, 2017.

Ho, Denise Y., and Jie Li. "From Landlord Manor to Red Memorabilia: Reincarnations of a Chinese Museum Town." *Modern China* 42, no. 1 (2016): 3–37.

Huang Zhangjin 黃章晉. "Fan Jianchuan: Bainian xinshi de minjian budaozhe" 樊建川百年信史的民間步道者 [Fan Jianchuan: A folk ambassador of the history of the past one hundred years]. *Fenghuang zhoukan* 227 (Aug. 2006): 14–19.

Huang Zhangjin 黃章晉. "Lishi de lingyizhong jilu fangshi" 歷史的另一種紀錄方式 [An alternative method of recording history]. *Fenghuang zhoukan* 227 (Aug. 2006): 20–23.

Kracauer, Siegfried. *The Mass Ornament: The Weimar Essays.* Cambridge, MA: Harvard University Press, 1995.

Kuhn, Anthony. "Chinese Red Guards Apologize, Reopening a Dark Chapter." National Public Radio (Feb. 2, 2014). http://www.npr.org/sections/parallels/2014/01/23/265228870/chinese-red-guards-apologize-reopening-a-dark-chapter.

Lee, Ching Kwan, and Guobin Yang, eds. *Re-envisioning the Chinese Revolution: The Politics and Poetics of Collective Memories in Reform China.* Washington, DC: Woodrow Wilson Center Press, 2007.

Leu, Siew Ying. "Cultural Revolution Museum Seeks 600,000 yuan for Extension." *South China Morning Post,* May 17, 2006. http://www.scmp.com/article/549184/cultural-revolution-museum-seeks-600000-yuan-extension.

Li, Jie. "Memorials and Museums of the Maoist Era: A Survey and Notes for Future Curators." In *Red Legacies in China: Cultural Afterlives of the Communist Revolution,* edited by Jie Li and Enhua Zhang, 319–54. Cambridge, MA: Harvard University Asia Center, 2016.

Li, Jie, and Enhua Zhang, eds. *Red Legacies in China: Cultural Afterlives of the Communist Revolution.* Cambridge, MA: Harvard University Asia Center, 2016.

Li, Li. *Memory, Fluid Identity, and the Politics of Remembering: The Representations of the Chinese Cultural Revolution in English-Speaking Countries.* Leiden: Brill, 2016.

Lim, Louisa. *The People's Republic of Amnesia: Tiananmen Revisited.* Oxford: Oxford University Press, 2015.

Liu Jiakun 劉家琨. "Anren Jianchuan bowuguan juluo sheji" 安仁建川博物館聚落設計 [Design of the Jianchuan Museum Cluster in Anren]. *Shidai jianzhu* 1 (2006): 37.

Mackinnon, Mark. "China's Cultural Revolution Museum: A Well-Kept Secret." *Toronto Globe and Mail,* July 22, 2010. http://www.theglobeandmail.com/news/world/chinas-cultural-revolution-museum-a-well-kept-secret/article1389357/.

Makinen, Julie. "Chinese Museum Builder Lets History Speak." *Los Angeles Times,* November 7, 2012. http://articles.latimes.com/2012/nov/07/world/la-fg-china-museums-20121108.

Mittler, Barbara. *A Continuous Revolution: Making Sense of Cultural Revolution Culture.* Cambridge, MA: Harvard University Press, 2013.

Mou Naihong 牟乃紅. "Fan Jianchuan he tade Jianchuan bowuguan" 樊建川和他的建川博物館 [Fan Jianchuan and his Jianchuan Museum]. *Dang jian* (June 1, 2014): 55–58.

Pan, Philip P. *Out of Mao's Shadow: The Struggle for the Soul of a New China.* New York: Simon and Shuster, 2008.

Pang, Laikwan. *The Art of Cloning: Creative Production during China's Cultural Revolution.* London: Verso, 2017.

Qiu Zheng 邱正. "Wei zhi jinianbei: Anren qiao guan" 未知紀念碑：安仁橋館 [As yet unknown monuments: The Anren Bridge Museum]. *Yishu jie* 2 (2013): 42–45.

Schoenhals, Michael, ed. *China's Cultural Revolution, 1966–1969: Not a Dinner Party.* Armonk, NY: M. E. Sharpe, 1996.

Song Rushan 宋如山, ed. *Zhongguo wenhua da geming shidian (1966–1976 nian)* 中國文化大革命事典 (1966–1976年). Hong Kong: Xianghui tushu, 2009.

Song Xiangguang 宋向光. "The Development of Private Museums in China." *Museum International* 60, no. 1–2 (2008): 40–48.

Song Xiangguang 宋向光. "Sili bowuguan fazhan xuyao shehui zhichi" 私利博物館發展需要社會支持 [The development of private museums requires social support]. *Zhongguo wenwu bao* (Sept. 15, 2006): 6.

Su, Yang. *Collective Killings in Rural China during the Cultural Revolution*. Cambridge: Cambridge University Press, 2011.

Sun Hongyan 孫洪艷. "Fan Jianchuan zhuanfang" 樊建川專訪 [Interview with Fan Jianchuan], *Kangri zhanzheng jinianwang*, November 18, 2016. http://www.krzzjn.com/html/40958.html.

Tatlow, Didi Kirsten. "Fate Catches Up to a Cultural Revolution Museum in China." *New York Times*, October 2, 2016. https://www.nytimes.com/2016/10/03/world/asia/china-cultural-revolution-shantou-museum.html.

Tatlow, Didi Kirsten. "Talking 'bout a Revolution." *South China Morning Post*, June 19, 2005. http://www.scmp.com/article/505060/talking-bout-revolution.

Wang Bing 王冰. "Hongse lüyou shangpin de geming: yi Dayi xiang Anren zhen Jianchuan bowuguan qun lüyou jinianpin wei li" 紅色旅遊商品的革命：以大邑縣安仁鎮建川博物館群紀念品為例 [The revolution in red tourism goods: The example of souvenirs at the Jianchuan Museum in Anren, Dayi County]. *Lüyou zonglan* (Aug. 2014): 208–9.

Wu, Guo. "The Social Construction and Deconstruction of Evil Landlords in Contemporary Chinese Fiction, Art, and Collective Memory." *Modern Chinese Literature and Culture* 25, no. 1 (Spring 2013): 131–64.

Xiao Shu 笑蜀. *Liu Wencai zhenxiang* 劉文彩真相 [The true face of Liu Wencai]. Xi'an: Shaanxi shifan daxue, 1999.

Xiao Shu 笑蜀. *Xin shixue: da dizhu Liu Wencai* 新史學：大地主劉文彩 [New historiography: Big landlord Liu Wencai]. Guangzhou: Guangdong renmin, 2011.

Xu Youyu 徐友漁. "Wenge bowuguan yu zhenshi jiyi" 文革博物館與真實記憶 [CR museum and real memory]. Originally published in *Qingnian baokan shijie* 青年報刊世界 1 (1996). http://www.baoxian.edu.gr/paper/sociology/001/2534.html.

Yang, Guobin. "A Portrait of Martyr Jiang Qing: The Chinese Cultural Revolution on the Internet." In *Re-envisioning the Chinese Revolution: The Politics and Poetics of Collective Memories in Reform China*, edited by Ching Kwan Lee and Guobin Yang, 287–316. Washington, DC: Woodrow Wilson Center Press, 2007.

Yang, Guobin. *The Red Guard Generation and Political Activism in China*. New York: Columbia University Press, 2017.

Yang Kelin 楊克林, ed. *Wenhua dageming bowuguan* 文化大革命博物館 [Cultural Revolution museum]. Hong Kong: Dongfang, 1995.

Ye Yonglie 葉永烈. "'Wenge bowuguan' zhi meng" 文革博物館之夢 [The dream of a Cultural Revolution Museum]. *Zhengming* 217 (Nov. 1995): 79–84.

Zhai Qiying 翟琦瑛. "Jianchuan bowuguan juluo guanzhong yanjiu" 建川博物館聚落觀眾研究 [A spectator study of the Jianchuan Museum Cluster]. MA thesis, Zhongyang meishu xueyuan, Beijing, 2014.

Zhao Biao 趙彪. "Bowuguan ziyuan yu luyou kaifa diaocha yanjiu: yi yi Chengdu Jianchuan bowuguan wei li" 博物館資源與旅遊開發調查研究——以成都建川博物館為例 [Research on museum resources and tourist development: A case study of the Jianchuan Museum]. MA thesis, Chongqing Normal University, 2014.

"Zhongguo gongchang dang zhongyang weiyuanhui guanyu jianguo yilai dang de ruogan lishi wenti jueyi" 中國共產黨中央委員會關於建國以來的若干歷史問題決議 [CCP

Central Committee resolution on certain party historical problems since the founding of the nation]. http://cpc.people.com.cn/BIG5/64162/71380/71387/71588/4854598.html.

Zhongguo siren bowuguan hangye fazhan baipishu, 2016 中國私人博物館行業發展白皮書 2016年度 [White paper on the development of the private museum industry in China, 2016]. Zhongguo siren bowugan lianhe pingtai, 2016. http://www.cpmup.cn/pdf/index.html.

Zhu, Tao. "Building Big, with No Regret: From Beijing's 'Ten Great Buildings' in the 1950s to China's Megaprojects Today." In *Red Legacies in China: Cultural Afterlives of the Communist Revolution*, edited by Jie Li and Enhua Zhang, 56–84. Cambridge, MA: Harvard University Asia Center, 2016.

Part II

Critical Memory and Cultural Practices

Reconfiguring Elite and Popular Discourse

6

Literary and Documentary Accounts of the Great Famine

Challenging the Political System and the Social Hierarchies of Memory

Sebastian Veg

Literature has long played an important role in political contexts with limited freedom of expression: it is typically able to broach "sensitive" political topics that cannot be dealt with directly, and it can also inflect the understanding of historical events in ways that contest the dominant narratives of the past. This function highlights literature's role in shaping the "collective memory" that emerges from an interplay of dominant and suppressed narratives. Literature's relative impunity is no doubt connected to the perceived "harmlessness" or frivolity of fiction in particular, which can provide a useful cover. At the same time, literature is endowed with a public dimension that enhances its social influence. Its unique role is well attested, of course, both in the long history of Chinese literature, and in the socialist context, in which literature contributed to sparking some important debates on the Mao era,[1] in particular by its strategic mobilization of "hidden transcripts" (James Scott). "The Scar" by Lu Xinhua, published as a wall newspaper in Fudan University in the spring of 1978, launched the movement of "scar literature," in which intellectuals who had suffered persecution or hardship during the Cultural Revolution expressed their grievances. This literary outpouring no doubt helped Deng Xiaoping to consolidate his power, but also made it urgent to clarify the limits of permissible debate, which Deng achieved through the 1981 Resolution on Party history.[2]

Today, in a situation in which the history of the People's Republic remains an object of academic and political contention, literature continues to be in a position to indirectly challenge certain tenets of official historiography, like for example the myth of the 1950s. As Michael Schoenhals has noted, while the 1950s were viewed in a negative light during Mao's final years, less than two years after his death they

---

1. See, for example, chapters by Rudolf Wagner, David Holm, and Geremie Barmé in *Using the Past to Serve the Present: Historiography and Politics in Contemporary China*, ed. Jonathan Unger (Armonk, NY: M. E. Sharpe, 1993).
2. For a fuller discussion of the 1981 resolution, see the editor's introduction to the present collection and Susanne Weigelin-Schweidrzik, "Party Historiography," in *Using the Past to Serve the Present*, 151–73.

had been rehabilitated as a golden age of "Seeking Truth from Facts."[3] It is therefore significant that several recent works have engaged directly and critically with the political crises of the 1950s.

Dealing with Maoism: The Compromise of the 1980s

"The Scar" set the tone for a certain type of writing, which was not contradicted by the 1981 Resolution, and continued to inspire new works throughout the 1980s. Many famous films of the 1980s also echoed its main themes. These works circumscribe political criticism to the Cultural Revolution episode (the only one that the Party condemned or "negated" unreservedly in the Resolution), but avoid discussing the political system or socialist ideology. They portray intellectuals as victims of the "ignorance" and violence of peasants, and of "mass democracy." Finally, they emphasize the Party's ability to correct its own mistakes and regain the people's trust. Despite enduring hardships, intellectuals remain loyal to the Party and eager to be reunited with it, usually thanking it for pardoning them. This was an elite narrative that suited both the Party and intellectuals throughout the 1980s and marked the reconciliation between them to move towards further "enlightenment and modernity."

The result of a limited collaboration and convergence of interests between intellectuals and the state, scar literature was of course not without its own ambiguities.[4] Only a small number of critical individuals found fault with the "scar" narrative early on for its elitism, and its inability to probe the intrinsic link between the mass violence of the Cultural Revolution and the socialist ideology and state institutions. Viewing Maoism as the expression of peasant tradition prevented from conceptualizing it as a distinctly modern form of totalitarian politics. Intellectuals continued to embrace the state and to rely on "rehabilitation" (*pingfan* 平反) and "redress" (*gaizheng* 改正) by their former persecutors.

Ba Jin, in an essay first published in the Hong Kong *Ta Kung Pao* on April 1, 1986, transcribes a conversation with a friend who, recalling a text written by Ba Jin on visiting the former concentration camp in Auschwitz, pleads for the establishment of a similar museum to commemorate the Cultural Revolution: "not because we won't let people forget past grudges . . . but to encourage ourselves to remember our responsibility . . . in bringing about this great catastrophe for several generations named 'Cultural Revolution.' Victims or perpetrators, old or new generation . . . all could come to this place to scrutinize themselves in a mirror and contemplate

---

3. Michael Schoenhals, *Doing Things with Words in Chinese Politics: Five Studies* (Berkeley: Institute of East Asian Studies, 1992), 79.
4. See, for example, Qin Liyan, "The Sublime and the Profane: A Comparative Analysis of Two Fictional Narratives about Sent-Down Youth," in *The Chinese Cultural Revolution as History*, ed. Joseph Esherick, Paul Pickowicz, and Andrew Walder (Stanford: Stanford University Press, 2006).

what we have personally done to advance or oppose the Cultural Revolution."[5] Ba Jin makes two important points that are implicitly critical of scar literature: the (quite daring) comparison between Maoism and Nazism, and the inextricable tangle of guilt and victimization, in which no participant can claim the innocence of pure victimhood. Commenting Ba Jin's work, Liu Zaifu, in a text published in *People's Daily* in September, endorsed Ba Jin's call for "repentance" (*chanhui* 懺悔; which also means "confession"), emphasizing three points: collective guilt for the backwardness of the Chinese nation, "survivor guilt" in view of sacrificed comrades like Lao She, and the need for an individual, self-searching repentance that, unlike in traditional culture, does not simply aspire to compliance with external norms.[6] Finally, in October, Liu Xiaobo criticized the literature of the "new period" for its "feudal ethics," its nostalgia for the socialist purity of the "seventeen years" (1949–1966), and its ultimate upholding and affirmation of the reeducation process that brings intellectuals closer to the proletariat.[7] Over the next few years, many writers were busy with more pressing issues. Only in the 1990s did individual works appear that were less formulaic, less official, and probed the boundaries of the 1981 Resolution. Wang Shuo's novella "Animals Are Wild" (Dongwu xiongmeng 動物兇猛, 1991, famously adapted for the screen by Jiang Wen) portrays a group of children taking advantage of the social breakdown of the Cultural Revolution for cynical enjoyment. Wang Xiaobo's "The Golden Age" (Huangjin shidai 黃金時代, 1993) desacralized Maoism by irreverently mocking the hardships of sent-down youth, and portraying intellectuals as consenting victims of socialism.

Throughout the initial phase of reflection, the 1950s, and in particular the famine, had been largely off-limits.[8] Land Reform was unreservedly eulogized.[9] This taboo began to be challenged in the late 1990s. The novel *A Starving Mountain Village* (Ji'e de shancun 飢餓的山村, 1994) by Zhi Liang was one of the first works to openly discuss the Great Famine of 1959–1961, and sold 200,000 copies in a few years. Susanne Weigelin-Schwiedrzik has argued that this novel marks the entrance of the famine into "communicative memory" (Jan Assman), after a long eclipse

---

5. Ba Jin, "Jinian" [Remembering], *Suixianglu xuanji* (Beijing: Sanlian, 2003), 53–54.
6. Liu Zaifu, "Xinshiqi wenxue de tupo he shenhua" [Breakthrough and deepening accomplishments of the new era literature], *Renmin ribao*, September 8, 1986, p. 7. The full text was later published as: "Wenxue yu chanhui yishi: Du Ba Jin de *Suixianglu*" [Literature and repentance: Reading Ba Jin's *Random Thoughts*] [Dec. 1986], *Liu Zaifu Ji* (Harbin: Heilongjiang Jiaoyu, 1988), 313–26.
7. See Liu Xiaobo, "Weiji! Xin shiqi wenxue mianlin de weiji" [Crisis! The literature of the new era faces a crisis], *Shenzhen Qingnianbao*, October 3, 1986. See also my French translation in Liu Xiaobo, *La Philosophie du porc et autres essais* (Paris: Gallimard "Bleu de Chine," 2011), 57–87, especially 64–70.
8. A few early works dealing with the famine and the Great Leap Forward are mentioned in Perry Link, *The Uses of Literature: Life in the Socialist Chinese Literary System* (Princeton: Princeton University Press, 2000), 254–55. A translation of Zhang Yigong's story "The Criminal Li Tongzhong" and other material can be found in the special issue "*Leaping to Disaster: Village Literature and the Great Leap Forward, Renditions,* 68 (2007). There were also a very small number of critiques at the time of the famine itself, such as the journal *Spark* (see Jean-Philippe Béja's chapter above).
9. See Brian DeMare's study of three novels dealing with the Land Reform (by Ding Ling, Zhou Libo, and Eileen Chang): "The Romance and Tragedy of Rural Revolution: Narratives and Novels of Land Reform in Mao's China," *Clio* 43, no. 3 (2014): 341–65.

attributed to the effects of trauma and cultural particularities.[10] In 1997, the fortieth anniversary of the Anti-Rightist Movement, in the wake of Deng Xiaoping's death, saw several influential publications.[11] He Guimei described these publications as a wave of "fin-de siècle nostalgia": in her view, intellectuals who had collaborated with the state and had seen their social status restored (but not their ideas rehabilitated) in the 1980s were now marginalized by economic reforms and consequently used these books to attack the state, seeking to promote their ideas within society.[12] However, they can perhaps more persuasively be seen as an attempt to further question the official narrative.

New Works of the 2000s: Shifting the Boundaries of Public Discussion

In the first decade of the new millennium, several individual works appeared that challenged some of the central tenets of the 1981 Resolution, and therefore the social consensus on the Mao era. The present chapter will focus on three particularly significant and influential ones that focus squarely on the 1950s. Yang Xianhui's *Chronicles of Jiabiangou* (first book version published in 2002) is a collection of reportage pieces, labeled as fiction but based on interviews with about one hundred rightists who survived the famine in the notorious Jiabiangou labor camp in Gansu in 1959–1960. Yang Jisheng's *Tombstone* (2008), a work of citizen journalism or citizen history, but also an interpretive essay in its own right, documents in unprecedented detail the circumstances of the Great Famine of 1959–1961. Yan Lianke's novel *The Four Books* (2010) is a fictionalized account of the famine set in a people's commune along the Yellow River.[13]

In several ways, these works displace the previous role of literature in shaping the memory of the Mao era. Perry Link, discussing memory and literature, distinguishes between the memory of perpetrators (who remember but want others to forget); victims (who usually fade into the background when literature tries to commemorate them); and bystanders, who easily develop amnesia. In particular, he discusses the "reverse magnet" syndrome, by which literary works attempting to publicly commemorate victims of the Mao era tend to deflect attention away from

---

10. See the translated extracts in *Leaping to Disaster: Village Literature and the Great Leap Forward*, *Renditions*, 68 (2007) and the discussion in Susanne Weigelin-Schwiedrzik, "Trauma and Memory: The Case of the Great Famine in the People's Republic of China (1959–1961)," *Historiography East and West* 1, no. 1 (2003): 41–67.
11. Niu Han and Deng Jiuping, eds., *Jiyi zhong de fanyoupai yundong* [Memories of the Anti-Rightist Movement] (Beijing: Jingji ribao, 1998).
12. He Guimei, "Shijimo de ziwo jiushu zhilu: 1998 nian 'fanyou' shuji re de wenhua fenxi" [The road to fin-de-siècle self-redemption: A cultural analysis of the 1998 "Anti-Rightist" book fever], *Shanghai wenxue* (April 2000): 71–76. She further argues that, to resist marginalization, intellectuals began to invent a collective identity rooted in liberalism, which she views as an expression of the "new liberal theology."
13. The following discussion of *Chronicles of Jiabiangou* and *Four Books* draws on two monographic articles that I have previously published in 2014, respectively: "Testimony, History and Ethics: From the Memory of Jiabiangou Prison Camp to a Reappraisal of the Anti-Rightist Movement in Present-Day China," *The China Quarterly* 218 (June 2014): 514–39, and "Creating a Literary Space to Debate the Mao Era: The Fictionalization of the Great Leap Forward in Yan Lianke's Four Books," *China Perspectives* 4 (2014): 7–16.

the heart of the events and focus on side issues or use techniques like "daft hilarity" (as Mo Yan does) to blur the focus.[14] The new works to some extent avoid the "reverse magnet" effect. They do not limit their criticisms to "hidden transcripts," allusions intelligible only to a group of insiders. Nor can they be brushed off as inauthentic, bourgeois commodifications of revolutionary history, as in Wang Ban's characterization of memory narratives in general, which he contrasts with "authentic" revolutionary epics in Lukács's sense.[15] While they may be seen as examples of "centrifugal" writing (Michael Berry), in which trauma cannot give rise to a new imagined community, they do not compensate for this lack through nostalgia, like many other Cultural Revolution narratives.[16] Yenna Wu has pointed to the new importance of "political prison narratives" after 1989, in which an aestheticization of the prison experience can be a way for former victims to regain agency and resist the monopoly of official discourses. By contrast, these texts—none of which is a memoir—resist such aestheticization and "enlightenment through pain."

The three works discussed below—despite their obvious differences—display remarkable commonalities. They deal frontally with the late 1950s, which were generally considered to be off limits for public criticism. This shift encapsulates a deeper challenge to the regime itself. Secondly, they question the social dichotomy of the "scar" narrative: intellectuals no longer appear as innocent victims but as collaborators of the regime, whereas the bulk of victims are shown to be ordinary, or even poor, rural or urban people. This represents a challenge to the narrative of the unbroken development of socialism and of a society becoming increasingly egalitarian after 1949. Finally, they qualify the author's own position: rather than presenting the author as a heroic victim searching for self-redemption, they each attempt, in different ways, to open a larger public debate on history.

These new approaches go beyond the classical, and perhaps somewhat rehashed, dichotomy between official history and critical memory. Although the question of reestablishing the "truth" remains at the horizon and is claimed by the authors, the present essay considers it from several different angles. Firstly, their works can be viewed as interventions into an embryonic public sphere, which have contributed to shifting the boundaries of public and private discourse about the Mao era. In authoritarian contexts, it has been observed that the state will try to "privatize" the expression of counter-hegemonic memory, while citizens or groups

---

14. Perry Link, "June Fourth: Memory and Ethics," *China Perspectives* 2 (2009): 4–17. Link has noted how the turn to modernism among another group of writers translated into the use of the surreal or the grotesque, which both expressed the trauma of the Mao years and avoided substantial engagement with the social mechanism of violence. Perry Link, "China: Novelists against the State," *The New York Review of Books*, November 15, 2015.
15. Ban Wang, "Epic Narrative, Authenticity, and the Memory of Realism," in *Re-envisioning the Chinese Revolution: The Politics and Poetics of Collective Memories in Reform China*, ed. Ching Kwan Lee and Guobin Yang (Washington, DC: W. Wilson Center Press, 2007), 193–216.
16. Michael Berry, *A History of Pain: Trauma in Modern Chinese Literature* (New York: Columbia University Press, 2011), esp. 260.

who express them will seek to share them and make them "public."[17] However, since the 1990s, the commercialization of the media, the progress of internet technology, and the growing accessibility of Chinese writings published outside China (whether physically or online), especially in Hong Kong, has contributed to creating a space in which discourses cannot be entirely controlled by the government.[18] Previously, counter-hegemonic historical narratives had to remain private (*samizdat*'s) or coded; now, by contrast, the boundaries have become porous and discourses that begin in semi-official areas may trickle into the mainstream media. Thus, the official designation "three years of natural disasters" (*san nian ziran zaihai*) has fallen out of use even in mainstream media, and has been progressively replaced by "three years of great famine" (*san nian da jihuang*).

Secondly, these texts have reconfigured the relationship between subaltern and elite discourses on the Mao era. Susanne Weigelin-Schwiedrzik connects the delayed memory of the famine with issues of class: many victims of the Cultural Revolution were elite members of the bureaucracy, while victims of the famine were mainly peasants, a disparity which in her view delayed wider acknowledgment of the victims of the famine with respect to those of Cultural Revolution.[19] A more critical memory of the Mao era necessarily calls into question the myth of the empowerment of the poor and downtrodden in China's post-1949 history. Intellectual elites, including writers, were deeply involved in the state's concerted effort to suppress the memory of the rural subaltern in Mao's China. Techniques like *suku* 訴苦, designed to empower the exploited, framed individual memories within a political discourse and erased individuality. These works are among the first to probe deeper into their own complicity with state ideology.

Through these two angles—publicness and social hierarchy—the present chapter attempts to open up new ways of approaching the relationship between literature and memory.

Reportage, Historical Investigation, Fiction

The books by Yang Xianhui, Yang Jisheng, and Yan Lianke span a continuum from asserted factuality (*Tombstone*) to asserted fictionality (*Four Books*), with *Jiabiangou* falling somewhere in between. However, this difference in genre does not preclude some deeper commonalities, in particular their critical assessment of the Mao years.

Yang Xianhui 楊顯惠 (b.1946) is a Gansu native who joined the Educated Youth movement as a volunteer when he graduated from high school in 1965. In the Gansu Production and Construction Corps, where he worked for six years, he

---

17. Rubie Watson, "Memory, History, and Opposition under State Socialism," in *Memory, History and Opposition* (Santa Fe: School of American Research Seminar Series, 1994), 10–12.
18. See Sebastian Veg, "New Spaces, New Controls: China's Embryonic Public Sphere," *Current History* 3 (2015): 203–9.
19. S. Weigelin-Schwiedrzik, "Trauma and Memory," 52.

came into contact with many former rightists who had been imprisoned in a deadly reeducation-through-labor camp named Jiabiangou. Yang later studied accounting and eventually transferred his residency to Tianjin, becoming a member of the Tianjin Writers Association, where he worked until retirement. In the 1990s, he devoted himself to interviewing the survivors of Jiabiangou and documenting the consequences of the famine. Based on approximately one hundred survivor interviews, he wrote a series of short pieces, which were serialized by the fiction journal *Shanghai Literature* from 2000.[20] Based on interviews but rewritten as reportage, their genre is hard to define and is often described as "documentary fiction" (*jishixing xiaoshuo* 紀實性小說). These stories were then collected and published in book form: seven stories appeared in 2002 under the title *Jiabiangou jishi* 夾邊溝記事; then nineteen were published in a second edition in 2003 under the title *Gaobie Jiabiangou* 告別夾邊溝, which was reprinted in 2008 under the first title *Jiabiangou jishi*. In content, they extensively document the absence of formal legality in the Anti-Rightist Movement, the techniques of dehumanization and the bodily experience of famine in labor camp, and the general moral breakdown in society under Mao. By initially working through a magazine, Yang was able to have his book published in China, and the full version of *Jiabiangou* went through three prints of respectively 10,000, 20,000, and 60,000 copies, although permission to reprint was withheld between 2005 and 2008, and the book, as well as his two other works, was reportedly removed from bookstores and electronic databases in July 2017.[21]

Yang Jisheng 楊繼繩 (b.1940) is a Hubei native who, after graduating from Tsinghua University in 1964, joined the state news agency Xinhua. From the early 1990s, and especially after he retired in 1996, he began documenting the circumstances of the Great Famine of 1959–1961. As a former high-ranking Xinhua journalist, he obtained many documents (3,600 folders from twelve archives) and interviewed many high ranking cadres. *Tombstone* (*Mubei* 墓碑), published in 2008 in Hong Kong, was too sensitive for mainland publication; nonetheless, many people bought copies in Hong Kong and took them back across the border, and the book also circulated on the Chinese internet in electronic version. Yang defines his work as that of an "unofficial historian":

> Traditional historians face restrictions. First of all, they censor themselves. Their thoughts limit them. They don't even dare to write the facts, don't dare to speak up about it, don't dare to touch it. And even if they wrote it, they can't publish it. And if they publish, they will face censure. So mainstream scholars face those restrictions. But there are many unofficial historians like me. Many people are writing their own memoirs about being labeled "rightists" or "counter-revolutionaries." There is

---

20. See Shao Yanjun, "Wenxue, zuowei yizhong zhengyan—Yang Xianhui fangtanlu" [Literature as a kind of testimony—a discussion with Yang Xianhui], *Shanghai Wenxue* 12 (2009): 91–96.
21. Solidot, "*Chronicles of Jiabiangou* and other works removed from electronic bookstores within China," *China Digital Times*, July 16, 2017, http://chinadigitaltimes.net/chinese/2017/07/solidot |《夹边沟记事》等多部书籍从国内电子商务网/.

an author in Anhui province who has described how his family starved to death. There are many authors who have written about how their families starved.[22]

While academics work within the system, it is possible (especially for a retiree) to work in an "unofficial" (*minjian*), "amateur," or "citizen" framework. *Tombstone* can be read as a work of history, but it is also an intervention on the nature of the Maoist system: the ubiquitous hierarchy and culture of fear, the uncontrollable dynamics of ideology, and the bureaucratic struggles and personal role of certain leaders.

Yan Lianke 閻連科 (b.1958 in Henan) also began writing critical fiction in the 1990s after having first pursued a career as a PLA writer. Some of his earlier fiction had already touched on the Mao era; *Four Books* 四書, published in 2010, was entirely devoted to the ideological campaigns of the Great Leap Forward and the ensuing famine. In a labor farm on the Yellow River (Zone 99), about one hundred sent-down intellectuals engage in production, tempering useless steel, then growing wheat to meet unrealistic targets, under the direction of the "Child," the camp leader. The novel stands out in its indictment of intellectuals' collaboration with the regime and its depiction of Maoism as a fanatical religion. In a *New York Times* op-ed titled "China's State-Sponsored Amnesia," Yan further criticized present-day writers' complicity with amnesia.[23] Yan attempted to publish the book in China but ultimately failed; after its publication in Hong Kong and Taiwan, it was, however, widely read and discussed in China.

The present chapter will discuss the rise of counter-hegemonic memories in literary and reportage writing of the early twenty-first century. Firstly, they challenge the exceptional character of certain historical episodes (like the Cultural Revolution) and in this manner reconnect the present situation with the entire history of the PRC. Secondly, they question the previous role of social class or elite privilege in shaping selective narratives of the Mao era. This shift translates into a twofold engagement with the narratives of "ordinary" people and a reflexive critique of intellectuals' own entanglement with the legitimization of official narratives. Finally, while they do not renounce a quest for "truth," they attempt to advance a more open and polyphonic view of history, by creating a space for public discussion.

Back to the 1950s: Questioning the Nature of the Regime

The 1950s were traditionally considered a danger zone for writers, and few books previously dealt with a decade closely tied to the political legitimacy of the regime. Yang Xianhui's stories are closely linked to the Anti-Rightist Movement, which caused the establishment of Jiabiangou as a *laojiao* 劳教 camp: "In the second

---

22. Ian Johnson, "Finding the Facts about Mao's Victims" (Interview with Yang Jisheng), *New York Review Blog*, December 20, 2010, http://www.nybooks.com/blogs/nyrblog/2010/dec/20/finding-facts-about-maos-victims/.
23. Yan Lianke, "On China's State-Sponsored Amnesia," *New York Times*, April 1, 2013, http://www.nytimes.com/2013/04/02/opinion/on-chinas-state-sponsored-amnesia.html.

half of 1957, the *laogai* 勞改 prisoners were moved out, and Jiabiangou became a reeducation through labor (*laojiao*) farm, in order to 'house' the extreme rightists exposed during the Anti-Rightist struggle in the administration units, enterprises and schools of Gansu province. . . . A total of 2,400 people (according to the official figure) underwent reeducation through labor there."[24] According to Yang's research, 60 to 80 percent of the inmates had died by the time the camp was closed in October 1961.[25] While the *laogai* system was essentially inherited from the Republican regime, the *laojiao* system, first proposed by the Central Committee during the Campaign to Cleanse Counterrevolutionaries (*sufan yundong* 肅反運動) in 1955, was specifically set up to serve the needs of the Anti-Rightist Movement, through a State Council Decision of August 3, 1957, and institutionalized as an administrative punishment that did not require a sentence from a judge.[26] The Anti-Rightist Campaign is described as an extra-legal dynamic that undermines formal socialist legality well before the Cultural Revolution. The rightist "hat" (*youpai de maozi* 右派的帽子), an administrative label imposed without formal criteria or possible appeal, is often used to simply dress up a personal vendetta.

Furthermore, while food self-sufficiency was a general principle of the Chinese prison system,[27] in Jiabiangou, in the middle of the Gobi desert, this principle simply served as a euphemism for a technique of deliberate starvation. Yang Xianhui's clinical descriptions focus on corporality rather than ideology, suggesting that the deprivation of basic humanity (eating vomit, "digging" in constipated inmates' bowels) may be the true objective of the *laojiao* system, a policy to break down dignity and reduce humans to self-destruction. In this manner, Yang Xianhui depicts the entire socialist system itself as underpinned by a dynamics of arbitrary and uncontrollable violence.

Yang Jisheng's book, in addition to a minute documentation of the famine, is also an interpretive essay that proposes a systemic assessment of the PRC state under Mao. The preface makes the author's stance clear by using the term "totalitarian" (*jiquan* 極權), referring to both then and now.[28] This term has long been frowned upon in China (although Arendt's *Origins of Totalitarianism* has been discussed for some time and a full translation was published on the mainland in 2008, the same year as Yang's book).[29]

---

24. Yang Xianhui, "Xiezuo shouji" [Writing notes], in *Jiabiangou jishi* (Tianjin: Tianjin guji, 2002), 355.
25. Interview with Yang Xianhui, November 29, 2011; see also Sebastian Veg, "Testimony, History and Ethics," note 16.
26. See Fu Hualing, "Reeducation through Labour in Historical Perspective," *China Quarterly* 184 (2005): 814.
27. Klaus Mühlhahn, *Criminal Justice in China: A History* (Cambridge: Harvard University Press, 2009), 277.
28. Yang Jisheng, *Tombstone*, trans. Stacy Mosher and Guo Jian (London: Penguin, 2013), 3, 22.
29. Hanna Alunte [Hannah Arendt], *Jiquan zhuyi de qiyuan*, trans. Lin Xianghua (Beijing: Sanlian, 2008). The term has, of course, also been criticized in the West, sometimes for valid reasons. Some confusion surrounds the term in Chinese, due in part to the homophony of the most widely used translation (*jiquan zhuyi* 極權主義 or "apex of power-ism") with another term that has the more banal meaning of "centralization of power" 集權. As the first term is not readily understood by laypeople, it is often confused with the second one. Some scholars (Xu Jilin) favor a different translation, like *quanquan zhuyi* 全權主義 ("total power-ism").

Yang understands the famine as a direct result of the political system: "The basic reason why tens of millions of people in China starved to death was totalitarianism," which takes two main forms. Firstly, the system is entirely dominated by ideology: "China's government became a secular theocracy that united the center of power with the center of truth."[30] The comparison between communist ideology and religious dogma suggests that famine was caused not by the economic situation but by prioritizing ideology over reality.[31] Although Yang's book compiles a lot of data that was already available in some form, the breadth of the material allows him to make revealing comparisons between provinces. He finds evidence for a correlation between the strength of the Anti-Rightist persecution and the scale of the famine, in particular in Henan and Gansu, where the Anti-Rightist persecution was severe and ongoing.[32] Secondly, just like Yang Xianhui, Yang Jisheng argues that dehumanization through humiliation or violence was used as a powerful political tool. For example, Guangshan, the county in Xinyang prefecture where the most people died of famine, also experienced severe mass violence.[33] Yang quotes an archival document describing how the head of the county secretariat (*shujichu shuji* 書記處書記) was labeled a "rightist deviationist" and "struggled" by county-level cadres in November 1959, as the famine approached its peak:

> Zhang was beaten bloody, his hair ripped out in patches, and his uniform torn to shreds, leaving him barely able to walk. On November 15, Zhang was handed over to commune cadres, by which time he could only lie on the floor while he was kicked and punched and had what remained of his hair torn out. . . . [On November 16] he had lost control of his bodily functions and could no longer eat or drink . . . On November 18 he was accused of pining for the return of Chiang Kai-shek and was dragged from his bed for more struggle. When he asked for water, he was refused. Around noon on November 19, Zhang Fuhong died.[34]

This type of political violence and dehumanization, not dissimilar from what is documented in Jiabiangou, contributed to spreading fear among the bureaucracy.

For Yang, dehumanization and violence make each member of the system into a two-faced Janus: "Regardless of what kind of person went into the totalitarian system, all came out as conjoined twins facing in opposite directions: either despot or slave, depending on their position respective to those above or below them."[35] Contrary to egalitarian ideals, the nature of the totalitarian system is strongly hierarchical: unthinkingly obeying leaders and violently bullying subordinates are the

---

30. Yang Jisheng, *Tombstone*, 17, 18, and 102.
31. Yang shows that in Henan, for example, where the famine was particularly devastating, there was enough grain in the silos to feed everyone. According to Yang's sources Xinyang had 2 billion kilograms available, see *Tombstone*, 46.
32. Yang Jisheng, *Tombstone*, 23.
33. Yang notes that over 400 people were beaten to death in Guangshan during the anti-hoarding campaign from October 1959 to June 1960, in which most cadres took part (*Tombstone*, 47).
34. Yang Jisheng, *Tombstone*, 24–25.
35. Yang Jisheng, *Tombstone*, 21.

rules of the system. Therefore, all members of society are both victims and perpetrators, innocent and guilty. "Old cadres from Xinyang told me: 'If you don't beat others, you would be beaten. The more harshly you beat someone, the more firmly you established your position and your loyalty to the Communist Party. If you didn't beat others, you were a right deviationist and would soon be beaten by others."[36] In this way, ideological campaigns molded a bureaucratic system dominated by fear of becoming a target of violence and of losing rank. When confronted with evidence of famine, cadres had a strong incentive to resort to ideology, deny the facts, and advance their career by disciplining those who raised the alert or using violence against them. When Mao finally recognized the difficulties in Henan, he ascribed them to feudalism and class enemies. After the center investigated Xinyang in late 1960, grassroots cadres, some of whom had tried to either draw their superiors' attention to the situation or to take remedial measures were scapegoated, and in some instances severely punished, while provincial secretary Wu Zhipu, who was instrumental in blocking news of the famine from reaching Beijing, came away relatively unscathed and was transferred to a new position, not having committed a "line error."[37]

Yan Lianke's *Four Books*, as suggested by the title, uses a formal parallel with the four "classics" but also with the four Gospels. Yan thus draws a deeper connection between religion and politics, questioning the nature of the Maoist state and the role of ideology. The religious parallel revolves around one of the four books in Yan's novel, titled "The Child of Heaven." The narration imitates the Bible, starting by narrating how "God [*shen* 神] separated light and darkness."[38] At the beginning, the main character, the camp commander called the Child, returns from the county town ("above" or *shangbian* 上邊) with "ten commandments," according to which the inmates must unquestioningly devote themselves to production, and "uncontrolled thinking is forbidden" (*jie luan si* 戒亂思).[39] Later, the Child attends a meeting at the district level where each camp leader tries to outbid the other in setting a higher production goal. The Child, disappointed by the target he is assigned, goes to the district secretary to show off his enthusiasm. At this moment, the secretary's face, in the Child's gaze, is bathed in "heavenly light" (*shen de guang* 神的光).[40] In this passage, hierarchy is imbued with divine authority: the Party secretary, an envoy from "above," imparts commandments that the Child unquestioningly and enthusiastically embraces. In this way, Yan allegorizes the cult of personality that radiated from the center of the system to its most far-flung corners. The parallel he draws

---

36. Yang Jisheng, *Tombstone*, 49.
37. Yang quotes a passage from a witness account documenting how, in front of a delegation from Beijing, Wu Zhipu berated a county secretary for not having alerted him to the situation earlier; the county secretary retorted that he had been persecuted for "rightist deviationism" when he tried. *Tombstone*, 56. This episode probably inspired Zhang Yigong's novella, "The Criminal Li Tongzhong" (see note 8 above).
38. Yan Lianke, *Sishu* (Taipei: Maitian, 2011), 30.
39. Yan Lianke, *Sishu*, 31.
40. Yan Lianke, *Sishu*, 69.

between ideology and a religious cult is designed to underscore the irrational nature of the whole political system.

Reintroducing Ordinary People

Historiography of the Mao era is traditionally tilted toward elite politics and factional conflicts. By contrast, a characteristic of the new writing about the Mao era is its interest in the experience of "ordinary" people. This reassessment that took place over the last decades questions the socially progressive nature of Mao's regime and the actual enfranchisement it was able to achieve for non-elite social groups. Of course, "ordinary people" is a vague category, since—in the CCP's perspective—it may encompass not only members of the "people" (workers, peasants), but also "enemies of the people" (Five Black Categories), many of whom were neither wealthy nor well-connected, but which the regime defined as "the old elite."[41] It can also encompass grassroots cadres, a social group with little higher education, hardly distinct from their constituents, especially in rural areas, and who in Yang Jisheng's view were made to take a large share of blame for the Great Famine.

While the number of designated "rightists" was officially set at half a million in 1978, some historians have argued that the "rightist hat" was applied much more widely, and for a longer period, extending throughout the Great Leap Forward.[42] By focusing on Jiabiangou, Yang Xianhui finds that many of the people designated as rightists had little or no connection with politics. Many were intellectuals only in the vaguest sense, and had difficulties understanding why they were targeted. Qi Shuying, a high school graduate who breaks off university studies to join the Party in 1949 and works as a low-level employee in the public security system, is sent to Jiabiangou simply for refusing her bureau chief's sexual advances.[43] In another case, in which a judge denounces his wife, the "rightist" label becomes a convenient way for a philandering husband to obtain a divorce. Since work units had to enforce quotas (for example, Lu Changlin in "The Clinic Director" refuses to do so and is taken in himself),[44] it was almost inevitable that random individuals would be caught up in the movement. In this way, Yang Xianhui inflects our understanding of the Anti-Rightist Campaign as having been directed as much against political elites critical of Party rule as against ordinary people without any particular privilege or political stance.

---

41. Class labels after 1949 were ascribed according to pre-1949 social status (*chushen*) and were never entirely revised. See Jean-François Billeter, "The System of 'Class Status,'" in *The Scope of State Power in China*, ed. Stuart Schram (London: SOAS, 1985), 127–69.
42. The highest estimate is 1.8 million. See Ding Shu, *Yang mou: Fan youpai yundong shimo* [An open plot: The bottom line on the Anti-Rightist Movement] (Hong Kong: Kaifang, 2006), 297–310.
43. Yang Xianhui, *Jiabiangou jishi* (Guangzhou: Huacheng, 2008), 390; Yang Xianhui, *Woman from Shanghai*, trans. Wen Huang (New York: Pantheon, 2009), 275.
44. Yang Xianhui, *Jiabiangou jishi*, 470; *Woman from Shanghai*, 264.

In *Tombstone*, Yang Jisheng highlights a related characteristic of the Maoist system: the rigorous hierarchy it introduced and enforced, separating the new communist elite and the toiling masses: "The regime considered no cost or coercion too great in making the realization of Communist ideals the supreme goal of the entire populace. The peasants bore the chief burden of realizing these ideals."[45] Unable to protest, tied to their land through the hukou system, the peasants very much remained the "subaltern" under Mao, despite the regime's lofty discourses of emancipation and well-staged *suku* meetings designed to praise the accomplishments of the new society. Cadre privilege and cadre abuse were only reinforced:

> As the quality and quantity of food declined, the communal kitchens became bastions of privilege for cadres, who always managed to eat their fill. By controlling the communal kitchens, cadres were able to impose the "dictatorship of the proletariat" on every individual stomach . . . the communal kitchens forced villagers to hand their food ladles over to these leaders; losing possession of their ladles, the villagers lost control of their very survival. . . . In the villages, the so-called dictatorship of the proletariat was in fact the dictatorship of the cadres, and those with the greatest power were able to inflict the greatest amount of arbitrary abuse.[46]

Accounts concur to note that cadres maintained excellent food supplies throughout the famine, which is also noted in the testimony from Jiabiangou. As one of the production brigade members in Xinyang interviewed by Yang Jisheng recalls, "We were swollen with starvation, while the cadres were swollen with overeating."[47] In Anhui, Yang documents the lavish lifestyle of even county-level cadres in Wudian Commune, Fengyang County, with lavish banquets organized while edema sufferers were locked out of sight.[48]

All in all, the three works considerably transform the expectations of public writing about the Mao era, and indeed the underlying mainstream understanding of Mao's regime among mainland readers. Victims of Maoism are not limited to political or intellectual elites. On the contrary, many victims are ordinary people with few or no prior political antagonisms with the party. The new social hierarchy, based on cadre privilege, is not unlike the old: rural laborers remain the voiceless subaltern class, and become easy victims for top-down political campaigns led by the new elites.

The Guilt of Intellectuals

In reflecting anew on the class structure of Maoist society, the three works break with the standard narrative of "elite victimization," in which loyal intellectuals claim

---

45. Yang Jisheng, *Tombstone*, 19.
46. Yang Jisheng, *Tombstone*, 21
47. Yang Jisheng, *Tombstone*, 45.
48. Yang Jisheng, *Tombstone*, 281.

to have been wronged by Mao, and request compensation.[49] Yan Lianke and Yang Xianhui investigate the complicity and guilt of intellectuals in abetting and intensifying the violence and dehumanization practiced by the regime.

It has been noted that the practice of *suku*, a narrative denouncing the living conditions of peasants in the "old society" that was institutionalized to highlight the accomplishments of the new regime, monopolized the discursive space and deprived the rural population of a framework to criticize the present regime.[50] In this sense, the *suku* form was a characteristic of scar literature, providing a space for complaining about the past in order to better celebrate the accomplishments of the present. In an interview, Yan Lianke argued that Cultural Revolution literature follows the model of *suku*, with intellectuals rather than peasants in the role of the innocent victims.[51] Klaus Mühlhahn, discussing the works of prison-camp literature (*daqiang wenxue* 大牆文學) by scar writers like Zhang Xianliang and Cong Weixi, points out that *yiku sitian* 憶苦思甜 (remembering bitterness to enjoy sweetness) was "inherent" in the genre.[52]

By contrast, Yan Lianke considers intellectuals as willing collaborators of the regime. In his novel, a character called the Writer, a famous intellectual who was designated by secret ballot by his colleagues to undergo reeducation, is eager to work with the authorities in informing on others and in furthering their utopian projects (growing oversized wheat by adding blood to the water is his idea). His character contrasts with the Scholar who resists collaborating, and remains in the camp reading Buddhist scriptures after the Child's death. The theme of cannibalism has been widely used in Chinese literature, both as a metaphor for the breakdown of (Confucian) social order in times of famine and social chaos, and more generally (most famously by Lu Xun) as a trope for the violence of social relations in a hierarchical society. In *Four Books*, the trope is inverted: after witnessing the death of Music, a woman he has reported on, the Writer is overcome by guilt and cuts off two chunks of his own flesh, one to be buried with Music, the other which he boils in broth and serves to her (starving) lover the Scholar as a plea for forgiveness. The consumption of human flesh thus becomes a means of repentance (*chanhui* 懺悔) for the intellectual, who is finally able to confront his own complicity with the system and understand his own role as a "cannibal." Yan has subsequently often

---

49. See Qin Hui, "Women gai zenyang fansi wenge" [How we should reflect on the Cultural Revolution], *Wenti yu zhuyi: Qin Hui wenxuan* (Changchun: Changchun Press, 1999), 10–11.
50. Gail Hershatter writes that, in China: "those we might call subalterns always already speak (and often understand their own experience) in the language of the state, which simultaneously recognizes their suffering, glorifies their resistance, and effaces any aspect of their history that does not clearly fall into these two categories." "The Subaltern Talks Back: Reflections on Subaltern Theory and Chinese History," *Positions* 1 (Spring 1993): 108.
51. Author's interview with Yan Lianke, Hong Kong, May 24, 2012.
52. See Klaus Mühlhahn, "Remembering a Bitter Past: The Trauma of China's Labor Camps, 1949–1978," *History and Memory*, 16, no. 2 (Fall/Winter 2004): 117.

used the term *chanhui* to refer to the need for intellectuals to atone for their "cannibalistic" role in the Maoist project.[53]

Cannibalism also appears in Yang Xianhui's collection, which uses similar moral dilemmas to explore the question of guilt. In Jiabiangou, intellectuals are the characters most likely to profess loyalty and confidence in the Party and the system, and to take the moral high ground, believing that wrongs will be righted if they dedicate themselves to sincerely reeducating themselves. By contrast, inmates from lower classes are often more critical of the state. In "The Train Conductor," the narrator Li Tianqing, a former detective in the local Public Security Bureau from a capitalist family, is scolded by Wei Changhai, a high-school graduate from the Lanzhou Rail Bureau, for his naïve beliefs:

> Why are you being such a fool? You've been kicked out of the Party long ago. Nobody thinks that you are still a Communist revolutionary, except you. You're an enemy of the people. You are receiving reeducation at a labor camp. You act like a foolish wife who prays for her treacherous husband to return. It's not going to happen. Even if we don't die of starvation, there's no end to our exile here.[54]

Wei Changhai sees the reality more clearly than Li and acts accordingly, freeing himself from all moral constraints to maximize his chances of survival; he is exposed by Li for cannibalizing the corpses of dead inmates, sparking outrage among the prisoners. However, the outrage slowly gives way to discussion: "In my cave, the majority agreed that he hadn't broken any laws. He had simply violated the moral code—but how could one clearly define moral standards in a reeducation camp like Jiabiangou?"[55] Li then feels remorse for his previous attitude of moral superiority—the intellectual's repentance—and worries that Wei will die in the pit he has been thrown into as punishment: "I was the one who had reported Wei. If he died, I would be a murderer. If I managed to survive, I would be haunted by guilt for the rest of my life. Wei had certainly done something terribly wrong, but he didn't deserve to die."[56] Li rescues Wei, who is able to redeem his immoral act: he saves Li from the fate of many other intellectuals in Jiabiangou by taking him along on his successful escape, and even carrying him through the desert when he can no longer walk.

Looking back, Li Tianqing has no simple answer to the ethical complexities of the situation: "I used to despise him for his lack of morals. I rescued him from the isolation cell for my own selfish reasons—I wanted to relieve my guilt. I could never have imagined that my unintended gesture of kindness would be met with

---

53. For example: "In *Four Books*, one intellectual deeply repents [*chanhui*], and that is the Writer, who is also an informant. His repentance is more or less unprecedented among contemporary Chinese intellectuals." In "Yan Lianke: Shenghuo de xiabian haiyou kanbujian de shenghuo" [Yan Lianke: Below life there is another invisible life], *Nanfang Zhoumo*, May 27, 2011, http://www.infzm.com/content/59605.
54. Yang Xianhui, *Jiabiangou Jishi*, 438; *Woman from Shanghai*, 80.
55. Yang Xianhui, *Jiabiangou Jishi*, 435; *Woman from Shanghai*, 77.
56. Yang Xianhui, *Jiabiangou Jishi*, 436; *Woman from Shanghai*, 78.

such deep appreciation."⁵⁷ Intellectuals can no longer take the moral high ground: without Wei's survival instinct, Li Tianqing would simply have died of famine at Jiabiangou. Li's act of first exposing Wei, then freeing him, is further qualified by the admission that he felt "guilty": he now understands that when he denounces Wei to the prison guards for cannibalism he is in fact revealing his complicity with a system which he still has faith in. In a world in which there are no black and white judgments, effectively breaking with the system may require moral deviance.

Yang Jisheng also engages with the complex issue of intellectuals' complicity. Throughout *Tombstone* he describes how higher cadres turn a blind eye to complaints, petitions, or letters seeking to raise alert about the famine: "Officials pandered to their superiors at the expense of the lives of ordinary people, and each level of officials put pressure on the next level down."⁵⁸ Yang, as a former journalist with Xinhua is of course not immune to this criticism. He tracks down and interviews a journalist named Fang Huang who in 1958 wrote a glowing article about "Sputnik fields" in Henan for *People's Daily*, which she has come to regret: "even though I had my doubts, I didn't dare express them; I just reported as fact what I had been told. Then it turned out to be false! To have been a journalist in this system leaves one feeling nothing but shame and regret."⁵⁹ Yang, although he lost his father to the famine, spent years working for the system and only reaches this realization after the democracy movement of 1989.⁶⁰ His somewhat ambiguous attitude is neatly encapsulated in his childhood memory of playing a game after watching a struggle session at which fourteen people are executed.

> After we went home, several other village boys and I played at struggling landlords. Quite to my surprise, my father pulled me into the house and gave me a thrashing. Later he told me that not all of those killed were bad men, and not all of those who beat them had any cause for grievance. He never took me to a struggle session again.⁶¹

This brief vignette can be read as a parable for the natural "complicity" with the system that children develop from the earliest age, and Yang's belated understanding of his own socialization within it.

From Individual Testimony to a Public Debate on History

The most interesting aspect of these three publications is without doubt their complex engagement with the embryonic public sphere in China. While more and more personal memoirs of the Mao era have been published by aging witnesses, including several by low- to mid-level cadres, many are private narratives, offering

---

57. Yang Xianhui, *Jiabiangou Jishi*, 439; *Woman from Shanghai*, 80.
58. Yang Jisheng, *Tombstone*, 34.
59. Yang Jisheng, *Tombstone*, 75.
60. Yang Jisheng, *Tombstone*, 12.
61. Yang Jisheng, *Tombstone*, 6.

a "personal version" (often a vindication) of events for the historical record. Their claim to publicness is in this way mitigated. By contrast, Yan, Yang and Yang's interventions, because they are not memoirs, displace the boundaries of the public and the private.

Yang Xianhui's work is the only one of the three under discussion that has been published in China. After the stories were serialized by *Shanghai Wenxue* under the liberal editor Chen Sihe, it became easier to collect them in a book. Yang's second collection, *Tales from Dingxi Orphanage* (Dingxi gueryuan jishi, 2007), also dedicated to the Great Famine in Gansu, received prizes and drew attention to Jiabiangou. Yang himself has stressed that his enterprise is not only personal (he was not a rightist and was too young to experience Jiabiangou), but aimed at sparking a discussion within society:

> The shock at hearing these rightists' stories never faded and, many years later, in 1997, I undertook to investigate the events of Jiabiangou. Every year for three years, I spent two or three months interviewing survivors and camp staff, reading archives, and traveled twice to Jiabiangou itself.... As an author, I am retelling the stories uncovered in my investigation in order to reopen a page in history covered by the dust of forty years, in the hope that such a tragedy cannot repeat itself, and in order to bring to those souls laid to eternal rest in the wilderness of the Gobi desert the consolation that history will not forget Jiabiangou. Scrutinizing the history of those who preceded us means scrutinizing ourselves.[62]

Since Yang was alerted to the tragic stories of Jiabiangou through his encounters with former inmates in the 1960s, he now aims to make these stories known to a wider audience ("reopen a page in history") in order to influence the future political direction of the country. This was ultimately the motivation for going to great pains to publish within China, which enabled the discussion and media interest that followed.

Yang Jisheng's attitude is quite similar, but the nature of the material contained in *Tombstone* made it impossible to publish on the mainland. Consequently, his preface gives less importance to the public aspect of the book, but underscores its meaning for history: "In this new century, I believe that rulers and ordinary citizens alike know in their hearts that the totalitarian system has reached its end.... With this book I erect a tombstone anticipating the ultimate demise of the totalitarian system. Through it, later generations will know that there was once a system established at a certain juncture of history in the name of 'liberating mankind' that in reality enslaved humanity."[63] The emphasis is on future generations rather than on present debates.

Although he quotes many preexisting private testimonies or memoirs, their juxtaposition produces a strongly polyphonic effect, which opens a historical debate

---

62. Yang Xianhui, "Xiezuo shouji" [Writing notes], in *Jiabiangou jishi* (Tianjin: Tianjin Guji, 2002), 355–56.
63. Yang Jisheng, *Tombstone*, 22.

on the responsibility for the famine. By allowing low-level cadres to "take the floor" and by placing their accounts of events side by side with the official version or those produced by higher-level cadres, Yang creates a new space for public discussion. In many cases, he shows how low-level cadres tried to alert higher authorities, or else to undermine them by allocating land to peasants for household cultivation,[64] but were criticized and struggled in the campaign against right deviationism after the Lushan conference. When the "communist wind" died down, they were often made to take the blame for the famine by higher leaders.

Yang probably did not expect the considerable echo his book encountered on the mainland. It was widely debated and discussed in academic fora, as well as in unofficial and authorized but more liberal journals like *Yanhuang Chunqiu*, which Yang was connected to as a member of the editorial board. Whole chapters were available for downloading on Chinese websites.[65] An academic controversy with the Marxist mathematician Sun Jingxian set alight social media.[66] *Nanfang Renwu Zhoukan*, a widely read liberal weekly, published a special issue in May 2012 with the title "Da Jihuang" (the Great Famine) and a graph of production statistics for 1959–1961 on the cover.[67] Although Yang's study was not directly referenced, its influence is obvious, showcasing the interplay between marginal publications and the mainstream public sphere, or the "centripetal" mechanism by which discussions find their way from specialized or overseas venues to the mainstream media on the mainland. This mechanism also highlights the limitations of the mainland's current censorship system.

Yan Lianke's novel also employs a polyphonic technique in its structure. The four "Books" are in fact four parallel accounts of the events in the fictional labor farm described by Yan, each of which is given a publication history.[68] In this manner, Yan allegorizes the social debates about the famine within the novel itself, contrasting an "internal Party document" published in the 1980s ("Records of Criminals") with a personal memoir published in 2002 ("The Old Course"), an anonymous work from a publisher specializing in myths and legends ("The Child of Heaven"), and a philosophical treatise preserved in the archives of the National Institute for Research on Philosophical documents ("New Myth of Sisyphus"). Each account presents a somewhat different view of the events: the informant's records published internally, the Writer's memoir which emphasizes repentance and atonement, the fable of the Red Child and his flowers and stars, and the cultural critique of Chinese civilization in "Sisyphus." Rather than replacing one "truth" about the famine (that it did not take

---

64. For example, Xi Daolong in Gansu or Zeng Xisheng in Anhui (*Tombstone*, 150 and 314).
65. For example, the chapter "Gansu bu gan" was available on a Sina blog when the present chapter was first written, now removed: http://blog.sina.cn/dpool/blog/newblog/mblog/controllers/apparticle.php?blogid=15d5540920102w25y.
66. See Wu Si's chapter in this collection, and Anthony Garnaut, "The Mass Line on a Massive Famine," *The China Story*, October 8, 2014, https://www.thechinastory.org/2014/10/the-mass-line-on-a-massive-famine/.
67. *Nanfang renwu zhoukan* no. 299, May 21, 2012, special feature, 34–51.
68. Yan Lianke, *Sishu*, 374.

place) with another, Yan's structural design showcases the importance of debate. Yan leaves it to the reader to navigate through the informant reports, allegorical narrative, self-introspection, and philosophical interpretation.

Like Yang Jisheng's study, Yan's book was not ultimately published in China, although he went to some effort to seek publication. Nonetheless, *Four Books* sparked notable public discussion on the mainland, in academic venues (it was launched at an open seminar at People's University in Beijing where Yan holds a position), in academic journals, where it was discussed by prominent scholars (Chen Xiaoming, Wang Binbin), and even in several mainstream media outlets, like *Southern Metropolis Daily*.[69]

Each of these three influential works contains a degree of internal polyphony, which was mirrored in the public discussions they provoked in China, sometimes filtering into the mainstream media. Through their internal structures, they break out of the memoir and personal reminiscence genre, and displace the boundaries of the private and the public. Through their external reception, they show that, paradoxically, it is no longer necessary to be published inside China to enter the Chinese public sphere.

Conclusion

The present chapter has argued that three works published in rapid succession in the first decade of the twenty-first century have contributed to shaping a new understanding of the Mao era. Although this discussion has taken place mainly within the intellectual sphere, it has occasionally filtered into the mainstream media. One of its most visible results is that the designation of the famine as "three years of natural disasters" has been slowly displaced by the new wording "three years of great famine."

Jiabiangou, *Tombstone*, and *Four Books* turn away from the well-circumscribed form of the "scar" narrative to probe the nature of Mao's regime, which is described as steeped in utopian ideology and violence. Turning away from elite politics and towards the stories of ordinary people, they question the regime's accomplishments in bringing about more social equality. They highlight the oppressive hierarchy of cadre privilege and the persecution or famine endured by countless members of the rural lower classes, showing that the Maoist elite continued to oppress the subaltern rural masses, as well as persecuting a new group of people who were disenfranchised by the new regime.

In this context, moral dilemmas are ubiquitous, and intellectuals in particular are often shown as complicit. The three authors break with the mold of the *suku* narrative, where critique is permissible if combined with a joyful affirmation of present progress, and the author seeks vindication and often revenge for having

---

69. See a more detailed discussion of the mainland reception in Veg, "Creating a Literary Space."

been among the downtrodden of yesterday. Here by contrast, authorship is not a form of personal revenge, but a self-reflexive exercise in assessing the author's own complicity and moral compromises.

Finally, the three writers are not former victims who recant and become heroes of their own personal memoirs, but observers who try to introduce a plurality of viewpoints despite the limitations imposed by censorship. The aim is not to replace a dominant narrative with a counter-hegemonic alternative, but to institutionalize a social space for debate, in which different voices and different stories can be heard. All three works, whether fictional of factual, are polyphonic in their internal structure. To varying degrees, they have displaced the boundaries of the public sphere in which their reception took place.

These writings may have begun to change the mainstream understanding of the nature of the PRC regime, establishing connections between the 1950s, the 1960s, and today. The famine has percolated into the mainstream media. However, critical narratives also remain strongly contested, whether through full-fledged denunciations on the internet led by "fifty-centers" (*wu mao dang*), active campaigns against "historical nihilism" within the bureaucracy, or through more respectable academic rebuttals, behind which can be glimpsed the heavy hand of the state.

Bibliography

"Da Jihuang." Special feature in *Nanfang renwu zhoukan*, no. 299 (May 21, 2012): 34–51.
"Yan Lianke: Shenghuo de xiabian haiyou kanbujian de shenghuo" [Yan Lianke: Below life there is another invisible life]. *Nanfang Zhoumo*, May 27, 2011, http://www.infzm.com/content/59605.
Arendt, Hannah [Hanna Alunte]. *Jiquan zhuyi de qiyuan*. Translated by Lin Xianghua. Beijing: Sanlian, 2008. 654 pp.
Ba Jin. "Jinian" [Remembering]. In *Suixianglu xuanji*, 53–54. Beijing: Sanlian, 2003.
Berry, Michael. *A History of Pain: Trauma in Modern Chinese Literature*. New York: Columbia University Press, 2011.
Billeter, Jean-François. "The System of 'Class Status.'" In *The Scope of State Power in China*, edited by Stuart Schram, 127–69. London: SOAS, 1985.
DeMare, Brian, "The Romance and Tragedy of Rural Revolution: Narratives and Novels of Land Reform in Mao's China," *Clio*, 43.3 (2014): 341–365.
Ding Shu. *Yang mou: Fan youpai yundong shimo* [An open plot: The bottom line on the Anti-Rightist Movement]. Hong Kong: Kaifang, 2006.
Fu Hualing. "Reeducation through Labour in Historical Perspective." *The China Quarterly* 184 (2005): 811–30.
Garnaut, Anthony. "The Mass Line on a Massive Famine." *The China Story*, October 8, 2014. https://www.thechinastory.org/2014/10/the-mass-line-on-a-massive-famine/.
He, Guimei. "Shijimo de ziwo jiushu zhilu: 1998 nian 'fanyou' shuji re de wenhua fenxi" [The road to fin-de-siècle self-redemption: A cultural analysis of the 1998 "Anti-Rightist" book fever]. *Shanghai wenxue* (April 2000): 71–76.

Hershatter, Gail. "The Subaltern Talks Back: Reflections on Subaltern Theory and Chinese History." *Positions* 1 (Spring 1993): 103–30.
Johnson, Ian. "Finding the Facts about Mao's Victims" (Interview with Yang Jisheng). *New York Review Blog*, December 20, 2010. http://www.nybooks.com/blogs/nyrblog/2010/dec/20/finding-facts-about-maos-victims/.
King, Richard, ed. *Leaping to Disaster: Village Literature and the Great Leap Forward*, Renditions, vol. 68 (2007).
Link, Perry. "China: Novelists against the State." *The New York Review of Books*. November 15, 2015.
Link, Perry. "June Fourth: Memory and Ethics." *China Perspectives* 2 (2009): 4–17.
Link, Perry. *The Uses of Literature: Life in the Socialist Chinese Literary System*. Princeton: Princeton University Press, 2000.
Liu Xiaobo. "Weiji! Xin shiqi wenxue mianlin de weiji" [Crisis! The literature of the new era faces a crisis]. *Shenzhen Qingnianbao*, October 3, 1986. (French translation in Liu Xiaobo, *La Philosophie du porc et autres essais* [Paris: Gallimard, "Bleu de Chine," 2011], 57–87.)
Liu Zaifu. "Xinshiqi wenxue de tupo he shenhua" [Breakthrough and deepening accomplishments of the new literature]. *Renmin ribao*, September 8, 1986, p. 7.
Liu Zaifu. "Wenxue yu chanhui yishi: Du Ba Jin de Suixianglu" [Literature and repentance: Reading Ba Jin's *Random Thoughts*]. *Liu Zaifu Ji*, 313–26. Harbin: Heilongjiang Jiaoyu, 1988.
Mühlhahn, Klaus. *Criminal Justice in China: A History*. Cambridge: Harvard University Press, 2009.
Mühlhahn, Klaus. "Remembering a Bitter Past: The Trauma of China's Labor Camps, 1949–1978." *History and Memory* 16, no. 2, Special Issue: Traumatic Memory in Chinese History (Fall/Winter 2004): 108–39.
Niu Han, and Deng Jiuping, eds. *Jiyi zhong de fanyoupai yundong* [Memories of the Anti-Rightist Movement], in 3 volumes: *Yuan shang cao* [Reeds on the steppe], *Liu yue xue* [Snow in June], *Jingji lu* [A thorny road]. Beijing: Jingji ribao, 1998.
Qin Hui. "Women gai zenyang fansi wenge" [How we should reflect on the Cultural Revolution]. *Wenti yu zhuyi: Qin Hui wenxuan*, 10–11. Changchun: Changchun Press, 1999.
Qin Liyan. "The Sublime and the Profane: A Comparative Analysis of Two Fictional Narratives about Sent-Down Youth." In *The Chinese Cultural Revolution as History*, edited by Joseph Esherick, Paul Pickowicz, and Andrew Walder. Stanford: Stanford University Press, 2006.
Schoenhals, Michael. *Doing Things with Words in Chinese Politics: Five Studies*. Berkeley: Institute of East Asian Studies, 1992.
Shao Yanjun. "Wenxue, zuowei yizhong zhengyan—Yang Xianhui fangtanlu" [Literature as a kind of testimony—a discussion with Yang Xianhui]. *Shanghai Wenxue* 12 (2009): 91–96.
Solidot, "*Chronicles of Jiabiangou* and Other Works Removed from Electronic Bookstores within China." *China Digital Times*, July 16, 2017. http://chinadigitaltimes.net/chinese/2017/07/solidot |《夹边沟记事》等多部书籍从国内电子商务网/.
Unger, Jonathan, ed. *Using the Past to Serve the Present: Historiography and Politics in Contemporary China*. Armonk, NY: M. E. Sharpe, 1993.

Veg, Sebastian. "Creating a Literary Space to Debate the Mao Era: The Fictionalization of the Great Leap Forward in Yan Lianke's *Four Books*." *China Perspectives, Remembering the Mao Era: from Creative Practices to Parallel History*, no. 4 (2014): 7–16.

Veg, Sebastian. "New Spaces, New Controls: China's Embryonic Public Sphere." *Current History* (September 2015): 203–9.

Veg, Sebastian. "Testimony, History and Ethics: From the Memory of Jiabiangou Prison Camp to a Reappraisal of the Anti-Rightist Movement in Present-Day China." *The China Quarterly* 218 (June 2014): 514–39.

Wang, Ban. "Epic Narrative, Authenticity, and the Memory of Realism." In *Re-envisioning the Chinese Revolution: The Politics and Poetics of Collective Memories in Reform China*, edited by Ching Kwan Lee and Guobin Yang, 193–216. Washington DC: W. Wilson Center Press, 2007.

Watson, Rubie. "Memory, History, and Opposition under State Socialism." In *Memory, History and Opposition under State Socialism*, 1–20. Santa Fe: School of American Research Seminar Series, 1994.

Weigelin-Schweidrzik, Susanne. "Party Historiography." In *Using the Past to Serve the Present: Historiography and Politics in Contemporary China*, edited by J. Unger, 151–73. Armonk, NY: M. E. Sharpe, 1993.

Weigelin-Schweidrzik, Susanne. "Trauma and Memory: The Case of the Great Famine in the People's Republic of China (1959–1961)." *Historiography East and West* 1, no. 1 (2003): 41–67.

Wu, Yenna, and Simona Livescu, eds. *Human Rights, Suffering, and Aesthetics in Political Prison Literature*, 1–16. Lanham: Lexington Books, 2011.

Yan Lianke. "On China's State-sponsored Amnesia." *New York Times*, April 1, 2013. http://www.nytimes.com/2013/04/02/opinion/on-chinas-state-sponsored-amnesia.html?_r=0.

Yan Lianke. *Sishu*. Taipei: Maitian, 2011.

Yang Jisheng. *Tombstone*. Translated by Stacy Mosher and Guo Jian. London: Penguin, 2013.

Yang Xianhui. *Jiabiangou jishi*. Guangzhou: Huacheng, 2008.

Yang Xianhui. *Woman from Shanghai*. Translated by Wen Huang. New York: Pantheon, 2009.

Yang Xianhui. "Xiezuo shouji" [Writing notes]. In *Jiabiangou jishi*. Tianjin: Tianjin guji, 2002.

7
Filmed Testimonies, Archives, and Memoirs of the Mao Era

*Staging Unofficial History in Chinese Independent Documentaries**

Judith Pernin

Introduction

Over the past twenty-five years, various writers, historians, artists, and journalists have addressed the history of the Mao era with a distinctive unofficial perspective.[1] This phenomenon is paralleled in the cinema circle, even though independent films on historical issues are still rare compared to those on contemporary topics such as urbanization, marginal and vulnerable groups, or rural politics. Emerging at the outset of the 1990s, but mostly produced at the turn of the 2000s, Chinese independent documentaries broke with the conventions of official film by emphasizing the position of the director as an author. Most record with a direct, subjective style the experiences of protagonists seldom represented in mainstream productions. Low budget and often self-produced, they circulate in China within the shrinking landscape of independent film festivals or other unofficial (*minjian* 民間) screenings. They are also distributed abroad in specialized or academic events, and some filmmakers, such as Wang Bing 王兵, have gained an important following on the international film festival and art scenes.

The first generation of independent documentary filmmakers—Wu Wenguang 吳文光, Wang Guangli 王光利, Duan Jinchuan 段錦川, and Shi Jian 時間—became active at the turn of the 1990s. Influenced by the 1980s cultural fever and intellectual debates, they were keen on questioning China's recent past and contemporary issues while renewing the approach of documentary cinema. In the aftermath of the 1989 democracy movement, the film projects they were working on in collaboration with national television stations came to a sudden halt. The political repression and

---

* This chapter is the result of my postdoctoral research (ANR-RGC project "New Approaches of the Mao Era," CEFC). It also draws on my PhD "*Pratiques indépendantes du documentaire en Chine. Histoire, esthétique et discours visuels*" (1990–2010) (Rennes: Presses universitaires de Rennes, 2015).
1. See the introduction above, "Trauma, Nostalgia, Public Debate."

increased control over the media and cultural industries prompted these filmmakers to step back from the film institutions and to definitely break away from official documentary aesthetics. This context of production partly explains why early independent documentaries were so few and far between during the 1990s, and why filmmakers carefully avoided sensitive historical issues. A notable exception was Wu Wenguang, who explored the impact of the Mao era on ordinary Chinese people early on. His interest for such a topic was already perceptible in his first film, *Bumming in Beijing*,[2] which encapsulated the despair of a generation of artists at the turn of the 1990s. Soon after, in *1966, My Time as a Red Guard* (1992, 165 min.), he directly interviewed five former participants in Cultural Revolution activism. In the 2010s, he filmed *Treatment* (2010, 80 min.) and *Investigating My Father in 1949* (2013, 60 min.), exploring his relationship to his late parents against the backdrop of Chinese history.

Until the advent of digital cameras at the turn of the 2000s, independent films on any topic remained rare. Very few works were produced until the mid-2000s when a wider and more diverse group of filmmakers emerged along with independent screenings and festivals. In 2004, Hu Jie 胡杰 made *Looking for Lin Zhao's Soul* (2005, 90 min.), which reconstructs the life of a female poet labeled as a rightist, then killed in jail during the Cultural Revolution. Because of this film on a sensitive topic, Hu Jie had to resign from his career as a journalist, and since then he has unveiled forgotten stories of political persecution in each of his documentaries. Although the impact of his filmworks is hard to assess given their limited audience, they should not be overlooked as they are widely discussed on social media and are very popular in activist groups.[3]

Other cinematic approaches exist among this small group of filmmakers interested in unofficial history. Renowned directors Wang Bing and Jia Zhangke 賈樟柯, who works at the edge of the independent circle, have both investigated socialist legacies (*24 City; I Wish I knew; West of the Tracks*),[4] and periods such as the Great Leap Forward (*Fengming, a Chinese Memoir*, 2007, 186 min.; *The Ditch*).[5] In the 2010s, younger independent filmmakers started to document their relatives' experiences during the Mao era on their own (Qiu Jiongjiong's 邱炯炯 *My Mother's rhapsody*, 2011, 106 min.; Meng Xiaowei's 孟小為, *The Camera of Socialist Country*,

---

2. *Bumming in Beijing – The Last Dreamers, Liulang Beijing – Zuihou de mengxiangzhe*, 1991, 150 min. The full references of Chinese independent documentaries on the Mao era appear in the appended filmographies. Other films—fictions and documentaries from China or other countries that do not directly address the Mao era appear in footnotes only.
3. See Judith Pernin, "Independent Documentaries and Online Uses in China: From Cinephilia to Activism," in *Post-1990 Documentary: Reconfiguring Independence*, ed. Camille Deprez and Judith Pernin (Edinburgh: Edinburgh University Press, 2015), 233–47.
4. Jia Zhangke, *24 City*, Ershisi Chengji, 2008, 107 min.; Jia Zhangke, *I Wish I knew*, Haishang chuanqi, 2006, 138 min.; Wang Bing, *West of the Track*, Tiexiqu, 2003, 551 min.
5. Wang Bing, *The Ditch*, Jiabiangou, 2010, 112 min. (fiction).

2013, 56 min.), or in the framework of the Folk Memory Project 民間記憶計劃,[6] a participative oral history initiative on the Great Famine.

As this brief description reveals, independent directors focus on personal stories overlooked, forgotten, or suppressed from official history. Typically, their films gather testimonies of personal hardships endured during sensitive times such as the Cultural Revolution or the Great Leap Forward, differing greatly from official productions in their content, approach, and their methodology. In contrast with mainstream documentaries, their narrative backbone is formed by testimonies from ordinary witnesses. In certain works, this oral history is presented along with other sources and materials, namely autobiographies, archival documents and images produced by official institutions, or pictures and memorabilia pertaining to the witnesses. Given the distrust of independent filmmakers for official documents and images, these materials are neatly distinguished in their filmic use. In stark contrast with official documentaries, independent filmmakers favor oral testimonies over official footage shot during the Mao era. Although theoretically sound, this preference is nonetheless complicated in practice by a set of parameters. First, it is at times impossible to document or represent certain historical events without relying on official documents, testimonies, or images. Secondly, recording oral history is a challenging task, as witnesses might be unwilling or unable to testify. Finally, formal choices need to be made in order to transmit effectively this unofficial history to an audience who may only have been exposed to official history. As independent filmmakers give a platform to bitter memories of the Mao era, their films' unorthodox view of the past might be rejected or considered untruthful and incorrect. Thus, they have to elaborate methods to persuade or convince the audience of the historical truth of the witnesses' discourse.

Besides contributing to our understanding of the past, this body of films also raises crucial questions regarding the production, aesthetics, and reception of unofficial historical discourses in China. What methods do independent filmmakers favor to record unofficial memories? How do oral testimonies interact with other materials on the Mao era, and what types of discourses are they producing? Finally, how do independent directors use film techniques to address the issue of historical truth?

This chapter aims to fill a disciplinary void between history and film studies and evaluate independent documentaries' contribution to historical debates on the Mao era. Its purpose is not to comment on historical events, but to observe how they are remembered and narrated by witnesses and transmitted in independent documentaries. Before analyzing more closely a selection of major works, I shall provide elements of context and introduce the main issues these documentaries raise with respect to historical and film debates.

---

6. This project is discussed later in the chapter. See also Zhuang Jiayun, "Remembering and Reenacting Hunger: Caochangdi Workstation's Minjian Memory Project," *The Drama Review* 58, no. 1 (2014): 118–40.

Independent Documentaries on the Mao Era: Overview and Challenges

Presenting an exhaustive review of independent documentaries on the Mao era is difficult given their discreet nature. The first task was to compile a filmography, by conducting research on the internet and social media, on the catalogues of independent film festivals, and, in some cases, by directly contacting filmmakers to obtain information about their works. Film copies were consulted in research institutions or during screenings. The general filmography appended to this chapter is titled "Independent documentaries on the Mao era (1992–2015)" and includes forty-four titles made by thirty-two filmmakers. In addition, thirty-five films from thirteen participants in the Folk Memory Project (2010–2014) appear in a separate filmography.

Altogether, these two filmographies amount to close to eighty films on the Mao era, out of a total of well over five hundred independent documentaries produced since 1991. Two documentaries on historical events were made as early as 1992— Wu Wenguang's *1966, My Time as a Red Guard* and *I Graduated!* (1992, 64 min.). Although the latter focuses on memories of the 1989 democratic movement and does not directly deal with the Mao era, it is included in the filmography for its implicit depiction of the period. These two early attempts were emulated only from the mid-2000s, with Hu Jie's investigative documentaries—*Looking for Lin Zhao's Soul*, mentioned above, and soon after with another film on the Cultural Revolution: *Though I am Gone* (2006, 70 min.).

A third and more consistent wave emerged after 2010, with eight films made in 2013 alone, the most prolific year so far. While the first documentaries were mainly focused on the Cultural Revolution—a sensitive but nonetheless officially criticized period discussed at length in 1980s scar literature—the topics became progressively more diverse. Recent films touch upon earlier periods such as the Land Reform, the Great Leap Forward, the Great Famine, and the Anti-Rightist Campaign. A few documentaries even go further back in time, beyond the scope of the period under scrutiny, shedding light on the transition between the Republican period and the Mao era. Xu Xin's 徐辛 *Pathway* (2012, 113 min.) records the memories of an army veteran labeled a counterrevolutionary in the 1950s despite his fighting during the war for liberation. Qiu Jiongjiong's *Mr. Zhang Believes* (2014, 270 min.) gives voice to a former progressive student who encountered similar misfortune during the Anti-Rightist Movement because of his family background.

At first sight, most of these documentaries resist the assignation of a well-circumscribed historical period. Unlike mainstream productions, they do not present an exhaustive narrative on a particular event, but rather, a record of the protagonists' memories as they emerge during conversations and daily activities. These documentaries investigate the Mao era from a contemporary perspective and are as such strongly rooted in the present time of the shooting. One of the difficulties in constituting this filmography was therefore to distinguish between documentaries focusing primarily on memories of the Mao era and those explaining contemporary issues by looking at their historical causes.

Some of the titles thus constitute borderline cases: Huang Wenhai's 黃文海 *We* (2008, 102 min.) gives a historical account of political activism in China through portraits of persons from various age groups; Zhu Rikun's 朱日坤 *The Dossier* (2014, 128 min.) narrates Tsering Woeser's late awakening to her Tibetan identity. The film starts by showing the writer and activist reading her personal dossier and recollecting her childhood during the Mao era. *Shanghai Youth* (Gao Zipeng 高子鵬 and Wu Meng 吳夢, 2015, 480 min.) is another case in point. The "political lexicon" published together with the film states: "This movie records [the rusticated youth's] later years as an attempt to reveal an episode of history that has completely changed the fate of a whole generation. But in fact, this episode is not concluded yet—we are still in the middle of it."[7] Indeed, in this eight-hour documentary, the directors film the ongoing struggle of Shanghai-born rusticated youth sent to Xinjiang who have not yet been fully rehabilitated. They regularly organize protests to claim a retirement pension consistent with their late relocation to their hometown. As they reach their sixties or seventies, they are still identified as "rusticated youth" and remain at odds with the current Shanghai administration. Unlike other cultural productions, they are therefore not filmed out of nostalgia,[8] but to shed light on the challenges some still face today.

Comparing past and present daily experiences is another common point of these films. In *Shanghai Youth* as in the Folk Memory Project and other films, filmmakers reveal how past difficulties remain acute for protagonists, which in turn stresses a sense of continuity between the Mao era and today. The loose adherence of these films to the genre of historical documentary and their emphasis on daily life, present time, and continuities has been noted by other scholars. Analyzing the "personal documentaries" dealing with the "haunting experience of socialism,"[9] Qi Wang attributes this to China's post-socialist nature, as well as to the identity of filmmakers such as Wu Wenguang, Wang Guangli, and even Wang Bing who belong to what she calls the "Forsaken Generation."[10] But the fact that post-1980s and post-1990s filmmakers are also engaged in filming memory indicates that generational distinctions are perhaps not entirely effective here.

Apart from offering counter-narratives of the Mao era, these documentaries also set themselves apart aesthetically by rejecting the expository mode[11]—a form

---

7. Gao Zipeng, ed., *Shanghai Qingnian Guanying Shouce* [A handbook to the documentary *Shanghai Youth*], (self-published, 2015), 3.
8. See Yang Guobin, "China's Zhiqing Generation: Nostalgia, Identity, and Cultural Resistance in the 1990s," *Modern China* 29, no. 3 (2003): 296.
9. Qi Wang, *Memory, Subjectivity and Independent Chinese Cinema* (Edinburgh: Edinburgh University Press, 2014), 12.
10. Wang, *Memory, Subjectivity and Independent Chinese Cinema*, 5.
11. For a definition of the various documentary modes, see Bill Nichols, *Introduction to Documentary* (Bloomington: Indiana University Press, 2010).

familiar to audiences around the world for its use of educational voice-over illustrated by visuals. Whereas Chinese official documentaries tend to paint history in broad strokes, following a clear periodization, and focusing on prominent political figures, independent documentaries shift our attention towards the local, "ordinary citizens" and "everyday history," giving voice to personal stories at odds with grand historical narratives. They seldom rely on archival footage from the Mao era, unlike compilation films (*wenxianpian* 文獻片) frequently broadcast on Chinese television. When independent filmmakers resort to archival footage, it is generally contrasted with witness's accounts:[12] filmed testimonies are presented as the authoritative narrative rather than the official archive, thus allowing usually silenced or marginal voices to become the main source of historical knowledge. This amounts to a complete reversal of value between archival documents and contemporary testimonies, and constitutes a fundamental challenge to official history writing.

This choice is not only fueled by opposition to official historiography nor caused by a mere aesthetic rejection of mainstream documentaries. It is also, and more importantly, the result of a lack of reliable archival materials on the Mao era. In a sense, the recent surge of independent documentaries on the Mao era is a direct reaction to a phenomenon of state-engineered amnesia, or what Paul Ricœur calls a "manipulated memory."[13] The Chinese project of state legitimization has generated an historical narrative that omits and distorts, while public discourses on the Mao era are limited, which influences collective and individual memories. The risks of repeating past mistakes because of history's gaps are acutely felt by independent filmmakers, and their films aim precisely at countering this form of amnesia. Filming *1966, My Time as a Red Guard* was for Wu Wenguang, who describes himself as "neither a participant, nor a clear-headed external observer,"[14] a way of understanding the Cultural Revolution as "the word Red Guard . . . had fallen into a historical abyss."[15] The documentary is an assemblage of interviews with five former Red Guards and excerpts from propaganda documentaries made during the Cultural Revolution. The film offers a nuanced portrait of Red Guards by inviting mature witnesses to share memories of their youth. Prompted by the filmmaker's questions, the use of personal memorabilia, and the reenactment of political songs, their emotional and corporal memory is reactivated, leading some to betray ambiguous feelings of nostalgia while at the same time expressing distance with the movement.

Since Chinese official history reflects the point of view of the ruling institutions, historians and independent filmmakers alike are confronted with "the fundamental

---

12. A notable exception is Mao Chenyu's 2013 film essay, where the filmmaker's voice acts as the witness's critical account: *I Have What? Chinese Peasant War: The Rhetoric to Justice* (2013, 103 min.).
13. Paul Ricoeur, *La mémoire, l'histoire, l'oubli* (Paris: Seuil, 2000), 216.
14. Wu Wenguang, "DV: Yi ge ren de yingxiang" [DV: Personal videos], in *Jingtou xiang ziji de yanjing yiyang* [The camera lens is like our own eyes], edited by Wu Wenguang (Shanghai: Wenyi chubanshe, 2001), 203.
15. Wu Wenguang, "DV: Yi ge ren de yingxiang," 211.

problem [of] constructing evidence where no documents exist."[16] Indeed, if past propaganda images are sometimes used as a contrast or a contextual aid in documentaries like *1966*, they certainly cannot provide insights on individual, lived experiences of the Mao era. To fill this gap, independent filmmakers produce their own records by interviewing ordinary witnesses of the Mao era and survivors of past political campaigns.

The renewed importance of personal accounts of historical experiences is by no means specific to China. In other national contexts where documentary films have been instrumental in transmitting a popular memory previously kept away from the public sphere,[17] studies in film and media have revealed the importance of ordinary people's memories not only to unveil concealed historical facts, but also to act as an agent of change in contemporary societies.[18]

Oral history has however its own issues, since it is based on subjective—and at times failing or distorted—memories of witnesses who are not experts, just "ordinary people." Because they are not sanctioned by institutions, popular memories also face an issue of legitimacy vis-à-vis mainstream discourses and official history. In China, they may generate distrust as filmmaker Hu Jie points out: some viewers do not accept his documentaries' version of history, especially when the films mainly rely on one witness's account.[19] Independent filmmakers' need to provide evidence and convince viewers has prompted them to find specific filming protocols and editing devices aimed at showing that the filmed testimonies are an authentic account of the subjective experience of the witnesses. This is in a way already addressed by the choice of medium—in contrast with fiction films, documentaries are theorized around scientific and legal concepts placing the audience in the role of "juror of the film as evidence."[20] Many prominent Chinese independent filmmakers such as scholar Ai Xiaoming 艾曉明 refer to documentary films as "evidence brought to the court of society," an idea shared by film historian Shan Wanli on etymological grounds.[21]

---

16. Paula Rabinowitz, "Wreckage upon Wreckage: History, Documentary and the Ruins of Memory," *History and Theory* 32, no. 2 (1993): 129. Expression qualifying Claude Lanzmann's *Shoah* (1985), and quoted here, with all contextual and historiographic specificities aside.
17. See, for instance, Rithy Panh's documentaries or *The Act of Killing* (2012, 115 min.) and *The Look of Silence*, Joshua Oppenheimer and et al. (2014, 103 min.).
18. Leshu Torchin, *Creating the Witness: Documenting Genocide on Film, Video, and the Internet* (Minneapolis and London: University of Minnesota Press, 2012); Joram Ten Brink and Joshua Oppenheimer, eds., *Killer Images: Documentary Film, Memory, and the Performance of Violence* (New York: Columbia University Press, 2013). See also Camille Deprez and Judith Pernin, eds., *Post 1990 Documentary: Reconfiguring Independence* (Edinburgh: Edinburgh University Press, 2015).
19. In an interview conducted in March 2015 in Nanjing.
20. Brian Winston, *Claiming the Real, the Documentary Film Revisited* (London: British Film Institute, 1995), 127–242. Full quote: "The legal tradition casts the documentarist as the witness to the original scene (and even more overtly, the interviewee as witness to data unfilmed or unfilmable). But science casts the documentary film audience as jurors of the film as evidence. Documentary mimesis is grounded in assumptions about the nature of evidence that come from using the camera as a scientific instrument," 141.
21. See interviews transcribed in Judith Pernin, "*Images en mouvement. Pratiques indépendantes du documentaire en Chine* (1990–2010)" (PhD diss., EHESS, 2012), 452–56 and 457–62, respectively.

Within the documentary film form, specific filmic protocols and mise-en-scène can further reinforce the perceived authenticity of the witness' accounts, and therefore legitimate (or not) their discourses. For instance, unveiling the filming process to show filmmaker and film subjects interacting, displaying undisputable documents and additional footage supporting the witness's claim, or revealing a close link between documents and discourses are common strategies to suggest the authenticity of documentary narratives. What editing and filming techniques do independent directors resort to in order to present their historical findings as consistent and truthful? I will investigate this issue by discussing various answers found by independent filmmakers while distinguishing their films according to the sources and materials they are based on: oral testimonies; archival images or objects pertaining to the witness; and written memoirs. This three-part distinction reflects the varying nature of material used and their historical and filmic value for the directors. Oral testimonies are recorded by the filmmakers and are usually the most trusted material, while official documents generally represent the least trusted sources. The editing of these films might therefore indicate a hierarchy between these materials and the filmmaker's distinctive view on history.

The documentaries discussed here have become over the years major references. Made by very different authors, they cover the entire period which saw independent documentaries develop (1992–2015), and are all successful in their own ways in articulating an unofficial historical discourse thanks to the memory of witnesses and compelling cinematographic means.

My analysis starts by examining representative works based on the most common source: oral testimonies. The staging of different types of filmed testimonies will be explored, and their significance regarding unofficial historical discourses will be assessed thanks to various examples.

The subsequent section is dedicated to filmed testimonies combined with the use of visual and personal archives (documents or objects belonging to the witness). *Though I am Gone*[22] gives an account of one of the first murders perpetrated by Red Guards thanks to the vivid testimony of the victim's widower, and rare historical materials.

Finally, I will discuss the relationship between written and filmed testimonies, with an analysis of two films based on or related to memoirs written by former Rightists. *Fengming, A Chinese Memoir*, is Wang Bing's second film. It is a minimal mise-en-scène of the oral testimony performed by a former journalist who was punished during the Anti-Rightist Movement and wrote a noted autobiography. As a counterpoint, Qiu Jiongjiong's recent docufiction, *Mr. Zhang Believes*, will allow a discussion on adapting and recording memoirs.

---

22. On this film, see also Jie Li, "Virtual Museums of Forbidden Memories: Hu Jie's Documentary Films on the Cultural Revolution," *Public Culture* 21/3 (2009): 539–54.

Against Amnesia: Filmed Testimonies, Ordinary Witnesses, and Engaged Filmmakers

All the documentaries included in the filmographies rely on oral testimonies. Far from being unquestionable and transparent, "an audiovisual testimony is always in some sense 'staged,' staged in that the interviewee would not be speaking if not for the occurrence of the filming, and staged in the sense of being put into a scene, a *mise-en-scène*."[23] To understand independent documentaries on the Mao era, it is necessary to analyze the filmed or "staged" testimonies they contain, and what Bhaskar Sarkar and Janet Walker call the "testimonial apparatus."[24] Since the apparatus implies a filming subject, a witness, and an audience, this section focuses on the choice of protagonists, the filming method, and the effect on the audience.

The controlled and elitist nature of official history explains why independent filmmakers have turned their cameras towards "ordinary people," that is, protagonists who do not belong to the leadership class, such as elderly villagers in the Folk Memory Project. Launched by Wu Wenguang and choreographer Wen Hui 文慧 in 2010, this participatory initiative aims at recording the rural population's experience during the Great Famine (1959–1961). The project was prompted by the looming disappearance of ageing witnesses considered to be the last living sources of popular memory on the Great Famine. Indeed, in the Chinese context, filming testimonies of survivors of political violence appears not only crucial to fill the gaps of official history, but also urgent, as witnesses are passing away without transmitting their experience. The Folk Memory Project is formed by filmmakers from the countryside who regularly return to their home villages to conduct interviews with old people. A series of documentary films, interview transcripts, diaries, and theatrical performances have been produced, documenting everyday life in the countryside now and in the past.[25] As most of the old people interviewed were telling their story for the first time[26] and no other documents on these individual cases exist, the collected testimonies constitute an important body of unofficial archives for a local history of the Great Famine.

---

23. See Janet Walker, "Rights and Return: The Perils of Situated Testimony after Katrina," in *Documentary Testimonies: Global Archives of Suffering*, ed. Bhaskar Sarkar and Janet Walker (London and New York: Routledge/AFI Film Readers, 2010), 85.
24. This concept was defined as an adaptation of "cinema studies' psychoanalytically informed 'apparatus theory' so as to conceive of testimony as a kind of ideological, institutional technology . . . that produces the details and emotions of suffering in and through the constitution of the spectator subject." See Bhaskar Sarkar and Janet Walker, "Introduction: Moving Testimonies," *Documentary Testimonies: Global Archives of Suffering*, ed. Bhaskar Sarkar and Janet Walker, 8–14.
25. The project's participants are also involved in actions aimed at alleviating problems such as pollution, poverty, or the lack of cultural activities and basic infrastructures in villages.
26. Except in Luo Bing's films featuring Luo Dingqi, a villager targeted during the Land Reform who wrote several volumes of memoirs. See Judith Pernin, "Performance, Documentary, and the Transmission of Memories of the Great Leap Famine in the Folk Memory Project," *China Perspectives* 4 (2014): 17–27.

Even when protagonists are presented as "ordinary," or happen to be the filmmakers' relatives,[27] their stories are far from anecdotal, as they depict acts of personal resistance, or everyday life during times of crisis. Similarly, independent documentaries feature forgotten individuals who fought for their ideals and are presented as counterexamples of the state and party leadership. In the opening monologue of *Looking for Lin Zhao's Soul*, Hu Jie recalls how he heard about the young Rightist executed during the Cultural Revolution, describing her resistance to the "lies and fears" created by the Anti-Rightist Movement. "Thinking by herself"[28] and keeping up writing even while in jail, she became a role model for him and inspired his subsequent works, including *Spark* (2013, 100 min.). Hu Jie's investigative style and choice of politically sensitive topics are akin to those of filmmakers such as Xie Yihui or Han Song who unveil unknown stories of political violence.[29]

To transmit these narratives, independent filmmakers had to create conditions allowing the filmed subjects to tell their experiences in a personal and subjective way. The Folk Memory Project documentaries precisely illustrate this point. At the outset, the young filmmakers knew close to nothing about the Great Famine, a topic almost absent from their high school history books and seldom discussed at home. Recording old peoples' memories was also no easy task, as their first rounds of films illustrated. The witnesses failed to remember, to express themselves clearly, or they turned to conventional speech patterns that only revealed a persistent ideological domination or a fear of testifying.[30] To circumvent these obstacles and gain the witness's trust, the filmmakers elaborated participative and performative strategies. Many sequences show them interacting with filmed subjects not as interviewers, but rather as relatives or social workers, even using the "performative mode"[31] to speak casually with the witnesses.[32] This stands in stark contrast with many oral-history film projects that rely on a systematic testimony apparatus from which the filmmaker seems "absent," so that the witness takes center stage.[33] Instead, Chinese independent filmmakers use a performative documentary mode that underlines their

---

27. See, for instance, Shen Jie, *Ghost Festival*, 2012, 45 min.; Meng Xiaowei, *The Camera of Socialist Country*, 2013, 56 min., Wu Wenguang, *Treatment*, 2010, 80 min.
28. Quoted from the film's opening monologue.
29. See Xie Yihui, *Rightist Li Shengzhao's hunger report*, 2012, 47 min.; Xie Yihui, *Juvenile Laborers Confined in Dabao*, 2013, 104 min.; Han Song, *Beida Wuyijiu*, 2013, 173 min.
30. As such, these films are vivid illustrations of sociologist Guo Yuhua's writings. See Guo Yuhua, "Xinling de jitihua: Shaanbei Jicun nongye hezuohua de nüxing jiyi" [Psychological collectivization: Cooperative transformation of agriculture in Jicun Village, Northern Shaanxi, as in the memory of women], *Zhongguo Shehui Kexue* 4 (2003): 79–92, available at *Ai Sixiang*, www.aisixiang.com/data/16601.html, and "Koushu lishi: Youguan jiyi yu wangque" [Oral history: On memory and forgetting], available at *Ai Sixiang*, www. aisixiang.com/data/16545.html (both accessed June 10, 2014). English partial translation: "Psychological Collectivization: Cooperative Transformation of Agriculture in Jicun Village, Northern Shaanxi, as in the Memory of Women," *Social Sciences in China* (2003): 48–61.
31. See Nichols, *Introduction to Documentary*.
32. See Pernin, "Performance, Documentary, and the Transmission of Memories of the Great Leap Famine in the Folk Memory Project."
33. See, for instance, Noah Shenker, *Reframing Holocaust Testimony* (Bloomington: Indiana University Press, 2015), 276.

presence in the testimony apparatus. Hu Jie's monologue at the outset of *Looking for Lin Zhao's Soul* and the wobbly images betraying his reactions are signs indicating his existence behind the camera. The filmmaker's personal and emotional engagement in the testimony apparatus means in most cases his endorsement of the witness's narrative. During the shooting process, many independent filmmakers form a bond with the protagonists, allowing them to behave spontaneously, which often means that they behave more emotionally as well. Filmed subjects are often seen bursting out in anger, fighting back tears, or expressing resentment. These marks of emotions, overt or subtle, play an important role in persuading the filmmaker and ultimately the audience of the testimony's authenticity. By contrast, the filmmaker's perceived absence from the testimonial apparatus and lack of engagement with the protagonist might indicate his or her distrust. To take an example from a "memory film" in the Cambodian context, in *Duch, Master of the Forges of Hell* (2012), Rithy Panh's testimonial apparatus is strikingly distanced and cold. The former director of the Security Prison 21 (S21) under the Khmer Rouge regime, Duch is first introduced to the viewer from behind the bars of the prison cell where he is awaiting trial. His narrative is not openly contradicted by the interviewer whose voice remains unheard throughout the film. Ultimately, the filmmaker's lack of empathy leads Duch to show signs of embarrassment and even to contradict himself, hence destroying his testimony's truth-value. Unlike this example, Chinese independent documentaries strive to demonstrate the authenticity of witness accounts by revealing the filmmaker's engagement in the testimonial apparatus. Visibly affected by "ordinary people's" memories of hardships during the Mao era, the filmmakers turn their emotional narratives into compelling testimonies for the audience too.

Testimonies, Archives, and Personal Memorabilia

Although independent testimonies are clearly considered by filmmakers as the most important historical material, objects, official images, and documents kept by protagonists as personal archives may play important roles too. While these various materials are all displayed for their historical and authenticating value, their use varies from film to film according to their status vis-à-vis official history. For instance, in *1966, My Time as a Red Guard*, Wu Wenguang uses propaganda images for expressive rather than merely illustrative or authenticating purposes. The film's fourth chapter is comprised of clips from the 1966 eight-part newsreels series *Chairman Mao Receives the Red Guards for the x time* (Mao Zhuxi di x ci jiejian Hongweibing) alternating with contemporary talking-head interviews with former participants. The faces of anonymous young Red Guards alternate with those of adult witnesses, most of whom are in their mid-forties, testifying about their experience. When the witnesses remember the August 1966 "meetings" with Mao on Tiananmen Square, they become increasingly emotional and begin using the slogans and gestures of their youth, in a faint echo to the group hysteria seen in the archival footage. The film's binary opposition between propaganda images and contemporary testimonies paints a nuanced portrait of aging activists who hold ambiguous views of their past.

The usual function of archive images and documents—representing the past in the contemporary context of the film, and giving historical weight to personal narratives—may also be complicated by their symbolic value as another film demonstrates.

Though I am Gone reveals how teacher and vice-principal Bian Zhongyun 卞仲耘 was beaten to death by high school students at the outset of the Cultural Revolution. Hu Jie's film combines two documentary efforts: the filmmaker's own footage and Wang Jingyao's (Bian Zhongyun's widower) photographic documentation of his late wife's murder. Hu Jie's investigation is based on Wang Jingyao's personal photographic archives and other material evidence, as well as on interviews with witnesses. This double documentary structure, exposed in the fast-paced editing of the opening sequence, is meant to strengthen the film's historical demonstration. Throughout the film, the intricate relationship between the two documentary efforts is consciously exposed for authenticating purposes. For instance, when Wang Jingyao guides Hu Jie through the school where Bian Zhongyun was beaten to death, Hu Jie's camera pans from Wang Jingyao's analog printed images to their site of origin, while Wang Jingyao's voice reconstitutes the crime scene on- and off-screen, indicating also how he took the pictures. In the editing of the sequence, the material quality of the photographs is emphasized by the camera's constant circulation between the photo albums, Wang Jingyao's hands pointing at them, and the very building in which they were shot. These situated testimonies identify the crime scene on the pictures with the site where the documentary is shot, and clearly present Wang Jingyao's photos as evidence.

This editing mode is related to Hu Jie's concern with proving the truthfulness of unofficial history to audiences primarily exposed to official narratives. The film's authenticating effort is further reinforced in the last part, shot in Wang Jingyao's apartment, as the old man decides to show Hu Jie the last material traces of his wife. In a room decorated with reproductions of famous Renaissance artworks, Wang Jingyao opens a suitcase and displays on the bed Bian Zhongyun's clothes and the bandages enveloping her body on her last day. While Wang Jingyao keeps talking on- and off-screen, the viewer is exposed alternatively to individual and family portraits of Bian Zhongyun, Wang Jingyao's photographic proofs, reproductions of artworks, and finally, to the traces on the fabric. For Wang Jingyao and Hu Jie, the final items constitute irrefutable evidence, since the painted insults, blood, and bodily fluid still visible on the stiffened pieces of fabric are a direct imprint of the victim's body and testify to the condition of her death with even more authority than indexical photographic evidence. But rather than mere judicial proofs, the mise-en-scène of the objects evokes the conditions of visibility of relics,[34] as Bian Zhongyun's clothes are preserved and kept away from the profane. Thanks to the reproducing ability of digital film, the stained clothes proving the "unique presence" of Bian Zhongyun "authenticated by contact" with her body, become a "disseminated presence, able to dispense her power everywhere."[35] If the personal archives and relics are integrated in the movie for their authenticating power, their staging and the Christian iconography reinforce the symbolical value of Bian Zhongyun's death, expressing Hu Jie and Wang Jingyao's critical stance on the Cultural Revolution. As the documentary ends on this visual memorial to Bian Zhongyun, Wang Jingyao's late wife becomes a martyr of communism, and the unofficial memories of "ordinary people" attain a status of a "sacred" yet secular historical truth.[36]

While in most independent documentaries personal archives are routinely used to prove unofficial narratives, in this film, they also hold the "sacred" qualities of relics. Besides proving Bian Zhongyun's ordeal, they commemorate a victim incarnating humanistic values opposed to the Cultural Revolution.

Documentary Staging and Adaptation of Memoirs

While the use of archives adds a symbolic layer or helps authenticate oral testimonies, further analytic complications arise when the filmed witnesses have already written memoirs on their experience. In this case, the documentary does not seem to be telling "anything new" that the text didn't previously reveal. What is then the role of filmic renditions of memoirs? The relation between these texts and their documentaries will be discussed in the two analyses below.

Wang Bing's *Fengming: A Chinese memoir* can be considered as a "documentary adaptation" of He Fengming's memoirs published in 2001,[37] in which she recalls her experience of the Anti-Rightist Movement. As young journalists based in Lanzhou during the Hundred Flowers campaign, He Fengming and her husband earnestly took part in the campaign only to find themselves harassed, punished, and then sent to two separate camps. There, they endured incessant labor and starvation, maintaining sporadic contact by correspondence. When He Fengming was finally allowed a conjugal visit in the early 1960s, she found out her husband had died a week before she arrived at his camp. Later, her rightist label continued to impede her career and basic survival, especially during the Cultural Revolution.

---

34. The editing alternating between Bian Zhongyun's photographic portraits and her "relics" evokes the Turin Shroud, an object bearing qualities pertaining to both figurative and imprinted artifacts. On imprints, see Georges Didi-Huberman, *La Ressemblance par contact* (Paris: Éditions de Minuit, 2008), 77.
35. Didi-Huberman, *La Ressemblance par contact*, 90.
36. Wang Jingyao claims that his "personal tragedy carries a more general significance." He adds that his interest in Christianity does not reflect a religious faith, but rather, a set of common values of "love and humanism."
37. He Fengming, *Jingli: Wo de 1957 nian* [My experience of 1957] (Lanzhou: Dunhuang wenyi chubanshe, 2001).

Interestingly, her tragic story had already been adapted by writer Yang Xianhui in a collection of novellas inspired by interviews with camp survivors.[38] This book was in turn adapted by Wang Bing in *The Ditch*, a neorealist fiction film taking place in Jiabiangou camp and featuring non-professional actors playing the role of prisoners with a striking form of distancing.[39] He Fengming's story has therefore circulated in various forms between her own memoirs, Yang Xianhui's book, and Wang Bing's two films, and one could wonder why this narrative remained significant for these different authors. Perhaps the first rendering of He Fengming's memoirs in a documentary form is the most intriguing of all, since it seems to be the closest to the original text, without however mentioning the existence of the book. I will focus on untangling the formal attributes of this documentary to reveal its specific contribution in transmitting He Fengming's story.

Like other documentaries made by Wang Bing,[40] *Fengming* is both a cinematographic achievement in itself, and a preparation to the fictional adaption of Yang Xianhui's book in *The Ditch*. As "research material," *Fengming* appears to be a direct recording characterized by temporal and spatial unity. In great contrast with other documentaries, history is only narrated by a single witness, without any additional archive footage or documents. However, this apparent simplicity hides a complex work of historical reconstitution and documentary mise-en-scène.

Wang Bing's editing creates the illusion of a continuous shooting process carried out over a whole night, by limiting cuts and restricting the variation of frames. At the same time, when He Fengming interrupts her narrative to go to the toilet, blow her nose, or switch on the lights, Wang Bing decides to keep filming. These mundane actions seem at first incongruous compared to the gravity of her testimony, but they reinforce the apparent continuity of the interview process, and therefore its perceived authenticity. Locating the testimony apparatus in He Fengming's very ordinary living room also conceals the staging of a testimony so crucial that it should "never" be interrupted, except for natural necessities. In this aesthetic framework, the slight variations of scales and angles, as well as two short inserts showing windows at sunset and sunrise are as much an attempt to recreate the supposed continuous chronological order of the shooting, as they are further evidence of interruptions.

Although orally communicated, He Fengming's memories are visibly based on a prior written account: she expresses herself with a consistency and an accuracy rarely seen in spontaneous testimonies.[41] Her attitude remains extremely stoic throughout the film, despite the tragic nature of her story. Wang Bing's minimal

---

38. Yang Xianhui, *Gaobie jiabiangou* [Farewell Jiabiangou] (Shanghai: Wenyi chubanshe, 2003), 549.
39. See Sebastian Veg, "The Limits of Representation, Wang Bing's Labor Camp Films," *Journal of Chinese Cinemas* 6, no. 2, (2012): 173–87. He Fengming's distanced personal account in the documentary has perhaps influenced the acting in *The Ditch*.
40. See Judith Pernin, "La persistance de la misère: *Les Trois sœurs du Yunnan* et *L'Homme sans nom*, études cinématographiques de Wang Bing," *Études Chinoises* 34-1 (2015): 45–72.
41. Compare, for instance, with the uncertainty of villagers in the Folk Memory Project.

filming style parallels the witness's contained attitude: his camera is kept at a certain distance from the protagonist during the testimony, briefly framing her up to the chest and shoulder during the most emotional anecdote, when she relates the moment that she learned that her husband died a week before her visit. Wang Bing's distancing is in tune with He Fengming's controlled oral performance that clearly reveals her memoir. However, the documentary does not merely consist in re-filming He Fengming's text. The film's apparent continuity heightens the testimony's perceived authenticity, while the ordinary film setting suggests that her painful experience of political violence wasn't unique. Indeed, in the epilogue she is seen answering a phone call from a fellow survivor, which highlights both that she is part of a group of survivors, and that her activities today are frequently linked to her experience in 1957.

Whereas He Fengming's memoirs are the unnamed source of Wang Bing's film, *Mr. Zhang Believes*[42] is more explicitly recognized as an adaptation. This unconventional docufiction draws from the autobiography of Zhang Xianchi 張先痴, a former rightist who spent over two decades in political camps. The title of the book, *China Gulag*,[43] is an explicit reference to Solzhenitsyn's *Gulag Archipelago*. Interestingly, *China Gulag* also proved inspiring to more than one filmmaker, as Hu Jie also shot a short documentary on the topic.[44]

Mr. Zhang Believes is Qiu Jiongjiong's attempts to express Zhang Xianchi's ironical conclusion on his experience as a political prisoner. Born in a wealthy family connected to the Kuomintang, Zhang Xianchi was a progressive student and a communist as a young man, decidedly opposed to his father's politics and lifestyle. Nevertheless, he was labeled a rightist because of his family background and the betrayal of friends and fellow writers. After two decades in the camps he definitely turned his back on his communist ideals, and became a "real rightist."

Mr. Zhang Believes roughly follows the chronological order of Zhang Xianchi's youth until his imprisonment. However, Qiu Jiongjiong's editing makes frequent transitions between various filmic materials: interviews, fictional adaptations of the autobiography, and other staged scenes conveying Zhang Xianchi's most intimate memories, as well as surreal sequences stemming from Qiu Jiongjiong's imagination. This complex movie would require more elaboration than this chapter allows. For the sake of clarity, I will focus on the relation between the original text, the staged sequences, and the interviews to discuss the use of textual and verbal sources.

---

42. This discussion is based on the director's cut (*Betrayal, the Story of Mr. Zhang* [*Chi*, 2014, 270 min.]). A shorter international version called *Mr. Zhang Believes* (2015, 135 min.) was screened at the Festival del Film Locarno in August 2015.
43. Zhang Xianchi, *Gelagu yishi* [Galug Anecdotes] (New York; Taipei: Fellow Press, 2007) was published in the United States and in Taiwan and circulates also on the internet. According to conversations with Qiu Jiongjiong in August 2014 in Beijing, the filmmaker first went to interview Zhang who gave him his book. After reading it, Qiu Jiongjiong promptly wrote a script based on the memoir and his interviews.
44. Hu Jie, *Gelagu zhi shu*, 2013, 38 min. Formally, this short is similar to *Though I am Gone*, with Zhang Xianchi's book in the role of Wang Jingyao's photographs, and his past belongings displayed as authenticating personal archives.

Strictly speaking, the film's documentary footage consists of the protagonist's testimony shot in Zhang Xianchi's home, in an informal setting allowing the old man to digress often and to speak subjectively rather than factually about his experience.[45] Shot from behind the interviewers, the black and white images are often half obstructed by curtains or other domestic elements, emphasizing the ordinary setting of the testimony apparatus, as well as distance with the filmed subject. But this mise-en-scène does not have the same effect as in *Fengming*. Here, the mundane setting highlights Zhang Xianchi's ironical distance with his personal tragedy and Qiu Jiongjiong's casual and at times provocative attitude towards the old man.

Zhang Xianchi's childhood and youth are depicted in staged sequences with two actors (a child and a young adult), and are adapted from his memoirs, or inspired by conversations between Qiu Jiongjiong, Zhang Xianchi, and Yang Wenting. Interestingly, these conversations were allegedly recorded by chance when the camera was supposed to be off.[46] This "stolen" material, whether staged or in a documentary form, expresses the most intimate stories, unveiling Zhang Xianchi's sentimental life and childhood in details that do not appear as such in his memoirs. The fictional sequences are shot on a Chinese opera stage located on a parking lot owned by one of Qiu Jiongjiong's relatives.[47] On this cheap and secretive film set, Qiu Jiongjiong manages to reconstitute Zhang Xianchi's Nanjing childhood home and various other places including exterior settings such as city streets and battlefields. Despite its makeshift and theatrical quality, the film set nonetheless renders vividly the atmosphere of Republican China and after, thanks to various characters such as Zhang Xianchi's childhood Japanese driver whose car is a painted replica on a wall.[48]

Qiu Jiongjiong's use of theatrical props in the fictional scenes reveals his interest in using a surrealist aesthetics to reconstitute past memories. One sequence shows Zhang Xianchi as a child reading a novel in a public library, while a cohort of camp prisoners, including himself as a young adult in the 1950s, enters the frame, silently warning him about his fate. Anachronisms and the splitting of characters into several actors are used in other surreal sequences, such as the prologue featuring several political figures and thinkers. Marx and Engels, Lenin, Stalin, and then Mao Zedong are discussing in the afterworld the necessity of violence to achieve revolution. Mao is the most unabashedly cruel of all, which suggests that this point will be illustrated later. Indeed, at the climax of the movie, Mao Zedong reappears, this time played by three different actors sharing the same filmic space, an empty

---

45. Another important documentary scene (in color this time) shows Zhang Xianchi and other former rightists reading the official texts and editorials causing their persecution.
46. See also this interview by Tang Zehui, "Ruhe Yizhuangyixie de jiang yi ge lao youpai de gushi?" [How to tell the story of an old rightist with both gravity and humor?], *Niuyue shibao Guoji shenghuo*, May 22, 2014, last accessed November 29, 2014, http://cn.tmagazine.com/film-tv/20140522/tc22chi/zh-hant/.
47. Qiu Jiongjiong comes from a family of Sichuan opera artists, and he is also a painter.
48. Another sequence describes his duties as a PLA soldier posted in a Yi minority village through a series of tableaux reminiscent of the mise-en-scène of silent film.

circus or a theater stage. As in the prologue, the actors are not an embodiment of Mao. Rather, they are "actors playing actors playing Mao,"[49] and their role is to caricature three distinct facets of the chairman. Later in the sequence, the filmmaker himself plays a short cameo role in the theater backstage area. While one of the actors playing Mao Zedong is putting makeup on his face, Qiu Jiongjiong, dressed in his everyday clothes, asks him about the meaning of the "Five Black Categories" and of "class origins." The director is quickly arrested and taken away by a group of soldiers, reminding us of the control over historical narratives, and perhaps also pointing at the risks of independent filmmaking.[50]

In *Mr. Zhang Believes*, the protagonist's memoirs have inspired the film script, and also the voice-over, which consists of direct quotes from the book, read by Qiu Jiongjiong in the first person. The interviews recorded by Qiu Jiongjiong provide yet another source of information complementing the autobiography without any overlapping, since they slightly differ both in terms of content and tone. Since Zhang Xianchi's memories are documented twice by the adaptation of the memoirs and by Qiu Jiongjiong's interviews, the whole film presents itself as a montage of mutually reinforcing cross-references. This strong backing allowed the filmmaker to choose an overtly unrealistic treatment for his fictional adaptation. The fictionalized scenes are clearly presented as playful reconstitutions, marking a reflexive and often comical distance with the historical narrative.

Qiu Jiongjiong's use of highly performative and theatrical means is of course in sharp contrast with the filmic treatment of memories in the above documentaries in which the filmmakers strive to legitimize unofficial narratives. Authenticating strategies are nonetheless present in *Mr. Zhang Believes*, even though, beside those contained in the documentary footage, they are used in a more playful way, and for expressive purposes. Acknowledging that staged scenes, especially the surreal ones, are historical fantasies gives the whole film an ironic tone. China's political past is depicted as a cruel circus where idealism is doomed. In this sense, archival photographs and objects, fake (on stage) or real (in the interviews), are not used for their indexical and authenticating power only, unlike in Hu Jie's films.

While documented and archival sources (personal items, memoirs, and direct testimonies) form the main material of the historical narrative contained in Chinese independent documentaries, forged images and artifacts can be summoned in these films to address, underline, or allude to a lack. Fake documents and theatrical props point to the lack of transmission of personal narratives of historical experiences. Nevertheless, the forgery is comically acknowledged, which helps to distinguish these props from historical items providing legitimate unofficial narratives.

---

49. Tang Zehui, "Ruhe Yizhuangyixie de jiang yi ge lao youpai de gushi?"
50. The cast includes independent filmmakers and/or film festival organizers, suggesting an analogy with 1950s intellectuals.

Conclusion

This overview of the various ways independent filmmakers engage with the Mao era has foregrounded the specificity and difficulties of working in a context of monopoly of official history over the plurality of personal memories. Because they aim at revealing untold stories, Chinese independent filmmakers have mainly focused on interviewing ordinary people and survivors of political violence. As a result, their films collect suppressed or forgotten memories and narratives seldom featured in mainstream media. By doing so, they challenge official history in its approach, method and narrative content.

To film the memory of individuals whose experience was never recorded, these filmmakers set out to work as independents, engaging affectively and personally with witnesses, and using personal items and archival documents to trigger remembrance and emotions. Their documentaries help reconstruct the struggles of important yet forgotten figures persecuted during the Mao era.

Because the unofficial status of their films might undermine their truth claim, independent filmmakers seek to demonstrate that they convey an authentic expression of the witness's experience of the Mao era. To do so, they use an array of strategies during the shooting and at the post-production stage. Many will emphasize the organic link between the film and its sources—written memoirs, archives, testimonies, and personal memorabilia—as in the case of Hu Jie's films, and to a certain extent, in Qiu Jiongjiong's docufiction. Most rely on a set of editing devices and a documentary mise-en-scène that unveil or recreate the filming conditions, show the interactions between witness and interviewer, and articulate these narratives in an emotional and therefore compelling manner (Folk Memory Project). The staging of testimonies reinforces their perceived authenticity by revealing a personal experience whose emotional content impacts the filmmakers and thus is able to be affectively transmitted to an audience (*Fengming*).

In a context of monopoly over history and distrust for historical narratives, it is not surprising that filmmakers work in series, or engage in participative projects, and that their films overlap and reference each other as well as literary works. More than just indicating shared interests across the literary and filmic field, the intricate relations between these works is further evidence of the perceived necessity of validating unofficial narratives by accumulation and cross-referencing. This is obvious in the method of some of the filmmakers: Hu Jie includes multiple interviews with various witnesses, choosing the most authoritative ones (usually, footage featuring direct witnesses; emotional testimonies; images containing material evidence such as archival objects, letters, and so on). The Folk Memory Project also relies on this strategy of authentication by accumulation of testimonies presented as evidence, ranging from transcribed interviews, diaries and personal notes written by the filmmakers, to documentary films and photographs. This accumulation of witness accounts and their artistic reenactments in theatrical performances produce a "body of evidence"[51] or unofficial archives that are not only aimed at preserving and transmitting the local experiences of rural populations during the famine, but also at mutually legitimizing themselves thanks to their great number.

Recording personal memories and translating them into various art forms is also a way of exorcising the historical traumas and political suffering of "ordinary witnesses." These documentary depictions seek to repair historical damage, and some give the filmed protagonists a heroic status on par with other figures favored by official history.

This process of rewriting history from a personal perspective is grounded in a critical view of the past and of the legacies of the Mao era as they manifest themselves today. This critique encompasses the official history's disregard for experiences of political suffering. Acknowledging the heavy toll of political history on ordinary people's lives, these filmmakers attempt to alleviate it to some extent, by recording their plight, giving them a space to express their grief and remember their life. This process often starts by turning the gaze towards family members and relatives, and other neglected witnesses of history.

An active approach to repairing the injustices of history is at play in the Folk Memory Project when participants film the whole process of finding out the names of famine victims in each village, in order to erect memorial stones commemorating them. Other filmmakers engage in a similar memorial endeavor. Hu Jie's *Though I am Gone*, discussed earlier, as well as his more recent *Spark*[52] both include sequences aimed at commemorating victims of political movements. *Spark* even ends with a list of names, a device that almost has become a trope of "activist" documentaries and videos on recent events.[53] The independent filmmakers' attempts at narrating a subjective history of the Mao era seem to be as much a "historiographic effort, as it is a grieving process . . . both for the collective memory and the individual memory."[54]

Bibliography

Boyle, Deirdre. "Trauma, Memory, Documentary, Re-enactment in Two Films by Rithy Panh (Cambodia) and Garin Nugroho (Indonesia)." In *Documentary Testimonies: Global Archives of Suffering*, edited by Bhaskar Sarkar and Janet Walker, 155–72. London and New York: Routledge/AFI Film Readers, 2010.

Cuau, Bernard. "Le lieu et la parole, Interview des Cahiers." In *Au sujet de Shoah: le film de Claude Lanzmann*, edited by Bernard Cuau, 292–99. Paris: Belin, 1990.

---

51. See Bhaskar Sarkar and Janet Walker, "Introduction: Moving Testimonies," in *Documentary Testimonies: Global Archives of Suffering*, ed. Bhaskar Sarkar and Janet Walker, 15.
52. Hu Jie, *Spark* 2013, 100 min.
53. Such as the 2008 Sichuan earthquake. See Ai Weiwei, *4851*, 2009, 87 min.
54. Paul Ricoeur, "Histoire et mémoire," in *De L'histoire au cinéma*, ed. Antoine de Baecque and Christian Delage, (Paris: Éditions Complexe, 1998), 23.

Deprez, Camille and Pernin, Judith, eds. *Post 1990 Documentary: Reconfiguring Independence*. Edinburgh: Edinburgh University Press, 2015.
Didi-Huberman, Georges. *La Ressemblance par contact*. Paris: Éditions de Minuit, 2008.
Gao, Zipeng 高子鵬. *Shanghai Qingnian Guanying Shouce* 上海青年觀影手冊 [A handbook to the documentary *Shanghai Youth*]. Self-published, 2015.
Guo, Yuhua 郭于華. "Psychological Collectivization: Cooperative Transformation of Agriculture in Jicun Village, Northern Shaanxi, as in the Memory of Women." *Social Sciences in China* (2003): 48–61.
Guo, Yuhua 郭于華. "Xinling de jitihua: Shaanbei yicun nongye hezuohua de nüxing jiyi" 心靈的集體化：陝北驥村農業合作化的女性記憶 [Psychological collectivization: Cooperative transformation of agriculture in Jicun Village, Northern Shaanxi, as in the memory of women], *Zhongguo Shehui Kexue* 4 (2003): 79–92. Accessed June 10, 2014. http://www.aisixiang.com/data/16601.html.
He, Fengming 和鳳鳴. *Jingli: Wo de 1957 nian* 經歷：我的1957年 [My experience of 1957]. Lanzhou : Dunhuang wenyi chubanshe, 2001.
Li, Jie. "Virtual Museums of Forbidden Memories: Hu Jie's Documentary Films on the Cultural Revolution." *Public Culture* 21/3 (2009): 539–54.
Nichols, Bill. *Introduction to Documentary*. Bloomington: Indiana University Press, 2010.
Pernin, Judith. "*Images en mouvement. Pratiques indépendantes du documentaire en Chine (1990–2010)*." PhD diss. EHESS, 2012.
Pernin, Judith. *Pratiques indépendantes du documentaire en Chine. Histoire, esthétique et discours visuels (1990–2010)*. Rennes: Presses universitaires de Rennes, 2015.
Pernin, Judith. "Independent Documentaries and Online Uses in China: From Cinephilia to Activism." In *Post-1990 Documentary: Reconfiguring Independence*, edited by Camille Deprez and Judith Pernin, 233–47. Edinburgh: Edinburgh University Press, 2015.
Pernin, Judith. "La persistance de la misère: *Les Trois sœurs du Yunnan* et *L'Homme sans nom*, études cinématographiques de Wang Bing." *Études Chinoises* 34–1 (2015): 45–72.
Pernin, Judith. "Performance, Documentary, and the Transmission of Memories of the Great Leap Famine in the Folk Memory Project." *China Perspectives* 4 (2014): 17–27.
Rabinowitz, Paula. "Wreckage upon Wreckage: History, Documentary and the Ruins of Memory." *History and Theory* 32, no. 2 (1993): 119–37.
Ricoeur, Paul. "Histoire et mémoire." In *De L'histoire au cinéma*, edited by Antoine de Baecque and Christian Delage, 17–28. Paris: Éditions Complexe, 1998.
Ricoeur, Paul. *La Mémoire, l'histoire, l'oubli*. Paris: Seuil, 2000.
Sarkar, Bhaskar, and Walker, Janet. "Introduction: Moving Testimonies." In *Documentary Testimonies: Global Archives of Suffering*, edited by Bhaskar Sarkar and Janet Walker, 8–14. London and New York: Routledge/AFI Film Readers, 2010.
Shenker, Noah. *Reframing Holocaust Testimony*. Bloomington: Indiana University Press, 2015.
Tang, Zehui 唐澤慧. "Ruhe Yizhuangyixie de jiang yi ge lao youpai de gushi?" 如何亦莊亦諧地講一個老右派的故事？ [How to tell the story of an old rightist with both gravity and humor?], *Niuyue shibao Guoji shenghuo*, May 22, 2014. Accessed November 29, 2014. http://cn.tmagazine.com/film-tv/20140522/tc22chi/zh-hant.
Ten Brink, Joram, and Oppenheimer, Joshua, eds. *Killer Images: Documentary Film, Memory, and the Performance of Violence*. New York: Columbia University Press, 2013.

Torchin, Leshu. *Creating the Witness: Documenting Genocide on Film, Video, and the Internet.* Minneapolis and London: University of Minnesota Press, 2012.

Veg, Sebastian. "The Limits of Representation, Wang Bing's Labor Camp Films." *Journal of Chinese Cinemas* 6, no. 2 (2012): 173–87.

Walker, Janet. "Rights and Return: The Perils of Situated Testimony after Katrina." In *Documentary Testimonies: Global Archives of Suffering*, edited by Bhaskar Sarkar and Janet Walker, 76–94. London and New York: Routledge/AFI Film Readers, 2010.

Wang, Qi. *Memory, Subjectivity and Independent Chinese Cinema.* Edinburgh: Edinburgh University Press, 2014.

Winston, Brian. *Claiming the Real, the Documentary Film Revisited.* London: British Film Institute, 1995.

Wu, Wenguang 吳文光. "DV: Yi ge ren de yingxiang" DV 一個人的影像 [DV: Personal videos]. In *Jingtou xiang ziji de yanjing yiyang* 鏡頭像自己的眼睛一樣 [The camera lens is like our own eyes], edited by Wu Wenguang, 200–205. Shanghai: Wenyi chubanshe, 2001.

Yang, Guobin. "China's Zhiqing Generation: Nostalgia, Identity, and Cultural Resistance in the 1990s." *Modern China* 29, no. 3 (2003): 267–96.

Yang, Xianhui 楊顯惠. *Gaobie jiabiangou* 告別夾邊溝 [Farewell Jiabiangou]. Shanghai: Wenyi chubanshe, 2003.

Zhang, Xianchi 張先痴. *Gelagu yishi* 格拉古軼事 [Galug anecdotes]. New York; Taipei: Fellow Press, 2007.

Zhuang, Jiayun. "Remembering and Reenacting Hunger: Caochangdi Workstation's Minjian Memory Project." *The Drama Review* 58, no. 1 (2014): 118–40.

Independent Documentaries on the Mao era (1992–2015)

General filmography

Compiled by author and date

Ai Xiaoming 艾曉明, Hu Jie 胡杰, *Painting for the Revolution*, Wei Geming Huahua 為革命畫畫, 2005, 56 min.

Cao Diao 曹雕, *Making friends with Mr. Zhang*, He Zhang Laoshi zuo pengyou 和張老師做朋友, 2015, 65 min.

Gao Zipeng 高子鵬, Wu Meng 吳夢, *Shanghai Youth*, Shanghai Qingnian 上海青年, 2015, 480 min.

Gu Tao 顧桃, Zhou Yu 周宇, *The Eclipse of the Gods / The Opaque God*, Shen Yi 神翳, 2011, 92 min.

Gui Shuzhong 鬼叔中, *To Relive*, Luopan jing 羅盤經, 2012, 109 min.

Han Song 韓松, *Beida Wuyijiu*, Beida Wuyijiu 北大五一九, 2013, 173 min.

Hu Jie 胡杰, *Looking For Lin Zhao's Soul*, Xunzhao Lin Zhao De Linghun 尋找林昭的靈魂, 2005, 90 min.

Hu Jie 胡杰, *Wo sui siqu* 我雖死去, 2006, 70 min.

Hu Jie 胡杰, *The East Wind State Farm*, Guoying dong feng nongchang 國營東風農場, 2009, 104 min.

Hu Jie 胡杰, *My Mother Wang Peiying*, Wo de muqin Wang Peiying 我的母親王佩英, 2011, 70 min.
Hu Jie 胡杰, *Spark*, Xinghuo 星火, 2013, 100 min.
Hu Jie 胡杰, *The Book of Gelagu*, Gelagu zhi shu 格拉古之書, 2013, 38 min.
Hu Jie 胡杰, Ai Xiaoming 艾曉明, *Red Art*, Hongse Meishu 紅色美術, 2007, 70 min.
Huang Wenhai 黃文海, *We*, Women 我們, 2008, 102 min.
Lin Xin 林鑫, *San Li Dong*, San Li Dong 三里洞, 2006, 172 min.
Liu Wei 劉偉, *The Sacrifice*, Xisheng 犧牲, 2012, 62 min.
Ma Zhandong 馬占東, *Hai shi wan*, Haishiwan 海石灣, 2011, 52 min.
Mao Chenyu 毛晨雨, *I Have What? Chinese Peasant War: The Rhetoric to Justice*, Yongyou, xin Zhongguo nongmin zhanzheng: xiucixue de zhengyi 擁有，新中國農民戰爭：修辭學的正義, 2013, 103 min.
Meng Xiaowei 孟小為, *The Camera of Socialist Country*, Xiongyali zhaoxiangji 匈牙利照相機, 2013, 56 min.
Peng Xiaolian 彭小蓮, Louisa Wei 魏時煜, *Storm Under The Sun*, Hong Ri Fengbao 紅日風暴, 2009, 137 min.
Qiu Jiongjiong 邱炯炯, *My Mother's Rhapsody*, Xuantang xianhua lu 萱堂閑話錄, 2011, 106 min.
Saipulla Mutallip, *Qarangghu Tagh: The Villages Afar*, Heishan: Yaoyuan de cunzhuang 黑山：遙遠的村莊, 2014, 90 min.
Shen Jie 沈潔, *Ghost Festival*, Gui jie 鬼節, 2012, 45 min.
Shu Haolun 舒浩侖, *Nostalgia*, Xiangchou 鄉愁, 2005, 70 min.
SWYC (The Structure, Wave, Youth, Cinema Experimental Group) 結構、浪潮、青年、電影實驗小組, *I Graduated!*, Wo Biye le 我畢業了, 1992, 64 min.
Wang Bing 王兵, *Fengming, A Chinese Memoir*, He Fengming 和鳳鳴, 2007, 186 min.
Wang Yunlong 王雲龍, *Comrades in arms*, Zhanyou 戰友, 2011, 90 min.
Wang Yunlong 王雲龍, *The Spokesman*, Daiyanren 代言人, 2013, 69 min.
Wang Yunlong 王雲龍, Han Yi 韓翊, *To Justify Bu Qinfu*, Huan Bu Qinfu yi meili 還卜琴父以美麗, 2011, 92 min.
Wu Wenguang 吳文光, *1966, My Time as a Red Guard*, 1966 nian, Wo de Hongweibing Shidai 1966年，我的紅衛兵時代, 1992, 165 min.
Wu Wenguang 吳文光, *Treatment*, Zhiliao 治療, 2010, 80 min.
Xie Yihui 謝貽卉, *Rightist Li Shengzhao's Hunger Report*, Youpai Li Shengzhao de ji'e baogao 右派李盛照的飢餓報告, 2012, 47 min.
Xie Yihui 謝貽卉, *Juvenile Laborers Confined in Dabao*, Dabao xiao laojiao 大堡小勞教, 2013, 104 min.
Xu Tong 徐童, *Shattered*, Lao Tang tou 老唐頭, 2011, 100 min.
Xu Xin 徐辛, *Karamay*, Kelamayi 克拉瑪依, 2010, 356 min.
Xu Xin 徐辛, *Pathway*, Daolu 道路, 2012, 113 min.
Xu Xing 徐星, *A Chronical of my Cultural Revolution*, Wo de Wenge biannianshi 我的文革編年史, 2007, 80 min.
Xu Xing 徐星, *Zuixing zhaiyao*, Zuixing zhaiyao 罪行摘要, 2013, 120 min.
Zhang Dali 張大力, *Looking For The Lost Veterans Of 1979 / My 1979*, Xunzhao 79 Yue Zhan Xiaoshi De Lao Bing / Wo De 1979 尋找79越戰消逝的老兵／我的1979, 2008, 180 min.
Zhang Ke 張珂, *Youth Cemetery*, Qingchun muyuan 青春墓園, 2005, 23 min.
Zhang Min 張民, *My Whole Life*, Wo zhe yi beizi 我這一輩子, 2007, 100 min.

Judith Pernin 159

Zhang Ming 章明, *60*, Liu shi 60, 2009, 184 min.
Zhong Jian 種鍵, *Try to remember?*, 2005, 60 min.
Zhu Rikun, *The Dossier*, Dang'an 檔案, 2014, 128 min.

Folk Memory Project

Filmography (2010–2015) by author and date

Compiled with the help of Caochangdi Workstation's artists in residence.

Guo Rui 郭睿, *Grandfather, Great Famine*, Yeye de jihuang 爺爺的飢荒, 2013, 75 min.
Guo Rui 郭睿, *The Rivers and Sisterhood*, Heliu he nüren de yinchang 河流與女人的吟唱, 2014, 72 min.
Hu Tao 胡濤, *Old People and My Village*, Shan Ga La 山旮旯, 2013, 70 min.
Jia Nannan 賈楠楠, *My Grandpa's Winter*, Jia Fukui de dongtian 賈夫奎的冬天, 2011, 30 min.
Jia Zhitan 賈之坦, *Revolution in Baiyun Village*, Yi da san fan zai baiyun "一打三反"在白雲, 2012, 80 min.
Jia Zhitan 賈之坦, *I Want to Be a People's Representative*, Wo yao dang renmin daibiao 我要當人民代表, 2013, 78 min.
Li Xinmin 李新民, *Back to Huamulin*, Huidao Huamulin 回到花木林, 2011, 75 min.
Li Xinmin 李新民, *Huamulin 2012*, Huamulin 2012 花木林 2012, 2012, 75 min.
Li Xinmin 李新民, *Huamulin, Boy Xiaoqiang*, Huamulin，xiaoqiang ah xiaoqiang 花木林，小強啊小強, 2013, 76 min.
Li Xinmin 李新民, *Huamulin zhi bei*, Huamulin zhi bei 花木林之碑, 2014, 70 min.
Luo Bing 羅兵, *Luo Village: I and Ren Dingqi*, Luojiawu: wo he Ren Dingqi 羅家屋：我和任定其, 2011, 80 min.
Luo Bing 羅兵, *Luo Village: Pitiless Earth and Sky*, Luojiawu: tiandi wu qing 羅家屋：天地無情, 2012, 75 min.
Luo Bing 羅兵, *Luojia Village: Farewell, Luojiang Bridge*, Luojiawu: yongbie luojiang qiao 羅家屋：永別落江橋, 2013, 73 min.
Shu Qiao 舒僑, *Shuangjing Village, I'm Your Grandson*, Shuangjing, wo shi ni de sunzi 雙井，我是你的孫子, 2012, 78 min.
Shu Qiao 舒僑, *Shuangjing Village, I Want to Marry You*, Shuangjing, wo yao jia gei ni 雙井，我要嫁給你, 2013, 74 min.
Shu Qiao 舒僑, *Shuangjing Village, I'm a paralyzed person*, Shuangjing, wo shi tanzi 雙井，我是癱子, 2014, 78 min.
Wang Hai'an 王海安, *Attacking Zhanggao Village*, Jingong Zhanggao cun 進攻張高村, 2012, 86 min.
Wang Hai'an 王海安, *Believing in Zhanggao Village*, Xinyang Zhanggao cun 信仰張高村, 2013, 71 min.
Wang Hai'an 王海安, *Poeming Zhanggao Village*, Shige Zhanggaocun 詩歌張高村, 2014, 70 min.
Wen Hui 文慧, *Listening to Third Grandmother's Story*, Ting San Nainai jiang guoqu de shiqing 聽三奶奶講過去的事情, 2011, 75 min.

Wu Wenguang 吳文光, *Investigating: My Father in 1949*, Diaocha: 1949 nian de fuqin 調查：1949年的父親, 2013, 60 min.

Wu Wenguang 吳文光, *Because of Hunger: Diary I by Wu*, Yinwei Ji'e：Wu Riji Zhi Yi 因為飢餓：吳日記之1, 2013, 90 min.

Wu Wenguang 吳文光, *Diaocha Fuqin: Dang'anjuan*, Diaocha Fuqin: Dang'anjuan 調查父親：檔案卷, 2014, 30 min.

Ye Zuyi 葉祖藝, *The Gleaners*, Shisui 拾穗, 2014, 94 min.

Zhang Mengqi 章夢奇, *Self-Portrait with Three Women*, Zihuaxiang he san ge nüren 自畫像和三個女人, 2010, 70 min.

Zhang Mengqi 章夢奇, *Self-portrait: at 47 km*, Zihuaxiang: 47 gongli 自畫像：47公裡, 2011, 77 min.

Zhang Mengqi 章夢奇, *Self-portrait: Dancing at 47 km*, Zihuaxiang: 47 gongli tiaowu 自畫像：47公裡跳舞, 2012, 77 min.

Zhang Mengqi 章夢奇, *Self-portrait: Dreaming at 47 km*, Zihuaxiang: 47 gongli zuomeng 自畫像：47公裡做夢, 2013, 77 min.

Zhang Mengqi 章夢奇, *Self-portrait: The Bridge at 47 km*, Zihuaxiang: sishiqi gongli jiaqiao 自畫像：47公裡架橋, 2014, 77 min.

Zhang Ping 張蘋, *Losing Home*, Gui jia 歸鄉, 2014, 39 min.

Zou Xueping 鄒雪平, *Children's Village*, Haizi de cunzi 孩子的村子, 2012, 85 min.

Zou Xueping 鄒雪平, *The Starving Village*, Ji'e de cunzi 飢餓的村子, 2010, 76 min.

Zou Xueping 鄒雪平, *Satiated Village*, Chi bao de cunzi 吃飽的村子, 2011, 88 min.

Zou Xueping 鄒雪平, *Trash Village*, Laji de cunzi 垃圾的村子, 2013, 82 min.

Zou Xueping 鄒雪平, *Shazi de cunzi*, Shazi de cunzi 傻子的村子, 2014, 80 min.

8
Visual Memory, Personal Experience, and Public History
The Rediscovery of Cultural Revolution Underground Art*

Aihe Wang

Introduction

The Chinese Cultural Revolution (officially dated 1966–1976) was the most defining episode of Mao's China. It dramatically exploded the inherent contradictions within and between the party-state and society, exerting a major impact on the direction of the post-Mao era, shaping both China's modernization and its discontent. For a subject of this magnitude, master narratives of it have become equally majestic and ideologically loaded. Deng Xiaoping and the CCP under his leadership passed the verdict in 1981 that the Cultural Revolution was "ten years of disaster and turmoil" resulting from Mao's mistake and the manipulations of Lin Biao and the Gang of Four; and that it only ended thanks to the CCP Central Committee, when it "decisively smashed" the Gang of Four after Mao's death.[1] This verdict has dominated China's official history and the cultural industry of memory alike, hindering alternative critical reflections.

The recent rediscovery of the underground culture that existed during the Cultural Revolution challenges this official verdict. Underground culture thrived and spread not *because* the Cultural Revolution ended, but right under the noses of Mao and the Cultural Revolution Leadership, contributing to the very *causes* of its ending. This article introduces an exemplary case of this underground culture, the Wuming (No name) painting group, and discusses the process of excavating this case for writing an alternative history of the life and culture of the Cultural Revolution. Exemplary of underground culture in the 1970s, the Wuming group was quickly forgotten and excluded from historical narratives of modern China and

---

* This chapter is part of a bigger project supported by a membership at the Institute for Advanced Study, Princeton, in 2013, provided in part by the Willlis F. Doney Membership Endowment; and by The French National Research Agency (ANR) / Hong Kong Research Grants Council (RGC) Joint Research Scheme, 2013–2016.
1. *Resolution on CCP History (1949–81)* (Beijing: Foreign Languages Press, 1981), 41–46.

Chinese art. The process of recent rediscovery of the group illustrates how visual materials and private memories could be productively used to generate collective memory, bringing into the public sphere the obscured and forgotten clandestine society, thus participating in the (re)writing of public history. This newly excavated group history provides a counter-narrative against the official verdict and other master narratives of the Cultural Revolution. It reveals an active and responsible historical agency unlike either the brainwashed masses or the powerless victims portrayed by those master narratives. In everyday life, workers gathered at dusk to make art, creating meaning that defied state orthodoxy. The private art they produced was an aesthetic critique of lived experience during Mao's era—a "rebellion of the heart" against the state's ruthless destruction of the private sphere. As a social formation, the group existed beneath the reach of the state, giving birth to a new kind of modern self. Private art as a social practice, the clandestine group as a social formation, and the new form of modern subjectivity that the art and group produced were all constitutive of the grassroots changes that irreversibly ended the Cultural Revolution and Mao's era.

The Wuming Painting Group

The Wuming painting group was active in Beijing between 1973 and 1981, with its prehistory traceable to 1962. Its fifteen or so members came from two generations and various manual labor jobs—in factories, construction, service, or sent-down farm work. The three elder Wuming painters became acquainted by 1962 and painted together at the very margin of society. During the Cultural Revolution, a younger generation grew up and were sent down to the countryside or assigned to work in factories. Deprived of self-determination, they painted as a way of inventing a self and a community. Some of the sent-down youth returned to the city, and the young painters gathered to paint together. This was the time when cultural salons of all kinds mushroomed. By 1973, twelve or so younger painters joined the older generation to form a larger group. The community, now with a clear group identity and divergent class backgrounds (red and black), met regularly to paint, listen to music, exchange ideas, circulate smuggled books and catalogues, and experiment with unorthodox painting. Together they produced several thousand oil paintings and held three underground or unofficial art exhibitions in 1974, 1979, and 1981.

Over the years, the Wuming group functioned as a vibrant cultural hub and a clandestine haven of artistic freedom. It was, first of all, a clearinghouse for book traffic. The artists gathered around books, especially world literature and philosophy, from Balzac, Victor Hugo, Roman Rolland, Tolstoy, Pasternak, Hemingway, and Whitman to Nietzsche and Sartre, as well as books that had been printed for internal circulation in order to carry out criticism campaigns. Crucial for their artistic experimentation, they also shared a body of art catalogues and reproductions, ranging from Michelangelo and Rembrandt to Corot, Monet, Van Gogh,

Cézanne, Picasso, Expressionism, and Fauvism, as well as Chinese literati artists such as Huang Gongwang, Ni Zan, and Ba Da. They embraced the two enemies of official art—Western modernism and Chinese literati aesthetics—studying and copying these reproductions, and collectively created a new form of modernist art—a private apolitical art—against an ultra-political era. These shared books and art catalogues not only nurtured their starved minds, but also formed an intellectual bond, a shared structure of knowledge, and a united front of transgression. Inside the group, they argued about art, recited poetry, played guitar, and listened to Western music.

Such cultural activities sometimes make sense only when viewed against the living social context. *Listening to Music in Secret*, painted probably in 1975 (Figure 8.1, see color plates), illustrates what such clandestine cultural activity was like at the time. The painting depicts one of the group gatherings at a private home to listen to Western music. Outside the room, a campaign against Western music was under way. In 1974, the Cultural Revolution leadership had initiated multiple campaigns against "music without titles," "black paintings," and so on, denouncing the restoration of the "black line of literature and art."[2] In February that year, the "Black Painting Exhibition" opened to condemn landscape paintings done in the traditional literati style—using the color black, with motifs of landscapes and animals.[3] In theater, the Shanxi opera *Going Up to Peach Peak Three Times* (Sanshang taofeng) triggered a similar campaign of criticism.[4] Also in 1974, the minister of culture wrote a series of articles denouncing European classical music as a weapon "to shape opinion to serve the bourgeoisie for seizing and consolidating political power." He accused untitled music of concealing bourgeois class content and said that even music dealing with themes of pine trees, fountains, and moonlight masked the "decadent, chaotic life and depraved sentiments of the bourgeoisie."[5] This was literally a time when, as Brecht once wrote, "to speak of trees is almost a crime."[6] It was in such a time that the Wuming group painted trees.

In such a time, 1974, the group held its first major underground exhibition.[7] They chose Zhang Wei's apartment because it was in a Soviet-style building with pitch-dark hallways and isolated staircases, making it easier to evade the neighborhood committee's surveillance. They delivered their paintings furtively, with

---

2. Frederick C. Teiwes and Warren Sun, *The End of the Maoist Era: Chinese Politics during the Twilight of the Cultural Revolution, 1972–1976* (Armonk, NY: M. E. Sharpe, 2007), 160.
3. Ellen Johnston Laing, *The Winking Owl: Art in the People's Republic of China* (Berkeley: University of California Press, 1988).
4. Richard Kraus, "Arts Policies of the Cultural Revolution: The Rise and Fall of Culture Minister Yu Huiyong," in *New Perspectives on the Cultural Revolution*, ed. William A. Joseph, Christine P. W. Wong, and David Zweig (Cambridge, MA: Council on East Asian Studies, Harvard University, 1991), 219–42; 229.
5. Quoted in Kraus, "Arts Policies," 230–31.
6. Bertolt Brecht, "To Those Born After" (An die Nachgeborenen), cited from Nadine Gordimer, *Living in Hope and History: Notes from Their Century* (New York: Farrar, Straus, and Giroux, 1999), 203.
7. The exact date of the exhibition is uncertain. For controversies about this date, see "Personal Recollection and Collective Memory" in this chapter.

some even planning a coded knock. Inside, about fifteen people gathered. No one can forget the zeal and exhilaration of that day and evening. The exhibition was open only to the small circle of close and trusted friends rather than to the public. However small and fragile, the underground exhibition created an altogether different kind of social space. For its participants, this was the rite of passage into true art and a clandestine art society. Against the state's atomization and divide and rule, this art community created a clandestine social space and a new form of solidarity. In this novel social space, artists from different classes, genders, and generations assembled, transgressing the boundaries set by the state. Here they celebrated human plurality and developed unique personal subjectivities, by way of creating an art form that completely sabotaged the reigning artistic doctrines of the party-state.

Over the many years of its existence, the group had remained informal, with no defined group membership or regulations, and with no name. On July 7, 1979, following the brief Beijing Spring, the group's first public exhibition opened in Beijing's Beihai Park. To hold this exhibition, the painters first had to name their group. After days of discussion and vetoing many proposals, the artists finally chose "Wuming," meaning "no name" or "nameless." This term did not signal the time of the group's birth, as did other groups' names, such as "New Spring" and "April." Nor did it declare avant-garde futurism, as did "Today" and "Stars." Instead, it was a retrospective description of a winding path stretching back into the nights of the Cultural Revolution. In an era when free association was a crime, the Wuming group had to be nameless, shapeless, and spontaneous.

Private Art

Representative of underground art and literature during the Cultural Revolution, Wuming art was private and apolitical, sharply contrasting with the official art of the time. Mao's decree that "art serves politics" had long been the ruling dogma, and socialist realism had become a set of crude stylistic dictates dominating all cultural domains. In painting, the genre had to be figural; the subject had to be revolutionary splendor symbolized by the ageless models of workers, peasants, and soldiers; images had to be "tall, grand, and complete" (*gao da quan*) and the style had to be "red, bright, and shining" (*hong guang liang*). Red symbolized the revolution, while the use of black indicated an artist's counterrevolutionary intentions.[8] Landscape served only as a background for these beaming figures, showing the abundant productivity brought by the red sun (Mao) or the victory of people conquering the earth under it. Art that did not strictly follow such stylistic dictates subjected an artist to incrimination.

---

8. Stefan Landsberger, "The Deification of Mao," in *China's Great Proletarian Cultural Revolution: Master Narratives and Post-Mao Counternarratives*. ed. Woei Lien Chong (Boulder, CO: Rowman and Littlefield, 2002), 139–84. Julia F. Andrews, *Painters and Politics in the People's Republic of China, 1949–1979* (Berkeley: University of California Press, 1994), 360.

In contrast, Wuming art was private and apolitical in subject matter, consciously excluding political content, avoiding political commentary, and rejecting the official doctrine that "art serves politics." The largest portion of Wuming paintings are landscapes, and most of them are about unpeopled, and unidentifiable, anonymous "nature." This subject allowed a complete negation of politicizing art, and an exploration of the private, subjective experience of individuals. One example is *Mist* (Figure 8.2). Zhang Wei painted *Mist* in 1974 at the site of Yuyuantan, a desolated park that became a key site for the Wuming painters. Zhang had by then returned to Beijing from his sent-down village, working as a loader for a truck team. In his spare time, he came to paint "nature." Here, the painter was facing the lake created by the PLA army, right outside Diaoyutai, the state guesthouse compound used as the headquarters of the Cultural Revolution leadership at the time. *Mist* transcends the lived social and political reality by erasing the human trace, creating a space that is not real and only minimally connected to this world. The abstraction of wintery sky and water covers the painting surface, its warm silky green yearning for spring, and the brush strokes move and circulate with air; with them nothing is actually frozen. Purplish gray tones signify the distant shore, alternating between appearing and disappearing, denoting a faint reflection in water or soft ice. The illusionary shore in the distance offers an opening, where the eyes must focus, where air from sky and water merge and disappear into an unknown world.

In the foreground, the place of human presence, is nonexistence. The only things recognizable are delicate tree twigs hanging from above or rising from below, but these "twigs" are not attached to trees or earth and have no materiality. Dangling and floating, coming from nowhere and going nowhere, they are calligraphic lines, one-off signatures that are unrepeatable. It reminds us of literati paintings but is a modern abstraction, in which fragmented and disconnected elements express subjective experience directly, threatening to abandon representation. Such abstraction, such cleansing of the "real" and the materiality of all things, opens a universe of imagination. This 10.5 cm tall, bookmark-sized surface creates an expansive, boundless vision, inviting and enchanting viewers into an idealized, ethereal world.

In paintings such as *Mist*, the very rejection of the political in a politicized context was itself a political action, giving apolitical art a political subtext. Small paintings of trees and flowers, water and moonlight, articulate private sensations and emotions, helping formulate unique individual subjective experience. Painting *Mist*, the painter created his subjectivity totally divorced from the state-assigned social identity of a truck loader. Pacific and non-confrontational, Wuming's private art projected a vision of the world opposing the state's orthodox vision of revolutionary modernity, substituting human harmony with nature for conquest of nature.

This underground private art was also distinct from the dissident art and political pop that thrived after 1980. A comparison of two iconic works illustrates this distinction. Wang Keping's political satire *Idol* was the most sensational work of the Stars' 1980 exhibition, provoking the greatest public and international excitement

(Figure 8.3). The icon of Wuming, on the other hand, was *Lotus* (Figure 8.4). Painted by Li Shan, the youngest female member of the group in 1976, it was put on the advertising boards for the 1979 group exhibition. The lotus is a traditional literati subject, symbolizing the purity of individual spiritual freedom elevated above the "filthy mud" of official politics. It is also an emblem of Buddhism and the Buddha's transcendent nature. Evoking this traditional Chinese symbolic structure, this painting is a modern picture, using imported oil painting as a medium and adopting the modernist vision of an individual experiencing light in a fleeting moment. It minimizes realistic details into a few purified colors and shapes. Whereas *Idol* evokes collective memories of official politics, *Lotus* presents an opposite icon, of a solitary individual spirit, rising above that mud and transcending into a private, purified inner world. The shocking effect of *Idol* on the crowds depended on traversing the very limit of tolerance set by the political authority of the time—taking over Mao's sacred space and satirizing his sacred image. *Lotus*, in its original A4 size, was meant to be viewed by private viewers in a private space, one at a time, within an arm's reach, inciting not a collective memory of Mao but a private experience of spiritual purification. This private subjectivity was further communicated to private viewers, creating a new kind of inter-subjective social transaction.

Small paintings of flowers and trees, therefore, could form a counterculture, or a challenge to state-orchestrated revolutionary modernity. By celebrating a free spirit and articulating private sensations and inner experience, this private art helped undermine the state's project of identity formation. To build Mao's communist utopia, the party-state strove to mold a revolutionary subject, the selfless New Man, through unprecedented thought reform, social conformity, and atomization of the individual. A propaganda poster of 1972, *We/You Must Become This Kind of Person* (or *Be This Kind of Person*), illustrates how art served to mold the New (Wo) Man (Figure 8.5). It uses socialist realism to represent a female worker-militia. Her body is laden with objective signs of her class identity. The army uniform answers Mao's call on the entire nation to learn from the People's Liberation Army, thus militarizing the society. She is holding a gun with one hand, the gun from which state power derives. Her other hand holds another weapon bestowed by the state, the red book containing Chairman Mao's thought, which is meant to be her thought and the viewers' as well. The Mao pin on her chest shows the figure's unwavering loyalty to the Great Leader. All signs signal not a personal identity, but the identity of an ideal type of revolutionary subject and communist successor. Above her is another female figure, the heroine from the model drama *Red Lantern* who was an orphan of communist martyrs. On her face engraved deeply is class hatred and determination for revenge. Her red clothes blend with the red flag behind, a flag dyed with the blood of the martyrs. Under the flag, on the face of the young worker-militia is the same emotion of class hatred and determination, which has been transcribed from the heroine to the new generation. Painted and viewed from a very low perspective, she stands as a towering figure for the entire population of youth to identify with and emulate. The title is a command: *We/You Must Become* the person in the painting, who in turn must become the heroine in the drama. Both figures face the same direction, looking outward toward the collective future, to the shared horizon. The poster served blatantly as a mold molding selfless subjects for the revolution.

One year after this poster's publication, the young Wuming painters were captivated by the image of a totally different youth emerging from Zhao Wenliang's portrait (Figure 8.6). Zhao's *Youth* of 1973 is an early landmark of the group's figural paintings, a portrait of his closest friend and fellow painter, Yang Yushu. In contrast to the generic model of the robust, bright, red, and shining revolutionary subject in official paintings, this portrait is a vivid likeness of a real, particular, unique person. This is a sharp turn from the ideal model, or mold, to a particular living individual. An important turn, one that is comparable to the earlier turn of European art and literature from ideal archetypes to particular, unique persons. Charles Taylor describes the eighteenth-century rise of the modern self, seen in the innovations of the modern novel, as part of the culture of modernity.[9] *Youth* evidences a similar turn, in 1973 China, towards a particular person in his detail. The turn was also a conscious one. Zhao Wenliang often spoke ill of official and academic art, describing it as "thousands of people sharing a single face." What he aimed for instead was a portrait of a particular person in his uniqueness. The subject, Yang Yushu, is meticulously portrayed in the prime of his youth. With his physical features presented in precise detail, the image brings the figure to life, as if he could start breathing and moving by a slight magical touch.

But this likeness is not an identificatory image of Yang Yushu's person, like an ID photo. Instead, it is a portrait of a person's inner world. It strips clean the figure's external social signs—no uniform, no armbands, and no identity of class, vocation, or social position. It reverses attention from objectifying signs to the subjective inner world, to his look. The look, again, gives no hint of expression, no class love, no class hatred, not even melancholy or defiance. He looks into the far distance past the right edge of the painting, into a self-directed space, a horizon not shared. The dark grey of the background extends to engulf the grey clothing that could not be more anonymous, giving no clue of when and where this moment could be. In this abstract time and space, in an abstract leaden grey, a third eye appears behind the figure, staring back and out at the viewer. Furthermore, the external likeness and the inner world collapse into each other. Such a precise portrayal reveals nothing about this person's relation to his external world, but solely presents an inaccessible interior. This is a different ideal—an ideal of an autonomous individual, presented in an autonomous portrait, standing in dire opposition to the masses of selfless New Men.

Turning toward the introspective inner world, *Wuming*'s private art opens up an entire world of intimacy for self-exploration. After a decade-long revolution against

---

9. The modern novel, Taylor says, departs from traditional archetypes and "breaks with the classical preference for the general and universal. It narrates the lives of particular people in their detail." Charles Taylor, *Sources of the Self: The Making of Modern Identity* (Cambridge, MA: Harvard University Press, 1989), 287.

"the flash of the private" and three decades of engineering of the soul, exploration of such a rich subjective experience of the inner world was a radical innovation. This art was a rebellion against the state's destruction of the private sphere, its invasion of family, and endless thought reforms. Countering the social conformity, these private paintings celebrated a free spirit and articulated private sensations and inner experience. They constructed a shelter, a refuge, in which an individual could evade the scrutiny of the state, to reflect on emotional and moral experiences and attend to body and soul in secrecy. Such private art thus gave rise to a new sense of modern subjectivity, asserting perspectives, emotions, sensations, and experience that were actually lived and felt. Depicting flowers and moonlight, mountains and waters, and portraits of friends and self, it silently created a modern self, fundamentally undermining the state programming of socialist subjects. Such private art was also produced in private time outside the official art apparatus, and circulated privately and discretely among friends within the group. When the private subjectivity was further communicated to private viewers, it created a new form of social space and human solidarity, and a new kind of inter-subjective social transaction, all counteracting against the state project of atomization of the individual.

Archaeology of the Image: The Forgotten History and Deposited Memory

While underground private art critiques revolutionary modernity, the private memory deposited in this art can also challenge the grand history of that modernity. But this has become possible only through a belated rediscovery. Almost immediately after its emergence into the public in 1979, apolitical underground art was forgotten by history, as newly rising dissident art and political pop attracted attention from global media and the art market. Scholars later attributed the rise of private art to post-1989 China, as part of a de-politicizing of society in the 1990s. Geremie Barmé sees 1989 as the turning point towards the "graying of Chinese culture."[10] Hou Hanru finds in the 1990s a new wave of artists abandoning ideology-centric art and seeking self-expression.[11] Only recently has the excavation of the underground art of Mao's era begun. In 2007, Gao Minglu identified Wuming's "art for art's sake" approach as belonging to an alternative undercurrent, what he calls an "aesthetic modernism" that has been marginalized throughout China's twentieth century, during which mainstream "social modernism" was dominant.[12] Wu Hung in 2010 observed that such private and apolitical art was in fact the majority of

---

10. See Geremie Barmé, "Graying of Chinese culture," in his *In the Red: On Contemporary Chinese Culture* (New York: Columbia University Press, 1999), 99–144.
11. Hou Hanru, "Towards an 'Un-unoffical Art': De-ideologicalisation of China's Contemporary Art in the 1990s," *Third Text* 34 (Spring 1996): 37–52.
12. Gao Minglu, "Xiandaixing Cuowei: Dui Zhongguo Dangdai Yishu Xushi De Fanxi" [Dislocation of modernities: Reflection on contemporary Chinese art narratives], in *Meixue Xushi Yu Chouxiang Yishu*, ed. Gao Minglu (Chengdu: Sichuan meishu chubanshe, 2007), 32–44.

Figure 8.1
Listening to Music in Secret—Für Elise, by Zhao Wenliang, 1975, 16.5 cm × 20 cm, oil on paper.

Figure 8.2
Mist, by Zhang Wei, 1975, 10.5 cm × 26.5 cm, oil on cardboard.

Figure 8.3
Idol, by Wang Keping, 1979, 67 cm × 40 cm × 15 cm, birch, stained.

Figure 8.4
Lotus, by Li Shan, 1978, 25 cm × 20 cm, oil on paper.

Figure 8.5
[We/You] Must Become This Kind of Person, by Shan Lianxiao, 1972, propaganda poster.

Figure 8.6
Youth, by Zhao Wenliang, 1973, 40.5 cm × 34.5 cm, oil on canvas mounted on three-ply board.

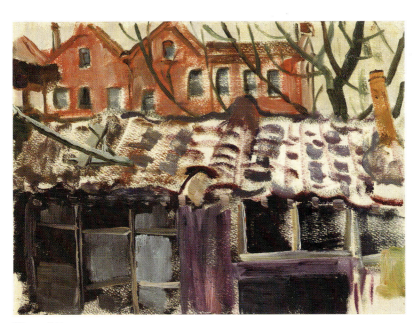

Figure 8.7
Home, by Wang Aihe, 1973, 19.6 cm × 27 cm, oil on paper.

Figure 8.8
Plowing 1, by Zheng Zigang, 1976, 27.2 cm × 39.2 cm, oil on paper.

Figure 8.9
Medicine, by Wang Aihe, 1978, 41.5 cm × 45.5 cm, oil on pasteboard.

what surfaced in 1979, yet has been omitted from the history of art altogether.[13] The Wuming painting group provides a key case for further exploring this private art and its engagement with revolutionary modernity and international modernism. A major retrospective exhibition of the group toured in Beijing, Shanghai, and Guangzhou in 2006–2007 with a companion book in Chinese.[14] Another exhibition, on the Wuming, Stars, and Caocao groups, was held in New York (2011) and Hong Kong (2013).[15] More far-ranging exhibitions (e.g., *Art and Revolution*, New York, 2009) and publications have started to include the Wuming group as part of the beginning of contemporary Chinese art.[16]

Contributing to the rediscovery of this underground art myself, I have conducted significant fieldwork, published a thirteen-volume catalogue of the primary Wuming artists (2009) and a number of scholarly articles, and am completing the first monograph in English on the subject.[17] My writing about underground art and art communities critically engages the existing public history of the Cultural Revolution, discovering the meaning of this art in that larger history while modifying the latter by bringing to light some of the obscured culture and life of everyday lived experience. Unlike conventional history writing, however, this project relies heavily on visual material and private memories. This is because the underground cultural movements left few written records. Out of fear of incrimination, people habitually erased or destroyed written records. Even the few painters who used to write diaries stopped during various political campaigns. Instead of writing, they stored their personal memory primarily in visual forms—the thousands of oil paintings produced underground during the Cultural Revolution, along with a small number of historical photographs.

In contrast to historical sources such as documents and archives, memories deposited in such visual forms are hidden, dormant, embodied, and unarticulated. The dichotomy between memory and history is well known. It has been repeatedly reenacted by many theories of modernity, so much so that it has become a convention to use the pair to sum up the contradictions of our modern time: memory is

---

13. Wu Hung, in conversation with the author at a joint archive and book launch by the Asia Art Archive and Museum of Modern Art, Hong Kong, September 7, 2010.
14. Gao Minglu, ed., *"Wuming": yige beiju qianwei de lishi* [The No-Name: A history of a self-exiled avant-garde] (Guilin: Guangxi shifan daxue chubanshe, 2006).
15. See Julia Andrews and Kuiyi Shen, *Blooming in the Shadows: Unofficial Chinese Art, 1974–1985* (New York: China Institute, 2011), 67–68. Julia Andrews and Kuiyi Shen, eds., *Light Before Dawn: Unofficial Chinese Art, 1974–1985* (Hong Kong: Asia Society, Hong Kong Center, 2013).
16. Melissa Chiu and Zheng Shengtian, eds., *Art and China's Revolution* (New York: Asia Society, in association with Yale University Press, 2008). Wu Hung, ed., *Contemporary Chinese Art: Primary Documents* (New York: The Museum of Modern Art, 2010). Julia Andrews and Kuiyi Shen, eds., *Art of Modern China* (Berkeley: University of California Press, 2012). Juliane Noth, "Landscapes of Exclusion: The No Name Group and the Multiple Modernities in Chinese Art in 1979," in *Negotiating Difference: Chinese Contemporary Art in the Global Context* (Weimar: VDG, 2012), 49–62.
17. Aihe Wang, ed., *Wuming (No Name) Painting Catalogue* (Hong Kong: Hong Kong Press, 2009). Aihe Wang, "*Wuming*: An Underground Art Group during the Cultural Revolution," *Journal of Modern Chinese History* 3 (2), (December 2009): 183–99.

backward looking and associated with the affective, the subjective, the traditional, and the communal, in contrast to history, which is forward looking and associated with rationality, objectivity, modernity, and the national/global.[18] My task here is to bring the two opposing categories into a dynamic cross-fertilization, using memory within and about underground art to critically interact with the grand history of Chinese modernity. The more I depend on memory in writing history, the more I realize that memory by itself is not history. It is unarticulated, embodied in the individual, and deposited in visual materials and the tangible; as such, it cannot enter historical discourse raw. A methodology of engaging memory, and visual memory in particular, must be perfected for bringing it into the writing of history.

To incorporate memory in the writing of this alternative history, I have developed what I call an archaeological approach, or an archaeology of the image. This archaeology has several basic procedures. The first is to evoke personal memories buried in the visual and tangible materials, by active recalling in front of the image. Second, these recollections of individuals are often fragmented and inconsistent, and need therefore to be compared with and tested against one another to synthesize a collective memory. With a regenerated collective memory, finally, writing a localized history of a community must actively engage and contest the grand history of the nation and modernity. The archaeology of the image, therefore, is a process of excavating memory from its visual, personal, and communal layers of deposit, in order to produce a counter-narrative that contributes to the (re)writing of public history.

My personal engagement with this project illustrates this archaeological process. As the author, I have a unique position relative to this subject, as both a participant in the past and a scholar in the present. I was an active member of the Wuming group. Between 1971 and 1983, from age seventeen to twenty-nine, I was a worker in a plastic factory, while painting secretly with the group after work. I participated in the very formation of the group and in all its major activities and exhibitions, and I witnessed its disintegration in the reform era. In 1983 I entered the Chinese Academy of Social Sciences as a graduate student in anthropology, and between 1986 and 1995 I pursued a joint PhD in the United States in anthropology and Chinese history. By 2006, when I revisited the case of Wuming, I was simultaneously an artist, a historian, and an anthropologist. My personal experience and memory provide me rich intrinsic knowledge, at the same time posing challenges of subjectivity and authenticity that are part and parcel of memory itself.

In 1983, when I stopped painting, the group had been dispersed, some other members had also changed professions, and some soon left China for the West. The existence of this clandestine private art was forgotten in the following decades. Studying and then working in the United States, I never mentioned my painting life to my teachers and friends, except for the very few. One of the few was Gao

---

18. For a summary of the discourse on memory and history, see Ban Wang, *Illuminations from the Past: Trauma, Memory, and History in Modern China* (Stanford, CA: Stanford University Press, 2005), 4–5.

Minglu, an art historian who came to study at Harvard before I graduated. I showed him some slides of my works around 1992. His first reaction: "your paintings are very private." Clearly this kind of painting did not have a place in the art-historical narrative of the time. Fourteen years later, in August 2006, Gao emailed me; a retrospective exhibition of the Wuming Painting Group was to open in October, and he, as the curator, had been trying to reach me as one of the group members. I rushed to Beijing to look for my paintings in my parents' house. In the attic, cardboard boxes were sealed with half an inch of dust. Inside, chronologically packed were paintings made between 1972 and 1981, wrapped with newspaper or prints of the time. My engagement with this project began.

As an artist, excavating such visual materials was first of all an act of awakening the memory. Opening each wrapping, the paint smelled fresh and the colors were vibrant. Hundreds of paintings, suddenly facing me, swept me off the ground, and took me back in time to relive my earlier experience. Curator Gao came the next morning, and selected paintings from this and that box, setting them aside for the exhibition. He was pulling out a small painting of a house. For a moment, I was not sure whose painting it was. Then, of course, I realized it was mine, and could only be mine. Reappearing suddenly, it evoked in me the most intimate emotions about the home of my youth, and that particular winter when the family was scattered, the windows broken, the stove extinguished . . . I was surprised at Gao's choice of a very private scene, a painting not even shown to my painter friends at the time, that was never meant as my "representative work." For the sake of exhibition, I named the painting *Home* (Figure 8.7). I did not realize at the time that the transformation of the painting had just begun—from unarticulated private memory to public visual art and source of history. With other selected paintings, *Home* has been shown in exhibitions in Beijing, Shanghai, Guangzhou, New York, and Hong Kong. Entering the public domain, these objects started lives beyond the control of their creator, acquiring meaning from pluralistic perspectives.

From one particular perspective, discussed below, I will analyze this painting to articulate my lived experience of the destruction of family and the private sphere on China's road toward a revolutionary modernity. For me, *Home* serves first of all as a visual deposit of personal memories. When reencountered across decades, it provoked memory from hibernation into action, the action of articulation and the creation of meaning.

Personal Recollection and Collective Memory

When Wuming's private art was excavated for public meaning, personal recollections of all the group members were activated to reconstruct collective memory. But memory about a collective is not itself collective memory, until it is shared. When the Wuming group shattered in the early 1980s, collective memory was also fractured, with its shards spread by individuals across the continents for a quarter of a century. Divergent life experiences through time and different positions in the present have created great discrepancies in personal memories. Between October 2006 and May 2007, when the retrospective exhibition was touring Beijing, Shanghai, and Guangzhou, fifteen or so artists had multiple reunions, in large and small groups, each engorged with passionate debates over the group history.

The fluidity and contested nature of memory has been a fact of life throughout this writing project. To reconstruct collective memory, I must put fragmented and contradictory personal recollections in relationship to one another, including my own, and insert them into the history of the revolution, letting the personal recollections, collective memory, and national history illuminate, test, and modify one another. This is necessary even for the most technical details, such as dating. To catalogue the hundreds of paintings in the Wuming catalogue, I relied on the artists to provide the date of each work, as well as its material, dimensions, and location of creation. Since most of the paintings were not dated at the time of completion, the artists often did not have firm dates. They do have a strong sense of relative chronology within their own bodies of work, based on how the subject and style evolved from one work to another, and when the group changed its painting sites. With a few firm dates serving as signposts, related to a historical or group event, each artist's work could be arranged into a relative chronological order. But the problem appears when works of different artists are put side by side.

During the retrospective exhibition, for example, Ma Kelu and I were standing in front of two small paintings we painted together, depicting a snow-covered bridge inside Beihai Park. We recalled a Chinese new year's holiday when we sneaked inside the park, then still closed to the public. We had mixed ourselves into a busload of visitors, who had been invited for an "internal visit," when the park was preparing to reopen to the public after years of closure. When was it? The labels next to the paintings gave two different dates: Ma's was dated 1975, and mine 1977.[19] Neither of us was certain of these contradictory facts, so I later checked the history of the park; it turns out it had been occupied by Mao's wife Jiang Qing until her arrest in October 1976, after Mao's death, and did not open to the public until 1977. So both paintings must have been made during the Spring Festival of 1977— an unusually precise fact, which could only be reconstructed by combining two artists' shared memories with factual historical records. This kind of deviation in memory seems trivial, but it shows the limitations of even the most basic and seemingly secure individual recollections. Only by synthesizing divergent memories and testing them against the larger history can personal memory credibly contribute to the writing of history.

By the same token, many such errors and inconsistencies in personal recollections could be productive when put in dynamic contact with one another and with the larger historical context. It was through discussion and debate over such

---

19. Gao Minglu, *"Wuming."* fig. 115 on page 62, and fig. 19 on page 161.

inconsistencies that we reconstructed the range of books and art catalogues we had shared. It was also through such interactions among conflicting memories that we tried to reconstruct our collective memory of the group's major events. One of the major disagreements about the group history has been the date of the first underground internal exhibition. This is the single event that all members commonly hold as the landmark for the group's final consolidation, and for many it was the rite of passage in formally joining a clandestine group. When I first noticed that the artists were dating this event to 1975, I checked back with Zhang Wei and Ma Kelu, who had both told me multiple times in the 1990s, when they lived in New York, that the exhibition had taken place on a holiday for the New Year of 1974, thus either January 1 or during the Spring Festival. Zhang had hosted the exhibition in his own home, and Ma was known for his good memory. "Why did you change your story?" I asked. They answered that after returning to China in 2005, they talked to the eldest of the group, Zhao Wenliang, who insisted that the exhibition took place in 1975. Out of respect, they followed Zhao's dating. During my interviews, I asked each person about this event, and most of them likewise remembered it happening in early 1974. But when Zhao Wenliang asserted that it was 1975 on public occasions in 2006, the painters accepted his date and changed their own story to form a consensus. Many thought such a difference in dating was too trivial to argue about, which exposes an important difference between the way artists and historians use and value memory.

For an individual or even the group as a whole, such dating is probably insignificant; but for writing the group history as part of the larger public history, the New Year (or Chinese New Year) of 1974 or 1975 presents two quite different historical moments. Putting conflicting personal recollections in relationship to one another and in a larger history, my own research shows that early 1974 is better supported. First of all, the exhibition did not include two painters, Du Xia and Liu Shi, who both joined the group in early 1974. Du Xia was certain about exactly when she joined: the winter after her boyfriend left Beijing to join the PLA's Air Force Political Art Troupe in the summer of 1973. By then, she had heard much about the underground exhibition that she had missed. Second, Ma Kelu and others recall that he had remarked during that exhibition that 1974 was perfect for our exhibition because it coincided with the centennial commemoration of the Impressionists' first unofficial exhibition in 1874. He would not have made such a comment in 1975. Third, Zhang Da'an, an old friend of Zhao who worked on a farm away from Beijing, told me the exhibition made a big impact on his own painting, evident in new types of works that he dated to 1974. Fourth, as far as all the artists could recall, the exhibited works only included paintings dated before 1974. Yang Yushu in 2008 criticized the young painters: "what did they exhibit at the underground exhibition? Dongjiaominxiang, Yuanming yuan, all the Western stuff." If it had been held during New Year of 1975, the young painters would have had very different paintings to show, since those sites had been mostly abandoned by then.

And Ma Kelu believes he would have exhibited works in an Impressionist style in 1975, as he was seriously studying Impressionism throughout 1974 and produced some major works. Finally, all these personal recollections can be tested against the larger historical context. Zhang Wei recalls the sharp contrast between the freedom created by the exhibition inside his home and the tense atmosphere outside caused by the Campaign of Criticizing Lin Biao and Confucius, which officially lasted from January to June of 1974. With all these reasons, New Year's day or the Chinese New Year of 1974 would be the more convincing date for the underground exhibition. When solid documentation is lacking and personal memories are in conflict, the best one can do is combine individual recollections in this way to find a most likely version of events; yet as a historian I know that version could be overthrown by the appearance of one solid document.

From Private Art to Public History

Using the archaeology of the image, I write about underground art and culture as a missing part of the national history of Mao's era. Most of my primary sources are paintings produced by the group, and the personal and collective memories evoked from these paintings. Analyzing these works of art, I weave art historical visual analyses—of the works' subjects, styles, and visual effects—with the artists' recollections generated from my fieldwork, and integrate personal and collective memories with my historical research. The visual art, personal memory, and national history engage one another in a mutual revelation. My analyses of the painting *Plowing* illustrates this methodology (Figure 8.8). The site of *Plowing* is a state farm near the Sino-Soviet border. My documentary research shows that this site used to be the sacred ancestral land for the Manchus of the Qing dynasty. In 1947, the Communist Party started to open this wilderness for mechanization of agriculture, using military and convict laborers. Shanhe Farm was one of the thirty-eight labor camps founded in the 1950s for this purpose. In 1969, masses of sent-down youth arrived as farm laborers to replace the convicts. They were organized in military units, and shared collective dormitories that had formerly been labor camps. The painter of *Plowing*, Zheng Zigang, spent ten years here. "From body to soul," he recalls, "we were all just there enduring." Visual analysis, however, shows something the national history does not. This pastoral scene does not represent the actual mechanized agricultural industry or the militant collective living. In contrast, it asserts individual emotion, energy, and freedom, demonstrating how painting created space for spiritual freedom even in a military agricultural camp:

> The vast black soil moves from the bottom upwards, with such a powerful force that it bends the horizon into a curve, slanting the sky in the direction of its motion. At the center is the source of all motion and energy—a single man driving two horses, plowing the land, his body the same color as the black soil, leaving behind long cuts deep in the earth. A lone man in nature, naked of any social signs, with his naked

animals, is dancing the primal dance of man living on the land. The perspective is from high and far away, the view of a free flying bird, a bird that is the painter and the viewer in one. The expressive brushwork, informal composition, contrasting colors and personal perspective together celebrate individual life and freedom. The energy and joy of the painting assert that the painter had not wasted his youth, but had overcome hardship to become a man of his own liking.

This visual analysis is supported by my interviews with the artist. The painter articulated in the interviews that "our landscape paintings have an element of anger and cynicism against the world. They no longer depict a reality but make a great deal of omissions and alterations." The painting thus produced "is no longer a real thing, but the painter's subjective experience." "Our works," he asserted, "can affirm and confirm our individuality, our spirit, and our talents." Who said we are escapist? "I am here creating something."[20]

This case illustrates that visual art and private memory do not simply verify or evidence national history that has already been written, but critically engage it, challenge it, and rewrite it. With the dynamic and critical cross-fertilization among the three, we now see that *Plowing* transfigured a sent-down youth into a self-reflective modern individual. Painting landscape articulated emotions and experience that were suppressed in a highly militant and puritan society. Painting thus became a counter against the state project that molded socialist subjects. Both the painter and the viewer rose as self-determining individuals with their own subjectivity, no more a socialist subject disappearing in the collective. Viewed today, with this memory recalled, the painted figure escapes the victimhood as portrayed by the post-Mao master narrative.

Subjectivity and Authenticity

Moving from visual and personal memory to the writing of public history, the most daunting challenge has been my own subjectivity, which is constantly in flux. As an artist active in the group back then and a historian and anthropologist now, I occupy multiple positions and identities, facing a formidable task of moving between memory and history, the personal and the collective, and subjective experience and objective analysis. While my "participation" as an artist and "observation" as an anthropologist cross four decades, anthropological "reflexivity" alerts me to be conscious about my own multiple identities and shifting subjectivity. At the beginning, this consciousness blocked me from writing altogether, until I made my own shifting subjectivity part of the story under study.

This challenge became insurmountable when it was time to write about my own paintings. Using images as a major source, I am writing a book that analyzes over seventy paintings produced in the group history by fourteen artists, including

---

20. Zheng Zigang, interviewed by Aihe Wang, Beijing, March 14, 2008.

myself. Analyzing works of other artists, I wrote as an anthropologist and historian. But when it was time to face my own paintings, I was literally wordless. I left them blank and moved on to discuss other people's paintings, until mine were the only ones left. Facing these, I simply could not put down the word "I," as the narrator describing that lived experience as a painter. It was impossible to claim that first person voice, and in that voice the authenticity of the first person experience, as if it were at all possible to step back into the same river from which those paintings had come. I was sharply conscious about how much a narrative account of my past experience was an act of recalling and reconstructing by my present self, rather than a voice from the past. In other words, it was "I" in the present that was talking, rather than that nineteen-year-old painter who finally got to say what was on her mind. My subjectivity has shifted, it has been remade, and there was no return to that original experience.

My narrative of the painting *Home* can serve to illustrate this shifting subjectivity, and how I resolved my wordlessness in front of the image (Figure 8.7). As mentioned above, *Home* is a painting I had completely forgotten. Forgotten also was the artistic intention, why I chose to paint it and to paint it that way, and what I was trying to achieve. When I finally wrote about this painting forty years later, in my study in Hong Kong, I was actively recalling the things that were important to me in the present, with the knowledge that this home had been demolished long ago, turned into a parking space on a wide street; that my father was dying of cancer; and that the family would never reunite under a single roof, even a broken one as in the painting. When I wrote, I was also informed by my academic training, with a sharp analytical focus on how Wuming art had responded to the state's revolutionary modernization. I therefore recalled from this painting the state's fragmentation of family and invasion of the private sphere, and read this painting as an artistic response that articulated emotional and subjective experiences resilient to that process. But I could not impose this present-based focus and interest—one of many possible ways of interpreting a painting—on that nineteen-year-old painter as her conscious artistic intention. To be honest to myself and to history, I finally found words when I used the third person voice, addressing that young painter whom I once was as "she." In front of *Home*, I recall:

> When she painted *Home* in 1973, it was an empty home like so many others. Her parents had been sent to two different provinces, the second elder brother had been sent to a third province for the Third Front Industry, and her eldest brother was living in his factory to carry out the revolution. She was assigned to work in a plastics factory, living mostly alone in this empty home.

To distinguish my understanding of the painting now from the original intention of the painter then, which was not possible to authentically recover in this case, I wrote about my understanding of it from a present perspective:

I understand this painting now as the ruin of the family and the ransacked emotional landscape of the painter. Looking out through her bedroom window is this scene that she contemplated every day. The home appears literally to be crumbling (the house as shown in this painting would in fact collapse in the earthquake three years later). A clay chimney above the semi-functional bathroom on the right looks about to fall, and some of the window panes of the central hallway and the communal kitchen to the left are broken, the black interior reminding one that the stove is extinguished and hasn't cooked a meal for seven in a long time. The tree in the neighboring yard, which shimmered with blossoms in the spring and shaded the afternoon sun in the summer, lends no protection now . . . There was not much left at home, and not much home left.

While the visual material eludes the original intention of the painter, it could evoke the strongest memory of the pain deeply buried in my unconscious. The painter at the time might not have been "expressing" it on purpose, but the painting has awakened it forty years later. I relive that moment through recollection:

> The strongest memory *Home* evokes in me today is not the poor condition of the house or the physical coldness inside it, but a psychological chill. If you stop your gaze and look into the windows, you see cold dark eyes staring straight at you like two black holes. I recall a girl spending long hours in a cold room alone, trying to put down cold words to denounce her parents who had been sent to faraway places. After she was assigned to the plastics factory in 1971, the head of the Communist Youth League from the factory's political work office periodically had a "heart-to-heart talk" with her: "As the daughter of a Rightist (mother) and a 'reactionary' intellectual (father), you should work on drawing a clear class line from your parents . . . you are to write thought reports monthly to denounce your parents and to report on how much progress you've made under re-education by the working class." So, in the empty home, she faced the task of composing condemnations of her parents, all the while struggling against the private emotions of missing them and her family.

By separating the person who recalls now as "I" and the person who painted then as "she," I disclaim the authenticity of my interpretation of this painting as the original and only meaning, while claiming my voice and perspective as an interpreter and scholar of the present. The shifts between the first and third personas give me the space and freedom to evoke memory deposited in the visual material, bringing into conscious analysis what was dormant or unconscious. Evoking memory from the visual, therefore, can fill the void in the narrative of the official history of the Cultural Revolution, the void in which the private, the personal, and the everyday family life of ordinary people has been erased by the narratives of elite politics and mass movements.

Besides the private and emotional life of individuals, another void in official histories of the Chinese revolution is the history of the human body. Consider that the Party-state was propagating revolutionary models to make the New Man, models from Zhang Side to Lei Feng, all so eager to sacrifice their young lives for the revolution. Consider that Mao's decree "fear not hardship, fear not death" was collectively chanted in front of any danger or harm. When death was taken so lightly, the suffering of the human body deserved not even to register. Personal memories deposited in visual images, however, have made it possible now for one to recall the experience of the body, thus to give a historical account of what the body had to pay for revolutionary modernity.

My own painting *Medicine* is about a body wounded by industrialization, hiding in the corner of its private struggle towards survival and recuperation (Figure 8.9). Reading this painting has been the most disturbing. Here again, the third person voice was the only voice with which I could write:

> This is a lonely corner of illness and isolation. In this private space, a lone person is struggling with the basic need of bodily survival, a struggle that no one could help.... During twelve years working in a plastics factory, the painter was sick for twelve of them. Her debilitating decline of health exhausted the wits of the modern hospitals, leaving her to the traditional wisdom of herbal medicine. For years she had been drinking three bowls of brown liquid a day, the herbal medicine boiled in the black clay pot depicted in the painting. Staring at the pot that was her everyday companion, the painter was contemplating her being saturated by the bitter liquid, like the saturated medicine pot itself. Ignorant about industrial pollution and its damage to the body, she was suffering without knowing the cause. Now better informed, I can see what had happened to a young female body caught up in industrialization typical of Marx's "primitive accumulation" that I read much later, and I can now find words to articulate the experience embodied in the medicine pot.[21]

The recalling was difficult, for it not only disturbed emotions, but also woke up the memory of the experience I had tried for years to actively forget, forget so as to live and to remake a life. For the sake of writing a history of the voiceless body, I now write, about the labor day and night, rotating around three shifts, making Mao's red book covers; about the body becoming parts of the machines, "nuts and bolts" screwed onto the revolutionary machines; about each breath breathing in the toxic concoction of chemicals; about the illness that possessed the body like a devil. Facing this painting, I recall, reliving the physical pain and inner suffering, each time choked with rage. I write, so as to give voice to the silent body, so as to leave a trace in public history of the price paid by the human bodies for revolutionary modernity.

---

21. For a fuller account, see Aihe Wang, "Hehuan Shu [Silk Tree]," in *Wuming (No Name) Painting Catalogue*, ed. Aihe Wang, vol. 7, 11–14.

Conclusion

Through an "archaeology of the image," a history of underground private art and communities has now emerged from oblivion. Excavating this forgotten history depended on the ongoing process of transforming visual art and personal accounts into collective memory, and eventually bringing them into the public sphere, partaking in the (re)writing of history. Such production of new historical knowledge challenges the post-Mao master narratives of the Cultural Revolution, closely interacting with both official and global narratives while challenging, modifying, and even subverting them.

This history of underground art reveals an active and responsible historical agency that is neither the brainwashed masses nor the powerless victims portrayed by the master narratives. Instead, it foregrounds the agency of the common people acting at the bottom of society and bringing change. In everyday life, workers gathered in dusk to make art, creating meaning that defied state orthodoxy. The private art they produced was a "rebellion of the heart" against the state's ruthless destruction of the private sphere and atomization of the individual. It reinvented a private refuge for the body and soul in which to subsist beyond state control. Its "inward turn" to the introspection of private and emotional experience gave birth to a new kind of modern self, who constituted social change. The underground group existed beneath the reach of the state, creating a new form of social formation and solidarity. The private art, the personal memory, and the clandestine community shall now be a valuable part of our common history.

Bibliography

Andrews, Julia. *Painters and Politics in the People's Republic of China, 1949–1979*. Berkeley: University of California Press, 1994.

Andrews, Julia, and Kuiyi Shen, eds. *Art of Modern China*. Berkeley: University of California Press, 2012.

Andrews, Julia, and Kuiyi Shen, eds. *Blooming in the Shadows: Unofficial Chinese Art, 1974–1985*. New York: China Institute, 2011.

Andrews, Julia, and Kuiyi Shen, eds. *Light Before Dawn: Unofficial Chinese Art, 1974–1985*. Hong Kong: Asia Society, Hong Kong Center, 2013.

Barmé, Geremie. *In the Red: On Contemporary Chinese Culture*. New York: Columbia University Press, 1999.

Chiu, Melissa, and Zheng Shengtian, eds. *Art and China's Revolution*. New York: Asia Society, in association with Yale University Press, 2008.

Gao, Minglu 高名潞, ed. *"Wuming": yige beiju qianwei de lishi* 無名：一個悲劇前衛的歷史 [The No-Name: A history of a self-exiled avant-garde]. Guilin: Guangxi shifan daxue chubanshe, 2006.

Gao, Minglu 高名潞. Xiandaixing Cuowei: Dui Zhongguo Dangdai Yishu Xushi De Fanxi "現代的錯位：對中國當代藝術敘事的反思 [Dislocation of modernities: Reflection on contemporary Chinese art narratives]." In *Meixue Xushi Yu Chouxiang Yishu* 美術與抽象藝術, edited by Gao Minglu 高名潞編, 32–44. Chengdu: Sichuan meishu chubanshe, 2007.

Gordimer, Nadine. *Living in Hope and History: Notes from Their Century*. New York: Farrar, Straus and Giroux, 1999.

Hou, Hanru. "Towards an 'Un-unoffical Art': De-ideologicalisation of China's Contemporary Art in the 1990s." *Third Text* 34 (Spring 1996): 37–52.

Kraus, Richard. "Arts Policies of the Cultural Revolution: The Rise and Fall of Culture Minister Yu Huiyong." In *New Perspectives on the Cultural Revolution*, edited by William A. Joseph, Christine P. W. Wong, and David Zweig, 219–42. Cambridge, MA: Council on East Asian Studies, Harvard University, 1991.

Laing, Ellen Johnston. *The Winking Owl: Art in the People's Republic of China*. Berkeley: University of California Press, 1988.

Landsberger, Stefan. "The Deification of Mao: Religious Imagery and Practices during the Cultural Revolution and Beyond." In *China's Great Proletarian Cultural Revolution: Master Narratives and Post-Mao Counternarratives*, edited by Woei Lien Chong, 139–84. Boulder, CO: Rowman and Littlefield, 2002.

Noth, Juliane. "Landscapes of Exclusion: The No Name Group and the Multiple Modernities in Chinese Art in 1979." In *Negotiating Difference: Chinese Contemporary Art in the Global Context*, edited by Birgit Hopfener, Franziska Koch, Jeong-hee Lee-Kalisch, and Juliane Noth, 49–62. Weimar: VDG, 2012.

Resolution on CCP History (1949–81). Beijing: Foreign Languages Press, 1981.

Taylor, Charles. *Sources of the Self: The Making of Modern Identity*. Cambridge, MA: Harvard University Press, 1989.

Teiwes, Frederick C., and Warren Sun. *The End of the Maoist Era: Chinese Politics during the Twilight of the Cultural Revolution, 1972–1976*. Armonk, NY: M. E. Sharpe, 2007.

Wang, Aihe, ed. *Wuming (No Name) Painting Catalogue*. Hong Kong: Hong Kong University Press, 2009.

Wang, Aihe. "*Wuming*: An Underground Art Group during the Cultural Revolution." *Journal of Modern Chinese History* 3.2 (December 2009): 183–99.

Wang, Ban. *Illuminations from the Past: Trauma, Memory, and History in Modern China*. Stanford, CA: Stanford University Press, 2005.

Wu Hung, ed. *Contemporary Chinese Art: Primary Documents*. New York: The Museum of Modern Art, 2010.

Part III

Unofficial Sources and Popular Historiography

New Discourses of Knowledge on the Mao Era

9
The Second Society

Frank Dikötter

In 1977 the economist Gregory Grossman proposed the term "second economy" to describe the many ways in which ordinary people in communist regimes created, bought, and sold goods to get around the widespread shortages caused by a command economy.[1] Many did so legally, for instance by working on private plots, but most of their activities were prohibited, from selling commodities on the black market to setting up underground factories.

While a second economy was quietly finding solutions to the problems created by central planning, a hidden, underground, largely invisible society lived in the shadow of the formal political system. Elemér Hankiss, a Hungarian sociologist, called it a "second society" in the early 1980s. Much as the informal economy was the inevitable counterpart of the official economy, the first society and the second society were two dimensions of most people's existence. Thanks to endless campaigns of ideological indoctrination, many individuals in communist regimes learnt how to parrot the party line in public and keep their thoughts to themselves. There must have been many subjects who were crushed by the relentless pressure to conform, just as there were true believers or pure opportunists who enthusiastically followed every twist and turn in official ideology. But some people developed two minds or two souls, one for public view, the other strictly private, to be shared with trusted friends and family only. Some were able to move to and fro between these two realms, while others sunk into apathy and depression, unable to reconcile the projected values of the world around them with their own beliefs.[2]

Under Mao, too, many people offered no more than outward compliance, keeping their innermost thoughts and personal feelings to themselves. Even at the height of the Cultural Revolution, when almost everything that strayed from Mao Zedong Thought was decried as "bourgeois" or "feudal," they managed to keep a

---

1. The core of this chapter is based on Frank Dikötter, *The Cultural Revolution: A People's Tragedy, 1962–1967* (London and New York: Bloomsbury, 2016), 285–300.
2. Elemér Hankiss, "The 'Second Society': Is There an Alternative Social Model Emerging in Contemporary Hungary?" *Social Research* 55, no. 1–2 (Spring 1988): 13–42. I much prefer the unedited version of this article, which can be found on the website of the Wilson Center, Washington DC.

diversity of cultural traditions alive. Much of this second society has escaped the gaze of historians, for the simple reason that it was carefully hidden from view and hence difficult to document. But over the past decade or so, a variety of primary sources have become available that allow us to get much closer to the hidden lives of a whole range of people. Party archives have declassified large numbers of files, and they contain a wealth of documentation, from detailed investigations into religious organizations in the countryside and surveys of prohibited activities in factories and workshops to police reports on black markets. They constitute the most important source used in this chapter. In line with other contributions to this volume, there are also alternative memories. These include, for instance, self-published memoirs written by the rank and file of the party or even by ordinary people, offering insights that cannot be gleaned from official accounts. There are also interviews with people from all walks of life, a few of which have been used here. This wealth of material, in addition to better known sources such as Red Guard memoirs, undermines the picture of complete conformity that is sometimes thought to have characterized the last years of the Mao era. If anything, it shows the extent to which ordinary people used the chaos caused by endless political purges to hollow out the party's ideology.

The second society developed well before the onset of the Cultural Revolution. Much as a black market appeared the moment the Communist Party started to clamp down on basic economic freedoms in 1950, social activities condemned by the new regime continued to survive away from public view. When community festivals were stigmatized and cult leaders sent to reeducation camps in the early years of liberation, popular religion went underground—quite literally. In north China underground chambers were built with tunnels long enough to connect strategic places throughout entire villages. In Hebei, some sectarian leaders took refuge for over four years in shelters several meters below the surface. Christianity and Buddhism also had great staying power, as their followers quietly dropped all visible signs of allegiance but clung to their faith. A literary inquisition in the early 1950s consigned entire collections to the pulping press, while even seemingly innocuous titles were taken off the shelves, but for many years people continued to read forbidden books in secret, sometimes with little interference.[3]

The leadership was very much aware of the extraordinary resilience of the old ideas and institutions it had tried to destroy wholesale after liberation. At the very heart of the Cultural Revolution was the acknowledgement that by 1966, despite seventeen years of communist rule, the old society continued to exist in the hearts and minds of many people. Underneath a surface of ideological uniformity lay a world of subcultures, countercultures, and alternative cultures that posed a threat to the Communist Party. In official parlance, once the socialist transformation of the means of production had been completed, a new revolution was required to liquidate once and for all the last remnants of feudal and bourgeois thought, or else

---

3. Frank Dikötter, *The Tragedy of Liberation: A History of the Communist Revolution 1945-1957* (London: Bloomsbury, 2013), 190, 199–203.

the forces of revisionism might very well prevail and undermine the entire communist enterprise.

But despite the house raids, the book burnings, the public humiliations, and all the purges, not to mention the ceaseless campaigns of reeducation, from study classes in Mao Zedong Thought to May Seventh cadre schools, old habits died hard. The Cultural Revolution aimed to transform every aspect of an individual's life, including his innermost thoughts and personal feelings, but in many cases it only managed to create the appearance of conformity. People fought deception with deception, lies with lies, and empty rhetoric with empty slogans. Many were great actors, pretending to go along, knowing precisely what to say when required.

* * *

Throughout the Cultural Revolution, propaganda trumpeted the importance of socialist education, both for young people who had never experienced the old world and for the older generation tainted by revisionist thoughts. But by the 1970s the educational system lay in shambles. Higher institutes of learning had all but closed down, with some of the best minds in the country confined to May Seventh cadre schools. As soon as they finished middle school, students were sent to the countryside for reeducation by the peasants.

The education dispensed in schools emphasized ideology. However, while children may have been able effortlessly to recite passages from the Little Red Book, the chaos of the Cultural Revolution did little to enhance their long-term academic development. In Nantong, near the river mouth of the Yangtze, some children could not tell when the People's Republic had been established. In Jiangning, also in Jiangsu, a few were unable to write their own names. This was the case with twenty of the fifty-four children in one class at the Dongtai Sancang commune. Forty of them could not write Arabic numbers.[4]

These were not isolated examples. In Shandong, one-third of all young people and 60 percent of adults were partly or entirely illiterate by the time that Mao Zedong died. In parts of the province, for instance the region of Linqin, half of all young people and two-thirds of all adults could not write their own name or read even a simple article from the *People's Daily*. These figures reflected a nationwide trend. As the State Council admitted, by 1978, as a result of the Cultural Revolution, the rate of illiteracy or semi-literacy reached 30 to 40 percent among children and youths of all age groups across China. In parts of the country it was more than 50 percent. Party members were no exception. In Hebei, regimented by 1.45 million cadres, one in three was illiterate. Few had graduated from high school.[5]

---

4. Jiangsu Provincial Archives, 4013-20-106, January 25, 1975, 1–3 and 38.
5. Shandong Provincial Archives, A29-4-47, Report from the Bureau for Education, May 15 and June 3, 1975, 75, 87 and 99; Shanghai Municipal Archives, B1-8-11, Report from the State Council, November 6, 1978, 14–16; Hebei Provincial Archives, 919-1-148, December 11, 1968, n.p.

But even as general literacy was on the decline, the opportunities to read forbidden literature paradoxically increased. Even at the height of the Cultural Revolution, as Red Guards went on a spree, trying to eradicate all signs of a feudal past, some of them quietly pocketed titles that attracted their attention. Many books were pulped or burnt, but quite a few found their way to a thriving black market. In Chengdu, as Jung Chang noted, all sorts of people could be found trading books, including "Red Guards who wanted to make some cash from the books they had confiscated; frustrated entrepreneurs who smelled money; scholars who did not want their books to be burned but were afraid of keeping them; and book lovers." Her brother went to the black market every day, trading his way up the ladder by selling books which he had obtained from a paper recycling shop. He read voraciously, at the rate of one or two volumes a day, but never dared to keep more than a dozen or so at any one time, all of them carefully hidden.[6]

These underground readers were soon joined by others, as people became increasingly disillusioned with politics. After March 1967 some of the students started withdrawing from factional warfare, joining the ranks of those referred to as the "free and unfettered." To keep themselves occupied, they turned to reading a whole variety of books that were beyond their reach before the onset of the Cultural Revolution. Zhai Zhenhua, who was expelled from her Red Guard organization, had her pick of all the forbidden books after she found an opening through the planks used to board up her school's library.[7]

Underground reading became even more common after the summer of 1968, as millions of young people exiled to the countryside circulated books among themselves to while away the long winter nights. Jung Chang, sent to a small village in Sichuan, had been given a whole stack of reading material by her brother. She was out in the fields every day, but itched to get back to them: "In the placidity of the village, in the hushed depth of the nights in my damp home, I did a lot of reading and thinking." Liang Heng, banned from Changsha, was lucky enough to be placed in a middle school, where he discovered a cache of books covered in dust and mildew in a storage room. His heart pounded, as a whole world of the imagination opened up to him: "My life changed completely."[8]

As the ideological climate relaxed in the wake of Lin Biao's death, the world of forbidden literature flourished yet further. While the contents of book shops changed very little, with row after row of works by Mao, Marx, Engels, Lenin, and Stalin, the range of books that circulated under the counter expanded enormously. Besides the banned books that had been rescued from private collections and public libraries, the state printed around a thousand translations of modern and contemporary writers for limited circulation, intended for the eyes of party members only.

---

6. Chang Jung, *Wild Swans: Three Daughters of China* (Clearwater, FL: Touchstone, 2003), 476–77.
7. Zhai Zhenhua, *Red Flower of China* (New York: Soho, 1992), 229–30.
8. Chang, *Wild Swans*, 552; Liang Heng and Judith Shapiro, *Son of the Revolution* (New York: Knopf, 1983), 201–2.

These books, too, found their way to the general public. The daughter of a leading official remembers that her father would lock the restricted books in a drawer, but failed to hide the key very well. She devoured Soviet novels, and was particularly struck by Ivan Shamiakin's *Snowy Winters*, dealing with the wrongful persecution of cadres in the Soviet Union. Jung Chang, on the other hand, relished Nixon's *Six Crises*, even if the translation came expurgated, while the descriptions of the Kennedy administration in David Halberstam's *The Best and the Brightest* made her marvel at the relaxed atmosphere of politics in the United States.[9]

One of the translations that had the biggest impact was William Shirer's *The Rise and Fall of the Third Reich*, as it offered striking parallels with the Cultural Revolution. Harry Truman's *Memoirs*, Milovan Djilas's *The New Class: An Analysis of the Communist System*, and Solzhenitsyn's *One Day in the Life of Ivan Denisovitch* were also welcome, helping readers to develop critical views of the communist revolution. The work of Trotsky, in a country where people were being shot for being Trotskyists, was also influential, not least his *The Revolution Betrayed: What is the Soviet Union* as well as *Stalin: An Appraisal of the Man and his Influence*. There were also notable literary works, including Albert Camus's *The Stranger*, Jack Kerouac's *On the Road*, Samuel Beckett's *Waiting for Godot* and J. D. Salinger's *The Catcher in the Rye*.[10]

Banned books were sometimes copied by hand. There were even reading groups exchanging forbidden material and gathering to discuss common interests. One network of readers based in Beijing, with correspondents in other parts of the country, boldly called themselves the Fourth International Counterrevolutionary Clique. Despite government suppression, these clubs continued to gain members, as a growing number of readers groped towards a critical perspective on the Cultural Revolution.[11]

Not all the literature that circulated was equally high-minded. On the black market, novels with erotic passages commanded the highest prices, proportionate to the degree of political danger. In this puritanical society, even Stendhal's nineteenth century classic *Le Rouge et le Noir* was considered erotic, and a copy could command the equivalent of two weeks' wages for an ordinary worker. Erotic novels were copied by hand and sometimes even crudely mimeographed with simple stencils or hand-cranked devices. At the height of the Cultural Revolution, many units had begun publishing their own bulletins or newspapers. Some of that equipment had escaped from the hands of the Mao Zedong Thought propaganda teams and

---

9. Li Jianglin, interview, September 7, 2014; Chang, *Wild Swans*, 593–94.
10. On these translations, see Guo Jian, Yongyi Song, and Yuan Zhou, eds., *The A to Z of the Chinese Cultural Revolution* (Lanham, MD: Scarecrow Press, 2009), 107; Mark Gamsa, *The Chinese Translation of Russian Literature: Three Studies* (Leiden: Brill, 2008), 24; Yang Jian, *Zhongguo zhiqing wenxue shi* [A literary history of educated youth] (Beijing: Zhongguo gongren chubanshe, 2002), chapters 4 to 6.
11. Guo, Song and Zhou, eds., *The A to Z of the Chinese Cultural Revolution*, 98–99.

was now being put to good use, as erotic novels and lewd songs circulated in factories, schools, and even government offices.[12]

One of the most widely read novels was *The Heart of a Maiden*, a story about a college girl and her sexual encounters with her cousin and other young men. The text was short and explicit, which may have accounted for its popularity. No one will ever know just how many copies circulated, but it may well have been one of the most studied texts after the Chairman's Little Red Book.[13]

* * *

Throughout the Cultural Revolution, people also continued listening secretly to foreign radio broadcasts, despite the risk of being denounced by a neighbor and sentenced for a counterrevolutionary crime. The extent of the practice was revealed during the "One Strike and Three Anti" Campaign in 1970, when millions of ordinary people were persecuted for the merest hint of discontent with the party, whether real or imagined. In one factory in Gansu, deep inside the hinterland, one in every fifty workers listened to radio programs broadcast from the Soviet Union, the United States, Taiwan, Hong Kong, Japan and India. There was also a Sichuan Underground Station and a Voice of the Liberation Army.[14]

Much as ordinary people had learnt how to use printing equipment at the height of the Cultural Revolution, quite a few students had taken classes in radio broadcasting. Gao Yuan, the head of his school's radio club in Zhengding, was able to build everything from the simplest single-diode receiver to seven-transistor radios. The best devices picked up signals from Moscow.[15]

Radio clubs soon became suspect, but there was a thriving black market in radio transistors and semi-conductors. On Fuzhou Street in Shanghai, young people keen to pursue their hobby could meet factory workers who stole the required parts. The authorities repeatedly tried to stamp out the trade, but to no avail.[16]

Their attempt to jam the Voice of America and radio signals from Taiwan was also futile. In the airwave war, no technology existed to prevent strong and stable signals from reaching most listeners. In an odd twist, by reducing the cost of a radio the regime actually made listening to shortwave programs from abroad easier. In the countryside, just before the onset of the Cultural Revolution, a set could cost the equivalent of a whole pig, a luxury few families could afford. The range varied from 300 to 500 kilometers, meaning that cities like Yining were out of range of the provincial capital Urumchi and did not enjoy daytime reception. In order to spread

---

12. See, for instance, Shandong Provincial Archives, A1-8-59, May 30, 1975, 3.
13. *Shaonü zhi xin* [The heart of a maiden], also called *Manna huiyilu* [Memoirs of Manna]; see Yang Dongxiao, "Wenge jinshu: 'Shaonü zhi xin'. Nage niandai de xingyuzui" [A book banned during the Cultural Revolution: "The Heart of a Maiden," the first pornographic novel hand-copied during the Cultural Revolution], *Renwu huabao*, no. 23 (2010): 68–71.
14. Gansu Provincial Archives, 129-6-48, May 26, 1970, 100.
15. Gao Yuan, *Born Red: A Chronicle of the Cultural Revolution* (Stanford: Stanford University Press, 1987), 29.
16. Shanghai Municipal Archives, B123-8-1044, May 6, 1974, 4–9.

Mao Zedong Thought, the price was cut by more than a third in following years, and by 1970 four-transistor radios were sold below cost of production in many parts of the country.[17]

Several years later, wired networks reached a majority of the population in entire provinces, supported by broadcasting stations in county towns and amplifying stations in people's communes. Even poor villagers were never far removed from the propaganda. In Hubei, in 1974, there were over 4.8 million loudspeakers, compared to a mere 180,000 prior to the Cultural Revolution. It was equivalent to almost one per household.[18]

Still, the din of the propaganda machine could not drown out a diversity of waves, local and foreign. Even in poor regions like Hainan, the subtropical island off the coast of Guangdong, people occasionally listened to the Voice of the Liberation Army, which was vehemently hostile to Mao Zedong. There was also a Voice of Communist Youth, which broadcast seditious slogans at irregular intervals throughout the day. The station was believed to be run by graduate students of Zhongshan University in Guangzhou. In Guangzhou itself, taxi drivers were openly tuning their radios to Hong Kong programs. They were not alone. By now, even dedicated party officials were lured by foreign radio, if only because they were keen to discover what was happening in their own country. The daughter of a high official one day walked into her parent's room without knocking on the door, only to hear a bright voice calling out: "This is radio Moscow!"[19]

Other social activities condemned by the state flourished. There were underground singing clubs, as people gathered under the pretext of singing revolutionary songs, only to perform forbidden plays and sing banned tunes. In the Shanghai Number Two Machine Tool Plant, a group of a hundred young workers played forbidden music every Friday in the winter of 1969–1970, attracting a lively audience from other factories.[20]

The old world made a comeback in the early 1970s, as people reconnected with pastimes decried as feudal or bourgeois by the Red Guards a few years earlier. The only widespread children's game by the time of Lin Biao's death was skipping, but soon enough whips and tops, hopscotch and diabolo could be seen in the streets of Beijing. The sale of traditional, painted silk kites was still restricted to foreigners, but some children knew how to fly ingenious contrivances made of strips of wood and bits of the *People's Daily*. Poker appeared in the narrow, winding alleys of the capital. Raising pigeons was repeatedly banned after 1966, although the birds could be seen racing across the sky with small bamboo pipes attached to their tail

---

17. Hebei Provincial Archives, Ministry of Trade, 999-4-761, May 18, 1966, 116–24; Shaanxi Provincial Archives, 215-1-1844, October 27 and November 20, 1970, 50 and 53–59.
18. PRO, FCO 21-1223, "China News Summary," September 25, 1974.
19. PRO, FCO 21-1089, "Overt Intelligence Reports, January to April 1972," June 1, 1973; PRO, FCO 21-1089, "Letter from Embassy," May 10, 1973; Li Jianglin, interview September 7, 2014.
20. Shanghai Municipal Archives, B246-2-554, January 12, 1970, 1.

feathers, producing an eerie, harmonious whistle. People started keeping birds in cages again, sometimes heading for the parks in the early morning to air their pets.[21]

Ordinary people became underground artists, seeking refuge from politics in art by painting in a manner deliberately detached from the "socialist realism" that shaped everything at the time, from the propaganda posters festooned on walls to the "people's art" officially sponsored by the party. Many were deliberately apolitical, trying to carve out a personal space in which they could reconnect with their inner selves. Their art was clandestine, but like the underground literary salons and singing clubs, informal groups of amateur artists shared their interests, using abandoned factories, deserted parks or private flats in buildings with adequate dark hallways and isolated staircases. Art books and exhibition catalogues were circulated, as people reconnected with everything Western from Michelangelo to Picasso, but also Chinese traditional paintings.

In Beijing some of these budding artists, all from very diverse backgrounds, came together in a group which only received a name much later: *Wuming*, or Nameless. "In an era when free association was a crime, the group had to be nameless, shapeless and spontaneous. There were no regulations, no membership, no unified artistic principles or style."[22] Many of them came from families defined as "class enemies" and had endured broken homes, ravaged schools and crumbling communities throughout the Cultural Revolution. They took to the brush, at first honing their skills by following the propaganda campaign and painting portraits of the Chairman. It was a good source of precious oil paint and linen canvas, which they used to begin experimenting in their spare time. Nature was a favorite theme, from peach blossoms and lilacs observed in the Botanical Garden to the sunsets seen from the Ming Tombs in the suburbs of Beijing. On one occasion, several members forged a letter of introduction to get past public security and made a trip to the seaside at Beidaihe on National Day. But they also painted from memory, carving a personal realm deep inside themselves. Wang Aihe, herself an accomplished painter and member of *Wuming*, remembers a fellow factory worker who stared for hours through the window, pondering how to paint a tree he could see in the distance.[23]

* * *

---

21. PRO, FO 21-969, Richard C. Samuel, "Play Games Not War," April 17, 1972; PRO, FO 21-969, M. J. Richardson, "Local Colour," October 3 and December 6, 1972.
22. Wang Aihe, "Wuming: An Underground Art Group during the Cultural Revolution," *Journal of Modern Chinese History* 3, no. 2 (Dec. 2009): 186.
23. See Wang Aihe's chapter in this volume, and Wang Aihe, "*Wuming*: Art and Solidarity in a Peculiar Historical Context," in *Wuming (No Name) Painting Catalogue* (Hong Kong: Hong Kong University Press, 2010), 7–9; see also Wang Aihe, "Wuming: An Underground Art Group during the Cultural Revolution," *Journal of Modern Chinese History* 3, no. 2 (Dec. 2009): 183–99; see also Julia F. Andrews, *Painters and Politics in the People's Republic of China, 1949–1979* (Berkeley: University of California Press, 1994), and Ellen Johnston Laing, *The Winking Owl: Art in the People's Republic of China* (Berkeley: University of California Press, 1988).

Religion also went underground, allowing people to remain secretly connected to their faiths, both organized creeds including Christianity, Buddhism, Taoism, and Islam, and folk religions with their local gods and ancestors.

Throughout the Cultural Revolution, there were even occasional spurts of popular protest. In Hebei, to take but one example, in 1969 Christians openly shouted "I don't believe in Mao Zedong, I believe in God!" Elsewhere in the province, slogans appeared on May Day, proclaiming "Celebrate God the Creator." But these were isolated incidents, quickly suppressed by the omnipotent military. In most cases, especially in the countryside, ordinary villagers carried on exercising their faiths in a quiet, indirect, nonconfrontational way.[24]

In many cases, religious leaders were impotent, but ordinary villagers continued with their beliefs. Ironically, denominations that had borne the brunt of persecution in the 1950s were better prepared for the onslaught of the Cultural Revolution. This was the case for Watchman Nee and the Little Flock, which had been one of the fastest growing native Protestant movements in China up to 1949, when it boasted as many as 70,000 followers. Within the first five years of liberation, most leaders of the Little Flock were arrested and the congregations systematically crushed. Watchman Nee died in prison in 1972. But ordinary followers viewed the persecution as a test of their faith, organizing cell groups and home meetings many years before the Cultural Revolution even began. A pragmatic tradition of clandestine worshipping allowed them to survive.[25]

Other organized religions resorted to similar strategies, adopting a decentralized approach with clusters of worshippers dispersed throughout the countryside. Lamas, imams and priests may well have been in reeducation camps, but ordinary followers stepped in to hold their communities together. They also recruited new members among the ever-growing number of victims of the Cultural Revolution, offering an explanation for their suffering, a sense of hope and sometimes a promise of salvation or inner peace. Most of all, with government offices in charge of religious affairs in turmoil, besieged by rebels or imploding under the weight of factional infighting, denominations of every hue resurfaced and reorganized themselves, laying a firm foundation for religious revival after the death of Mao Zedong.

Local gods were also stubborn, subverting attempts by the state to replace them with the cult of Mao. In some villages, local festivals and public rituals were discontinued, while temples were closed down, but many villagers continued to worship at a small shrine or altar inside their home. They offered incense, repaid vows, invoked the spirits or otherwise communicated with a whole variety of local gods away from the public eye, from ancestral spirits, patron deities and rain gods to fertility goddesses. The ultimate act of subversion was probably to turn the Chairman

---

24. Hebei Provincial Archives, 919-1-290, May 31, 1969, 54–55.
25. Joseph Tse-Hei Lee, "Watchman Nee and the Little Flock Movement in Maoist China," *Church History* 74, no. 1 (March 2005): 68–96; see also Chen-yang Kao, "The Cultural Revolution and the Emergence of Pentecostal-style Protestantism in China," *Journal of Contemporary Religion* 24, no. 2 (May 2009): 171–88.

himself into a local deity. But larger statues also survived, even as temples were often demolished or turned into granaries. In some cases they were moved from one place to another, until by 1972 local communities felt it safe enough to give them a more permanent home. Sometimes a temple was built with collective funds under the pretense of establishing a school, a trend that could be observed throughout Pingliang county in Gansu, and no doubt in other parts of the country.[26]

Folk culture, often intertwined with local religion, also remained resilient, even at the height of the Cultural Revolution. Jiang Qing had made one of her first public appearances at the Peking Opera festival in the summer of 1964, determined to reform traditional opera, one of the most popular art forms in the countryside. Soon enough she banned all opera with the exception of six revolutionary plays and two ballets which glorified the People's Liberation Army and Mao Zedong Thought. The Eight Model Operas appeared on posters, postcards, stamps, plates, teapots, vases and calendars. They were played by special performing troupes in schools and factories. Zhai Zhenhua, who was sent to Yan'an to till the fields, was lucky enough to be selected by a travelling troupe. They presented their show to factory workers and commune peasants on crude stages in open fields. "The audience was usually large but applause was sparse. The opera was never really welcomed anywhere except, believe it or not, at Yan'an University." She may have overstated the case, but her experience clearly shows how state-sponsored operas were far from receiving universal acclaim, even in the countryside.[27]

But despite all the state propaganda, some communities still went ahead and stuck to their own traditions. In 1968, several villages joined forces in Zhejiang and organized huge gatherings around a performance of traditional opera, with cigarettes and wine laid out on hundreds of tables for honorary guests and local families alike. In Jiangxi, a much poorer province than Zhejiang, there were also occasions on which thousands of people gathered openly to enjoy a traditional play. In parts of the countryside, commune members routinely celebrated traditional festivals and prayed to the local gods and spirits. Some villages had a common fund to allow dragon boat competitions, which were attended by large crowds, as pigs were slaughtered and food was spread on the tables in a conspicuous display of consumption. By the early 1970s, besides opera performers, a whole range of traditional specialists, including folk musicians, geomancers, spirit mediums and fortune tellers, were making a living in the countryside.[28]

* * *

---

26. Gansu Provincial Archives, 91-7-283, May 26, 1974, 1–7.
27. Zhai, *Red Flower of China*, 226–27; see also Barbara Mittler, "'Eight Stage Works for 800 Million People': The Great Proletarian Cultural Revolution in Music; a View from Revolutionary Opera," *Opera Quarterly* 26, no. 2–3 (Spring 2010): 377–401.
28. Hebei Provincial Archives, 919-1-185, Report from the Ministry of Grain, January 23, 1968, 24–25; Shandong Provincial Archives, A1-8-24, Report from the Public Security Bureau, November 20, 1973, 46; Shaanxi Provincial Archives, 194-1-1317, April 25, 1968, 59.

Underground churches are sometimes called house churches, as small groups of believers gathered secretly in private homes to share their faith. While religion could no longer openly function as a social bond holding communities together, it survived as a more personal, private experience, retreating from the church, the temple or the mosque into the realm of the home. Paradoxically, as the Cultural Revolution attacked the very notion of privacy as a bourgeois concept, people from all walks of life tried to turn their homes into fragile islands of freedom. This was not easy, especially in the cities where apartments and houses were often shared by several families, while prying neighbors and gossip were a nuisance everywhere. Still, literary salons, reading clubs and underground artists, like religious believers, sometimes managed to gather clandestinely in a private home, even if they had to change venues regularly to avoid detection.

But it was families rather than religious groups or underground clubs that stubbornly perpetuated their beliefs in the relative privacy of their home. The educational system may have been in disarray, but home schooling allowed some parents to instill the values they cherished into their offspring. Across the country, millions of children were not allowed to go beyond elementary education because of their bad class background. Not only were they spared much of the state propaganda, but family members sometimes educated them at home. Mothers in particular played an important role, drawing on a rich culture of family education, since their status in the traditional household had often depended on the academic success of their offspring. Liu Wenzhong, who belonged to a family ostracized as "counterrevolutionaries" in Shanghai, was schooled at home and taught to value human rights and democracy.[29]

Well before liberation, a whole range of traditional skills were also developed and transmitted through family ties. Sometimes several households or even entire villages specialized in producing paper umbrellas, cloth shoes, silk hats, rattan chairs, wicker creels or twig baskets for the market. Throughout the Cultural Revolution some families continued to pass on their expertise, from crafting protective charms and printing popular almanacs to making paper lanterns. Many other occupations were family-based, for instance martial arts, traditional theatre or opera singing.

The family, of course, endured sustained attack during the Cultural Revolution. Some households were divided right through the middle, as members pledged allegiance to different factions or were caught up in the shifting currents of local politics. Senseless and unpredictable purges were designed to cower the population and rip apart entire communities, producing docile, atomized individuals loyal to no one but the Chairman. Family members were expected to denounce each other at public struggle meetings, and spouses were often enjoined to seek a divorce when their partners were shipped away to the gulag. Most of all, particularly in the cities, many households were ruthlessly broken up, as their members were sent to

---

29. Liu Wenzhong, *Fengyu rensheng lu: Yige canji kuqiu xinsheng ji* [A record of my stormy life] (Macau: Aomen chongshi wenhua, 2004), 40.

different parts of the countryside. Children were wrenched away as soon as they graduated from middle school, their parents sometimes split up and confined to different reeducation camps. Ordinary workers ended up in improvised factories on the Third Front, while government employees were reeducated by the peasants in Mao Zedong Study Classes or May Seventh Cadre Schools. In Sichuan, Jung Chang's parents were separated and held in two different labor camps, while her four siblings were tilling the fields in remote villages far away from Chengdu.

But China has one of the world's most complex kinship systems, fine-tuned over many centuries by a sophisticated lexicon with separate designations for almost every family member according to their gender, relative age, lineage and generation. Filial piety was a linchpin of Confucian ethics, while extended families in the form of clans and lineages formed the backbone of a millennial empire that only collapsed in 1911. As a result, families proved to be remarkably resilient. In some cases, they actually became closer. Jung Chang and her siblings learnt how to look after each other, and became more united by frequently visiting their parents in camp.[30]

The strength of the family bond was clearly demonstrated by the paucity of children who actually denounced their parents. Propaganda was replete with examples of young pioneers who chose loyalty to the state above duty to a parent. In the Soviet Union the case of Pavlik Morozov, a teenage boy killed by relatives in 1932 for having informed on his own father, became a cause célèbre. Though mythical, the story was endlessly exploited by the state. In the cult of Pavlik Morozov, children were encouraged to replace the family bond with one fealty alone, namely to Stalin.[31]

Propaganda in China was equally vociferous. Already during the Socialist Education Campaign in the early 1960s, the slogan "Father is Close, Mother is Close, but Neither is as Close as Chairman Mao" was inculcated into every child. As one student noted, "We were drilled to think that anyone, including our parents, who was not totally for Mao was the enemy." Parents themselves encouraged their children to conform to official ideology, recognizing that this was the best option to safeguard their future.[32]

Yet in the Soviet Union, fanatical denunciations of parents were actually rather unusual. Even fewer cases can be documented for the Cultural Revolution. Those rare children who actually informed on their own relatives were often ostracized. Ma Dingan, who reported his father for dealing in ration coupons on the black market, was expelled from his home, repudiated by the villagers and confined to an abandoned temple, and even local party officials refused to have anything to do with him.[33]

---

30. Chang, *Wild Swans*, 576; on the family during the Cultural Revolution, see also Zang Xiaowei, *Children of the Cultural Revolution: Family Life and Political Behavior in Mao's China* (Boulder, CO: Westview Press, 2000).
31. Orlando Figes, *The Whisperers: Private Life in Stalin's Russia* (New York: Picador, 2007), 300.
32. Chang, *Wild Swans*, 330.
33. Gansu Provincial Archives, 91-7-351, July 1975, n.p.

An even more striking case is that of Zhang Hongbing, who as a boy aged fifteen shopped his own mother, demanding that she be shot for her counterrevolutionary crimes. The party granted his wish. The woman, whose only crime was to have thrown portraits of the Chairman into the fire, was executed by firing squad. The son became the object of a cult, briefly celebrated for his revolutionary fervor by the local party committee, before being persecuted himself as the son of a counter-revolutionary element. For decades Zhang was tormented by a guilty conscience, finally coming forward in 2013 to make a public confession in the hope of assuaging his pain. By going public he discovered that he was the only case of a son who had actually demanded the death penalty for a close relative. In China as in the Soviet Union, more often than not the norm for young people was to renounce family members rather than denounce them.[34]

Even outside the family, an old code of loyalty occasionally survived, as people stood by their friends or colleagues. Jung Chang was allowed to visit her father on a regular basis thanks to a squad leader in his late twenties who did his best unobtrusively to improve the lot of the people he knew. One translator working in Beijing remembers how she was shunned by her colleagues at work after she became a victim of the campaign to cleanse the class ranks in 1969. But their family members, all living in the same compound, carried on as if nothing had happened, helping her with discreet gifts of rationed items. As memoirs and interviews amply testify, there were also random acts of kindness among complete strangers.[35]

In its effort to atomize society, the regime took sword and fire to traditional social bonds, but it failed to suffocate the family. Not only did family ties endure, but new bonds were forged. The regime frowned on romantic relationships, and married couples rarely displayed their affection in public during the Cultural Revolution. Love was considered a decadent, bourgeois emotion, and sex was taboo. Many students grew up in sheer ignorance of the most basic physiological facts. Zhuo Fei, for one, was terrified that she might become pregnant after sharing a bicycle with a young man, but she was too afraid to ask anybody, even her own relatives. Rae Yang, a Red Guard from Beijing who had relished the opportunity to go and work in the countryside in Manchuria, put it in a nutshell: "We did not have sex or even think about it. Sex was bourgeois. No doubt about it! In my mind, it was something very dirty and ugly. It was also extremely dangerous. In the books I read and the movies I saw, only the bad guys were interested in sex. Revolutionaries had nothing to do with it. When revolutionaries fell in love, they loved with their hearts. They didn't even touch hands."[36]

---

34. The most extensive interview and research on Zhang Hongbing appears in Philippe Grangereau, "Une mère sur la conscience," *Libération*, April 28, 2013, 5–7.
35. Chang, *Wild Swans*, 574; Pamela Tan, *The Chinese Factor: An Australian Chinese Woman's Life in China from 1950 to 1979* (Dural: New South Wales: Roseberg, 2008), 157.
36. Zhuo Fei, *Yingzujie mingliu zai wenge de gushi* [Celebrities from the British concession in Shanghai during the Cultural Revolution] (Hong Kong: Mingbao chubanshe youxian gongsi, 2005), 249.

But like so many other students banned to the countryside, Rae learnt quickly by watching the farm animals. She was put in charge of breeding boars, having to guide their quivering genitals into a sow's vagina. "It was like watching pornographic movies day in and day out." Others found out by reading *The Heart of a Maiden*. Once Lin Biao vanished, young people began to meet socially and quietly pair up, seeking privacy away from collective dormitories and crowded dining halls. In Manchuria, with temperatures plunging to thirty degrees below zero, young couples on state farms had little choice but to take to the great outdoors. Despite the cold they persisted, rushing back to the dormitories to embrace the heaters after less than twenty minutes.[37]

On the other hand, for students who did not work on agricultural collectives controlled by the army, living among the villagers instead, the opportunities for sexual encounter were much greater. In some cases young people even lived together, a practice unimaginable in the cities. A few had children out of wedlock, refusing to marry for fear of being stuck in the countryside forever.

But most of all, except for students from the cities, the vast majority of people in the countryside were far less coy about sex. When they first arrived among their peasant hosts, quite a few young students were taken aback by their open display of affection. One day Wang Yuanyuan, a sixteen-year-old girl sent to Inner Mongolia, saw a couple making love by the side of a ditch and reported the affair to the brigade leader. "The old peasants, though, didn't treat it as anything and just laughed." As with so many other aspects of folk culture, the Cultural Revolution ran no more than skin deep.[38]

It is commonplace to note that not just the economy, but also culture was revived under Deng Xiaoping, even though he officially identified Marxism-Leninism and Mao Zedong Thought as one of the four cardinal principles on the Communist Party. As this chapter suggests, however, the foundations of this revival are not to be found in the policy decisions of one man, but in the secret, hidden activities of many millions of ordinary people who subverted the ideological strictures of the one-party state, often at great personal risk. The second society, like the second economy, appeared as early as the 1950s, although paradoxically it thrived during the last years of the Cultural Revolution. It grew because, on the one hand, more people than ever before became targets of the indoctrination campaigns unleashed by the "revolutionary party committees" under military control that took over the party and the state after the summer of 1968. But on the other hand, once the role of the military was drastically curtailed after the Lin Biao incident in September 1971, the power and credibility of the party as a whole suffered a huge blow. The Chairman was forced to turn to the party officials denounced as "capitalist roaders" at the height of the Cultural Revolution, but the clout and prestige they once wielded was now gone. The Cultural Revolution, by unleashing a frontal attack on cadres at all

---
37. Rae Yang, *Spider Eaters: A Memoir* (Berkeley: University of California Press, 1997), 197 and 248–49.
38. Emily Honig, "Socialist Sex: The Cultural Revolution Revisited," *Modern China* 29, no. 2 (April 2003): 143–75.

levels, had undermined the very organization of the party. Vast numbers of people used the opportunity to quietly hollow out Marxism-Leninism and Mao Zedong Thought. In effect, they buried Maoism even before the Chairman died.

But there is another way of looking at the so-called era of reform that followed the death of Mao Zedong, one in which the keyword is not so much "reform" but "stalemate." A year before the fall of the Berlin Wall, Elemér Hankiss observed that the second society never exists independently from official ideology. The two spheres encroach on each other "in an inextricable and mutually parasitic way." It is not only that the second society, like the second economy, provides an indispensable safety valve, compensating for the dysfunctions of the one-party state. More importantly, the second society is, at times, allowed to become a testing ground for new organizational principles or policy decisions before they are formally introduced in the first society. An example he provides is the relatively peaceful development of social groups who clamored for the preservation of traditional landmarks and monuments in Hungary. Their aims were finally incorporated and legitimized by the one-party state, although militant ecological organizations were mercilessly stamped out.

But the key point that Hankiss makes is that this uneasy relationship, while providing a small measure of freedom of choice, dignity, and independence for countless individuals, can also prevent the development of a truly open and transparent society. The very existence of a second society, much like that of the second economy, is precisely what allows the ruling elite to indefinitely postpone meaningful reforms. What emerges is a series of "vicious hybrids and low-efficiency mixes," from "quasi-corporatism" and "quasi-pluralism" to the "quasi-market." This form of hybridization is detrimental to the interests of everybody, from the very top of the social hierarchy to the bottom, even though all have a stake in it. While this did not happen in Hungary, where the communist regime collapsed by the end of 1989, one wonders whether "stalemate" rather than "reform" might not be the keyword to understanding political developments in China after 1978.

Bibliography

Andrews, Julia F. *Painters and Politics in the People's Republic of China, 1949–1979*. Berkeley: University of California Press, 1994.
Chang, Jung. *Wild Swans: Three Daughters of China*. Clearwater, FL: Touchstone, 2003.
Dikötter, Frank. *The Cultural Revolution: A People's Tragedy, 1962–1967*. London and New York: Bloomsbury, 2016.
Dikötter, Frank. *The Tragedy of Liberation: A History of the Communist Revolution 1945–1957*. London and New York: Bloomsbury, 2013.
Figes, Orlando. *The Whisperers: Private Life in Stalin's Russia*. New York: Picador, 2007.
Gamsa, Mark. *The Chinese Translation of Russian Literature: Three Studies*. Leiden: Brill, 2008.
Gao, Yuan. *Born Red: A Chronicle of the Cultural Revolution*. Stanford: Stanford University Press, 1987.

Hankiss, Elemér. "The 'Second Society': Is There an Alternative Social Model Emerging in Contemporary Hungary?" *Social Research* 55, no. 1–2 (Spring 1988): 13–42.

Honig, Emily. "Socialist Sex: The Cultural Revolution Revisited." *Modern China* 29, no. 2 (April 2003): 143–75.

Jian, Guo, Yongyi Song, and Yuan Zhou, eds. *The A to Z of the Chinese Cultural Revolution.* Lanham, MD: Scarecrow Press, 2009.

Kao Chen-yang. "The Cultural Revolution and the Emergence of Pentecostal-Style Protestantism in China." *Journal of Contemporary Religion* 24, no. 2 (May 2009): 171–88.

Laing, Ellen Johnston. *The Winking Owl: Art in the People's Republic of China.* Berkeley: University of California Press, 1988.

Liang, Heng, and Judith Shapiro. *Son of the Revolution.* New York: Knopf, 1983.

Lee, Joseph Tse-Hei. "Watchman Nee and the Little Flock Movement in Maoist China." *Church History* 74, no. 1 (March 2005): 68–96.

Liu, Wenzhong. *Fengyu rensheng lu: Yige canji kuqiu xinsheng ji* [A record of my stormy life]. Macau: Aomen chongshi wenhua, 2004.

Mittler, Barbara. "'Eight Stage Works for 800 Million People': The Great Proletarian Cultural Revolution in Music; a View from Revolutionary Opera." *Opera Quarterly* 26, no. 2–3 (Spring 2010): 377–401.

Tan, Pamela. *The Chinese Factor: An Australian Chinese Woman's Life in China from 1950 to 1979.* Dural, New South Wales: Roseberg, 2008.

Wang, Aihe. "*Wuming*: Art and Solidarity in a Peculiar Historical Context." In *Wuming (No Name) Painting Catalogue.* Hong Kong: Hong Kong University Press, 2010.

Wang, Aihe. "Wuming: An Underground Art Group during the Cultural Revolution." *Journal of Modern Chinese History* 3, no. 2 (Dec. 2009): 183–99.

Yang, Dongxiao. "Wenge jinshu: 'Shaonü zhi xin'. Nage niandai de xingyuzui" [A book banned during the Cultural Revolution: "The Heart of a Maiden," the first pornographic novel hand-copied during the Cultural Revolution]. *Renwu huabao*, no. 23 (2010): 68–71.

Yang, Jian. *Zhongguo zhiqing wenxue shi* [A literary history of educated youth]. Beijing: Zhongguo gongren chubanshe, 2002.

Yang, Rae. *Spider Eaters: A Memoir.* Berkeley: University of California Press, 1997.

Zang, Xiaowei. *Children of the Cultural Revolution: Family Life and Political Behavior in Mao's China.* Boulder, CO: Westview Press, 2000.

Zhai, Zhenhua. *Red Flower of China.* New York: Soho, 1992.

Zhuo, Fei, *Yingzujie mingliu zai wenge de gushi* [Celebrities from the British concession in Shanghai during the Cultural Revolution]. Hong Kong: Mingbao chubanshe youxian gongsi, 2005.

10
Case Files as a Source of Alternative Memories from the Maoist Past*

Daniel Leese

When searching for alternative sources to rescue the complexity of historical developments during the first thirty years of the People's Republic of China from the Procrustean bed represented by the 1981 party resolution, documents from the Chinese political-legal sector remain a largely untapped reservoir. Judicial records or documents compiled in the course of administrative investigations, here broadly referred to as "case files," are probably perceived as one of the least likely sources to extract individual memories about the Maoist era. As crucial components of the Chinese Communist Party's (CCP) "organs of dictatorship" (*zhuanzheng jiguan* 專政機關), courts, public security organs, or makeshift institutions during campaign periods sought to document criminal acts rather than to preserve alternative accounts of the past. Yet these case files often contain various traces of contested memories that touch upon issues ranging from everyday life to competing standards of norm-abiding behavior. These traces of individual voices from the Maoist era often take the form of verbatim quotations. They furthermore include first person narratives in the form of confessions, spanning up to two decades within a changing political environment. Despite their enforced nature, the case records represent a specific type of "ego-document"[1] and offer glimpses of alternative memories or at least about ways of framing certain events according to current norms of discourse. While their veracity can seldom be ascertained, because few of the individuals mentioned have left traces in official archival memory, these problems are not unique to judicial records.

In the case of early modern Europe, legal documents have provided the basis for several classical studies on heterodox thought or the art of persuasively turning an act of crime into a convincing story in order to receive royal pardon.[2] There

---

* The author gratefully acknowledges funding by the European Research Council (ERC grant agreement no. 336202) and the Bavarian Academy of Sciences. Valuable research assistance was provided by Wang Baigulahu.
1. Winfried Schulze, ed., *Ego-Dokumente. Annäherung an den Menschen in der Geschichte* [Ego-Documents: Approaching Man in History] (Berlin: Akademie Verlag, 1996).
2. See, for example, Carlo Ginzburg, *The Cheese and the Worms: The Cosmos of a Sixteenth-Century Miller*

are similar records of incredible bravery, stubbornness, and noncompliance still waiting to be explored in Chinese archives. This chapter, however, is not devoted to reconstructing the mental cosmos of an extraordinary individual. It rather aims at showing three different ways of tracing memories of ordinary people, sometimes of subaltern status,[3] through the prism of case files. All documents formed part of the attempt to reverse millions of "unjust, false, and mistaken" (*yuan, jia, cuo an* 冤假錯案) verdicts in the early reform era.[4] The cases thus touch upon the lives and memory of individuals who came into conflict with the authorities during the tumultuous period of the Cultural Revolution.

After briefly outlining the difficulties of working with sources from the Chinese political-legal sector, the first case study explores how the sparse amount of ego-documents contained in the file of a "speculator" allows us to reconstruct some aspects of life on the fringes of Chinese society in the Maoist period. The second case highlights the importance that quotations as legal evidence may have in assessing previous perceptions of Chinese politics. It analyzes investigations into the veracity of certain political statements of a former "extreme rightist" (*jiyou fenzi* 極右分子) after the Cultural Revolution. Finally, the repeated confessions of a factory worker regarding his rebel activities during the Cultural Revolution are discussed in order to show how the memory of certain events is adapted over time to fit changing discursive frameworks.

The respective case files differ enormously in terms of their internal organization and the amount of space devoted to first-person accounts. While some contain hundreds of pages of explanation and justification, others mainly consist of a few administrative forms. In all instances, caution has to be applied with regard to ascribing a higher truth-value to these individual statements as opposed to interpretations offered by state actors in form of either administrative or judicial verdicts. While some of the accused would stick to a certain fact, even if it would result in a higher penalty, most individuals were less interested in historical truth than in reducing their sentences. Still, the often chaotic, multivocal perspectives springing from the case files allow us to gauge the complexity of social reality in Maoist era China that has all but vanished from the official version of history set down by the resolution.

(Baltimore: Johns Hopkins University Press, 1980) and Natalie Zemon Davis, *Fiction in the Archives: Pardon Tales and Their Tellers in Sixteenth Century France* (Cambridge: Polity Press, 1988).

3. On the difficulty of tracing the voice of marginalized individuals in history see especially Gail Hershatter, "The Subaltern Talks Back: Reflections on Subaltern Theory and Chinese History," *Positions* 1 (1993): 103–30.
4. See Daniel Leese, "Revising Political Verdicts in Post-Mao China: The Case of Beijing's Fengtai District," in *Maoism at the Grassroots: Everyday Life in China's Era of High Socialism*, ed. Jeremy Brown and Matthew D. Johnson (Cambridge, MA: Harvard University Press, 2015), 102–28.

Case Files from the Late Maoist period

Research based on political-legal documents from the Maoist past is beset with various difficulties. With the exception of a very brief phase in the mid-1950s, the legal sector did not gain any meaningful independence from the executive political branch, most notably the public security sector, and is often linked to sensitive political campaigns.[5] Thus unlike the rich materials of the Shaan-Gan-Ning Border Region High Court held by the Shaanxi Provincial Archives in Xi'an,[6] which was accessible at least for a brief period of time, judicial files on post-1949 developments have generally remained off limits. Even today, case files from the Maoist period are seldom stored in regular archives. They are mostly held by professional or working archives (*zhuanye* or *gongzuo dang'an* 專業／工作檔案), whose function, like in the case of Western court archives, is not to serve the public or historical scholarship but to guarantee the functioning of the respective bureaucracy.[7] There tends to be an occasional overlap with the holdings of regular archives, but because no uniform rule applied to a transfer of files previously, archival findings are often based on coincidences. This holds especially true for the Cultural Revolution, when archives came to serve as weapons in political conflicts ("dead archives have to be used in lively fashion").[8] However, this may also be seen as an advantage for present-day research, because the state's regulating and filtering functions were greatly complicated by the tumultuous character of the movement.

Additionally, individual case files contain a large amount of personal information that was never intended to be made available for a wider public or to be preserved for posterity. While personality and privacy rights played a minuscule role in Maoist era China, by now archival regulations place much greater emphasis on the protection of personal identities. The Archives Law only vaguely hints at this problem and primarily mentions the necessity to protect state and party secrets,[9] but archival practice in recent years has been characterized by a growing awareness of protecting the identities of ordinary citizens. Researchers are thus confronted with a dilemma: case files provide a welcome antidote against generalizing accounts of how "the masses" felt or behaved, yet one has to be careful not to engage in a

---

5. The most comprehensive account is still Han Yanlong, ed., *Zhonghua renmin gongheguo fazhi tongshi* [Comprehensive history of the judicial system of the People's Republic of China], 2 vols. (Beijing: Zhongyang wenxian chubanshe, 1998).
6. See Xiaoping Cong, *Self-Determination: Marriage, Law, and Gender Construction in Revolutionary China, 1940–1960* (Cambridge: Cambridge University Press, 2016).
7. For the distinction between different archival categories, policies, and practices, see Vivian Wagner, *Erinnerungsverwaltung in China. Staatsarchive und Politik in der Volksrepublik* [Memory governance in China: State archives and politics in the People's Republic] (Cologne: Böhlau, 2006).
8. Beijing shiju bangongshi, "Guanyu quan ju dang'an gongzuo cunzai de yixie wenti ji jin yi bu jiaqiang dang'an gongzuo de yijian" [Opinions on some problems in the whole bureau's archival work and on how to strengthen archival work], April 1978, 3. All unpublished documents cited in the following have been archived by "The Maoist Legacy Project" at the University of Freiburg.
9. See especially §21 and §22 of the 1987 Archives Law, accessed June 1, 2017, http://www.npc.gov.cn/wxzl/gongbao/2000-12/06/content_5004486.htm.

second victimization of individuals or their offspring by way of publicizing highly personal information.

After the Cultural Revolution extended discussions began on how to deal with the content of individual case files that contained "fake" or "black" materials used to frame certain individuals. In November 1979, the CCP Center demanded a standardized procedure in dealing with the multitude of case materials.[10] Documents with historical relevance were to be sorted out and preserved, while most Cultural Revolutionary criticism materials were either to be destroyed or, in case of confessions, to be returned to the former defendants. Many high-ranking party members were unhappy that not all personal materials from the period were to be discarded. In a speech before the Central Disciplinary Inspection Commission in January 1980, Zeng San, recently restored to his position as director of the Central Archives, explained the reasons. While about 85 percent of the materials would be removed from the files, some important documents of more general character were to be kept for historical reasons. Otherwise later generations would be unable to reconstruct the reasons for the purge of the alleged "Gang of Four." Therefore some "black" materials, also on certain high-ranking cadres, were to remain in the archives. However, these were to be strictly separated from the personal dossiers that continued to serve as basis of individual evaluation and never be used to frame party members again, unless China would fall prey to yet another period of dictatorial rule, in the case of which framing and blackmailing would happen anyways.[11]

The distinction between valuable historical materials and "black materials" was never clear-cut and led to enormous differences in handling case files by the respective authorities. The Central Archives came to argue in favor of preserving larger quantities of materials.[12] Yet in many regions a larger number of documents were "weeded out" than demanded.[13] The "great cleansing" of the Cultural Revolutionary case files after 1978 thus resulted in unforeseen disclosures, as parts of the files were not destroyed but returned, kept, or sold as waste paper. The three examples in this chapter are all based on such discarded documents. Although the cases might

---

10. "Zhonggong zhongyang, guowuyuan pizhuan guojia dang'anju guanyu chuli 'Wenhua da geming' yundong zhong xingcheng de yuan, jia, cuo an neirong de wenshu cailiao de yijian" [Opinion of the State Archives Bureau concerning the disposal of written materials dating from the 'Great Cultural Revolution' Movement the contents of which bear upon unjust, false, and mistaken cases circulated with a comment by the CCP Center and State Council], Zhongfa [1979] No. 81, November 3, 1979.
11. "Zeng San tongzhi guanyu Zhonggong Zhongyang, Guowuyuan (1979) 81 hao wenjian de ji dian shuoming" [Some explanations of Comrade Zeng San on Document (1979) No. 81 circulated by the CCP Center and the State Council], January 11, 1980, in *Dang'an gongzuo wenjian huiji* [Collection of documents on archival work], No. 2, ed. Guojia dang'anju bangongshi (Beijing: Dang'an chubanshe, 1985), 55–57.
12. "Guojia danganju dui zai lici zhengzhi yundong zhong xingcheng de han you cuan, jia, cuo an neirong de wenshu cailiao chuli de fuxin" [Reply of the State Archives Bureau regarding the handling of written materials from various political campaigns that include content related to unjust, false, and mistaken cases], Guodangfa (1980) No. 369, August 21, 1980, in *Dang'an gongzuo*, 58–59.
13. Zhongyang bangongting, Guowuyuan bangongting zhuanfa guojia danganju, "Guanyu 'Wenhua da geming' zhong xingcheng de dang'an cailiao chuli wenti de baogao" [Report on the problem of handling archival materials produced during the 'Great Cultural Revolution'], Ting (dang) fa (1982) No. 83, November 5, 1982.

appear random at first sight, they stand for vast numbers of structurally similar cases reviewed in the late 1970s and early 1980s. Most case files today only exist in fragmented form and seldom provide a comprehensive picture. However, despite their fragmented nature the documents offer insights about individual ways of remembering past events rarely mentioned in official histories of the Maoist era. These include heroic tales of pointing out social or political grievances, petty neighborhood quarrels mirroring problems of communal living, and practices of informing on others.

Traces of an Unruly Life

In early July 1962, authorities in Dalian, a port city in the northeastern province of Liaoning, picked up a woman selling household goods on a busy road intersection. While in the immediate aftermath of the Great Leap Forward markets had been briefly institutionalized for certain agricultural products, this did not apply to the unregistered vending of commodities. The conversation was recorded as follows:

> What do you sell?
> – Various commodities.
>
> Where did you get them from?
> – From the Western Harbor shop.
>
> How long have you been doing this?
> – For more than a week.
>
> How large is your family?
> – Seven people, one earner, 51 yuan per month.
>
> From which place have you been laid-off?
> – [I have been] laid-off on 28 May from the Aquatic Products Processing Factory.
>
> Don't you know that it is illegal to simply sell stuff?
> – I know, but I have no choice.
>
> You know that it is wrong, but still you keep doing it?
> – I have nothing else to do.[14]

The woman had been affected by the great retrenchment after the Great Leap Forward, as millions of factory workers were laid off in order to reduce the burden on state budgets.[15] A copy of this conversation ended up in the case file of her husband, Mr. Li, as we shall call him, as he became an investigation target for economic crimes. His case file is a fairly typical example of materials weeded out during the "great cleansing" of the archives after the Cultural Revolution. The 100-page file contains only those materials deemed useless after 1978: evidence in

---

14. "Chaolu shichang guanlisuo weifa chuli de dang'an cailiao" [Copy of archival materials on the Market Control Office's handling of illegal activities], July 9, 1962.
15. Compare Nara Dillon, *Radical Inequalities: China's Revolutionary Welfare State in Comparative Perspective* (Cambridge, MA: Harvard University Press, 2015), 255.

the form of witness statements, case reports by various authorities, images of his personal belongings from a house raid in 1968, and four confessions dated 1965 to 1969. Furthermore, there are several appraisal sheets monitoring the success of his thought reform process between 1970 and 1974. Most of the materials are handwritten, often on coarse paper. There is no final organizational "conclusion" (*jielun* 結論) on how his case was handled after Mao's death, as these documents were probably included in his personal dossier later.

It is difficult to detect Li's individual voice in the case file. From several administrative forms, which he filled out during different periods, we learn that he was born in 1920 and was categorized during Land Reform as being of poor peasant class background. He had a primary school education and a checkered work biography that included ten years as a shop clerk (1937–1947) in Dalian, before returning to his native county in Shandong to work as a peasant. By early 1956, he found work in the office of a major dockyard in Dalian, where he was tasked with preparing hot drinking water. It was here that he seems to have carved out a small niche for himself by engaging in bartering and trading small quantities of leftover goods such as wastepaper, glass, or old ropes. No one later claimed that Li had stolen items from the factory. He rather had noticed the value of certain discarded objects, purchased them from the relevant departments at a low price, and made his cut when reselling them to garbage traders or in case of the ropes to slaughterhouses.[16] In the diction of the time, this behavior constituted the crime of "speculation and profiteering" (*touji daoba* 投機倒把).[17]

Li's first, very brief confession (*jiaodai cailiao* 交代材料) dates from February 18, 1965. He does not engage in justification of his deeds, but matter-of-factly explains the reasons why his wife started selling household goods back in 1962:

> It started in July and August 1962. Because my wife was laid-off from her factory on 28 May 1962, she had nothing to do, and we had difficulties making ends meet. Therefore we started selling household items at different places. We had round mirrors, big mirrors (square), small chains, combs, electric batteries, gaiters, nail clippers, aluminum spoons, kettles, pots, handbags, tobacco pipes, big and small hair pins, pencil cases, soap (black), needles, poker cards, fire lighters, small knives, leather cushions, small leather balls, maybe a few more things, but nothing important. My wife bought and sold these items on a daily basis. She got them from a department store and a factory cooperative by means of queuing.[18]

---

16. "Jieshao qingkuang" [Explanation of the situation], November 12, 1963.
17. "Speculation and profiteering means to extract state or collective goods and materials with the motive of reaping exorbitant profits. It includes acts such as carrying out illegal buying and selling, long-distance trafficking, the organization of underground businesses (underground factories, shops, construction teams), as well as undertaking other illegal economic activities," see Zhonggong zhongyang wenxian yanjiushi, ed., *Jianguo yilai zhongyao wenxian xuanbian* [Selection of important documents since the founding of the PRC], vol. 18 (Beijing: Zhongyang wenxian chubanshe, 1998), 12.
18. "Guanyu Li XX jiaodai cailiao" [On Li XX's confession materials], February 18, 1965.

The profit from selling these household goods, which at the time were constantly in short supply even in a city such as Dalian, was small but steady. According to Li, a mirror bought for 1.4 yuan could be resold for 1.8 yuan to people who had no time or patience to wait in line. Over the course of two years, the Li family was able to earn a sizable income from their black market activities.

The file also contains various items in the form of "accusation letters" (*jianju xin* 檢舉信), written by neighbors, which informed the authorities about the new affluence of the Li family. The letters mainly targeted the leader of the local residential small group (*jumin xiaozu* 居民小組) for having taken Li's side in various local conflicts. These include snippets of contemporary quarrels. Here Li's voice is occasionally rendered through quotations by his neighbors, such as: "One day I went to [Li's] home to borrow some money. He gave me the money, then seized the chance, drew close to me and said: 'In our unit, you should be wary of Mr. Song. He is good at stealing. He stole oysters from Old Yuan, and blankets from others. Later he stole two of my water barrels.'"[19] The letter writer accused the residential committee leader of not having reigned in Li's activities because he had accepted a loan of 100 yuan from Li and thus had compromised himself.[20] One of the neighbors alerted Li's factory and informed them about his purchase of a new watch, a radio, leather shoes, and serge trousers. The factory therefore sent someone to check on Li to make sure that his family was still entitled to receive social welfare. Li's good relation with the leader of the residential small group seems to have paid off initially. As one accusation letter quotes the group leader: "Whoever reported this to the factory should come forward and sincerely confess. If no one volunteers information, I myself will go to the factory and get the name. No one should play tricks. I guarantee that after two months, the factory will provide [Li with] social welfare payments again. [This is what happened two months later.]"[21]

Li's patron came under attack when anti-corruption efforts were stepped up in late 1963 as part of yet another Five-Anti Campaign in the cities, while the Four Cleanups movement sought to root out economic crime in the countryside. Li himself became the target of local investigations through the local Security Protection Group (*zhibao zu* 治保組). A case was built and the Li family speculation profit estimated at 1,800 yuan.[22] Li only admitted having earned an extra 100 yuan, which he upgraded to 320 yuan during investigations during the Cultural Revolution. He was officially labeled a "speculator," and worse still, he was confronted with evidence unearthed from Kuomintang "enemy archives" in his home county, which found him to be a "historical counterrevolutionary" (*lishi fangeming* 歷史反革命) who had managed to "slip through the net." Li accordingly had been

---

19. "Guanyu Li XX zai wo yuanli jinchang jinxing tiaobo lijian, shanfeng dianhuo, touji daoba, yong dongxi bannong shifei" [On how Li XX frequently played one person off against another, stirred-up trouble, engaged in fraudulent purchase and resale, and used objects to make mischief], October 14 [1963].
20. "Jianju xin" [Letter of accusation], October 14 (1963).
21. "Jianju xin," October 14 (1963).
22. "Zhengming cailiao" [Evidence materials], November 8, 1963.

an accomplice to murdering an alleged communist spy back in 1948.²³ Li's older confessions regarding the homicide were not weeded out and thus are not part of the file. The record shows that Li was treated surprisingly leniently: He was charged as a "counterrevolutionary" but without being permanently labeled (*bu dai maozi* 不戴帽子). Here the benefits of a good class background paid off. Offenders with bad class backgrounds routinely faced much higher charges. After having been subject to "critical education" (*piping jiaoyu* 批評教育) in his unit, Li was allowed to continue working under "mass supervision" (*qunzhong guanzhi* 群眾管制).

The final three confessions all date from the Cultural Revolution period. As far as the records reveal, Mr. Li's life routine seems not to have been disturbed by the movement at first. He publicly made a point of his changed lifestyle by wearing only worn-out garments and living mainly off social welfare. Occasionally, he seems to have sold fish, raised in barrels in his backyard. Yet the confiscation of his additional income seems to have made him bitter. Conflicts with law enforcement grew more frequent. After being reprimanded several times for intentional hit-and-run accidents with his bicycle, he came into serious trouble in August 1967. Mr. Li admitted that he had used the opportunity of a public film screening (the *Ice Sisters*, a 1959 sports movie) to sexually molest a female comrade. In a confession dated from 1969, he remembered the incident as follows:

> I entered the venue from the side to take a look. There were some kids surrounding a female "tiger" [*nüren huzi* 女人虎子].²⁴ At this point, my thoughts were centered on enjoying indecent behavior [*wan liumang* 玩流氓]. I thus pushed my hand into a women's sleeve to fondle his [her] breasts. This was detected by a kid sitting nearby. I was arrested and brought to the public security bureau. . . . In October 1967 my crime of hooliganism was made public at a big meeting.²⁵

Despite all these wrongdoings, "poor peasant" Li was able to continue working under mass supervision until the local leadership singled him out as a potential target during the campaign to "cleanse the class ranks" (*qingli jieji duiwu* 清理階級隊伍) in the fall of 1968. His house was searched for incriminating evidence and the search produced a large number of potentially incriminating items, including 193 yuan in cash, old silver coins, 150 meters of cloth (obtained though social welfare), twenty overcoats, stacks of unkempt wool, three watches, fishing nets, as well as other items deemed bourgeois such as three metal cauldrons.²⁶ The file includes two photographs of the items as they were put on public display as an example of Mr. Li's rotten morals.

---

23. "Dui fangeming fenzi Li XX de zonghe cailiao" [Comprehensive materials on counterrevolutionary element Li XX], 1963–1974, 7.
24. Local slang word in Shandong province for a mentally handicapped individual.
25. "Li XX jiaodai cailiao" [Confession materials of Li XX], January 24, 1969, 10–11.
26. "Guanyu Li XX bei chachao de wuzi chuli yijian" [Opinion on how to handle the materials confiscated from Li XX], May 25, 1969, 9.

For the temporary institution in charge of the investigation, the case was clear. Li was a counterrevolutionary who had intentionally "vilified socialism" (*chouhua shehui zhuyi* 醜化社會主義) by way of putting on a show of poverty while hoarding public goods.[27] He was said to have embezzled no less than 975 yuan of social welfare. With the exception of the goods needed for daily life, all items were confiscated. The previously paid welfare was to be recharged by way of deducting it from his monthly wage, a fact he publicly lamented and contested. Upon being questioned about his motives, Li did not resort to an elaborate defense but simply stated: "I did this for economic reasons. History has produced [me], this rotten piece of flesh."[28] Even at the high tide of the Cultural Revolution, the confessions remained nearly completely devoid of sloganeering and never indulged in excessive self-criticism beyond stating and accepting the obvious facts.

This time Li received an official label as counterrevolutionary and was sent-down to engage in supervised labor in a rural production team roughly 60 kilometers north of Dalian. Here he spent the following six years carrying manure, guarding pigs, or engaging in other agricultural tasks. According to the annual review reports by the local production team, attempts at remolding his morals and character were not deemed successful. While there are no more written confessions, the reports make clear that Mr. Li did not engage in outright resistance. Yet he showed no insight into his previous wrongdoings nor did he accept his status as criminal in his everyday activities.[29] The 1973 review explicitly mentions his stubbornness and dishonest (*bu laoshi* 不老實) attitude toward remolding. He was said to always choose the lightest work tasks, to prefer sleeping to political meetings, and under the pretense of illness to refrain from working altogether.[30] The annual case review produced the same result: Given the failure to remold his thinking and to thoroughly accept his crimes, his label was not to be removed. The case file ends in late 1974. The later case reviews, the release form, and the final decision were probably added to his personal dossier at his later work unit.

The case file is interesting for several reasons. It is a fairly straightforward account about life on the fringes of society in the aftermath of the Great Leap Forward. The case file reveals a type of resilience toward socialist remolding that is not based on political viewpoints but upon individual quirks and the nonacceptance of socialist norms in daily life. The major political campaigns of the day clearly affected Li's life, yet in a way unaccounted for by common narratives of the late Maoist years. He went through the motions of publicly stating his guilt, but otherwise dragged his feet and remained unenthusiastic about socialist reeducation. The information on the existence of illegal exchanges and the misappropriation of

---

27. "Dui fangeming fenzi Li XX zonghe cailiao," 1.
28. "Li XX jiaodai cailiao," 10.
29. "Pingshen silei fenzi Li XX ziliao" [Evaluation materials on Four-Type Element Li XX], December 29, 1972, 17.
30. "Silei fenzi jianding" [Appraisal of Four-Type Elements], December 27, 1973, 16.

social welfare provides insights into common phenomena to be expected in any bureaucratic system and are a welcome antidote to perceiving the Maoist era solely in terms of political campaigns. The case further reveals that even during the high tide of the Cultural Revolution, administrative sentencing in urban centers continued in comparatively orderly fashion and that, especially in case of individuals with good class background, the standards of adjudication were not always drastically different from earlier years. Not least, it provides us with insights into everyday practices of informing on neighbors and the manifold conflict lines within local residential groups. It is fairly certain that Li was released after Mao's death as part of the official policy change toward the roughly twenty million individuals labeled as "four types of people," who were no longer regarded as class enemies.[31] Maybe Mr. Li's economic clout led to a successful career in the reform period, when making profit was no longer regarded as vice but as a desirable skill.

"Speech Crimes" as Alternative Memory

The second case study relies on a fairly extensive revision report as well as corroborating evidence collected in late February 1979 by judicial personnel of a district Middle People's Court in Shenyang, capital of Liaoning. The court personnel had teamed up with members of a local factory party committee to review the complex case of a fifty-four-year-old factory worker, who we shall call Mr. Song. The investigation group combined different expertise because the accused had received both administrative and criminal sentences. In 1958, he had been labeled an "extreme rightist" by his work unit party committee, a designation reserved for offenders in important positions with the potential of harming the CCP dictatorship.[32] The harsh verdict was clearly related to his former position as editor at a major provincial publishing house and the potential influence his status had granted him. The same year, his case at the suggestion of the provincial party committee leadership was taken to court. At the outset of the Great Leap Forward, the Shenyang City Middle People's Court sentenced Song to a four-year prison sentence as a "bad element" (*huai fenzi* 壞分子), a vague designation that after 1957 came to signify both criminal offense and a political label for dubious, yet politically harmful behavior, including illicit sexual relationships.[33] While the report does not mention the evidence for these earlier convictions, the combination of judicial and administrative punishment, as well as the double labeling as rightist and bad element was complicating matters. Song's lamentation about the two labels and their permanent status ("There is no

---

31. Xiao Donglian, *Lishi de zhuangui: Cong boluan fanzheng dao gaige kaifang (1979–1981)* [Turning point in history: Re-examination of the Cultural Revolution and the policy of reform and opening] (Hong Kong: Chinese University Press, 2008), 127.
32. See also Eddy U, *Disorganizing China: Counterbureaucracy and the Decline of Socialism* (Stanford: Stanford University Press, 2007), 136.
33. Compare Yang Kuisong, "How a 'Bad Element' Was Made: The Discovery, Accusation, and Punishment of Zang Qiren," in *Maoism at the Grassroots*, 19–20.

way out. A political label is worse than a criminal sentence.") was later cited as evidence for his criminal behavior. After having served his sentence, the former editor remained a "bad element" and "rightist" and was sent to work as a mason in a Shenyang factory under supervision of the masses.[34]

The 1979 revision report merely lists these previous sentences and notes the fact that the Provincial Publication Bureau had recently removed the label of "extreme rightist." The investigation team was thus mainly concerned with charges brought against Song by the military committee in control of the public security sub-bureau in his factory in April 1970 during the "One Strike, Three Anti" (*yi da, san fan* 一打三反) Campaign. After being held in custody for over a year without access to legal advice, the military control commission had sentenced Song as a "bad element resisting reform" to a ten-year prison sentence "according to the law," yet without mentioning any specific regulations or statutes. The charges had been twofold: Song was accused of "spreading reactionary sayings in a big way, attacking our party and the socialist system, and reestablishing the credits of the renegade, traitor, and scab Liu Shaoqi."[35] He was further said to have incited and masterminded the flight of two convicts from the local study class, a euphemism for the reestablishment of the party-military dictatorship through supervised study. Song had accepted the charges in mid-1971 after intense interrogations and been sent to prison.

Song appealed this sentence in early January 1979 and claimed that he had been framed and had confessed his guilt only under duress. The appeal immediately prompted the formation of an investigation team. The fast response was possibly due to the fact that Liaoning was among the provinces with the greatest turnover in terms of political leadership. The new provincial leaders thus faced fewer difficulties in investigating previous verdicts. The case review was complicated by the fact that the military control committee had not left any case files with the exception of the verdict and an accompanying short report. Therefore, the group had to collect all evidence anew, including the questioning of ten contemporary witnesses.

Song's case is especially interesting due to the importance attached to certain statements he was said to have made during previous years. The report lists about a dozen of these "speech crimes," which Song was said to have committed mostly at home or in the company of friends and neighbors, who later had informed on him. By way of relying on Song's and the witnesses' memories, the investigation team tried to establish the veracity of every single utterance, some ten years after the actual speech context and carefully compared the wording in each instance.

The statements reveal alternative perceptions of social and political reality at the time of the Cultural Revolution. Song was said to have criticized the movement by claiming: "While many people have died, not a single problem has been solved with the exception of expelling Liu Shaoqi from the party. It is a complete waste

---

34. "Guanyu kangju gaizao de huai fenzi Song XX an de fucha baogao" [Re-examination report on the case of the bad element resisting reform Song XX], February 23, 1979, 1.
35. "Guanyu kangju gaizao de huai fenzi Song XX an de fucha baogao," 1.

of labor and money. While Liu Shaoqi was at the helm, we had everything. Since his fall from power, we have nothing." It is noteworthy that both the informant and Song himself confirmed the statement years later, though with slightly different wording. Song remembered having said: "I had a wrong perception of the Cultural Revolution. Many people hung themselves in public parks; quite a few were beaten to death. Especially many young people died in the Cultural Revolution. The Cultural Revolution did not solve any problems and society at the time was rather chaotic. ... Workers did not work, peasants did not farm, and students did not study. I said that while Liu Shaoqi was still around, it was at least possible to buy things. After Liu Shaoqi was struck down, there was nothing to be purchased anymore."[36] The investigation group concluded that the sentences did not constitute a crime but mirrored a lack of understanding of contemporary developments. The same held true for references made by Song about the alleged nepotism in Mao's family, by having wife and nephew helicoptered to high-level political positions, and his comments about China's growing international isolation with only Albania and Vietnam as remaining partners. He had furthermore criticized the campaign to "cleanse the class ranks": "What does cleansing the [class] ranks mean? It is Chairman Mao taking Stalin's old road by exaggerating the purge of counterrevolutionaries."[37] In all these instances, the dominant mode of explanation by 1979 allowed previous criticism to be pardoned on grounds of having been directed against the influence of the Gang of Four, albeit unknowingly.

Competing evidence appeared with regard to the policy of rusticating Red Guards. Song was quoted in the verdict with the following lines: "No one volunteered to be sent to the countryside. The educated youth went to the villages, but they did not really work. After returning to [Shenyang], many of them committed crimes. With each youth sent down, they [the CCP] created an additional enemy."[38] The informant revealed upon renewed questioning that he had made up the statement: "[Song] only said that sending the students down to the villages does not make sense. At the time, the propaganda teams handled matters fairly strictly and we did not get to sleep several nights. What I wrote does not accord with the facts. I added this sentence when I wrote the accusation materials." The investigation team therefore opined that this utterance could not be pinned on Song. The same held true for the case of supposed utterances regarding the clashes on Zhenbao Island in 1969, which Song was said to have termed an instance of "political swindling" from both sides. The derogatory content of the previous speech acts could no longer be proven and was thus discarded as criminal evidence.

Two further quotations are of special interest. Both were now deemed to be "extremely wrong" but no longer said to constitute a crime. According to an informant, Song had compared the Chinese to robots: "The Chinese, especially

---

36. "Guanyu kangju gaizao de huai fenzi Song XX an de fucha baogao," 2.
37. "Guanyu kangju gaizao de huai fenzi Song XX an de fucha baogao," 7.
38. "Guanyu kangju gaizao de huai fenzi Song XX an de fucha baogao," 3.

the Northeasterners, have a very strong slave mentality. They are like robots: Once you wind them up, they continue moving. Today, they strike down this person, the next day someone else, without asking why."[39] The investigation group decided not to question the specific wording of this statement but to evaluate it against the background of Cultural Revolutionary struggles. It was declared an improper comparison without criminal intent. More problematic was another statement of Song recorded in his file: "In this society one fares best as a deaf-mute, because it is impossible to say good things, even less bad things. One has to completely act against one's conscience. The Chinese do not have any kind of liberty; it is only permissible to breathe. No other country or society is like this."[40] Song claimed to have uttered only the first half of the quotation and to have addressed both factional struggles and the fact that by wearing a political label he had little freedom left. While in prison he had been regarded as a small criminal, in society he was perceived as a major enemy. The investigation group tried to adopt Song's perspective of being wrongly labeled for decades and did not question the veracity of the claim as such. Instead, his words were explained as the outcome of personal discontent.

By providing alternative explanations for every previous "speech crime," the investigation group attempted to reestablish procedural justice based on a comprehensive evaluation of evidence within a broader discursive framework that allowed for blaming all previous policy blunders on the Gang of Four. Memories of certain speech acts played a major role in reversing the former sentence. The investigation group finally advised the local party committee to clear Song of all the aforementioned charges. This held also true for the second major crime, the supposed planning of the escape of two study class members from his commune. After having spent a total of fourteen months in interrogation between April 1970 and June 1971 without any possibility to obtain legal protection, Song had finally admitted to this crime, which was corroborated by the testimonies of the two escapees, who had been caught shortly after. In his appeal, Song stated that the confession had been made under duress. The group questioned the former escapees again, one of who admitted that they had consciously framed Song in order to receive a lighter sentence. Given the fact that Song had already been labeled as political criminal, they correctly assumed that the authorities would rather trust their word than his. At home, they had justified their acts to their wives by way of referring to the saying "great men have to be ruthless" (*wu du bu zhangfu* 無毒不丈夫).[41] Based on the review of all evidence, the investigation group characterized the verdict as a miscarriage of justice and advised the local party committee, who had the final say, to correct the sentence and to completely rehabilitate Song. There can be little doubt that the suggestions were followed through, as the party envisioned intellectuals to play an important role in the reform period.

---

39. "Guanyu kangju gaizao de huai fenzi Song XX an de fucha baogao," 4.
40. "Guanyu kangju gaizao de huai fenzi Song XX an de fucha baogao," 6.
41. "Guanyu kangju gaizao de huai fenzi Song XX an de fucha baogao," 8.

This case is much closer to the accustomed memories of oppressed intellectuals during the Cultural Revolution. The quotations, deriving both from the late Maoist period and the immediate aftermath, to a certain degree mirror our expectations of dissenting opinions under Maoist rule. Yet an advantage of the original case files over the manifold memoir literature is presented by their close proximity to the actual events, the insights into the specific procedures of revising verdicts, as well as the original, partly idiosyncratic quotations, untainted by changed speech conventions or the attempts at refashioning a certain image. The case also clearly reveals the changing truth standards in judicial work that allowed for interpreting the same utterances in very different ways once the specter of looming class struggle had been removed. Finally, it is noteworthy how much time and effort the investigation group invested in reevaluating the charges in order to reach reversal of the previous verdict deemed "just" in the changed political landscape. Every recorded speech crime was reevaluated yet again and the investigations produced both similarities and variances along lines previously not be expected. Memory during the review process obviously not only served strategic functions of minimizing personal involvement but also related to questions of personal honesty and procedural justice.

Confessions and Memories of a Rebel

The third case deals with a worker rebel at the Beijing Capital Steel and Iron Works (*Shoudu gangtie gongchang* 首都鋼鐵工廠), one of China's most prestigious factories at the time. The case covers two thick hand-written volumes of about 150 pages each. The files consist mainly of several series of confessions, interrogation records with testimonies, as well as administrative verdicts spanning fifteen years from 1971 to 1985. The worker, termed Wang in the following, was defined as Cultural Revolutionary perpetrator after the end of the mass mobilization period and subjected to meticulous scrutiny. Born in 1938 and of poor peasant class background, he had been a worker in a sub-factory of Shougang. By the early Cultural Revolution, Wang became a worker representative and by mid-1967 vice-leader of the "East is Red Headquarters Combat Group" (*Dongfang hong zongbu zhandouzu* 東方紅總部戰鬥組), one of three competing mass organizations to emerge within the factory in 1967. His tasks as rebel leader were manifold. He organized workers for citywide activities, participated in power seizures, conducted rebel networking, and engaged in violent struggles with competing groups. Wang furthermore helped to organize the staging of public humiliation rallies of former high-ranking leaders such as Peng Zhen. He does not seem to have been a powerful political thinker as there are no charges regarding specific word crimes or political views. From the documents he emerges as a third-level rebel leader, well below the likes of national figures such as Wang Hongwen, yet associated with more famous rebels such as "East is Red" leader Zhang Zhaoqing.[42]

Wang's case materials are interesting from several perspectives, including changing narrative frameworks, the reliability of supposedly factual information on Cultural Revolutionary developments, and the definition of Cultural Revolutionary perpetrators. Wang was subjected to three rounds of investigations altogether. These were conducted at the factory and did not include formal judicial organs but rather administrative bodies such as study classes, temporary campaign offices, and the local party committee. The first round of interrogations took place between 1971 and 1972 as part of the attempt to uncover "May 16th Elements" (*wu yi liu fenzi* 五一六分子),[43] an alleged conspiracy against Premier Zhou Enlai based on no factual evidence whatsoever. By 1970, the campaign was consciously employed to detain former contenders to CCP power, including rebel leaders, as the later chairman of the Beijing Revolutionary Committee Wu De admitted.[44] The second round of investigations stretched from April 1978 to January 1979, mostly still under the general leadership of Hua Guofeng, as part of the "reveal, criticize, investigate" (*jie pi cha* 揭批查) campaign. Finally, his case was reviewed yet again between 1984 and 1985 as part of the attempt to purge "three types of people" (*qingli san zhong ren* 清理三種人) from the party ranks, notably those with "factionalist thoughts," adherents of the Gang of Four, and those who had committed acts of violence during the Cultural Revolution.[45]

Wang's statements clearly mirror the changing objectives and circumstances of the investigations. In the first round, the oppressive character of the study class is documented by the lengthy handwritten confessions, the expressions of personal guilt, and the strong political rhetoric inherent in the statements. The interrogators were predominantly interested in the existence of rebel networks, individual and organizational details, and the background of specific events such as factional struggles. The file thus contains fairly comprehensive information on the organization of local factional violence, the storming of the Beijing Public Security Bureau in late January 1967 (for which Wang later had to assume primary responsibility) or the formation of the "Seize Liu Shaoqi Liaison Station" in July/August 1967, which championed no less than 1,800 participating groups.[46] It furthermore provides an

---

42. Zhang turned highly critical against the system and in 1977 was tried and sentenced for allegedly having attempted a counterrevolutionary conspiracy alongside former Middle School Red Guard leader Li Dongmin, see Mi Hed, ed., *Huiyi yu fansi: Hongweibing shidai fengyun renwu* [Remembering and rethinking: Influential persons from the Red Guard period] (Hong Kong: Zhongguo shuju, 2011), 208–13.
43. Compare Roderick MacFarquhar and Michael Schoenhals, *Mao's Last Revolution* (Cambridge, MA: Belknap Press of Harvard University Press, 2006), 221.
44. Zhu Yuanshi, ed., *Wu De koushu: Shinian fengyu jishi; Wo zai Beijing gongzuo de yixie jingli* [Wu De's recollections: An account of the ten years of turmoil; some experiences of my work in Beijing] (Beijing: Dangdai Zhongguo chubanshe, 2004), 71.
45. For an overview, see Hong Yung Lee, *From Revolutionary Cadres to Party Technocrats in Socialist China* (Berkeley: University of California Press, 1991), 245–53.
46. "Wang XX jiaodai cailiao" [Confessions materials of Wang XX], September 10, 1971, 15.

insider's account of the burning of the British Mission from the perspective of a key activist, who according to his testimony not only helped to seize a member of the legation for public humiliation but also joined in the torching of the building. Wang meticulously describes the organization of straw and gasoline, the logistical background of having different groups join in the action under the leadership of foreign ministry rebel Yao Dengshan:

> Around 20 August 1967 the core group gathered and Zhang Zhaoqing said: 'Currently, Beijing municipality is preparing to organize a city-wide action that is to force the British ambassador back home as well as to burn down the British Mission. Great Britain is an imperialist state. We cannot cooperate with imperialist states. . . . They have seized our territory in Hong Kong and refuse to return it. . . . The action will not be enacted in the name of the state or the government, but will appear as self-organized movement by the revolutionary masses. But the CCP Center knows about it, Qi Benyu supports it. . . .' As we arrived at the embassy [sic], there were already about 2,000 people gathered. . . . Under the leadership of five or six people from the Foreign Ministry and with the help of others, we forced our way into the British Mission. In the third room on the second floor, we found the British *chargé d'affaires*, at least, that is what the people from the Foreign Ministry told us. We wanted him to engage with us in public discussion, [and we] shouted slogans at him, but he did not move. Finally, we shoved him out. . . . We placed straw and wood in a room behind the entrance and poured gasoline on it. Zhang Zhaoqing lit the fire and as soon as it burned, we left the building.[47]

The details of the action are embedded within a general framework through which Wang constantly downplays his responsibility, for example by way of emphasizing the leading role played by Zhang Zhaoqing as well as the guiding function of Cultural Revolution Small Group member Qi Benyu. Wang twisted his narrative of every action to provide the interrogators with the sought for information on the alleged May 16 conspiracy, for example by claiming that it was Qi's suggestion to compile "black materials" against Zhou Enlai in August 1967. He further ascertained that they organized the writing of posters and criticism materialism against Zhou Enlai, whom they referred to as "China's Kosygin" in analogy to the Soviet Chairman of the Council of Ministers Alexei Kosygin. The criticism within the "black materials" accordingly had been mainly directed at Zhou's economist tendency regarding the importance of expertise and planning, while neglecting the role of worker activism and political education as emphasized in the 1960 "Angang constitution."[48] In short, Zhou was a "time bomb" within the proletarian headquarters that needed to be defused.[49]

---

47. "Wang XX jiaodai cailiao," 30–37. For the account of the British chargé d'affaires Donald Hopson, see MacFarquhar and Schoenhals, *Mao's Last Revolution*, 225–26.
48. "Wang XX jiaodai cailiao," 27.
49. "Wang XX jiaodai cailiao," 23.

The descriptions of the events are always followed by one or two paragraphs, in which the political character of the confessions is particularly strong. Wang repeatedly admits his guilt of having unknowingly been a part of the May 16 conspiracy. The ending lines often include far-fetched connections to fit the event into contemporary speech conventions, especially in the case of attacking Liu Shaoqi:

> The "Seize Liu Station" was a big conspiracy conducted by the Yang-Yu-Fu, Wang-Guan-Qi May 16th Counterrevolutionary Conspirative Clique.[50] The intention was to conduct a counterrevolutionary coup, to overthrow the dictatorship of the proletariat, and to reestablish capitalism. With regard to "Seize Liu Station," seizing Liu was fake, protecting Liu was real. It used the pretext of seizing Liu Shaoqi in order to secretly spearhead the attack against Chairman Mao, against the Party Center with Chairman Mao as its head and Vice-Chairman Lin as his deputy, and against Premier Zhou. The aim was to rely on the "Seize Liu [Station]" to conduct a counterrevolutionary coup.[51]

These sections of the confession are less interesting in terms of their factual content, rather than in terms of the speaking conventions. They mirror the shifts in political discourse and the revealing ways in which individuals relied on formalized speech to render their admissions of guilt meaningful in a certain political setting. Simultaneously, at least in the case of Wang, he tried to shift the blame for the actual misdeeds on others. He was nevertheless found guilty of being a member of the May 16 clique, and was labeled a counterrevolutionary, but he stayed on at the local factory to work under mass supervision.

The second round of investigations was conducted under the auspices of temporary political organs in his factory in 1978. By this time, the May 16 conspiracy was no longer of interest. During the interrogations, Wang claimed that with the exception of having taken part in storming the Beijing Public Security Bureau, most of his statements, especially those regarding the compilation of "black materials" on Zhou Enlai, had been the result of forced confessions.[52] As other witnesses also withdrew their statements, the local party committee felt compelled to clear Wang of these specific charges, yet warned him: "If one of these major problems will be corroborated by new evidence in the future, the responsibility will be on Wang alone." The focus thus shifted to other questions, especially to his role in harming factory cadres during conflicts between the rebels and the military control committee in the summer of 1967, when under his leadership two cadres had been taken

---

50. The names refer to military leaders Yang Chengwu, Yu Lijin, Fu Chongbi all purged in March 1968, as well as Wang Li, Guan Feng, and Qi Benyu, former Cultural Revolution Small Group members purged between August 1967 and February 1968, compare Guo Jian, Yongyi Song, and Yuan Zhou, *Historical Dictionary of the Cultural Revolution* (Lanham: Scarecrow Press, 2006), 347–48 and 377–78.
51. "Wang XX jiaodai cailiao," 21.
52. "Guanyu Wang XX zai jie pi cha yundong zhong yiliu wenti de qingshi baogao" [Report with request for instruction concerning the left-over problems of Wang XX during the campaign to reveal, criticize, and investigate], January 18, 1979.

prisoner and, as Wang confessed after several months, been subjected to torture.[53] The interrogators were mainly interested in who took part in the beatings and who organized the sessions, pressing for names and details. The questions were repeated dozens of times over a period of months, with each round producing new details to be seized upon later. Wang's strategy remained similar: He selectively remembered details, actively directed the blame upward, and adapted his narrations to the changed political circumstances:

> My mistake of having interrogated Xi and Miao is of severe nature. It cannot be separated from the counterrevolutionary revisionist line of the Gang of Four. It has been determined by my [contemporary] standpoint and views. Because I was poisoned by the Gang of Four, I actively served their counterrevolutionary revisionist line. They viewed the old cadres as an obstacle in their conspiracy of seizing state power, incited a left-extremist ideological position and engaged in beating, smashing, and looting in the name of "attacking with words, defending with force".
> . . . I am determined to draw lessons from my mistakes and want to even better receive help offered by my leaders and comrades, thus increasing the knowledge of my deficits.[54]

Wang was found guilty of having ordered the illegal arrest of the two cadres, of "obstructing the Cultural Revolution" by way of harming production and engaging in factional struggles, as well as being the "black backstage boss" of the power seizure at the Beijing Public Security Bureau.[55] The other charges could not be proven. Unlike in the case of Mr. Song, the invocations of the evil influence of the Gang of Four did not lead to a complete rehabilitation in Wang's case. While his counterrevolutionary label was removed, he was still said to have committed "severe errors" and remained on the watch list of the local party committee. Unlike most "victim" cases, his 1979 reversal ends by stating that given the lack of evidence the case could "only be dealt with like this: If further problems are found in the future, the case should be handled anew."[56] Former rebel leaders were not to be let off the hook easily.

During the third round of interrogations as part of the campaign to purge "three types of people" in the early 1980s, there were no more confessions or public declamations of guilt. After the local party committee had received central-level orders to search for Cultural Revolutionary perpetrators,[57] they subjected those workers with a dubious past to renewed questioning. As the party committee drew up a

---
53. "Guanyu pohuai Xi, Miao buchong cailiao he hecha cailiao" [Additional materials and examination materials on harming Xi and Miao], July 19, 1978, 43–48.
54. "Guanyu pohai Xi XX, Miao XX" [On harming Xi XX and Miao XX], July 5, 1978, 79–81.
55. "Zonghe cailiao" [Comprehensive materials], 7. November 1978, 91–92.
56. "Guanyu Wang XX jietuo de qingshi baogao" [Report with request for instructions regarding the release of Wang XX], March 1, 1979.
57. "Zhonggong zhongyang guanyu qingli 'san zhong ren' ruogan wenti de buchong tongzhi" [Additional notification of the CCP Center regarding important questions in the purging of the "Three Types of People"], Zhongfa [1984] No. 17, July 31, 1984.

first number of suspects, Wang was placed first on the list.[58] His attitude, however, was perceived as commendable. The files by now include fairly elaborate charts on the organizational structures of the different rebel groups in the factory during the Cultural Revolution, the respective responsibilities of local leaders, and a narrative history of major incidents with local involvement. The detailed reconstructions served the evaluation of the trustworthiness of individual workers. Past misdeeds and recent behavior were compared in order to define potential mischief-makers.

The political climate was very different though. Wang submitted seven testimonies on specific subjects, in which he basically disclaimed knowledge of any particular misdeeds, especially the participation in violent activities. Ultimately, the review committee therefore decided to uphold the former conclusion of Wang having committed "severe errors" as the investigations did not yield further evidence. They ended their report with a bleak account of how the cooperation of both former perpetrators and victims had developed in the course of the investigations. Previous suspects had either recanted their former confessions or "used the phrase 'I don't remember' as a pretense not to reveal the real situation"[59] as soon as critical issues were at stake. The review committee specifically mentioned Wang as an example of this attitude. Yet Cultural Revolutionary victims were also hesitant to discuss previous events with the investigators: "People who were previously beaten also have ideological misgivings. They fear that the situation might change again and that there might be repercussions."[60] By 1984, not everyone was convinced that the political tide had turned for good.

Conclusion

By way of looking at case files of three individuals, this chapter has used political-legal documents as a prism to probe for alternative memories of the late Maoist era. The cases revealed glimpses of everyday life in the Maoist period, contested limits of admissible speech, and strategies of twisting confessions according to current modes of political discourse. The files also include snippets of older discourses, the specificity of which offers insights into contemporary speech conventions as well as the changing categories of defining deviant behavior. The case records are of historical value both for what they describe and how they describe it. While historical truth remains elusive, the case files document changing frames of remembering certain events and political campaigns over time. Despite the manifold difficulties in assessing political-legal documents from the Maoist era, these cases are highly valuable sources for understanding how ordinary people lived and remembered

---

58. "'Wenge' zhong you wenti de renyuan fenxi" [Analysis of people having had problems during the 'Cultural Revolution'], December 29, 1984.
59. "Guanyu luoshi Zhongfa [1984] 17 hao wenjian qingkuang fanhui" [Feedback on the situation of implementing Central Document (1984) No. 17], September 17, 1984, 4.
60. "Guanyu luoshi Zhongfa [1984] 17 hao wenjian qingkuang fanhui," 5.

these extraordinary times, which otherwise would be completely obliterated from the official version of history.

Bibliography

All unpublished sources have been archived at the Maoist Legacy Project at the University of Freiburg. Single documents within the three case files only appear in the footnotes with full titles.

Archives Law, 1987. Accessed June 1, 2017. http://www.npc.gov.cn/wxzl/gongbao/2000-12/06/content_5004486.htm.

Beijing shiju bangongshi. "Guanyu quan ju dang'an gongzuo cunzai de yixie wenti ji jin yi bu jiaqiang dang'an gongzuo de yijian" [Opinions on some problems in the whole bureau's archival work and on how to strengthen archival work]. April 1978, unpublished document.

Case file Li, 1962–1974.

Case file Song, 1979.

Case file Wang, 1971–1985.

Cong, Xiaoping. *Self-Determination: Marriage, Law, and Gender Construction in Revolutionary China, 1940–1960*. Cambridge: Cambridge University Press, 2016.

Davies, Natalie Zemon. *Fiction in the Archives: Pardon Tales and Their Tellers in Sixteenth Century France*. Cambridge: Polity Press, 1988.

Dillon, Nara. *Radical Inequalities: China's Revolutionary Welfare State in Comparative Perspective*. Cambridge, MA: Harvard University Press, 2015.

Ginzburg, Carlo. *The Cheese and the Worms: The Cosmos of a Sixteenth-Century Miller*. Baltimore: Johns Hopkins University Press, 1980.

Guojia dang'anju bangongshi, ed. *Dang'an gongzuo wenjian huiji* [Collection of documents on archival work], No. 2. Beijing: Dang'an chubanshe, 1985.

Han Yanlong, ed. *Zhonghua renmin gongheguo fazhi tongshi* [Comprehensive history of the judicial system of the People's Republic of China], 2 vols. Beijing: Zhongyang wenxian chubanshe, 1998.

Hershatter, Gail. "The Subaltern Talks Back: Reflections on Subaltern Theory and Chinese History." *Positions* 1 (1993): 103–30.

Jian, Guo, Yongyi Song, and Yuan Zhou, eds. *Historical Dictionary of the Cultural Revolution*. Lanham: Scarecrow Press, 2006.

Lee, Hong Yung. *From Revolutionary Cadres to Party Technocrats in Socialist China*. Berkeley: University of California Press, 1991.

Leese, Daniel. "Revising Political Verdicts in Post-Mao China: The Case of Beijing's Fengtai District." In *Maoism at the Grassroots: Everyday Life in China's Era of High Socialism*, edited by Jeremy Brown and Matthew D. Johnson, 102–28. Cambridge, MA: Harvard University Press, 2015.

MacFarquhar, Rocderick, and Michael Schoenhals. *Mao's Last Revolution*. Cambridge, MA: Belknap Press of Harvard University Press, 2006.

Mi Hedu, ed. *Huiyi yu fansi. Hongweibing shidai fengyun renwu* [Remembering and rethinking: Influential persons from the Red Guard period]. Hong Kong: Zhongguo shuju, 2011.
Schulze, Winfried, ed. *Ego-Dokumente. Annäherung an den Menschen in der Geschichte* [Ego-documents: Approaching man in history]. Berlin: Akademie Verlag, 1996.
U, Eddy. *Disorganizing China: Counterbureaucracy and the Decline of Socialism.* Stanford: Stanford University Press, 2007.
Wagner, Vivian. *Erinnerungsverwaltung in China. Staatsarchive und Politik in der Volksrepublik* [Memory governance in China: State archives and politics in the People's Republic]. Cologne: Böhlau, 2006.
Yang, Kuisong. "How a 'Bad Element' Was Made: The Discovery, Accusation, and Punishment of Zang Qiren." In *Maoism at the Grassroots: Everyday Life in China's Era of High Socialism*, edited by Jeremy Brown and Matthew D. Johnson, 19–50. Cambridge, MA: Harvard University Press, 2015.
Xiao, Donglian. *Lishi de zhuangui: Cong boluan fanzheng dao gaige kaifang (1979–1981)* [Turning point in history: Re-examination of the Cultural Revolution and the policy of reform and opening]. Hong Kong: Chinese University Press, 2008.
"Zhonggong zhongyang, guowuyuan pizhuan guojia dang'anju guanyu chuli 'Wenhua da geming' yundong zhong xingcheng de yuan, jia, cuo an neirong de wenshu cailiao de yijian" [Opinion of the State Archives Bureau concerning the disposal of written materials dating from the "Great Cultural Revolution" Movement the contents of which bear upon unjust, false, and mistaken cases circulated with a comment by the CCP Center and State Council], Zhongfa [1979] No. 81. November 3, 1979, unpublished document.
Zhongyang bangongting, Guowuyuan bangongting zhuanfa guojia danganju, "Guanyu 'Wenhua da geming' zhong xingcheng de dang'an cailiao chuli wenti de baogao" [Report on the problem of handling archival materials produced during the "Great Cultural Revolution"], Ting (dang) fa (1982) No. 83. November 5, 1982, unpublished document.
"Zhonggong zhongyang guanyu qingli 'san zhong ren' ruogan wenti de buchong tongzhi" [Additional notification of the CCP Center regarding important questions in the purging of the "Three Types of People"], Zhongfa [1984] No. 17. July 31, 1984, unpublished document.
Zhonggong zhongyang wenxian yanjiushi, ed. *Jianguo yilai zhongyao wenxian xuanbian* [Selection of important documents since the founding of the PRC], 20 vols. Beijing: Zhongyang wenxian chubanshe, 1992–1998.
Zhu, Yuanshi, ed. *Wu De koushu: Shinian fengyu jishi; Wo zai Beijing gongzuo de yixie jingli* [Wu De's recollections: An account of the ten years of turmoil; some experiences of my work in Beijing]. Beijing: Dangdai Zhongguo chubanshe, 2004.

11

Popular Memories and Popular History, Indispensable Tools for Understanding Contemporary Chinese History

The Case of the End of the Rustication Movement

Michel Bonnin

The writing of the history of the People's Republic of China poses specific problems due to the opacity of the actions of its government and of the control it imposes on the media. As this control does not concern only the present but also the past, historians find it difficult to get access to sources outside the limited official ones. This is particularly true for the Maoist period, when control of the media and opacity were the most severe. Fortunately, since the 1990s, unofficial memoirs and historical studies have provided very useful elements to correct and complete what could be known through official channels.

This chapter will show on a specific topic (the abrupt end of the rustication movement) that unofficial sources can provide a solid foundation to write a history of the 1978–1980 period radically different from the official one. Without these materials, we would miss the important change that took place at this time in the relationship between state and society. This chapter argues that the rebellion of the rusticated youth was decisive in the brutal ending of the rustication policy and the massive return of these youths to the cities. By their actions, they broke the monopoly of the Party on political initiative. Use of unofficial sources is thus essential to fully understanding this turning point in the history of the People's Republic. They are not only the only reliable source on the concerns and feelings of the people (in this case the rusticated youth and their parents), but also an indispensable tool to complete and rectify an official history, which is often sketchy and distorted due to propaganda considerations both at the time and nowadays.

To give an example of the importance, even the absolute necessity, of using popular memory and popular historical publications to understand Chinese contemporary history, I shall take in this chapter the example of the history of the rusticated youth (*zhiqing* 知青, abbreviation of *zhishi qingnian* 知識青年) movement or the rustication (*xiaxiang* 下鄉) movement (*zhishi qingnian shangshan xiaxiang yundong* 知識青年上山下鄉運動, in full). This topic is considered by the authorities as "sensitive" (as is the case for many episodes of the history of China under Mao), but it is not considered to be one of the most sensitive. It can therefore be considered fairly representative of a general situation and similar demonstrations could certainly be made for most aspects of the history of the PRC. I shall specifically examine in this chapter the sudden end of the *xiaxiang* movement (including the massive return of urban youths sent to the countryside who were still there at the end of the 1970s) and its only exception: that of the Shanghai rusticated youth sent to Xinjiang.

In my book, *The Lost Generation*, I incorporate a wide array of materials, official and unofficial, to present and interpret the history of the *xiaxiang* movement. I study it from the double point of view of the authorities and of the population concerned. It is in my view the only way to understand what really happened at the time, since the interaction between state and society was particularly at stake in this movement, which purported to transform into peasants, potentially for the rest of their life, millions of urban-educated youth arriving at the end of their secondary schooling.[1]

The Official Version of History: Eulogy to Deng Xiaoping

The rustication movement appeared on a small scale in the 1950s, began to be institutionalized in the early 1960s, and became almost universal and acquired a new political meaning at the end of 1968. It lasted with ups and downs until 1980. If you look only at official materials of the time, it would be simply impossible to understand why it came abruptly to a halt between the end of 1978 and 1980 (about seven million *zhiqing* came back to the urban areas during this period). A few problems were sometimes acknowledged officially but, basically, this policy was presented as successful and as stirring great enthusiasm among the population, especially among the rusticated youth. The official press was full of articles about *zhiqing* models expressing their determination to stay in the countryside and work hard for the development of China's socialist agriculture. If we look at later official accounts of the movement, even when they acknowledge more fully the problems it caused, they give the impression that the authorities, having "liberated their thinking" after the arrest of the Gang of Four and the reemergence of Deng Xiaoping, simply ordered the immediate end of the movement.

In the official narrative of the reform era, Deng Xiaoping gets full credit for the rapid solution of this long-standing problem. Having understood that the crux of the question was youth employment, he ordered officials to enlarge employment

---

1. Michel Bonnin, *The Lost Generation: The Rustication of China's Educated Youth (1968–1980)* (Hong Kong: Chinese University Press, 2013). On this topic, see also Thomas Bernstein, *Up to the Mountains, Down to the Villages: The Transfer of Youth from Urban to Rural China* (New Haven, CT: Yale University Press, 1977) and Pan Yihong, *Tempered in the Revolutionary Furnace: China's Youth in the Rustication Movement* (Lanham, MD: Lexington Books, 2009).

capacities. This was done seriously and in a few years almost all youth, including former rusticated youth and newcomers to the labor force, found jobs in the cities.[2] In a historical TV drama about Deng Xiaoping, forty-eight episodes broadcast at prime time in 2014 and now accessible on the internet,[3] the grandfatherly figure is even portrayed as saying with benevolence "Rang wawamen huilai ba" 讓娃娃們回來吧 ("Let the kids come back").[4] There is no record that Deng ever said those words. Although the series is presented as historical, and the main characters are supposed to be based on real historical figures using real names, there are many distortions of facts and clearly invented characters replace real ones. For example, the name of the official sent by the central authorities to inspect the situation in Yunnan where rusticated youth had begun a protest movement is not the real one,[5] and the rusticated youth who makes an appeal to Deng is not the person who really sent the first collective letter to him, but the son of one of Deng's close subordinates. There is no mention of the large protest movement launched by the Yunnan *zhiqing*. The reason for these distortions certainly lies in the desire to sing the praise of Deng Xiaoping and to show that thanks to the wisdom of the Party and of its new great leader, everything was always under control even in this troubled period when China embarked in a new direction (the series covers the important transition period from October 1976 to October 1984). At the decisive moment, a simple sentence pronounced by the wise leader, alerted by a close person about the difficulties of the masses, could solve all the problems of the populace. This narrative is in line with the traditional image of the benevolent and honest official, the model being the famous Bao Qingtian, who was revered by the Chinese people as a kind of savior. Deng Xiaoping was indeed called Deng Qingtian by numerous petitioners who came to Beijing in 1978–1979 in order to seek redress of their grievances from the Maoist period.

But thanks to other information, coming from both official sources of the time and from popular memory, we can obtain a much more authentic and complex

---

2. See, for example, Luo Junsheng, "Deng Xiaoping zhongjie zhishi qingnian shangshan xiaxiang yundong" [Deng Xiaoping puts an end to the Rustication Movement of Educated Youth], *Dangshi zonglan* ["The scan of the CCP history"], no. 12 (2004): 4–10, and Wan Qiang and Lin Rong, "Deng Xiaoping yu zhishi qingnian shangshan xiaxiang yundong" [Deng Xiaoping and the rustication movement], *Dangshi Wenyuan* [Texts on the party history], no. 11 (2004): 34–37.
3. *Lishi zhuanzhe zhong de Deng Xiaoping* [Deng Xiaoping at a turning point of history], 48 episodes TV drama, 2014 (director: Wu Ziniu). See detailed presentation in Chinese at: http://www.tvmao.com/drama/L2MvKiU=/.
4. This sentence has been quoted in many articles about this series. See, for example, Xu Diye, "Rang Deng Xiaoping tongzhi he women yidao shenghuo zai naduan lishi zhong" [Let Comrade Deng Xiaoping live together with us in that historical episode], http://news.163.com/14/0808/09/A346HH8300014AED.html.
5. This is probably because this cadre, named Zhao Fan (at the time, head of the Land Reclamation Bureau), and not Deng Xiaoping, was considered by many Yunnan *zhiqing* as their savior. They later invited him to Chengdu, and even wanted to erect an arch to his glory but he declined. When he died in Beijing in 2010, they took part in great numbers in his funeral. (Many websites of former *zhiqing* show pictures of Zhao's funeral and of his visit to Chengdu.) In his memoirs published in 2003, he clearly expressed the shock he felt when seeing hundreds of *zhiqing* kneeling and weeping in front of him, and resorting to hunger and thirst strike to show their determination (see note 13).

picture of this period, a dramatic one, full of uncertainties, which saw not only a radical change in the economic orientation of the regime, but also the first important emergence since 1949 of an outburst in social protest which was largely successful.

The Tug-of-War between the Authorities and the Zhiqing

If we look at the official materials of the time, we can clearly see that there was some hesitation on the part of the authorities in 1978, since the *People's Daily* published only eleven articles on the *xiaxiang* topic that year, whereas it had published dozens or even hundreds in the preceding years. 1978 was the year that many Maoist policies were beginning to be challenged and when new radically different policies were prepared. It is true that speeches made by Deng Xiaoping in 1978 reducing the rustication movement to a problem of employment, destroyed its Maoist rationale (the necessity of reeducating the urban educated youth and of preventing them from becoming revisionist intellectuals or bureaucrats), and then opened the road for an end to the movement.[6] But, it did not mean that this policy would be rapidly interrupted, since the employment situation was acknowledged to be difficult. Moreover, it did not mean that all rusticated youth in the countryside would be allowed to come home, especially to come home quickly.[7] In fact, the exceptional length (forty-one days) of the national Working Conference on the rustication policy, which finally opened on October 31 after having been postponed since Mao's death in 1976, and which lasted until December 10, shows that it was difficult for leaders and cadres in charge to reach a consensus.

According to the conclusions of that conference published on December 15, *xiaxiang* was considered only a means to solve the employment problem, and as a consequence it would come to an end in the future when the employment situation in the urban areas was improved, but for the time being smaller numbers of young people would still be sent to the countryside with better conditions. Those still in the villages would be authorized to come back little by little, according to employment opportunities and the duration of their stay, with priority given to those who had been rusticated before 1972. As for those who were sent to state farms (two million altogether, of which 1.6 million were still there), they were not considered *zhiqing* any longer, but state employees, and so could not go back to the cities.[8]

---

6. The first attack by Deng on the Maoist conception of youth training had been the restoration of exams for university entrance at the end of 1977. According to Mao's "Revolution in education," after secondary school, all students had to be either peasants, or workers, or soldiers for at least two years, before being able to eventually enter university on mainly political (and not academic) criteria.
7. I have shown that the end of the 1970s was the period in the whole history of China when the largest number of young urban people were attaining the age of employment. To my knowledge, this was never publicly acknowledged by Chinese officials nor by Chinese scholars. It seems, however, important to show that a policy which was supposed to be directed mainly at alleviating the problem of urban employment stopped suddenly, exactly at the most difficult period in history for employing all urban youth. See Bonnin, *The Lost Generation*, 401–2, especially Figure 4.
8. See Bonnin, *The Lost Generation*, 137–39. The rusticated youth were either sent to villages, where they had no

All official materials published from the end of 1978 to the end of 1979 show that the authorities exerted many efforts to implement the decisions of the conference. Local conferences were organized to discuss them and an important propaganda effort in favor of *xiaxiang* filled the media. But these efforts did not bear much fruit, since in 1979 only one-third of *zhiqing* who were supposed to go to the countryside were actually sent, while most of the rusticated youth already in the countryside went back to the cities en masse during that year, in a kind of irresistible movement later called unofficially the "wind of return" (*huicheng feng* 回城風 or *fancheng feng* 返城風). Then, after the usual articles on the organization of the annual *zhiqing* departures at the beginning of 1980, this topic disappeared from the press and in fact the movement died altogether, without any official obituary.[9]

The reason for this sudden end and for the return of the *zhiqing* to the cities (including those from the state farms who were not supposed to do so at any time) cannot be found in official materials but can be pieced together using unofficial sources.

What happened was the conjunction of a new political situation, in which ordinary people discovered that some well-established policies could suddenly be challenged, and a very deep and long suppressed discontent bordering on despair among the so-called "educated youth," who had been in fact deprived of education and who were less and less youthful as time passed. Almost all of them were dissatisfied with their fate. Although every rusticated youth was forced to sign up as "volunteer", many of them had only gone to the countryside because they had seen no alternative, no way to resist in Mao's time. Even those who had initially been real volunteers felt that they had been cheated by romantic and rosy pictures of their future life. As soon as they arrived in their new surroundings (or after a few months there), they had been disappointed by the realities of the "socialist countryside" and by the not so altruistic and revolutionary mentality of the "poor and lower-middle peasants." They had lost their urban residence permit, equivalent to a guarantee for basic necessities, and had to face endless difficulties for food and housing while working very hard without leisure or cultural activities. In the Yunnan farms, those conditions had not significantly improved along the years. After some time, the youth had seen other *zhiqing* going back home or to other urban areas, to be workers or students, very often because they had "a good daddy" or the means to corrupt a cadre. As they did not want to stay in the countryside, they could not marry there, which jeopardized their sentimental and sexual life. When going back for rare holiday visits to their families, they had to spend many days in transportation and, when they finally arrived in their home cities, they were treated as bumpkins by their former friends or relatives, whereas they never were really accepted as country people by the peasants. They were often victims of arbitrariness or violent

---

fixed salary but shared the harvest according to work-points earned, or to state or military farms where they were given a monthly salary.
9. Bonnin, *The Lost Generation*, 170–76.

treatment by local cadres, especially the girls who were easy preys for male bullies. A substantial number of rapes occurred on the military farms of Yunnan, and in 1973 the central authorities executed officers responsible for the record numbers of rapes. Healthcare was also very bad in the countryside, especially in the border regions, where illness or work accidents led to the death or crippling of a substantial number of *zhiqing*. All these pent-up frustrations led to the feeling that if any opportunity arose to go back home, it should be grasped at all costs.

From Passive to Active Resistance: Sources at Our Disposal

Passive resistance to the movement had indeed existed from the beginning, and became more obvious with time passing. *Zhiqing* tried very hard to find ways to be recruited as workers, students, or soldiers. Very often, this could only be obtained through string-pulling or outright corruption of cadres in charge. Others pretended to be ill and showed doctor's certificates obtained by money to go back home. Some even injured themselves, in order to be declared inapt for agricultural work. There was an upsurge of these methods in 1978. We know from interviews and written memoirs that throughout that year, many *zhiqing* succeeded in arranging their return to the city through corruption (of doctors or cadres; this was later confirmed when official numbers were published in different publications such as collections of statistics and provincial annals (*shengzhi*).[10] The rustication policy was a decisive factor in the worsening of social mores, in the spreading of official corruption, and in the emergence of an underground culture among China's youth during the 1970s.[11] But what precipitated the end of the movement was the open resistance of the *zhiqing*. This was made possible by the new political atmosphere of 1978–1979 and by the hesitations of the authorities, which even *zhiqing* living in remote areas were able to feel, albeit after some delay.

The first and the most influent example of active resistance was that of the Xishuangbanna educated youth. However, another spontaneous and unrelated movement in Mengding, in another part of Yunnan, was also instrumental, as we shall see.

At the time, the only official mention of the Xishuangbanna movement was an article on the front page of the *People's Daily* of February 10, 1979. Ten representatives of the Xishuangbanna *zhiqing* were received on January 4 in Beijing by Wang Zhen, who was in charge of this domain in the Politburo. The *People's Daily* published the scolding of the representatives by Wang Zhen and the repenting telegram

---

10. In 1978, return to the cities for health and family difficulty reasons more than trebled over 1977 (*Zhongguo laodong gongzi tongji ziliao, 1949–1985* [Beijing: Zhongguo tongji chubanshe, 1987], 111). Many provincial annals published from the end of the 1980s until now provide similar statistics at the provincial level and note the sudden easing of this kind of returns. A partial list of these annals can be found in Bonnin, *The Lost Generation*, 467–69.
11. See Bonnin, *The Lost Generation*, chap. 11, 337–85.

that three of them had sent to him on January 23 saying that they were back to Xishuangbanna and that the strike was over.

But thanks to other, unofficial materials, we know that at the very time when the *People's Daily* published this article, on the ground all *zhiqing* were leaving Yunnan en masse to go back to their cities. This irony has to be explained, and can only be understood through two unofficial sources.

One is the historical testimony of officials who were at the time in charge of this question, and who later wrote unofficially. The most important is Gu Hongzhang (he published in 1996 with other people, including other former cadres, two books on the *xiaxiang* policy that give a rather detailed account of the main events of this movement seen from the point of view of the government),[12] but Zhao Fan's more personal testimony also provides interesting complements.[13] Although former officials wrote these books, they are not themselves official and could at best be considered semi-official. They were based on official materials, but their authors decided by themselves to publish them and encountered some difficulties in doing so. In one of the two books published by Gu Hongzhang et al., a leaflet was inserted reporting these difficulties and expressing the authors' gratefulness for the help of a member of the Research Centre on the Party History of the Central Committee (which has advisory power concerning the censorship of books on contemporary China). Those books were in the end approved by the Ministry of Labor and published by an official publisher. Another high-level cadre who was linked to the Rustication policy, Xu Fa also published two books on the topic.[14] Their unofficial character is shown by the fact that they have no publisher name and no book number. This is the case for many interesting recollections and memoirs, which are thus published as *samizdat* (in Chinese: *ziyin*, or self-published). Those books are sold or given away directly by the authors but in some cases they can be bought on the internet, except when they are particularly disliked by the censorship organs. Sometimes, the authors buy a book number in Hong Kong and pretend that their book was published there, even as it is, in fact, printed secretly in China. The reason that Xu Fa's books are unofficial is probably because they are critical of some of the historical assessments concerning *xiaxiang* expressed in the two Gu Hongzhang books. The first of Xu Fa's books (published in 1998, soon after the publication of the two books by Gu) is a direct critical commentary on the two Gu books. Xu himself took part in the planning of the books, but later disagreed with Gu on the general orientation

---

12. Gu Hongzhang and Hu Mengzhou, eds., *Zhongguo zhishi qingnian shangshan xiaxiang shimo* [History of the rustication of Chinese educated youth] (Beijing: Zhongguo jiancha chubanshe, 1996); Gu Hongzhang and Ma Kesen, eds., *Zhongguo zhishi qingnian shangshan xiaxiang dashiji* [Chronicle of the rustication of chinese educated youth] (Beijing: Zhongguo jiancha chubanshe, 1996). Gu Hongzhang was a high level leader of the Central Educated Youth Bureau.
13. Zhao Fan, *Yi zhengcheng* [Remembering the journey of my mission] (Beijing: Zhongguo nongye chubanshe, 2003). Zhao Fan was vice-minister of agriculture and head of the Agricultural Reclamation Bureau.
14. Xu Fa, *Wo suo zhidao de zhiqing gongzuo* [What I know about the work concerning the educated youth] (no publisher, 1998); Xu Fa, *Yi bo san zhe—Xu Fa jingli jishi* [Twists and turns: Recording of Xu Fa's experience] (Beijing: no publisher, 2008).

and quit. It is interesting because it provides additional information on historical facts that were not recorded in the other books.

The other source for our knowledge concerning the rustication movement consists of the testimonies and historical publications of the *zhiqing* themselves, either in books or articles published by them or through interviews with historians working in an unofficial function. One of them, Liu Xiaomeng, who is a researcher on the Manchu dynasty at the Chinese Academy of Social Sciences, has made the most important contribution.[15] Concerning more precisely the end of the movement, his book of oral histories gives invaluable information through the interviews of some leaders of the *zhiqing* protest movements of that period.[16] Of course, directly interviewing the leaders and participants in these movements is an excellent source of information, which can be compared to printed sources. That is what I have done with Ding Huimin, leader of the Xishuangbanna movement, and Ye Feng, leader of the Mengding movement, as well as with some other participants, in September 2008 and December 2009.

Other books written by former *zhiqing* who were active in the Yunnan movement are also very useful,[17] as are books about the Xinjiang movement, which I shall present later. Apart from printed materials, a lot of memoirs are published electronically on a large number of websites managed by former *zhiqing*. There are also unofficial historical debates on these websites or in blogs about the interpretation of the rustication movement. A few electronic magazines publish academic papers on contemporary history and evade censorship, since they are only distributed to limited lists of specialists.[18] Documentary films constitute another important source for the history of the movement and of its turbulent ending. In this domain, Phoenix TV, based in Hong Kong but mainly run by mainlanders, has done a lot of work. Different films have been made on the rustication movement, each one covering one region or one topic. Even if the films have been shot in China, the fact that the producer is a Hong Kong company provides a much wider space to speak about "sensitive" topics like the Yunnan protest movement. Most of these are accessible on the internet. Apart from that, a mainland film company linked to the *People's Daily* has also made a very interesting series of twenty documentary films. Because of censorship, they were ultimately not able to show this series on Central Television,

---

15. Liu Xiaomeng, *Zhongguo zhiqing shi: Dachao (1968–1980)* [History of the Chinese educated youth: The great tide, 1968–1980] (Beijing: Zhongguo shehui kexue chubanshe, 1998). Liu Xiaomeng, *Zhongguo zhiqing koushushi* [Oral history of the Chinese educated youth] (Beijing: Zhongguo shehui kexue chubanshe, 2004).
16. This source and some other unofficial sources are quoted in Bin Yang, "'We Want to Go Home!' The Great Petition of the *Zhiqing*, Xishuangbanna, Yunnan, 1978–1979," *The China Quarterly* 198 (June 2009): 401–21.
17. Qu Bo and Luo Xiaowen, eds., *Jufeng guaguo yaredai yulin* [A hurricane passed over the subtropical forest] (Beijing: Zhongguo guoji shiyejia chubanshe, 2006). Zou Shengyong, ed., *Jianzheng lishi* [Witness to history] (Hong Kong: Zhongguo wenhua yishu chubanshe, 2008).
18. To this author's knowledge, the two most important ones concerning the Cultural Revolution and the Rustication Movement are *Jiyi* (Remembrance) produced in Beijing by Qi Zhi (penname of Wu Di) and *Zuotian* (Yesterday) produced in Chongqing by He Shu. Their archives until December 2016 can be accessed on the site of the PRC History Group: prchistory.org. See Jean-Philippe Béja's chapter in this volume.

but they have made it available to the public as a box of ten VCDs including the printed script.[19]

The Real Petitioning Movement "to Go Back Home"

Thanks to semi-official and unofficial sources, we can form a rather detailed and vivid picture of the interaction of officials and petitioners during this protest movement. We learn that on October 18, 1978, a Shanghai *zhiqing*, Ding Huimin, after some discussions with other *zhiqing*, publicized an open letter addressed to Deng Xiaoping asking for the right for *zhiqing* to go back to their cities. He knew that a national conference on the rustication policy would be held soon and, like many other *zhiqing*, he felt that the political situation was favorable. The letter was quickly signed by one thousand *zhiqing*, but did not produce the result they were hoping for. Then, a strike was organized in which 50,000 *zhiqing* took part and a delegation was sent to Beijing, while another was blocked in Kunming by local authorities. The successful delegation arrived at the time of the Democracy Wall movement. They began petitioning in front of the railway station and then on Tiananmen Square as soon as they arrived, asking to be received by the two highest leaders, Hua Guofeng and Deng Xiaoping. They clearly stated their main demand as: "We want to go back home" (*Women yao hui laojia qu* 我們要回老家去). They went to the Democracy Wall at the Xidan crossroads and posted *dazibaos* there.[20] Then, as mentioned earlier, some of them were received on January 4 by Wang Zhen, who scolded them and asked them to go back and stop the strike. The reason why the reality on the ground was the reverse of the impression given by the *People's Daily* article published later is that, on December 25, two days before their arrival to Beijing and about ten days before Wang Zhen's meeting with the representatives, a high-ranking cadre, Zhao Fan, had already been sent to Yunnan to investigate and calm down the *zhiqing*. And Zhao was moved by what he learned of the real situation of the *zhiqing* in the Yunnan farms and also by their despair and their determination. He was then able to convince the leaders that it was better to let the *zhiqing* go back to their cities. He was helped by the fact that leaders at the places of origin of the *zhiqing* (Sichuan, Shanghai, Beijing, and Kunming) accepted the idea of taking back their own *zhiqing* in different batches. Sichuan, then headed by reformist leader Zhao Ziyang, took the lead, which put pressure on the others. The details of this trip became known later through the testimonies both of officials and of the *zhiqing* rebels. Visiting different farms in Xishuangbanna, Zhao was confronted by hundreds of kneeling and weeping *zhiqing*, showing their determination by shouting slogans and giving

---

19. The series was sold under the title *Laosanjie—Yu gongheguo tong xing* [The three graduation years—Walking together with the Republic] (Nanjing: Nanjing yinxiang chubanshe, 2001). It seems to be now out of stock.
20. This author was able at the time to take photos of these posters. Some of the photos were published in Victor Sidane (collective penname), *Le Printemps de Pékin* (The Peking spring) (Paris: Gallimard [coll. Archives], 1980).

him banners like the one presented to him in a farm in Mengla which was covered with the bloody fingerprints of the local *zhiqing*, saying: "If we cannot go back to our birthplace, we shall die with a remaining grievance" (*Bu hui guxiang, si bu ming mu* 不回故鄉，死不瞑目).[21] And it appeared that Xishuangbanna was not the only place where there was a petitioning movement. One movement, which also had an influence on Zhao Fan, took place in Mengding, about one thousand kilometers away from Xishuangbanna. It was unrelated to the first movement, but the petitioners were able to reach indirectly Zhao Fan while he was in Xishuangbanna after a telephone conversation with authorities in Beijing. Zhao Fan then rushed to the place by car. One unofficial book gives many details on the hunger (and even thirst) strike in Mengding, as well as on Xishuangbanna and other places. It also presents many little-known aspects of the life of the rusticated youth working in the Yunnan farms.[22]

If we relied only on the article on the front page of the *People's Daily* of February 10, we would then obtain a completely erroneous image of the Yunnan movement and its consequences. By publishing the article more than one month after the meeting between Wang Zhen and the delegates actually took place, the authorities were probably trying to "save face"[23] and to discourage other *zhiqing* from organized protest action to get back home during the very sensitive period of the Chinese New Year, when many *zhiqing* were allowed to visit their family. But, this was not successful, because protest movements burst out in twenty-one of the twenty-nine provinces at that time. Although the official press never mentioned the success of the Yunnan *zhiqing* protest movement and the actual discarding of the decisions of the National conference concerning the exclusion of the *zhiqing* working on farms from the *zhiqing* category, it was largely known by word of mouth, since the desperate desire of the *zhiqing* to come home was then the hottest topic of discussion in Chinese cities and towns. In fact, even this propaganda trick backfired in the case of the Shanghai *zhiqing* living in Xinjiang, since it alerted those very isolated *zhiqing* about the efforts of their Yunnan counterparts and triggered among them the desire to launch a similar movement.[24]

A New State-Society Relationship and Its Limits: The Fate of the Shanghai *Zhiqing* in Xinjiang

In studying the last period of the rustication movement, we can observe a turning point in the state-society relationship in China. Under Mao, the rule was that

---

21. Zou Shengyong, *Jianzheng lishi*, 51.
22. Qu Bo and Luo Xiaowen, eds., *Jufeng guaguo*.
23. During the January 4 meeting with Wang Zhen, the Minister of Civil Affairs, Cheng Zihua, who was also taking part, said to the representatives: "When you get back there, do not say that your strike was victorious." Precisely because it was . . . (Zou Shengyong, *Jianzheng lishi*, 140).
24. Interview with Ouyang Lian.

initiative was the monopoly of the official side, society being only able to react to official decisions, by obeying (sometimes with excessive enthusiasm to show loyalty) or, on the contrary, by using passive resistance. Both unofficial materials written by former high-ranking cadres and those written by former *zhiqing* show that at the end of the 1970s, both sides were able to take initiatives and that, very often, it was the authorities who reacted to the spontaneous actions of the *zhiqing*. And in many cases, they were not able to impose their decisions on the *zhiqing*. This is similar to what happened with the collapse of collective agriculture in the countryside, which went faster and further than the authorities had first planned. It can be said, then, that the sudden interruption of the long-standing rustication movement resulted from the conjunction of a weakening of the authorities' determination and of the strengthening of the determination of the *zhiqing* to go back to their cities after having spent a large part of their youth in places where they did not feel at home and where they saw no future.

It is in this context that the "wind of return," took place everywhere in China, not only in Yunnan.[25] But, through unofficial materials we also know that this success story of the popular resistance of the rusticated youth suffered an exception. The Shanghai *zhiqing* who were sent to Xinjiang before the Cultural Revolution tried to imitate the Yunnan *zhiqing* through a similar petitioning movement, which went on for a very long time. It began in February 1979 in Xinjiang, then a delegation was sent to Beijing in mid-April, and after many ups and downs, including a large hunger strike in the streets of Aksu in temperatures reaching negative 23 degrees, it was severely suppressed in December 1980, although the local authorities had already accepted to let the *zhiqing* go back to Shanghai with their residence certificate. Some leaders of the movement were imprisoned for a few years and the large majority of the remaining 30,000 Shanghai *zhiqing* were forced to stay in Xinjiang. Most of them went back illegally from the mid-1980s on, but had to live for many years in miserable conditions, without residency permits and without jobs.[26]

---

25. Bonnin, *The Lost Generation*, 148–54. The fact that, at the end of 1978, the authorities had already decided to launch a limited war against Vietnam (close to Yunnan) probably played a role in the decision to solve quickly the problem of the Yunnan *zhiqing* movement, but in different political circumstances, it could have on the contrary led the authorities to strike rapidly and decisively against it. We shall probably have to wait until the Central archives are open to know for sure the relative weight of this concern in the happy ending of the Yunnan protest movement. Zhao Fan should have known something about this concern, but does not say a word about it in his memoir. This could mean either that it was not important, or that it was important, but considered as a State secret.

26. See details of this movement in Liu Xiaomeng's books, especially *Zhongguo zhiqing koushu shi*, and in Xie Mingan, *Xinjiang Shanghai zhishi qingnian shangshan xiaxiang sishinian dashiji* [Forty years' chronicle of the rustication of Shanghai educated youth to Xinjiang] (Zhuhai: Zhuhai chubanshe, 2008), as well as Wang Liangde et al., *Gebi shen chu de nahan* [Cries coming from the heart of the Gobi Desert] (Hong Kong: Zhongguo wenhua yishu chubanshe, 2008). See also (in French) Michel Bonnin, "Shanghai et l'héritage douloureux du maoïsme: le destin de la 'génération perdue'" [Shanghai and the painful legacy of Maoism: The fate of the "Lost Generation"], in *Shanghai*, ed. N. Idier (Paris: Robert Laffont, 2010), 931–72.

Relying on different materials, mostly unofficial but also official, we can try and answer the question: why this exception?[27] My conclusion is that it was a central decision, mainly motivated by the desire to keep on the ground as many Hans as possible in this region of restive "national minorities." Wang Zhen, who had a personal interest in the military farms of this region, which were his main political capital, played a decisive role in convincing Deng Xiaoping of the necessity to keep the *zhiqing* there, and of restoring the Xinjiang Production and Construction Corps, which he had founded and which had been dismantled like all other Production and Construction Corps in the 1970s.[28] It should be noted that one reason for their failure is also the fact that the Xinjiang *zhiqing* began their movement a bit late and very mildly at the beginning, which made them miss the best political opportunity of the end of 1978 through the beginning of 1979. Since February and more clearly since March 1979, Deng Xiaoping, who had already won the battle against Hua Guofeng and the conservative leaders, became less tolerant toward the expression of the demands of the masses. On March 30, he imposed respect for the Four Cardinal Principles, among which was the (absolute) leadership of the Chinese Communist Party. Strict political limits were thus imposed on reforms, and some leaders of the democratic movement were arrested. But this did not prevent the massive return of *zhiqing* from taking place during 1979–1980, nor did it stop the sporadic reemergence of the Democracy Wall movement, at least until October 1979.

The question of the Xinjiang *zhiqing* is then a specific one, and requires specific explanations. Of course, the failure of their movement of petitioning to go back home shows the limits of the political change that took place at the end of the 1970s. Although, since 1978, the Party has been able to take into account the desires of specific groups of the population, it has retained the right to impose its views by force for some reasons it considers superior. The Xinjiang *zhiqing* were then deprived officially by Central Document 91 of 1981 of their status of *zhiqing*, which posed a lot of problems to them. Even until now, their difficulties are not yet totally solved, although they are all over the age of seventy. Over the last ten years, some of them have continued petitioning the authorities, demanding different kinds of compensation, some demanding also the abrogation of Document 91.[29] Others, or the same ones, have made a contribution to the saving of their memory and the recording of the history of their movement, through books or through articles published on websites[30] although for those who are still fighting to obtain an improvement of their fate, this period is not yet closed, not yet history.

---

27. Yang Bin also raises this question in his paper ("We Want to Go Home!" 414). He is right to say that the success of the Yunnan movement was something new, but he insists on the specificity of the Yunnan situation and treats Yunnan as the exception, whereas the exception was in fact the failure of the Xinjiang *zhiqing*. In all other places the *zhiqing* were allowed to go back home.
28. Michel Bonnin, "Shanghai ou l'héritage douloureux du maoïsme."
29. The different petitioning leaflets and court documents which they have produced are also an interesting source of unofficial material, which I have used in my research.
30. See, for example, the books by Xie Mingan and Wang Liangde et al. quoted in note 26.

Cautiously Optimistic Conclusion

It is then mainly thanks to the different unofficial materials quoted above that we can understand why the authorities had to solve the problem of the Rustication policy (because of the huge discontent it caused in the population and the trouble it had become even for the cadres in charge) and why they could not implement their plan of a gradual halt of the rustication policy and of a gradual return of the *zhiqing* excluding those who had been sent to state and military farms.

The real experience and the real feelings of the millions of rusticated youth were clearly exposed only after the end of the movement, but even before that, in fact even before Mao's death, some knowledge of this reality and some expressions of the rusticated youth's discontent were known outside China, especially thanks to the existence of Hong Kong, where the press published articles written and sent by people inside the mainland or who had arrived in Hong Kong legally or illegally.[31] Interviews of *zhiqing* having escaped to the then British Colony were also a good source for getting information unavailable in the official Chinese publications.[32] These articles sent to the Hong Kong press and the "little narratives"[33] of the interviewees were the first expressions of the aspiration to a popular memory which is now flourishing on the mainland. In the 1970s, when some scholars, including this author, were doing this kind of interviewing, they were often criticized for using "biased" sources by those who preferred to rely only on official sources. But, it was later proved that many official sources were in fact much more "biased" than the unofficial ones. To give an example concerning the *zhiqing*, there were official "*zhiqing* songs" expressing the determination of the youth to overcome all hardships and work for socialism in the countryside. But, thanks to popular memory, it was later discovered that the *zhiqing* in the countryside never sang those songs. They sang songs written by them, which were full of nostalgia for their places of origin and much less positive concerning the meaning of their stay in the countryside. The first place where those real "*zhiqing* songs" became known was in Hong Kong.[34]

Since the 1990s, the aspiration of the generation of the Cultural Revolution to an authentic memory and an honest history of the period of their youth has become more and more obvious. There are now many outstanding contributions

---

31. It is in a Hong Kong magazine (*Nanbeiji*, no. 70, March 1976) that the first open rebellion of a large group of *zhiqing* was first reported. It happened on Mount Baiyun, near Guangzhou, in 1974. See Bonnin, *The Lost Generation*, 389–91.
32. Many scholars used this kind of interviews in their studies on Maoist China to obtain authentic information, completing and correcting the materials provided by official media. A partial list of works largely based on interviews of refugees in Hong Kong can be found in Michael Frolic, *Mao's People* (New Haven, CT: Harvard University Press, 1980), 257.
33. In a book published in French in 1979, Jean-François Lyotard contrasted the "grand narratives," designed to give a unified meaning and legitimation to everything from politics to science, with the "little narratives" or "private narratives" which do not pretend to explain everything but are full of authenticity and rich of inventiveness. See Jean-François Lyotard, *The Post-Modern Condition: A Report on Knowledge* (Minneapolis: University of Minnesota, 1984).
34. On these songs, see Bonnin, *The Lost Generation*, 349–54, 383–84.

made through different channels. On the other side, the ambition of the authorities of controlling the writing of history and the recording of memory is unabated, but even if the social impact on the new generations of the distorted history presented in a TV drama series like "Deng Xiaoping" is much greater in quantitative terms, the existence of pieces of real history contained in different forms of popular memory and historical recording seems to guarantee that those in the future who will want to know will be able to know. This is comforting for historians and a great satisfaction for those who lived through that period.

Bibliography

Bernstein, Thomas. *Up to the Mountains, Down to the Villages: The Transfer of Youth from Urban to Rural China*. New Haven, CT: Yale University Press, 1977.

Bonnin, Michel. *The Lost Generation: The Rustication of China's Educated Youth (1968–1980)*. Hong Kong: Chinese University Press, 2013.

Bonnin, Michel. "Shanghai et l'héritage douloureux du maoïsme: le destin de la 'génération perdue'" [Shanghai and the painful legacy of Maoism: The Fate of the "Lost Generation"]. In *Shanghai*, edited by N. Idier, 931–72. Paris: Robert Laffont, 2010.

Gu Hongzhang, and Hu Mengzhou, eds. *Zhongguo zhishi qingnian shangshan xiaxiang shimo* [History of the rustication of Chinese educated youth]. Beijing: Zhongguo jiancha chubanshe, 1996.

Gu Hongzhang, and Ma Kesen, eds. *Zhongguo zhishi qingnian shangshan xiaxiang dashiji* [Chronicle of the rustication of Chinese educated youth]. Beijing: Zhongguo jiancha chubanshe, 1996.

Laosanjie—Yu gongheguo tong xing [The three graduation years—Walking together with the Republic]. Nanjing: Nanjing yinxiang chubanshe, 2001 (a series of 10 VCD with a booklet).

Lishi zhuanzhe zhong de Deng Xiaoping [Deng Xiaoping at a turning point of history], 48 episodes TV drama, 2014 (director: Wu Ziniu). Detailed presentation in Chinese at: http://www.tvmao.com/drama/L2MvKiU=/.

Liu Xiaomeng. *Zhongguo zhiqing koushushi* [Oral history of the Chinese educated youth]. Beijing: Zhongguo shehui kexue chubanshe, 2004.

Liu Xiaomeng. *Zhongguo zhiqing shi: Dachao (1968–1980)* [History of the Chinese educated youth: The great tide, 1968–1980]. Beijing: Zhongguo shehui kexue chubanshe, 1998.

Luo Junsheng. "Deng Xiaoping zhongjie zhishi qingnian shangshan xiaxiang yundong" [Deng Xiaoping puts an end to the Rustication Movement of Educated Youth]. *Dangshi zonglan* ("The scan of the CCP history"), no. 12 (2004): 4–10.

Lyotard, Jean-François. *The Post-Modern Condition: A Report on Knowledge*. Minneapolis: University of Minnesota, 1984.

Pan Yihong. *Tempered in the Revolutionary Furnace: China's Youth in the Rustication Movement*. Lanham, MD: Lexington Books, 2009.

Qu Bo, and Luo Xiaowen, eds. *Jufeng guaguo yaredai yulin* [A hurricane passed over the subtropical forest]. Beijing: Zhongguo guoji shiyejia chubanshe, 2006.

Sidane, Victor (collective penname). *Le Printemps de Pékin* [The Peking spring]. Paris: Gallimard (coll. Archives), 1980.

Wan Qiang, and Lin Rong. "Deng Xiaoping yu zhishi qingnian shangshan xiaxiang yundong" [Deng Xiaoping and the rustication movement]. *Dangshi Wenyuan* [Texts on the Party history], no. 11 (2004): 34–37.

Wang Liangde et al. *Gebi shen chu de nahan* [Cries coming from the heart of the Gobi Desert]. Hong Kong: Zhongguo wenhua yishu chubanshe, 2008.

Xie Mingan. *Xinjiang Shanghai zhishi qingnian shangshan xiaxiang sishinian dashiji* [Forty years' chronicle of the rustication of Shanghai educated youth to Xinjiang]. Zhuhai: Zhuhai chubanshe, 2008.

Xu Diye. "Rang Deng Xiaoping tongzhi he women yidao shenghuo zai naduan lishi zhong" [Let Comrade Deng Xiaoping live together with us in that historical episode]. http://news.163.com/14/0808/09/A346HH8300014AED.html.

Xu Fa. *Wo suo zhidao de zhiqing gongzuo* [What I know about the work concerning the educated youth]. No publisher, 1998.

Xu Fa. *Yi bo san zhe—Xu Fa jingli jishi* [Twists and turns: Recording of Xu Fa's experience]. Beijing: no publisher, 2008.

Yang, Bin. "'We Want to Go Home!' The Great Petition of the Zhiqing, Xishuangbanna, Yunnan, 1978–1979." *The China Quarterly* 198 (June 2009): 401–21.

Zhao Fan. *Yi zhengcheng* [Remembering the journey of my mission]. Beijing: Zhongguo nongye chubanshe, 2003.

Zhongguo laodong gongzi tongji ziliao, 1949–1985 [Statistical materials about labor and salary in China, 1949–1985]. Beijing: Zhongguo tongji chubanshe, 1987.

Zou Shengyong, ed. *Jianzheng lishi* [Witness to history]. Hong Kong: Zhongguo wenhua yishu chubanshe, 2008.

Contributors

(By order of chapter)

Jean-Philippe Béja is a senior research fellow emeritus at CNRS, Centre d'études et de recherches internationales (CERI-Sciences-Po) in Paris. He has been the scientific director of the CEFC in Hong Kong, and a visiting scholar at CASS institute of sociology. A political scientist, he specializes on relations between society and the Chinese Communist Party, and has extensively published on China's pro-democracy movement, as well as on Hong Kong politics. Among his major works is *A la recherche d'une ombre chinoise: le mouvement pour la démocratie en Chine (1919–2004)* (2010). He has edited *The Impact of China's 1989 Tiananmen Massacre* (2011) and co-edited with Fu Hualing and Eva Pils, *Liu Xiaobo, Charter 08 and the Challenges of Political Reform in China* (2012). He edited and partly translated an anthology of Liu Xiaobo's works, *La philosophie du porc et autres essais* (2011).

Wu Si, born in 1957, is currently the chair of the Unirule Institute of Economics. After graduating in 1982 from the Chinese Department of People's University, he worked as an editor for ten years at *Farmer's Daily* (Nongmin Ribao). He worked for seventeen years at *Yanhuang Chunqiu*, where he held the positions of chief editor and acting publisher. His main works include *Chen Yonggui: Mao's Peasant, Implicit Rules: The True Game in China's History,* and *The Law of Blood Feud: The Game of Survival in China's History*.

Jun Liu is an associate professor in the Department of Media, Cognition, and Communication and the Centre for Communication and Computing at University of Copenhagen, Denmark. His research areas cover political communication, information and communication technologies, and political sociology. He has articles published in *Mass Communication & Society*, *Television & New Media*, *Social Movement Studies*, and *China Perspectives*, among others. His research has won several awards, including the Best Dissertation Award, the Information Technology and Politics Section of American Political Science Association (2014), and the Best Paper Award, the 2014 International Communication Association Mobile Preconference.

Kirk A. Denton is professor of Chinese literature at The Ohio State University. He specializes in the fiction and literary criticism of the Republican period (1911–1949) and in Chinese museums and issues of historical memory. Denton's works include *Modern Chinese Literary Thought: Writings on Literature, 1893–1945* (edited collection, 1996) and *The Problematic of Self in Modern Chinese Literature: Hu Feng and Lu Ling* (1998). He is co-editor, with Michel Hockx, of *Literary Societies in Republican China* (2008) and editor of *The Columbia Companion to Modern Chinese Literature* (2016). He has published several articles and a book—*Exhibiting the Past: Historical Memory and the Politics of Museums in Postsocialist China* (2014)—on Chinese museums. Denton is editor of the journal *Modern Chinese Literature and Culture* and manager of its sister MCLC Resource Center (http://u.osu.edu/mclc/).

Sebastian Veg is a professor (directeur d'études) of intellectual history and literature of twentieth-century China at the School for Advanced Studies in Social Sciences (EHESS), Paris and an honorary professor at the University of Hong Kong. He was director of the French Centre for Research on Contemporary China (CEFC) in Hong Kong and publisher of *China Perspectives* from 2011 to 2015. His interests are in twentieth-century Chinese intellectual history, literature, and political debates.

Judith Pernin is a visiting scholar at the Center for Chinese Studies (Taiwan National Central Library). Her PhD from the School for Advanced Studies in Social Sciences (EHESS, France) is entitled *Moving Images, Independent Practices of Documentary in China (1990–2010)* (Rennes University Press, 2015). She is also the co-editor of *Post-1990 Documentary, Reconfiguring Independence* (Edinburgh University Press, 2015).

A factory worker and member of the *Wuming* (*No Name*) underground art group during the Chinese Cultural Revolution, **Aihe Wang** received her PhD in history and anthropology from Harvard University in 1995. Since then, she has taught at Purdue University (USA) and the University of Hong Kong. Her research spans the fields of Chinese history and anthropology, with topics ranging from ancient cosmology to modern totalitarianism, and to art, subjectivity, and community in Mao's China. Representative publications include *Cosmology and Political Culture in Early China* (second edition, 2006) and the *Wuming (No Name) Painting Catalogue*, thirteen volumes (2010). Her single-authored research articles are published in *Society*, *China Perspectives*, *Twenty-First Century*, *The Journal of Chinese Philosophy and Culture*, *Journal of Modern Chinese History*, *Asia Major*, *History of Chinese Philosophy*, *The Bulletin of the Museum of Far Eastern Antiquities*, and *Journal of East Asian Archaeology*. She was a residential member of the Institute for Advanced Study in Princeton (2013), working on a book project on underground art during the Cultural Revolution.

Frank Dikötter is chair professor of humanities at the University of Hong Kong and Senior Fellow at the Hoover Institution. Before moving to Asia in 2006, he was professor of the modern history of China at the School of Oriental and African Studies, University of London. He has published a dozen books that have changed the way we look at the history of China, most recently a "People's Trilogy" that documented the impact of communism on the lives of ordinary people during the Mao era. The first volume, *Mao's Great Famine*, won the BBC Samuel Johnson Prize for Non-Fiction in 2011 and was translated into thirteen languages. *The Tragedy of Liberation: A History of the Chinese Revolution 1945–1957* was shortlisted for the Orwell Prize in 2014. *The Cultural Revolution: A People's History, 1962–1976* concludes the trilogy and was published in May 2016.

Daniel Leese is professor of modern Chinese history and politics at the University of Freiburg. He is the author of *Mao Cult: Rhetoric and Ritual during China's Cultural Revolution* (2011) and *Die Chinesische Kulturrevolution, 1966–1976* (2016).

Michel Bonnin is a professor at the School for Advanced Studies in Social Sciences (EHESS), Paris. From 2011 to 2014, he was director of the Sino-French Studies Centre at Tsinghua University (Beijing). Since 2015, he has been teaching Chinese contemporary history at the Chinese University of Hong Kong. In the 1970s in Hong Kong, he met a group of former rusticated youth from Guangdong Province and published in French a book of interviews concerning their experience. During the 1990s, he was the director of the French Research Centre on Contemporary China and of the journal *China Perspectives*, which he both founded in Hong Kong. In 2004, he published in French a book giving a global presentation of the rustication movement of China's educated youth. It had two Chinese editions published in Hong Kong and Beijing and an English edition entitled *The Lost Generation: The Rustication of China's Educated Youth (1968–1980)* ("Choice Outstanding Academic Title, 2014").

Index

agency (concept): 119, 162, 179.
Ai Weiwei: 95, 155.
Ai Xiaoming: 12, 143, 157–58.
Annals of the Yellow Emperor (Yanhuang chunqiu): 2, 10, 11, 14, 26–30, 32, 40, 43–60, 132.
Anren: 80, 87–88, 90–91, 93, 96, 104–10.
Anti-Rightist Campaign (Anti-Rightist Movement): 2, 5, 23, 25, 28, 29, 32–35, 37, 41, 46, 50, 96, 118, 121–24, 126, 134–36, 140, 144, 146, 149.
April 5 (1976): 5, 6, 51.
archives (archival): 2–3, 12–13, 35–36, 63, 66, 69, 71, 72, 75, 98, 101, 121, 124, 131–32, 142, 144–45, 147–57, 169, 184–85, 188–89, 191–92, 194, 200–203, 205, 218, 219, 227–28, 230.
Arendt, Hannah: 123, 134.
art: 3, 12, 24, 50, 80, 82, 87, 88, 107, 109–10, 137, 155, 158, 161–80, 190, 192, 198, 199, 236.
authenticity: 10, 65, 67–69, 74–75, 77, 119, 136, 144, 147, 150–51, 154, 170, 175–77, 232.
autobiography: 2–3, 13, 16, 26, 37–38, 86, 139, 144, 151, 153.

Ba Jin: 81, 82, 105, 107, 116–17, 134–35.
bad element: 27, 32, 37, 46, 208–9, 219.
Beckett, Samuel: 187.
Beihai Park: 164, 172.
Beijing: 1, 2, 8, 25, 30, 31, 34, 35, 41, 51, 56–57, 68, 82, 84, 90, 92, 111, 125, 133–34, 138, 151, 162, 164–65, 169, 171–73, 175, 187, 189–90, 195, 198, 200–201, 212–16, 218–19, 222, 225, 227–30.
Bian Zhongyun: 148–49.
black market: 183–84, 186–88, 194, 205.
body (human): 4, 7, 40, 69, 73, 148–49, 166, 168, 174, 177–79.

Camus, Albert: 187.
cannibalism: 44, 71, 128–30.
Caocao (painting group): 169.
Caochangdi (Documentary Film Workstation): 12, 14, 139, 157, 159.
case files: 199–218.
CCP (Chinese Communist Party): 13–15, 21–22, 24, 26–28, 30, 35, 38, 44–45, 47, 49–50, 52, 54–55, 57–58, 66–67, 71–73, 79, 81, 93–94, 96, 102, 105, 110, 125–26, 161, 174, 184, 196, 199, 202, 208, 210, 213, 214, 216, 219, 231.
CCP Central Document Research Office: 44
CCP Central Party History Research Office: 26–27, 45, 72, 79, 226.
Chang, Jung: 186–87, 194–95, 197.
chanhui (confession, repentance): 53, 117, 128–29, 132, 135.
Chen Duxiu: 27, 47.
Chen Xiaolu: 2, 83.
Chiang Ching-kuo: 30.
China Central Television (CCTV): 93, 227.
Chinese Academy of Social Sciences (CASS): 32, 43–44, 59, 70, 170, 227.
Chinese Communist Party: *see* CCP.
civil society: 3, 10, 16, 33, 47.

Index

class background: 162, 193, 204, 206, 208, 212.
class struggle: 23, 68, 212.
cleanse the class ranks (*qingli jieji duiwu*) campaign: 51, 195, 206, 210.
Clinton, Bill: 25.
collective memory: 3, 6, 8, 16–18, 24, 62–64, 77–79, 88, 109–10, 115, 119, 155, 162, 163, 166, 170–74, 179.
commemoration: 4, 6, 14, 21, 35, 62–63, 67, 68–69, 71, 75–77, 82, 100–101, 116, 118, 149, 155, 173.
communicative memory: 117
community: 3, 6, 8, 10, 62, 119, 162, 164, 169–70, 179, 184, 190–93.
counter-memory: 16, 63, 77.
counterrevolutionaries (including Campaign against): 26, 46, 50–51, 121, 123, 164, 187–88, 193, 195, 205–6, 207, 210, 213, 215–16.
Cultural Revolution: 1–3, 5–6, 8–18, 21–23, 26, 29, 32–35, 38, 41, 46, 50–51, 53–55, 64, 68, 79–89, 92–110, 115–17, 119–23, 128, 135, 138–40, 142, 144, 146, 148–49, 156, 158, 161–80, 181–98, 200–219, 227, 230, 232.

Dalian: 203–5, 207.
dazibao: 23, 228.
Democracy Wall (1979): 5, 228, 231.
Democratic Progressive Party (DPP): 92.
democratization: 30, 33, 40.
Deng Xiaoping: 5, 23, 41, 51, 55, 82, 93, 115, 118, 161, 196, 221–23, 228, 231, 233–34.
Ding Dong: 30.
Ding Huimin: 227–28.
diorama: 101–2.
dissident art: 165, 168.
Djilas, Milovan: 187.
documentary film: 2, 12, 21, 38, 66, 71, 81, 90, 93, 103, 106, 108, 137–60, 227.
dossier (*dang'an*): 141, 159, 202, 204, 207.
Du Daozheng: 26–27, 29–30, 47, 49.
Du Xia: 173.

Educated Youth (*zhiqing*, sent-down youth, Rusticated Youth): 2, 7–8, 13, 17, 17, 24, 34, 84, 86, 96, 100–101, 116–17, 120, 135, 141, 157, 162, 174, 175, 187, 198, 210, 220–34; employment problem: 221, 223; passive resistance (*zhiqing*): 225, 230; songs: 232; "wind of return": 224, 230.
ego-document: 199.
evidence: 124–25, 143, 148, 150, 154–55, 200, 203, 205–6, 208–11, 213, 215–17.
exhibition: 8, 81–82, 85, 89, 90, 92, 94–96, 98, 99–108, 162–66, 169, 170–74, 190.

Fan Jianchuan: 80–81, 86–91, 93, 95, 98, 101, 103–5, 107–10.
Feng Jicai: 98.
Feng Zhe: 104–5, 107.
Fengming: A Chinese memoir: 12, 144, 149–52, 154, 156, 158.
filmed testimony: 145–47, 150–52.
Five-Anti Campaign: 23, 50, 205.
Five Black Categories: 2, 15, 46, 126, 153.
Folk Memory Project: 12, 14, 139–46, 150–56, 159–60.
folk religion: 191.
forbidden literature: 186–87.
Four Cleanups: 50, 205.
Four Types of People: 207–8.

Gang of Four: 6, 22, 23, 51, 161, 202, 210–11, 213, 216, 221.
Gao Yuan: 188, 197.
General Administration of Press and Publication (GAPP), State Administration of Press, Publication, Radio, Film and Television (SAPPRFT): 29, 47, 54–57.
Gorbachev, Mikhail: 22.
Great Famine: 2, 9, 10–12, 17, 28, 38–39, 43–46, 50, 59, 62, 64, 65–67, 70–79, 115–36, 145–46, 159.
Great Leap Forward: 8, 11, 16, 21, 25, 28, 38–39, 46, 50, 84, 96, 105, 117–18, 122, 126, 135–36, 138–40, 203, 207–8.

Grossman, Gregory: 183.
Gu Hongzhang: 226, 233.

Halberstam, David: 187
Hankiss, Elemér: 183, 197–98.
He Duoling: 100.
He Fengming: see *Fengming*.
He Shu: 34, 41, 227.
hidden transcripts: 6, 10, 115, 119.
historical knowledge: 13, 61–64, 69, 74–76, 142, 179.
historical memory: 49, 81, 201, 108.
historical nihilism: 14, 25, 41, 44, 57, 59, 134.
Holocaust: 4, 16, 146, 156.
Hong Kong: 169, 171, 176, 188–89, 214, 226–27, 232.
Hong Zhenkuai: 43–44, 59.
Hou Jun: 101.
Hu Feng: 25, 32, 50.
Hu Huishan: 94–95.
Hu Jie: 2, 38, 138, 140, 143–44, 146–49, 151, 153–58.
Hu Yaobang: 6, 23, 41.
Hua Guofeng: 213, 228, 231.

independent documentaries: 2, 12, 137–60.
individual: 2, 9–11, 13, 31, 40, 46, 51, 62, 66, 69–71, 74–76, 100, 116–18, 120, 126–27, 130, 142–43, 145–46, 148, 154–55, 165–68, 170–75, 177, 179, 183, 185, 193, 197, 199–204, 206–8, 213, 215, 217.
intellectuals: 5–9, 11–14, 16, 23–26, 30, 36, 39, 42, 46, 48, 50, 82, 115–20, 122, 126, 127–30, 133, 137, 150, 163, 177, 211–12, 223.
internet: 1–3, 9–11, 14, 19, 24, 26, 29, 31, 34, 41, 43, 45, 47, 61–79, 110, 120–21, 134, 143, 151, 157, 222, 226–27.
Isozaki Arata: 90

Jia Zhangke: 138.
Jiabiangou (Reeducation through Labor Camp): 10, 12, 118, 120–24, 126–27, 129–31, 133, 136, 138–50, 157.

Jianchuan Museum Cluster (Jianchuan Museum): 80–111; Anren Bridge Museum: 105–7, 109; China Heroes Statues Square: 93–94; Daily Life Hall: 101–2; Badges, Clocks, and Seals Hall: 98–99, 102–4; Educated Youth Hall: 100; Flying Tigers Hall: 92, 95; Mirror Museum: 99.
Jiang Qing: 23, 64, 79, 110, 172, 192.
Jiang Wen: 117.
June Fourth (1989): 24, 27, 55, 119, 135.
justice (injustice): 81, 89, 105–6, 123, 135, 142, 155, 158, 211, 212.

Kerouac, Jack: 187.
Kunming (Yunnan): 86, 228.
Kuomintang, KMT, Nationalist Party: 21–22, 27–28, 38, 50, 54, 92–93, 95, 151, 205.

label (political): 26–27, 32, 37–38, 44, 50, 121, 123–24, 126, 138, 140, 149, 151, 205–9, 211, 215.
Land Reform: 2, 7, 15, 21, 23, 34, 41, 50, 117, 134, 145, 204.
Lei Feng: 62, 64, 67–68, 72, 74, 77–78, 178.
Lenin: 22, 23, 32, 52–53, 152, 186, 196–97.
Li Shan: 166.
Liao Bokang: 83.
Liao Gailong: 45, 59.
Liaoning: 203, 208–9.
Lien Chan: 92.
Lin Biao: 6, 23, 51, 161, 174, 186, 189, 196.
Lin Zhao: 2, 38, 138, 140, 146–47, 157.
Lin Zhibo: 66, 73, 75.
literacy: 185–86.
Liu Jiakun: 90–91, 109.
Liu Shahe: 98.
Liu Shaoqi: 51, 209–10, 213, 215.
Liu Shi: 173.
Liu Wencai: 87–88, 110.
Liu Xiaobo: 40–41, 56, 117, 135, 235.
Liu Xiaomeng: 227, 230, 233.
Liu Zaifu: 117, 135.
Long March: 50.

Looking at History (*Kan lishi*, also *National History*): 2, 26, 30.
Looking for Lin Zhao's Soul: 2, 138, 140, 146–47, 157.
Lu Xinhua: 115.
Lu Xun: 128.
Lyotard, Jean-François: 232–33.

Ma Kelu: 172–74.
main melody film: 94.
Mao badges: 86, 98, 99, 106.
Mao Zedong (person): 5, 8, 15, 22–23, 29, 32–33, 39, 41, 45, 50–51, 53, 59, 62, 66–68, 82–83, 86, 101, 125, 128, 147, 152–53, 161, 164, 166, 180, 183, 185–86, 189, 191, 194, 197, 210, 215, 221, 229.
martyr: 83–84, 95, 105, 149.
May 16 circular: 1, 51.
May 16 conspiracy: 213–15.
May Seventh Cadre Schools: 185, 194.
Medvedev, Roy: 22.
memoirs: 3, 12–13, 16, 26, 35–36, 66, 70, 73, 82, 119, 121, 130–34, 138, 144–45, 149–54, 158, 184, 187–88, 195–96, 198, 212, 220, 222, 225–27, 230.
Memorial (association): 22, 31, 33.
memory: *see* collective memory, communicative memory, counter-memory, historical memory, popular memory, public memory, social memory.
Mengding (Yunnan): 225, 227, 229.
Mengla (Yunnan): 229.
minjian (*see also* unofficial): 3, 30, 31, 36, 108, 122, 137, 139, 157.
mnemonic (practices): 62–63, 65–66, 69–71, 75–76, 78.
modernism: 119, 163, 166, 168–69.
modernity: 8, 15, 116, 165–71, 178.
monopoly: 6, 24, 34–35, 40, 71, 75, 119, 154, 220, 230.
Morozov, Pavlik: 194.
Mr. Zhang Believes: 140, 144, 151, 153, 157.
Museum of Modern Chinese Literature: 82.
Museum of the Cultural Revolution: 81–82, 85.

museum supermarket: 81, 91.
museum: 9–11, 14, 17, 64, 69, 80–111, 116, 144, 156.
music (*see also* opera): 71, 93, 162–63, 189, 192, 198.

Nanfang Media Group (Southern Media Group): 10, 56, 129, 132, 134.
National Museum of China: 82, 86.
neoliberalism: 81, 83, 89, 97, 107.
New Left: 8, 50, 59.
New Man: 166, 177.
1966, My Time as a Red Guard: 2, 138, 140, 142, 147, 158.

official art: 162–64, 168.
official history (official narrative): 1–3, 5, 8, 10–11, 13, 17, 21–23, 26–27, 29–31, 40, 43, 46, 48, 59, 62–64, 66–75, 81–82, 87, 89, 92–92, 95, 102–3, 105–6, 115, 118–20, 122–23, 132, 139, 142–45, 147–48, 154–55, 161, 177, 179, 184, 194, 197, 199, 200, 203, 218, 220–26, 228–32.
one-party rule: 24–28, 37, 196–97.
One Strike, Three Anti Campaign: 29, 188, 209.
opera: 152, 163, 192–93, 198.
oral history: 1–4, 13, 31, 139, 143, 146, 227, 233.
Orwell, George: 24.

painting: 12, 80, 100, 157, 161–80, 190, 198.
Pan Yihong: 221, 233.
Peng Dehuai: 28, 39, 42.
Peng Qi'an: 85.
Peng Zhen: 212.
People's Commune: 8, 16, 39, 73, 89, 103, 105, 118, 124, 127, 185, 189, 192, 211.
People's Daily: 1, 48, 61, 66, 76, 78, 103–4, 117, 130, 135, 185, 189, 223, 225, 225, 226–29.
People's Liberation Army (PLA): 50–51, 58, 65, 78, 92–93, 122, 140, 152, 165–66, 188–89, 192, 196.

perpetrator: 106, 116, 118, 125, 212–13, 216–17.
personal archives: 144, 147, 149, 151.
petitioning: 228–31.
Phoenix TV: 48, 93, 103, 103, 227.
popular memory: 3, 5, 8–12, 15, 46, 61, 77, 143, 220, 222, 232–33.
private art: 162, 164–71, 174, 179.
private museum: 80–81, 89, 107, 111.
propaganda: 7, 21, 28, 56, 61, 67–69, 74, 87, 94, 96, 104, 106, 142–43, 147–48, 166, 185, 187, 189, 190, 192–94, 210, 220, 224, 229.
protest: 5, 61, 127, 141, 191, 222–23, 227–30.
provincial annals (*shengzhi*): 225.
public history: 162, 169–70, 173–75, 178.
public memory: 11, 43, 46, 49, 53–54, 57, 63, 64, 77–78.
public sphere: 4, 6, 9–13, 16, 31, 46, 119–20, 130, 132–34, 136, 143, 162, 179.

Qi Benyu: 214–15.
Qi Zhi: *see* Wu Di.
Qiu Jiongjiong: 151–53, 158.
Qu Qiubai: 27.

radio: 29, 56, 61, 188–89, 205.
rebels (Cultural Revolution): 102, 191, 200, 212–17, 228.
Red Guards: 2, 24, 34–35, 40, 51, 83–84, 101, 109–10, 138, 140, 142, 144, 147, 158, 184, 186, 189, 195, 210, 213, 219.
reeducation through labor (*laojiao*): 10, 21, 26, 37, 117, 121–23, 128–29, 134, 158, 184–85, 191, 194, 207.
reenactment: 4, 142, 154.
Reform and Opening: 6, 52–53, 55, 197, 208, 211, 219, 221.
reform through labor (*laogai*): 32, 123.
rehabilitation (*pingfan*): 1, 13, 16, 22–23, 26–27, 41, 51, 83, 116, 118, 141, 211, 216.
religion: 7, 51, 103, 122, 125, 128, 149, 166, 184, 191–93, 198.

Remembrance (*Jiyi*): 2, 26, 34–35, 41, 83, 227.
remolding: 207.
Rent Collection Courtyard: 87–88.
resistance (under Mao era): 6, 12, 21–22, 38–40, 42, 51, 128, 146, 207, 225, 230.
"Resolution on certain questions in the history of our Party since the Foundation of the PRC" (1981 resolution): 5, 6, 15, 23, 34, 43, 52, 55, 102, 111, 115–18, 161, 180, 199, 200.
revolutionary subject: 166–67.
rightist: 2, 5, 10, 15, 21, 23–26, 28–29, 32–41, 46, 50, 52, 96, 118, 121–26, 131, 134–36, 138, 140, 144, 146, 149, 151–52, 156, 158, 177, 200, 208–9.
Roginsky, Arseny: 22, 33.
Rustication Movement (*shangshan xiaxiang yundong*): 220–23, 227, 229, 230, 233–34 (*see also* Educated Youth).

Salinger, J. D.: 187.
samizdat (*ziyinshu*, self-printed books): 2, 9, 11, 17, 26, 36, 38, 120, 226.
scar literature (*shanghen wenxue*): 6–7, 11, 100, 115–17, 119, 128, 133, 140.
schooling system (home schooling): 193, 222.
sex: 195–96, 198.
Shamiakin, Ivan: 187.
Shandong: 185, 188, 192, 204, 206.
Shanghai: 13, 86, 102, 121, 141, 156–57, 169, 171–72, 185, 188–89, 193, 195, 198, 221, 228–31, 233–34.
Shanghai Youth: 141, 156–57.
Shao Yanxiang: 98.
Shapingba Park: 83–84.
Shenyang: 208–10.
Shirer, William: 187.
Sichuan: 31–32, 37, 43, 59, 80, 87, 90, 98, 152, 155, 186, 188, 194, 228.
social media: 1, 9, 11, 14, 61–79, 132, 138, 140.
social memory, social remembering: 11, 62–66, 69, 75–79.

Index

socialist realism: 164, 166, 190.
Solzhenitsyn, Aleksandr: 151, 187.
Song Binbin: 2, 83.
Southern Media Group: see *Nanfang*.
speculation and profiteering: 29, 204–5.
speech crimes: 208–9.
staging: 7, 15, 137, 144, 149, 150, 154, 212.
Stalin: 13, 16, 22, 32–33, 52–53, 152, 186–87, 194, 210.
Stars (Painting Group): 164–65, 169.
state (or military) farms: 196, 223–25, 228–32.
subjectivity: 53, 141, 157, 162, 165–66, 168, 170, 175–76.
suku (narrating bitterness): 7, 120, 127–28, 133.
Sun Jingxian: 43–45, 59, 132.

Taiwan: 30, 56, 70, 92, 122, 151, 180.
Tan Chanxue: 24, 38–41.
Tang Jianguang: 30–31.
Though I am Gone: 140, 144, 148, 151.
Three-Anti Campaign: 50.
Tiananmen democracy movement (1989): 9, 11, 25, 33, 109 (*see also* June Fourth).
Tie Liu: 24, 31–34, 40–41.
Tiny Scars of the Past (*Wangshi weihen*): 26, 31–33.
trauma: 1, 3–4, 6–7, 9, 11, 15, 17–18, 21, 81–82, 89, 105, 107, 118–20, 128, 134–37, 155, 170, 180.
Trotsky: 27, 50, 187.
Truman, Harry: 187.
TV drama (about Deng Xiaoping): 222, 233.

underground: 2–4, 6, 13, 16, 26, 50, 161–65, 168–70, 173–74, 179–80, 183–84, 186, 188–91, 193, 198, 204, 225.
underground art, artists: 161–80, 190, 193, 198.
underground clubs: 193
underground reading: 186, 190.
unjust, false, and mistaken verdicts: 13, 200, 202, 219.

unofficial: 1–3, 9–14, 17, 23, 25–27, 29, 30–33, 35–37, 40, 46, 64, 121–22, 132, 137–39, 144–45, 148–49, 153–55, 162, 169, 173, 179, 181, 220–21, 224, 226–32.
USSR: 22, 49, 54, 67, 72, 187–88, 194–95.

victim: 6–8, 13–14, 22–24, 26, 28–29, 31–33, 36–37, 40, 46, 58, 94–95, 104, 107, 116–20, 122, 125, 127–28, 134–35, 144, 148–49, 155, 162, 175, 179, 191, 195, 202, 216–17, 224.

Wang Aihe (paintings): 178, 190, 198.
Wang Bing: 12, 137–38, 141, 144, 149–51, 156–58.
Wang Keping: 165.
Wang Qishan: 33.
Wang Shiwei: 27.
Wang Shuo: 117.
Wang Xiaobo: 117.
Wang Zhen: 225, 228–29, 231.
War of Resistance against Japan (War of Resistance): 21, 27, 50, 87, 89–90, 92–95, 108.
War of Resistance Memorial Hall: 92.
Watchman Nee: 191, 198.
Weibo: 14, 44, 61–79.
Wen Jize: 27, 29, 42.
Wenchuan Earthquake: 89, 94–95, 155.
Wu De: 213, 219.
Wu Di: 34–35, 41, 227.
Wu Wenguang: 2, 12, 137–38, 140–42, 145–47, 157–58, 160.
Wuming (No Name): 161–62, 164–72, 176, 178–80, 190, 198.

Xi Jinping: 33, 35.
Xiao Ke: 27, 47.
Xie Tao: 28, 32, 42, 52, 59.
Xing Tonghe: 90.
Xinjiang: 13, 56, 141, 221, 227, 229, 230–31, 234.
Xinyang incident (Anhui): 124–25, 127.
Xishuangbanna (Yunnan): 225–29, 234.

Xu Fa: 226, 234.

Yan Lianke: 11–12, 24, 42, 118, 120, 122, 125, 128–29, 132, 134, 136.
Yan'an: 27, 35, 50, 192.
Yang Jisheng: 2, 10, 12, 14–15, 28, 30, 42–43, 48, 59, 60, 72, 79, 118, 120, 121–27, 130–31, 133, 135–36.
Yang, Rae: 195–96, 198.
Yang Xianhui: 12, 118, 120–21, 123–24, 126, 128–31, 135–36, 150, 157.
Yang Yushu: 167, 173.
Yanhuang Chunqiu: see *Annals*.
Yao Dengshan: 214.
Ye Feng: 227.
Yue Minjun: 83.
Yunnan: 51, 100, 150, 156, 222, 224–31.
Yuyuantan Park: 165.

Zhai Zhenhua: 186, 192, 198.
Zhang Hongbing: 195

Zhang Lei: 97–98.
Zhang Side: 178.
Zhang Wei: 163, 165, 173–74, 239.
Zhang Xianliang: 98, 128.
Zhang Yimou: 21, 83.
Zhang Yonghe: 90, 105.
Zhang Zhaoqing: 213–14.
Zhang Zhixin: 23.
Zhao Fan: 222, 226, 228–30, 234.
Zhao Wenliang: 167, 173.
Zhao Ziyang: 27, 29, 228.
Zheng Zigang: 174–75.
Zhi Liang: 117.
Zhou Enlai: 6, 51, 213–15.
Zhou Gucheng: 27.
Zhu Rongji: 25.
Zhuo Fei: 195, 198.